The Human Tradit

MW00483950

CHARLES W. CALHOUN
Series Editor
Department of History, East Carolina University

The nineteenth-century English author Thomas Carlyle once remarked that "the history of the world is but the biography of great men." This approach to the study of the human past had existed for centuries before Carlyle wrote, and it continued to hold sway among many scholars well into the twentieth century. In more recent times, however, historians have recognized and examined the impact of large, seemingly impersonal forces in the evolution of human history—social and economic developments such as industrialization and urbanization as well as political movements such as nationalism, militarism, and socialism. Yet even as modern scholars seek to explain these wider currents, they have come more and more to realize that such phenomena represent the composite result of countless actions and decisions by untold numbers of individual actors. On another occasion, Carlyle said that "history is the essence of innumerable biographies." In this conception of the past, Carlyle came closer to modern notions that see the lives of all kinds of people, high and low, powerful and weak, known and unknown, as part of the mosaic of human history, each contributing in a large or small way to the unfolding of the human tradition.

This latter idea forms the foundation for this series of books on the human tradition in America. Each volume is devoted to a particular period or topic in American history and each consists of minibiographies of persons whose lives shed light on that period or topic. Well-known figures are not altogether absent, but more often the chapters explore a variety of individuals who may be less conspicuous but whose stories, nonetheless, offer us a window on some aspect of the nation's past.

By bringing the study of history down to the level of the individual, these sketches reveal not only the diversity of the American people and the complexity of their interaction but also some of the commonalities of sentiment and experience that Americans have shared in the evolution of their culture. Our hope is that these explorations of the lives of "real people" will give readers a deeper understanding of the human tradition in America.

The HUMAN TRADITION in AMERICA
1865 to the Present

THE HUMAN TRADITION
IN AMERICA
1865 TO THE PRESENT

No. 17
The Human Tradition in America

Edited by
Charles W. Calhoun

A Scholarly Resources Inc. Imprint
Wilmington, Delaware

© 2003 by Scholarly Resources Inc.
All rights reserved
First published 2003
Printed and bound in the United States of America

Scholarly Resources Inc.
104 Greenhill Avenue
Wilmington, DE 19805-1897
www.scholarly.com

Library of Congress Cataloging-in-Publication Data

The human tradition in America: 1865 to the present / edited by
    Charles W. Calhoun
        p. cm. — (The human tradition in America ; no. 17)
        ISBN 0-8420-5128-7 (alk. paper) — ISBN 0-8420-5129-5 (pbk. :
alk. paper)
        1. United States—History—1865—Biography. I. Calhoun,
Charles W. (Charles William), 1948–   . II. Series.
E663.H85 2003
920.073—dc21

                                                            2003007501

♾ The paper used in this publication meets the minimum requirements
of the American National Standard for permanence of paper for printed
library materials, Z39.48, 1984.

For

John A. Garraty,

mentor

and

doyen of American biography

About the Editor

Charles W. Calhoun received his B.A. from Yale University and his Ph.D. in history from Columbia University. He is a professor of history at East Carolina University, Greenville, North Carolina, and a past president of the Society for Historians of the Gilded Age and Progressive Era. His research specialty is the politics of the Gilded Age. His books include *The Human Tradition in America from the Colonial Era through Reconstruction* (2002), *The Gilded Age: Essays on the Origins of Modern America* (1996), and *Gilded Age Cato: The Life of Walter Q. Gresham* (1988).

Contents

Introduction

Charles W. Calhoun

The distinct character of each human being is the distillation of a unique set of experiences: biological inheritance, placement and movement in particular surroundings, interaction with other people, successes enjoyed, disappointments borne, accidents endured, plans fulfilled, dreams thwarted. Each of us is the sum of what we have gone through. The same is true of nations, which are aggregates of individuals. Certainly, the physical setting—geography, topography, climate—has much to do with the course of a nation's history, but it is humans' interaction with that physical circumstance and with one another that marks out a country's destiny. Some individuals—a George Washington, an Eleanor Roosevelt, a Martin Luther King—have loomed large in the forging of American destiny. But it is the premise of this volume that other, lesser known Americans have played a vital role as well in the definition of the nation.

Traditionally, when historians have ranged beyond the examination of well-known and influential historical actors, they have explored the impact of large, seemingly impersonal forces and developments such as demographic change, industrialization, urbanization, and secularization. In the past fifty years of historical inquiry, statistical analysis has provided a powerful tool for depicting the contours of these forces. Yet, more and more, scholars have come to recognize that each of these large movements represents countless small deeds and decisions by individual Americans, sometimes acting in concert, sometimes acting alone. The purpose of this book is to telescope the lens from the wide-angle group portrait down to the focused individual closeup.

In the nineteen brief biographies presented here the emphasis is less on representativeness than on variety. These stories illustrate how truly diverse the American experience has been. Yet the very centrality and pervasiveness of this diversity point to two other themes that have dominated American history and that implicitly connect these essays. First, the diversity is not simply a matter of idiosyncratic individuals; it exists also in the tremendous heterogeneity of the groups that have constituted the nation's population. From the initial contact between indigenous peoples and migrant Europeans, a central fact of American life and civilization has been the encounter of distinct groups of people of widely varying origins and cultures. Many of the life stories presented here illustrate the differing ways in which Americans have negotiated and contested the boundaries between racial and ethnic groups.

Second, at the heart of the American story is the persistent tension between liberty and community. Americans have placed a high premium on dynamic individuality, on the right of each person to chart his or her own destiny. Yet they have never adopted liberty as license or the right to flout the legitimate requisites of the community. They have embraced the pursuit of happiness as a basic tenet, but they have also conceived that pursuit as limited by the rights of other individuals and the larger community, where ideally the rights and interests of all are mediated for the common good. Again, many of the lives portrayed in this volume illuminate the multiplicity of ways that Americans have coped with these paradoxical impulses.

The unfolding of these two themes grew increasingly complex in the decades after 1865 and throughout the twentieth century. The Industrial Revolution transformed the American economy and the life of labor. A vastly expanded immigration flow continued to diversify the nation's population. Modernity carried with it challenges to long-standing notions about gender relations and sexual identity. The burgeoning economy with a concomitant growth in trade and the rise of global capitalism thrust the United States onto the world stage. As a world power, the nation assumed enormous new responsibilities that profoundly affected the lives of its citizens. Complexity, strife, and struggle became the hallmarks of industrial and postindustrial America.

In the view of many contemporaries and later observers, the Civil War stood as the great watershed in the nation's history, bringing to a close what some supposed to be an American Arcadia and heralding the coming of the modern industrial society. Trying to cope with the war's impact consumed the lives of many of its participants, for none more so than for George E. Pickett and LaSalle Corbell Pickett, the subjects of the first essay. In reality, the war seemed to have unhinged both Picketts. George never got over his monumental failure at Gettysburg and increasingly lost control over himself, to the point of sanctioning an unwarranted mass execution of Union prisoners in North Carolina that almost earned him prosecution as a war criminal after the war. LaSalle saw some of the war's destruction firsthand, and she must have watched with profound horror the psychological desolation of her husband as well as the annihilation of her society. She spent much of the postwar years constructing an idealized, if not totally fictional, portrait of George Pickett and even invented supposed correspondence from her husband. Nor were her many publications entirely consistent. While she dutifully praised her husband as brave and chivalrous, she also sometimes depicted him as pacifistic compared with her own purported strength and boldness. Her works promoted a revanchist interpretation of the war's origins and meaning and buttressed the burgeoning Lost Cause myth of the benign Old South, which, as the nineteenth century drew to a close, did much, in the name of sectional reconciliation, to undermine the liberty of the freed slaves and their descendants.

Securing that new liberty in the postwar decades was a consuming passion for Benjamin Singleton. An escaped slave who had lived in the North for two decades, Singleton returned during the war to Union-occupied Nashville, Tennessee, there hoping to rebuild his life in freedom. But as the hopes of Reconstruction faded and legal restrictions and other impediments hindered blacks' progress, he began to explore the possibility of African Americans' relocation outside the South. Singleton saw land as the key to the former slaves' advancement, but economic hard times and resistance by whites rendered blacks' acquisition of land virtually impossible in the old slave states. In the mid-1870s he mounted a recruitment effort to encourage southern blacks to migrate to Kansas, and thousands had moved there by the end of the decade. Calling himself the father of the Kansas Exodus, Singleton became a leading spokesman for the state's new residents and told a U.S. Senate committee that migration was the only defense against oppression in the South. When blacks encountered continuing discrimination in Kansas, Singleton launched an advocacy group known as the Colored United Links, but the group proved shortlived. Finally, convinced that America offered little hope for blacks' progress, he advocated migration to Africa, but again his effort attracted little support among either whites or blacks. In the end, Singleton's peripatetic efforts at reform simply exemplified the frustrations blacks encountered as second-class citizenship tightened its grip on their existence in the late nineteenth century.

Although many African Americans agreed with Singleton that land ownership was the great elixir for their troubles, others sought betterment in the South's cities, including the thousands who settled in

Washington, DC. Again these former slaves found their hopes largely dashed in the years after the Civil War, but the nation's capital did witness a burst of urban renewal that was largely the work of one man, Alexander R. Shepherd. A native Washingtonian, Shepherd rose rapidly from a plumber's apprentice to a wealthy contractor and developer. In 1871, President Ulysses S. Grant made him head of the city's new Board of Public Works, a position from which he built an influential political machine. But Shepherd's ambitions were less political than entrepreneurial, with a refurbishing of Washington as his central purpose. In a few short years he guided the construction of hundreds of miles of paved roads, sidewalks, sewer lines, water mains, and natural gas lines together with new markets and new schools. But Shepherd's drive to build quickly drove up expenditures and inflated contractors' profits, at enormous cost to the city and the federal government. An 1874 congressional investigation highlighted Shepherd's lax management and shady dealings, and these findings were compounded by the shoddy nature of some of his projects. The achievements and liabilities of Shepherd's program boosted the movement for greater federal fiscal support for the city's development balanced by closer congressional supervision. Shepherd himself lost power in Washington, and he relocated to Mexico to pursue silver mining enterprises. Though no longer active in Washington's advancement, he left a paradoxical legacy that embodied both the possibilities and the pitfalls of urban improvement.

The rapid growth of Washington and other cities in the late nineteenth century owed much to migration not only from abroad but also from the nation's agricultural hinterland. Industrialization, the transportation revolution, and other broad secular trends profoundly affected American farmers, leaving them in an almost constant state of crisis from the Civil War to the end of the century. Farm protest rumbled throughout the era and reached a crescendo in the 1890s Populist movement. One of the most remarkable among that movement's leaders was the "Kansas Pythoness," Mary Lease, who knew firsthand the hardscrabble life as the wife of a failed businessman and farmer in the 1870s and 1880s. Entering reform activism through the temperance and woman's suffrage movements, she had by the late 1880s joined both the Knights of Labor and the Farmers' Alliance. Her speaking talents quickly became apparent, and in 1890 she gave 160 speeches on behalf of Populist candidates in Kansas, where the new party won five of the state's seven congressional seats and put one of their own in the Senate. The triumph inspired Populists elsewhere, and Lease soon found herself speaking at rallies around the country. But she believed that the momentarily successful Kansas Populists did not appropriately reward her efforts with public office, and she soon split with the state party's leadership. Opposing Populist fusion with the Democrats in 1896, she somewhat grudgingly spoke for presidential candidate William Jennings Bryan in 1896, and after his loss she began to identify herself as a socialist. At age forty-eight, having earlier studied law, she divorced her husband and moved to New York City, where she practiced law, taught, and worked for women's suffrage and reproductive rights. Although her fame and influence as a brilliant Populist orator were relatively shortlived, Lease's career foreshadowed later, more successful efforts to redefine American liberty with women as equal participants in public life.

At the end of her varied career, Mary Lease recalled her service in the National Birth Control League as among her most important work: recognizing the primacy of the issue of women's right to govern their own bodies. Finding ways to enhance that liberty was the central aim that Clelia Duel Mosher pursued throughout her long medical career. Born into a family of physicians, Mosher early determined to study medicine and challenge prevailing assumptions about women's health. Early in her career she conducted studies that demonstrated the harm women suffered from the culturally mandated custom of wearing multilayered clothing and constrictive corsets. She also challenged the notion that women's biological makeup, particularly menstruation, affected their psychological and intellectual development and thus limited the kinds of work they could pursue.

Mosher's work on breathing and menstruation catapulted her to national prominence in her profession. In retrospect, however, her most notable contribution was a survey of female sexual attitudes. Over a period of nearly three decades she interviewed forty-five women concerning their sexual practices. Her findings challenged notions that women engaged in sexual relations only for reproduction, but her middle-class respondents also were careful to claim a spiritual dimension, which placed heightened affection with their husbands over coarse physical pleasure. She also discovered a widespread use of birth control despite the legal and societal strictures against it. In 1923 she published *Woman's Physical Freedom*, in which she told postmenopausal women that their changed condition, rather than being debilitating, released them to engage in more active lives outside their homes. Throughout her career, Mosher practiced for herself the most fundamental tenet she preached for women generally—that they should chart their own lives.

If women in the late nineteenth and early twentieth centuries who wished to chart their own lives felt restricted by law and custom, so also did African Americans of both sexes. Since the end of Reconstruction, blacks in the South, where most of them still resided, found their lives largely circumscribed by well-defined legal and social boundaries. And yet those boundaries were not entirely impenetrable. Historian Paul Conkin recalls the stories of two black men, Zachariah Bennett and Amon Hays, who managed to carve out successful lives in nearly all-white communities in East Tennessee. Born a slave and skilled at breeding and training horses, Bennett earned and saved enough money in freedom to buy a 100-acre farm in 1892. His frugality and hard work netted him sufficient wealth to lend money at high interest rates to less fortunate, or less ambitious, white farmers. When he died in 1910 his will assigned a portion of his estate to the local white church and the remainder to a board of white trustees for the erection and maintenance of a large granite monument, which stands to this day as testimony to his prosperity and his status among his white neighbors.

Amon Hays led a more complex life. The only black man in an all-white community, he got on well with his neighbors. He owned a small farm and enjoyed modest prosperity, but he also enjoyed a good time. He played the fiddle, and at his home he hosted Saturday-night square dances where nearly all the revelers were white. During the 1920s he operated a moonshine still with a white neighbor. He lived to an old age respected by his white neighbors. Indeed, only whites were pallbearers at his funeral, and he was laid to rest in a white cemetery. The lives of Black Zack and Uncle Amon suggest a submerged alternative course in a time of generally grievous race relations.

Blues singer Gertrude "Ma" Rainey navigated the troubled waters of race in a way that earned her greater renown than Amon or Zack but in other ways proved ultimately less satisfying. Born into modest circumstances in Georgia, Gertrude was singing professionally before she turned eighteen, when she married the manager of a traveling minstrel show, William "Pa" Rainey. She joined her husband's act as "Ma" Rainey and the name stuck. Throughout her three-decades-long career, she sang in minstrel shows, tent shows, circuses, honky-tonks, and vaudeville theaters before audiences that were all black, all white, or segregated with whites in one section and blacks in another. In 1923 she began recording for Paramount Records, which produced a growing line of "race," or black, records. Rainey's career flourished until sound movies and the Great Depression killed both Paramount and black vaudeville.

She retired from singing in the mid-1930s and died a few years later in obscurity. While Rainey's repertoire included a wide range of songs, her specialty was the blues. This "down and dirty" genre bewailed personal troubles—lost love, hard luck, the perils of drink, trouble with the law—but usually stopped short of overt social protest. Nonetheless, by focusing on the miseries of the underside of life that plagued many of their race, Rainey and other black blues singers presented a telling indictment of blacks' living conditions.

Protest lay at the center of labor and feminist leader Pauline Newman's life, and it was unrelenting. Born to Jewish parents in Lithuania in the early 1890s, Newman showed her assertiveness early, demanding that she be given the same education and religious training that boys received. Immigrating with her mother and sisters to New York in 1901, she immediately started work in a factory at age nine. Depressed by the miserable working conditions, she found solace in reading and writing. Drawn to the ideals of socialist trade unionism, she soon began to describe garment workers' plight in the *Jewish Daily Forward* and similar papers. Like other exponents of Jewish socialism, she espoused a politico-economic philosophy rooted in the Old Testament and Karl Marx and in workers' harsh experiences. While still in her teens she campaigned for women's suffrage not only as an end in itself but also as a means to support women workers. In 1909–10 she led a citywide strike of women garment workers, which won her appointment as the first woman general organizer for the International Ladies' Garment Workers' Union (ILGWU). After the disastrous Triangle Shirtwaist fire killed many of her friends, she became an inspector for the New York Factory Investigating Commission, a position that gave her entry into the reform circles of the state's Democratic Party. As an advocate of labor's interests, she moved easily into the world of lobbying and legislative politics, regarding an alliance with government as indispensable for workers' protection. Entering into a lifelong partnership with a female political ally who had a child, Newman also became a pioneer in the construction of gay family life. She took a post as the ILGWU's Health Education director and frequently advised governments on labor issues, but when no political office was forthcoming for her, she returned to labor union organizing. With that work and through her later years she nurtured a new generation of women labor leaders.

Although Pauline Newman fervently believed that workers must fight for themselves, she also saw government as an agent of economic inclusiveness for the broad community of American workers, and during the 1930s she continually prodded the Roosevelt administration to do more for labor. The devastating depression of that decade gave rise to an array of economic and social nostrums sponsored by a host of would-be reformers, including the gifted orator and eventual right-wing zealot, Gerald L. K. Smith. Born in Wisconsin in 1898, Smith became a Disciples of Christ preacher and soon exhibited great power in the pulpit and as a fundraiser. In 1929 he moved to Louisiana, where, shifting his focus from saving souls to social reform, he enlisted in several causes. He caught the eye of Senator Huey Long, who put him in charge of organizing the national Share Our Wealth Society, which advocated a radical redistribution of wealth from the richest Americans to those mired in poverty.

After Long's assassination, Smith cast about for a new movement. In 1936 he momentarily backed the Union Party presidential candidacy of William Lemke against Franklin D. Roosevelt but soon underwent a political metamorphosis, emerging as a vehement anti-Communist. He formed a group known as the Committee of One Million, whose avowed purpose was to defend private property, Christianity, and American democracy, but in effect Smith became a mouthpiece for the capitalist class. Based in Detroit, he launched a national radio program that netted him thousands of dollars per week in donations from listeners who tuned in to his virulent attacks against Communists, labor unions, and Jews. Failing to gain any influence in the Republican Party, Smith ran for president in 1944 as the nominee of the America First Party and in several succeeding elections on the Christian Nationalist ticket. Both these "parties" were Smith's personal vehicles and echoed his hypernationalism, isolationism, and rabid racism. Although his popularity declined after the 1940s, Smith continued to rail against Jews, African Americans, homosexuals, Communists, liberals, and any others who violated his notion of the American creed. He lived on till 1975, but by then most of his countrymen had rejected the message of this "preacher of hate."

At the height of his influence, however, many Americans shared Smith's intolerance. No instance showed this bigotry more clearly than the relocation of more than 100,000 Japanese Americans from the West Coast early in World War II. Ordered by President Roosevelt in the wake of the Pearl Harbor attack, this forced resettlement represented an egregious infringement of liberty in the imagined defense of the larger "American" community. Among this policy's victims were Rose and Benji

Hara, who were driven from their home on Terminal Island, California, and placed in what amounted to a concentration camp in Arizona. They and their fellow Nisei internees found bleak conditions in their desert camp, but they moved swiftly to create a functioning community by launching an elected government and a school system for the children. After a year and a half the resourceful Benji Hara parlayed his competence as a radio operator into permission to relocate in the East, where he eventually found work at a Long Island electronics firm that made radio equipment for the armed forces. Here, Hara's draft status was changed from the medically ineligible 4-F to the completely eligible 1-A, and the former internee found it necessary to apply for a draft exemption based on his war industry work—a turn of events that neatly underscored the absurdity of the internment program. After the war, Hara rose in the electronics firm, served ably in the Coast Guard Auxiliary, and otherwise lived as a model citizen. Fifty years after he and his family entered the internment camp, the U.S. government apologized and provided a partial restitution of $20,000.

The intolerance of the sort experienced by the Haras in the West had been endemic in the South for centuries, but the civil rights movement of the midtwentieth century called upon Americans to make a fundamental shift in how they related across racial lines. In 1954, in *Brown v. Board of Education*, a unanimous Supreme Court struck down racial segregation in the nation's public schools. It soon became clear, however, that implementing that decision would require a long, hardfought struggle. Among the most stalwart of the soldiers in that front-line fight was Daisy Bates of Little Rock, Arkansas. The murder of Daisy's mother by a white man had filled her as a child with animosity for whites, but her adoptive parents taught her to turn that hatred against segregation and the other forms of discrimination. She and her husband launched a newspaper, the *Arkansas State Press*, which soon became the state's leading voice for blacks' rights. In 1952, at age thirty-eight, Daisy Bates became president of the Arkansas conference of the National Association for the Advancement of Colored People (NAACP). After the *Brown* decision, with the federal government reluctant to act and the state government overtly hostile, implementation of desegregation at Little Rock's Central High School fell to Bates and other community leaders. When their attempts to escort nine black students into the school met the resistance of a mob, they desisted until President Dwight Eisenhower mobilized national guard and regular army troops to uphold the Court's mandate.

Besides being the principal strategist for the desegregation effort, Bates served as a counselor and advocate for the students. Although she and her allies became the targets of intimidation, lawsuits, and threats of violence, she repeatedly implored authorities to protect the students who continued to suffer harassment. The next year the state's governor closed the city's public schools, but they were reopened some months later. Daisy Bates remained active in the civil rights cause, working for the NAACP, the Democratic National Committee, and the Johnson administration's antipoverty programs. She lived long enough (until 1999) to see her chief aims fulfilled and to receive the thanks of a grateful state and nation for her work. From the grinding intolerance of her childhood to her own celebration as a national leader, she witnessed a profound change in the nature of American liberty and community.

At the March on Washington on August 28, 1963, when Martin Luther King Jr. gave his "I Have a Dream" speech, Daisy Bates was the sole female to give a principal address. On that day, the only white speaker was Walter Reuther, a prominent advocate of civil rights who had long used his leadership in the labor movement to campaign for social justice. Born into a working-class family in Wheeling, West Virginia, Walter learned radical precepts at his socialist father's knee before moving at age nineteen to Detroit, where he became a diemaker at the Ford Motor Company. He kept his skilled job when the Great Depression hit, but when his empathy for the thousands of his unemployed coworkers impelled him into the city's socialist movement, Ford fired him. After an eighteen-month sojourn in the Soviet Union, he returned to the United States more determined than ever to organize laborers in the United Auto Workers (UAW). Under the benign umbrella of New Deal prolabor legislation, the union grew rapidly, and Reuther rose rapidly to president. Abandoning socialism, he joined the Democratic Party and became a fervent supporter of Franklin Roosevelt and advised his administration on labor issues. Aiming to put the UAW in the vanguard of a more economically democratic America, Reuther used tough negotiations with management and occasional strikes to win substantial wage increases, pension plans, medical insurance, and other benefits. A leading voice in the Democratic Party, he called for greater government action to ensure economic equity.

Those calls elicited little response until the 1960s, when Reuther swung the UAW behind the civil rights movement, not only on behalf of racial equality but of economic and social justice as well. Reuther ardently supported Lyndon Johnson's War on Poverty programs. But his hopes for real progress soon turned sour, as racial tension within the union undermined support for civil rights, and the Vietnam War drained resources out of the antipoverty programs. After initially supporting the war, Reuther turned against it and sought to capitalize on the protest culture of the late 1960s as a way to reinvigorate labor's cause. This effort was cut short by his death in a plane crash in 1970.

Reuther's turnabout on the Vietnam War followed a familiar path. Many Americans were initially convinced that the country's involvement in Southeast Asia represented a struggle for their own ideals of freedom and self-government, only to conclude that in its purposes and its conduct the war had become a betrayal of those ideals. The war as a failing operation abroad and as a divisive issue at home had a profound impact on the nation as a whole and on the lives of countless individuals. Professor Elizabeth Weber recounts the profound sorrow caused by the death in combat of her brother, Army Spec. 4 Bill Weber. Born into an academic family in Minnesota, Bill took little interest in school despite his high intelligence. Music was at the center of his life and at times seemed his whole reason for being. He flunked out of the University of Minnesota in 1967, was soon drafted, and in less than a year was dead, the victim of a Vietcong sniper. The death devastated his family, but the hurt was compounded a month later when members of Weber's company massacred the villagers of My Lai, in part to avenge his death. For Bill's parents, the incident deepened their opposition to the war, and they thought that President Johnson and other American leaders should be the ones tried for war crimes. Elizabeth, always a model student, became a countercultural dropout. She eventually returned to school, but she could not shake her hatred of the government or her distrust of people generally. A trip to the site of her brother's death in Vietnam did not erase her bitterness.

One month after Bill Weber's death, Minnesota Senator Eugene McCarthy nearly defeated Lyndon Johnson in the New Hampshire Democratic presidential primary. The heart of McCarthy's campaign was his opposition to Johnson's Vietnam War, and the senator's New Hampshire "victory" not only reflected the strength of the antiwar movement but also inspired many more people to join it. Not all opponents to the war were countercultural peaceniks; solid, middle-class citizens were also committed to the pursuit of peace and justice at home and abroad. One of this latter group was Professor Otto Feinstein of Wayne State University in Detroit. Born the son of East European Jews in Vienna in 1930, Otto along with his family abandoned Austria after the Nazi takeover and arrived in New York in 1940. The Holocaust—and the loss of many relatives to it—implanted in Otto a deepseated commitment to social justice and democracy. This commitment grew during his student days at the University of Chicago, where he studied international relations and took part in local politics. In 1960 he joined the faculty at Wayne State and soon became active in the liberal wing of the Democratic Party as well as in national organizations for the study of peace and war. When Johnson escalated the war in the mid-1960s, Feinstein emerged as a leader in organizing academic protest against it. Working within the Democratic Party, he threw his support to McCarthy and headed his Michigan campaign. Feinstein also used his liberal magazine, *New University Thought*, to promote academic participation in the campaign as well as in the Concerned Democrats, a reform movement within the party. After McCarthy lost the nomination to Hubert Humphrey, who in turn lost the election to Republican Richard Nixon, many academics who had joined the McCarthy crusade abandoned political activism. Less disillusioned, Feinstein scaled back his participation, but in the ensuing years he continued to pursue his core goals regarding peace and justice at home and abroad through a variety of university outreach programs.

In the same years that Otto Feinstein and his allies were protesting American policy in Southeast Asia, another struggle in pursuit of justice was unfolding in the agricultural fields of California. There the United Farm Workers (UFW) led by César Chávez employed strikes, boycotts, and other means of protest against the oppressive conditions that field laborers had suffered for decades at the hands of the growers and landowners. Chávez was born in 1927 in Arizona to parents who owned a small ranch and a grocery store. Losing their property during the Great Depression, the family moved to California and subsisted as part of the migrant agricultural workforce. After a stint in the Navy during World War II, Chávez returned to migrant work, but during the 1950s he signed on as an organizer for a political action group, the Community Service Organization, concentrating on voter registration campaigns. By the early 1960s he had begun to focus his energies on the plight of farm laborers and founded the Farm Workers Association, which evolved into the UFW.

Even though the group attracted national attention and won some notable victories over the growers, the farmworkers' movement under Chávez's leadership suffered from internal contradictions that eventually undermined its effectiveness. Inherent conflicts marked Chávez's role as an organizer of workers and as an ethnic role model for Chicano college students and others who aided the movement. The organization itself split over tactics—whether to stress strikes or boycotts as the way to wring concessions from growers. Moreover, Chávez drew fire from within the UFW when he sought to impose upon its members his own Catholic values and a hierarchical structure reminiscent of that of the Church. And, as a Mexican American, Chávez strongly opposed competition from illegal aliens from Mexico, but in doing so he increasingly alienated his fellow Mexican-heritage citizens who were being joined by relatives from across the border. After his sudden death in 1993, Chávez continued to be regarded as a hero for the causes and people he championed, but in some ways his accomplishments were more shadow than substance.

Along with Chávez's labor struggles, antiwar protests, and demonstrations for civil rights, the tumultuous decade of the 1960s witnessed the flowering of yet another mass effort for reform, the women's liberation movement. One of the important literary figures in that effort was Alix Kates Shulman. Born to middle-class parents in 1932, Alix Kates showed some early signs of rebellion as a teenager before heading off to graduate school in philosophy. Although she did well, she abandoned an academic career for marriage. After her first marriage failed and a second one to Martin Shulman, with whom she had two children, turned sour, she increasingly felt trapped in the traditional woman's role. After attending a women's liberation meeting in 1967, she immediately turned to feminism as the key to understanding her own frustrations.

With a raised consciousness, she grasped the notion that the oppression felt by women was not an individual matter but rather a circumstance that derived from society's treatment of women as a class. She took part in rallies and demonstrations and began to write articles supporting the movement. She also turned to fiction, writing the movement's first important novel, *Memoirs of an Ex-Prom Queen*, a best-selling satire about a young woman obsessed with gaining men's approval. Her later novels dealt with such characters as female revolutionaries, runaway girls, homeless women, and women who stay married for the sake of their children. After the women's liberation movement had begun to fade (in part because of its successes), Shulman wrote a memoir of her summers alone on an island in Maine, where she sustained herself both emotionally and physically by living off the natural foods that the island and its waters provided. Her latest work, about caring for her dying parents, speaks of reconnecting with the family she had left in her youth in a quest for personal freedom. All told, Shulman's life has provided a remarkable example of the transformative power of the feminist movement in defining women's liberty and their status in the American community.

During the 1960s and 1970s, while women such as Alix Kates Shulman fought for gender liberty and equality in the American community, another group, American Indians, struggled to preserve their distinctiveness as a nation and a culture separate from the American community. At the forefront of this movement were members of the Lakota tribe of the Pine Ridge reservation in South Dakota, among whom was Mary Crow Dog, a member of the American Indian Movement (AIM). The principal target of Mary Crow Dog and other activist Indians was the federal government's policy of assimilation, begun in the nineteenth century, whereby Indians were to be shorn of their tribal identity (and most of their lands) and transformed into independent American citizens. In the midtwentieth century, Congress had sharpened this policy with legislation to terminate tribes as legal entities and to break up Indian nations, and with other laws to relocate some Indians to cities. Assimilation's aim to turn tribal reservation dwellers into prosperous citizens failed miserably, and Indians who lost their lands sank into abysmal poverty. In 1968, Indian activists created AIM to seek educational and economic opportunities and to fight against discrimination.

Mary Crow Dog had been born Mary Brave Bird on the Pine Ridge reservation in 1953. As a child she experienced the grinding poverty of her people, and as a student in white-run Indian boarding schools she bridled at the attempts at forced assimilation. In 1971 she joined AIM and began participating in demonstrations. The most significant was an occupation in 1973 of Wounded Knee, South Dakota, as a protest against the pro-government chairman of the Pine Ridge reservation. AIM had earned a reputation in government circles as a radically dangerous organization, and the occupiers soon found themselves besieged by a heavily armed government force. Midway through the 71-day ordeal, Crow Dog gave birth to a son, but the protest netted little except a heightened federal effort to squelch AIM. Most of AIM's goals remained unreached in the ensuing years, but the Indian movement did succeed in raising the consciousness of white Americans about the need to preserve rather than destroy the Indian heritage.

In the general movement to reconstruct definitions of liberty and equality, one other group—gays and lesbians—rose to fight for acceptance in the diverse American community in the last decades of the twentieth century. The progress their movement achieved, as well as the perils they encountered, are illustrated in the life and death of gay rights activist Harvey Milk. Born on 1930 in suburban New York, Milk recognized his own homosexuality as a teenager, but he kept it a secret while he charted a successful career on Wall Street. Socializing in the New York theater world and producing a couple of successful plays helped Milk shed his essential conservatism for more liberal political views as well as a liberated personal style. Settling permanently in San Francisco in 1972, he soon moved to the forefront of local radical gay activism. Opening a camera shop in a gay neighborhood, he earned a reputation as an effective community organizer, not only in the interest of gays but of others needing representation as well. In 1977, after two unsuccessful tries, he won election to the city's board of supervisors and claimed victory not only for gays but also for all minorities. Two months after taking office he won passage of a gay rights ordinance. But Milk's achievements did not come easily. The gay rights movement in San Francisco and across the nation confronted a persistent and virulent antigay backlash. Still, in the fall of 1978 he successfully led a statewide election effort to defeat a referendum barring gays from teaching in public schools. But in less than a month after that triumph, Milk and Mayor George Moscone were murdered by an antigay former fellow supervisor with whom Milk had often clashed. Milk's crusading voice was thus stilled, but the cause of gay rights lived on.

Harvey Milk's move to San Francisco in search of liberty and equality represented an implicit acknowledgment of the long-held belief that the West has something to teach Americans about how they should lead their lives. At least since the days of Frederick Jackson Turner, historians and other observers have explored the formative influence of the frontier. Among the West's most important lessons is that of environmentalism, and in the twentieth century few public figures were more determined environmental advocates than Supreme Court Justice William O. Douglas. Born in Minnesota, Douglas moved as a child to Washington State, where his family's poverty instilled in him a deep and abiding class consciousness. In a determined effort to build his strength after a mild case of polio, Douglas as a boy took to vigorous hiking in the foothills of the Cascade Mountains and thereby formed an enduring reverence for nature and the outdoor life. He also compensated by hard work in school, which took him to Columbia University Law School in the 1920s. In the following decade he enjoyed a meteoric public career that culminated in his appointment to the Court. By the 1950s, safely ensconced in his judicial job, Douglas became a vocal exponent of environmental causes. In addition to leading protest hikes, he wrote several environmentalist books that warned of man's threat to various ecosystems. Moreover, although his work on the bench ran the gamut of legal issues, he emerged as "the environmental justice" in cases such as one in 1967 when his opinion blocked a power project on the Columbia-Snake River system. Most often, Douglas's environmentalist voice was heard in the Court's minority. Even so, his dissents and other work proved enormously influential in educating Americans about the value of and the threats to their natural heritage.

The environmentalism of William Douglas essentially underscored the notion that we are all riders on the Earth together. Since 1865, circumstances have made that journey for Americans at once easier and more complex. The last century and a half have witnessed the transformation of the country from a largely localized, agricultural, and traditional society to one that is national, industrial, and modern. Yet, these years have seen the persistence of the two fundamental themes traced here: the continuing effort to accommodate the disparate peoples who constitute the American nation, and the ongoing contention between the impulse toward liberty and the mandates of community. With a vastly expanded immigration, the U.S. population has become even more diverse, and the conundrum of mediating among the multiplicity of peoples has become even more acute. The career of liberty has gone forward, sometimes haltingly, toward a wider range for freedom and opportunity, although their full scope for all Americans is yet to be achieved. In the modern era, as in the earlier centuries, the nation's evolution has represented the summation of countless acts and choices by individuals, each forming a part of the human tradition in America.

The essays included here were drawn from other volumes in the Human Tradition in America series. Notes at the foot of the first page of each chapter give their source. I am grateful to the individual chapter authors and the volume editors.

1

LaSalle Corbell Pickett
"What Happened to Me"

Lesley J. Gordon

LaSalle Corbell Pickett simultaneously overstepped and affirmed the accepted role of a woman in midnineteenth-century America. The wife of the tragically famous but hapless Confederate general, George Pickett, she used both her status as his widow and her own considerable literary talents during the decades after the Civil War to remake her own and her husband's past, forging an idealized version. In doing so, she was moving beyond the conventional role assigned to women in the mid-1800s. Yet at the same time, she validated the cultural norms of her society, for the idealized Sallie Pickett of her retouched memories was far more meek and retiring than the forceful woman who made her husband a hero after the fact and herself "the child-bride of the Confederacy."

Lesley J. Gordon, who presents LaSalle Pickett's story, is an associate professor of history at the University of Akron, author of *General George E. Pickett in Life and Legend* (1998), coeditor, with Carol K. Bleser, of *Intimate Strategies of the Civil War: Military Commanders and Their Wives* (2001), and coauthor of *This Terrible War: The Civil War and Its Aftermath* (2003).

In her 1917 autobiography, *What Happened to Me*, LaSalle "Sallie" Corbell Pickett described a dream she had soon after the end of the Civil War when she and her infant son were traveling by train to Canada to rejoin her husband, ex-Confederate major general George Pickett. The sound of the train had kept her up much of the night, she wrote, reminding her "of the sound of the executioner's axe. All night long it rose and fell through seas of blood—the heart's blood of valiant men, of devoted women, of innocent little children." When LaSalle finally drifted off to sleep near morning, she dreamed that "it was I who had destroyed the world of people whose life blood surged around me with a maddening roar, and that I was destined to an eternity of remorse."[1]

Portions of this chapter have been taken from Lesley J. Gordon, *General George E. Pickett in Life and Legend* (Chapel Hill: University of North Carolina Press, 1998). © 1998 University of North Carolina Press. Reprinted by permission of the University of North Carolina Press.

In this passage and throughout her many published writings, LaSalle Corbell Pickett blended the personal story of her life with a public re-telling of war and defeat. In this excerpt, she blamed herself for the suffering and death that all of America, not just her native South, endured in its bloody civil war. But Pickett was no unimpassioned chronicler of events that had occurred decades before, nor was she a helpless victim. As the widow of a famed Confederate general, she claimed a personal role in the dramatic saga of Southern defeat. Despite the passive title of her autobiography, Pickett wrote in a decidedly active and powerful voice. She outlived her husband by five decades, supporting herself and her son with a lucrative career—touring the United States, giving lectures, writing ten books and numerous articles, visiting veteran reunions, and bringing her "firsthand" account to a national audience.

Although Pickett insisted on the veracity of her recollections, scholarly research shows that she fabricated much of her published writings. She lied about her age, lied about her husband's defeats and failures, and lied about her contemporaries. She erroneously presented herself as a child in many of her writings, so that, it would seem, she could better hide the assertiveness and independence she attained as a successful writer and single mother. In writing of the past, she transformed herself into a "child wife," highlighting her husband's strength and masculinity and emphasizing her own delicacy and fragility. Pickett smoothed over embarrassing aspects of the past, using the shield of widowhood to protect her husband's memory and deflect any challenges to her own authority.[2]

Yet there is still "truth" in the emotionally charged words Pickett wrote. Her mix of fact and fiction provides important insights into the war's meaning for a white Southern woman. Underneath her Victorian romanticism and occasional morbidity was a strong-willed woman desperate to make order out of war's chaos. The voice telling these stories spoke of real anguish, true despair, and a steely determination to set things right again.

LaSalle Corbell was eighteen years old in 1861. The first of nine children, she had spent her childhood at her family home in Nansemond County, Virginia. Her parents, John David and Elizabeth Phillips Corbell, were wealthy slaveholders and owned a sizable plantation. War shattered her family's peaceful existence, and Sallie's life, like that of so many of her contemporaries, was never the same.[3]

War first touched LaSalle while she was a student at Lynchburg Female Seminary in Lynchburg, Virginia. She was not attending the elite academy to expand her intellectual capacities; as the eldest daughter of a large Tidewater planter, she was learning how to be a cultivated white Southern lady and preparing to assume the traditional role of devoted wife and mother.[4]

Pickett's published memoirs vividly recalled the early days of secession and crisis. Her autobiography recounted how she and her classmates clustered excitedly in their schoolrooms, believing "that we knew something of war." They cheered at the sight of the first Confederate national flag and felt confident that their brothers, fathers, uncles, and male friends soon would come home, safe and victorious, from the battlefront. They also held a springtime festival to raise money for knapsacks to equip a local rifle company. LaSalle admitted to her postwar readers that she, like so many other Southerners, believed the war would be relatively bloodless and quick. "We saw then," she remembered, "only the bonfires of joy and heard the paeans of victory."[5] Her impression changed when she met a man wounded in battle: "I began to feel that war meant something more than the thrill of martial music and shouts of victory." In retrospect, she stated that "not only soldiers in the field had obstacles to encounter; they loomed in the pathway of the school-girl."[6]

Historians have recently explored the ways in which white elite Southern women such as LaSalle Pickett tried to reinvent themselves during this time of great social crisis. Traditional gender roles no longer sufficed, and new ones were created, tried on, and tested by war.[7] Pickett's wartime recollections showed a young woman eager to play an active role in the conflict, but often frustrated by conventional attitudes and restrictive gender expectations.

In one story, Pickett told of visiting her uncle Col. J. J. Phillips in camp on the day of the famed naval battle between the *Virginia* and the *Monitor* in early March 1862. When her uncle readied a dinghy to join in the action, Pickett begged to accompany him. " 'No, No!' he shouted. 'Go Back.' " Unshaken by his refusal, she took a seat in his small vessel when he turned his back. As her uncle realized that she had defied him, "a look of horrified amazement" came over his face. According to Pickett, he declared, " 'You needn't think I am going to try to keep you out of danger, you disobedient, incorrigible little minx. . . . It would serve you right if you were shot.' " Pickett attested that she had given little thought to the danger she faced, wanting only to get a good view of the fight.[8]

LaSalle Pickett claimed that the Battle of Seven Pines "brought the war closer to me than any other had yet done."[9] In 1862 she went to

Richmond to spend her summer vacation, unable to return to her Tidewater home because it was caught behind Federal lines. This time she did not have to go looking for action, for Northern troops came dangerously close to the Confederate capital. Her portrait of a city reeling from its first brush with enemy invasion is riveting. She wrote to readers of *Cosmopolitan*: "If I could lay before you the picture of the Richmond of those battle-days, you would say that I had written the most powerful peace argument ever penned." Emphasizing the terrible sights and sounds the Richmond citizenry witnessed during the two-day battle, she described the Confederate capital "shaking with the thunders of the battle while the death-sounds thrilled through our agonized souls." Carts loaded with the wounded and the dead crowded the streets, and most residences were open to the injured. Women and children found that the horror of war had come directly into their homes: "Women, girls, and children stood before the doors with wine and food for the wounded as they passed." Soldiers and civilians flooded into Capitol Square, anxiously awaiting news of loved ones, and black crepe was draped on doorways and windows. Remembering a mother who lost her son at Seven Pines, Pickett declared, "Sometimes the Richmond of those days comes back to me now, and I shudder anew with terror."[10]

Her writings mixed traditional gendered reactions to war, blending the stereotypical feminine repulsion to fighting with the equally stereotypical masculine fascination with battle. She often depicted herself at the forefront of the action, impervious to the danger surrounding her. It appeared that she could not pull herself from the violence. In one account, she told readers of accompanying George as he inspected the lines. As shells began to explode dangerously close, her husband pleaded with her to leave:

> "No indeed," I said. "I'm not a bit afraid, and if I were do you think I would let Pickett's men see me run?"
>
> "Come, dear, please! You are in danger, useless danger, and that is not bravery."

Despite his entreaties, she stayed at the front, snatching a pair of field glasses to gaze across the lines and allegedly catching a glimpse of General Grant and his wife.[11]

In another story, Pickett spoke of witnessing the decapitation of a young officer just after he, too, had warned her of the danger she faced in visiting the front. She watched him "riding in that graceful way which the Southerner has by inheritance from a long line of ancestors who have been accustomed to ride over wide reaches of land."[12] Regretting her "obstinate resistance to his appeal" that she take shelter, she was mortified to see his death. "Impulsively I sprang from my horse," she wrote, "and ran and picked up the poor head, and I solemnly believe that the dying eyes looked their thanks as the last glimmering of life flickered out."[13] This was a strange portrait, indeed—an officer's wife standing defiant to the dangers of battle.

Most of LaSalle Pickett's books and articles had a decidedly martial tone to them. In *The Bugles of Gettysburg*, *Pickett and His Men*, and her serialized *Cosmopolitan* article, "The Wartime Story of General Pickett," she became an official military historian. Perhaps this explains why she unabashedly plagiarized large portions of a staff officer's book for her own writings. Realizing that veterans might question a woman's authority to speak of battle, she inserted a male author's voice for the purely military passages. Pickett insisted to readers that she had a right to publish battle narratives; after all, as a general's wife, she had loyally shared in his victories and his defeats. "My story has been so closely allied with that of Pickett and his division," she wrote in *Pickett and His Men*, "that it does not seem quite an intrusive interpolation for me to appear in the record of that warrior band." She asked, "How could I tell the story, and the way in which that story was written, and not be part of it?"[14]

She believed her wartime romance with George Pickett and their subsequent marriage justified her role as historian of this grand American saga. In her published recollections, she never failed to include details of her whirlwind courtship and the marriage to her "Soldier." It is unclear exactly when their courtship began. LaSalle always maintained that she fell in love with George in 1862 when she first met him on a beach in eastern Virginia. Certainly by the spring of 1863, there was supporting evidence from witnesses of a budding romance. It was apparently during the 1863 Suffolk campaign that things really began to heat up. LaSalle described to readers how George saw her nightly after she went to stay with her aunt some ten miles from his command. "Here when all was quiet along the lines," LaSalle attested, "my Soldier would ride in from his headquarters almost every night between the hours of sunset and sunrise to see me—a ride of about thirty miles."[15]

Two officers corroborated LaSalle's assertions. Col. William Dabney Stuart of the Fifty-sixth Virginia complained to his wife that his division commander was "continually riding off to pay court to his young love, leaving the division details to his staff."[16] And Maj. G. Moxley Sorrel criticized George's "frequent applications to be absent" to see his lover. These nightly rides were long, and the major general did not return to his command until early the next morning. Sorrel sensed that even George's close friend James Longstreet, the corps commander, was irritated with Pickett's constant requests to leave camp, and he recounted how Pickett once asked him (Sorrel) for permission instead. The staff officer declined. He felt he could not justifiably take responsibility for a major general's absence should the division move or be attacked. "Pickett went all the same," Sorrel wrote, "nothing could hold him back from that pursuit." He concluded, "I don't think his division benefited from such carpet-knight doings on the field."[17]

LaSalle Pickett also shared her wartime romance with postwar readers by publishing a collection of letters George allegedly sent her from the battlefront. As already mentioned, scholars have seriously questioned whether her husband actually penned these letters. Comparing them to LaSalle's other published writings and a staff officer's history of Pickett's division, they accuse her of fabricating the letters' contents because the published correspondence contains information George could not have known at the time the letters were purportedly written. Scholars have also pointed to the emotional and romantic tone of the published letters as betraying LaSalle's authorship. Some have wondered if LaSalle heavily edited original letters.[18]

It does seem likely that Pickett constructed the bulk of these missives herself, perhaps basing them loosely on some original love letters George sent her. Her other writings repeatedly stressed her husband's devotion to her, even in the thick of battle. This published collection of wartime letters made her Soldier speak for himself and thus bolster her claims. Even the title is telling: *The Heart of a Soldier: As Revealed in the Intimate Letters of Genl. George E. Pickett CSA.*

While Pickett yearned to be at the forefront of battle, these letters show her husband was growing weary of war. In one of the published letters, George declared: "Oh, my darling, war and its results did not seem so awful till the love for you. Now—now I want to love and bless and help everything, and there are no foes—no enemies—just love for you and longing for you."[19] Until the war ended, LaSalle attested that her husband frequently interrupted important military operations to write her. In another published letter, he pleaded to know why she had quipped "never mind" to him at their last meeting. "It troubled me all night," he declared. "I wanted to follow after you and ask you what you meant, but couldn't. I would have jumped on Lucy [his horse] and ridden in to Petersburg and found out if it had been possible for me to leave. I was so troubled about it that I was almost tempted to come in anyhow." He wondered if he had hurt her feelings by telling her she need not come to the front anymore, that he had enough men to do soldiers' work: "Were you aggrieved because your blundering old Soldier told you there was no necessity for your coming out to bring dispatches, any longer, that, thank heaven, the recruits and reinforcements were coming in now and that we could manage all right?"[20]

In the published Pickett letters, George appeared more impatient to marry than LaSalle. In one, he urged: "So, my Sally, don't let's wait; send me a line back by Jackerie saying you will come. Come at once, my darling, into this valley of the shadow of uncertainty, and make certain the comfort if I should fall I shall fall as your husband." According to LaSalle, he suggested that they "overlook old-time customs" and marry immediately in his camp. She hastily explained to her postwar audience that some might disapprove of the impropriety of his proposal, noting that for those who knew of the "rigid system of social training in which a girl of that period was reared," it would not be "strange that a maiden, even in war times, could not seriously contemplate the possibility of leaving home and being married by the wayside in that desultory and unstudied fashion." LaSalle felt bound by "social laws" even if George did not, and she convinced him to wait.[21] But her lover was a professional soldier and high-ranking general and had to go where orders sent him. "Cupid does not readily give way to Mars," she stated to her readers, "and in our Southern country a lull between bugle calls was likely to be filled with the music of wedding bells."[22]

Pickett naturally chose to include a description of her wedding day in her writings, and it was a dramatic one. She alleged that she and George had difficulties just getting to the Petersburg church. Unable to obtain a furlough, George instead received permission for "special duty" to leave the front, and LaSalle and her family had to sneak across enemy lines, traveling by ferry and train to reach Petersburg from Chuckatuck. LaSalle's father, two uncles, and a female chaperone accompanied her; her mother had to stay behind to care for her baby brother. At the church, she reunited with George, his brother Charles, and his faithful Uncle Andrew and Aunt Olivia. Finally, after a brief but dramatic delay in obtaining the marriage license, George and LaSalle married on September 15, 1863. She recalled: "I felt like a child who had been given a bunch of grapes, a stick of candy. Oh I was happy."[23]

A honeymoon was out of the question, but the couple allegedly managed a festive reception in the Confederate capital. The Picketts' personal celebration became public: LaSalle claimed that several Confederate luminaries attended the party, including President and Mrs. Jefferson Davis, members of Davis's cabinet, and officers in Lee's army. There was also plenty of food, drink, and dancing. "If people could not dance in the crises of life," LaSalle explained to her postwar audience, "the tragedy of existence might be even darker than it is."[24]

In reality the man whom LaSalle Corbell married in 1863 was deep in a personal and professional crisis. A West Point graduate and brevetted Mexican War veteran, George found himself ill prepared for civil war. His former comrades and the nation he had pledged his life to defend became the hated enemy. As the violence escalated, he grew more disturbed. He complained repeatedly, showed flashes of quick anger, and failed when left with any sort of autonomy on the field. As a brigadier general, he was a zealous and aggressive fighter, but when promoted to division commander in October 1862, he seemed overwhelmed with his responsibilities. At Gettysburg, he watched in stunned disbelief as his division shattered itself in a desperate attempt to break the Union line. George never forgot Gettysburg: He brooded over the loss of his division, blaming everyone but himself. He increasingly felt a demise of control and began to perceive the North as uncivilized and demonic.[25]

Soon after his marriage to LaSalle Corbell, George showed further evidence of this loss of personal and professional restraint. When he failed to reclaim Union-held New Bern, North Carolina, in February 1864, he turned his rage on a group of Union prisoners, former members of the North Carolina home guard. Pickett ordered a hasty court-martial and execution of these men, mocking the pleas of Federal officials and ignoring the anguish of the victims' family members. Later, this episode would nearly earn Pickett indictment for war crimes by the U.S. government.[26]

Readers of LaSalle Pickett's books and articles will find no mention of this troubled, angry man. Instead, her Soldier was loving and sensitive, courageous and chivalrous. Her literary George Pickett was not perfect, to be sure, but LaSalle used her morally superior female sex to monitor his weakness for drinking and swearing. But as destruction and chaos raged around them, she said, love and serenity thrived within their union. The wartime marriage Pickett described in her books and articles was, indeed, a haven in a heartless, senseless world.[27]

Pickett's memoirs contain several examples of her efforts to seek "rifts of sunshine to break the gloom."[28] In the bloody summer of 1864, while General Pickett and his men faced grueling siege warfare, LaSalle insisted that "there was no lack of social diversions. In a small way we had our dances, our conversaziones and musicales, quite like the gay world that had never known anything about war except from the pages of books and the columns of newspapers. True, we did not feast."[29]

Pickett set the final chapter of her wartime story in Richmond in April 1865. Separated from her husband during the Confederacy's final days of existence, she waited in the Southern capital, anxious for news. On April 2, 1865, the Confederate government abandoned Richmond, and the next day, Union troops entered the city. Pickett described her terror and fear as she found herself alone with her baby son. Her slaves had long gone, and rumors circulated that her Soldier was dead. Fires set by Confederates spread, and frenzied crowds looted stores and warehouses. Broken furniture, shattered glass, and other wreckage filled the muddy streets. LaSalle likened the experience to a "reign of terror": "The yelling and howling and swearing and weeping and wailing beggar description. Families houseless and homeless under the open sky!"[30] The surreal, hellish picture was made complete by the presence of black Union soldiers. She recalled that "they were the first colored troops I had ever seen, and the weird effect produced by their black faces in that infernal environment was indelibly impressed upon my mind."[31]

An unexpected visitor supposedly came in the midst of the terror. One day after Richmond fell, Pickett answered a knock at her door and saw before her a "tall, gaunt, sad-faced man in ill-fitting clothes, who asked with the accent of the North: 'Is this George Pickett's place?' " President Abraham Lincoln had presumably stopped by to pay her a personal visit during his tour of the fallen Confederate capital. As pure fantasy, the account illustrates the delusive pathos of Pickett's latter-day recollections, as well as her overinflated sense of self-importance. Nonetheless, she shrewdly played to her postwar audience's renewed feelings of reunion and Lincoln nostalgia. It made a great story.[32]

All of LaSalle Pickett's published memories of her war experience and marriage were carefully presented. Deliberately crafting her literary self and that of her husband for national consumption, she followed the Southern plantation tradition initiated by authors such as Thomas Nelson Page and Joel Chandler Harris. When she described the antebellum South, she celebrated "de good ole times 'fo' de wah," putting herself and her husband in a setting that featured paternalistic slaveowners and loyal, passive slaves. Her racist images were eagerly bought up by the white reading public, North and South, at the turn of the twentieth century.[33]

Besides sheer profit and celebrating the Lost Cause, LaSalle Pickett seemed to have had additional personal motives for publicly recounting her wartime experience. As a Confederate general's wife, she could only celebrate her husband; it would have been highly unacceptable for her to write anything negative about him or her marriage. So instead, she cloaked the suffering and difficulties she must have endured in the conventional role of loving wife and mourning widow. She sought to conform to acceptable gender roles by emphasizing her husband's courage and bravery and de-emphasizing her own autonomy and strength. The resulting picture was a contradictory one: Her husband often appeared in her writings as pacifistic and emotional, and she seemed reckless and bold, eager to be in the thick of battle yet sickened by war's destruction and chaos. Pickett struggled to make sense out of it all decades after the war ended. "Years away from that time of anguish and terror," she wrote, "I awaken suddenly with the crash of those guns still in my ears, their fearful sounds yet echoing in my heart, only to find myself safe in my soft, warm bed."[34] Haunted by these images, she wondered if she were "destined to an eternity of remorse."[35]

Few historians have taken LaSalle Pickett or her published works seriously, for she was overtly dishonest about her husband's failings and difficulties and about people she allegedly met and events she allegedly witnessed. Yet should historians question the sorrow she described? Should they doubt the disturbing nightmares that she told readers she continued to suffer years after the war ended? After all, men such as James Longstreet and George McClellan publicly exaggerated and stretched the "facts" of their wartime experiences. Clearly, LaSalle Pickett's recollections of the Civil War pose difficult questions for modern readers to consider. The line between fact and fiction in her writings is often so blurred that it is nearly impossible to separate myth from reality. But her reconstructed memory of her Civil War experience tells us a great deal about the war's lasting meaning to one of its singular participants. It tells us about powerful gender conventions during and after the war. And it tells us of a woman seeking desperately to stake a personal claim for a painfully uncivil past.

Notes

1. LaSalle Corbell Pickett, *What Happened to Me* (New York: Brentano's, 1917), 216. This chapter is drawn from the author's larger study of the Picketts, *General George E. Pickett in Life and Legend* (Chapel Hill: University of North Carolina Press, 1998).

2. Obituaries in the *Confederate Veteran* 39, no. 4 (April 1931): 151, and the *Washington Post*, March 23, 1931, refer to Pickett as the "Child Bride of the Confederacy." She called herself a "child wife" in her autobiography, Pickett, *What Happened to Me*, 189. The age discrepancy appears in U.S. Census Office, 7th Census of the United States, 1850: Population Schedules, Nansemond County, Virginia, and U.S. Census Office, 8th Census of the United States, 1860: Population Schedules, Nansemond County, Virginia. Both census records list Pickett's age as five years younger than she later claimed to be in her autobiographical writings.

3. U.S. Census Office, 7th Census of the United States, 1850: Population Schedules, Nansemond County, Virginia, and U.S. Census Office, 8th Census of the United States, 1860: Population Schedules, Nansemond County, Virginia; obituaries in *Confederate Veteran* 39, no. 4 (April 1931): 151, *New York Times*, March 23, 1931, and *Washington Post*, March 23, 1931.

4. Pickett, *What Happened to Me*, 83; Dorothy T. Potter and Clifton W. Potter, *Lynchburg: "The Most Interesting Spots"* (Lynchburg, VA: Progress Publishing Co., 1976), 1; Christie Anne Farnham, *The Education of the Southern Belle: Higher Education and Student Socialization in the Antebellum South* (New York: New York University Press, 1994), 72–73, 174; Anne Firor Scott, *The Southern Lady: From Pedestal to Politics, 1830–1930* (Chicago: University of Chicago Press, 1970), 71.

5. Pickett, *What Happened to Me*, 89–92; George Morris and Susan Foutz, *Lynchburg in the Civil War: The City, the People, the Battle* (Lynchburg, VA: H. E. Howard, 1984), 10.

6. Pickett, *What Happened to Me*, 89–90.

7. Drew Gilpin Faust, *Mothers of Invention: Women of the Slaveholding South in the American Civil War* (Chapel Hill: University of North Carolina Press, 1996); LeeAnn Whites, *The Civil War as a Crisis in Gender: Augusta, Georgia, 1860–1890* (Athens: University of Georgia Press, 1995); Catherine Clinton and Nina Silber, eds., *Divided Houses: Gender and the Civil War* (New York: Oxford University Press, 1992).

8. Pickett, *What Happened to Me*, 99–100.

9. LaSalle Corbell Pickett, *Pickett and His Men* (Atlanta, GA: Foote and Davies, 1899), 170.

10. LaSalle Corbell Pickett, "The Wartime Story of General Pickett," *Cosmopolitan* 56 (January 1914): 178–80. Pickett repeated this same passage in her 1917 autobiography, *What Happened to Me*, 104–8; see also idem, *Pickett and His Men*, 170–74.

11. Pickett, *What Happened to Me*, 143.

12. Pickett, *Pickett and His Men*, 361.

13. Pickett, *What Happened to Me*, 144–45. An abbreviated form of this story is included in her *Pickett and His Men*, 360–61, but Pickett left out any mention of her retrieving the head.

14. LaSalle Pickett, *Pickett and His Men*, 7. For discussion of her plagiarism, see Gary Gallagher, "A Widow and Her Soldier: LaSalle Corbell Pickett as Author of the George E. Pickett Letters," *Virginia Magazine of History and Biography* 94 (July 1986): 335–37.

15. Pickett, *What Happened to Me*, 121.

16. Quoted in William A. Young Jr. and Patricia C. Young, *56th Virginia Infantry* (Lynchburg, VA: H. E. Howard, 1990), 74.

17. G. Moxley Sorrel, *Recollections of a Confederate Staff Officer* (1905; reprint ed., Dayton, OH: Morningside, 1978), 153.

18. Gallagher, "A Widow and Her Soldier," 329–44; Glenn Tucker, *Lee and Longstreet at Gettysburg* (Indianapolis: Bobbs-Merrill Co., 1968), 44– 45; George R. Stewart, *Pickett's Charge: A Microhistory of the Final Attack at Gettysburg, July 3, 1863* (Boston: Houghton Mifflin Co., 1959), 297–98; Douglas Southall Freeman, *R. E. Lee: A Biography*, 4 vols. (New York: Charles Scribner's Sons, 1935), 4:563.

19. LaSalle Corbell Pickett, ed., *The Heart of a Soldier: As Revealed in the Intimate Letters of Genl. George E. Pickett CSA* (New York: Seth Moyle, 1913), 65–66.

20. Ibid., 125.

21. Ibid., 75–76.

22. Pickett, *What Happened to Me*, 124.

23. Quoted in Arthur Crew Inman, *The Inman Diary: A Public and Private Confession*, ed. Daniel Aaron, 2 vols. (Cambridge, MA: Harvard University Press, 1985), 1:328; wedding details gathered from Pickett, "The Wartime Story of General Pickett," 764, and idem, *Pickett and His Men*, 320–21; also *Richmond (Virginia) Dispatch*, September 22, 1863.

24. Pickett, *Pickett and His Men*, 320–21; see also idem, *What Happened to Me*, 126–29.

25. Douglas Southall Freeman, *Lee's Lieutenants: A Study in Command*, 3 vols. (New York: Charles Scribner's Sons, 1942), 1:158–59, 192, 242–43; Ezra Warner, *Generals in Gray: Lives of the Confederate Commanders* (Baton Rouge: Louisiana State University Press, 1959), 239–40.

26. Freeman, *Lee's Lieutenants* 3:xxxvi; Warner, *Generals in Gray*, 239–40.

27. Pickett, *What Happened to Me*, 136; see also Pickett, *Pickett and His Men*, 326.

28. Pickett, *What Happened to Me*, 141.

29. Pickett, *Pickett and His Men*, 357; see also idem, *What Happened to Me*, 141.

30. LaSalle Corbell Pickett, "The First United States Flag Raised in Richmond after the War," in *The Fourth Massachusetts Cavalry in the Closing Scenes of the War for the Maintenance of the Union*, ed. William B. Arnold (Boston: n.p., n.d.), 19–22, quote from p. 21.

31. Pickett, *What Happened to Me*, 164–65. See also idem, "My Soldier," *McClure's Magazine* 30 (March 1908): 563–71; Richard N. Current, ed., *Encyclopedia of the Confederacy*, 4 vols. (New York: Simon and Schuster, 1993), 3:1331.

32. Pickett, *What Happened to Me*, 167–70.

33. LaSalle Corbell Pickett, *Jinny* (Washington, DC: The Neale Co., 1901), 59.

34. Pickett, *Pickett and His Men*, 343.

35. Pickett, *What Happened to Me*, 216.

2

Benjamin "Pap" Singleton
Father of the Kansas Exodus

Gary R. Entz

In 1879 the news that thousands of impoverished former slaves were abandoning their southern homes in search of a better life in Kansas stunned many white Americans. For black southerners, however, this mass migration was anything but surprising. They were free in name, but emancipation had not resulted in economic or political freedom. White landlords had used the sharecropping system to keep black tenant farmers in perpetual debt and bound to the land. Moreover, by a variety of means, conservative white southerners had deprived African Americans of the right to vote. Thus, for black southerners, the westward migration not only represented a search for economic opportunity but also a means for asserting their autonomy, protecting their citizenship rights, and articulating their opposition to white supremacy.

Few people understood this better than a former slave named Benjamin "Pap" Singleton. Beginning in 1875, Singleton urged black southerners to migrate to the West, and two years later he led the first group of black settlers to Kansas. With only limited financial resources, however, most of the black agricultural settlements in the West collapsed. Embittered by this failure, Singleton concluded that African Americans could only achieve economic independence and political autonomy if they separated completely from the United States. Thus, instead of encouraging black southerners to migrate to the West, Singleton embraced Pan-Africanism and began to urge them instead to settle in Africa.

Gary R. Entz earned his Ph.D. from the University of Utah, Salt Lake City, in 1999 and is assistant professor of history at McPherson College, McPherson, Kansas. His "Zion Valley: The Mormon Origins of St. John, Kansas," *Kansas History* 24 (Summer 2001), won the Western History Association's 2002 Arrington-Prucha Prize for best article in Western Religious History.

Benjamin Singleton was born into slavery in 1809 near Nashville in Davidson County, Tennessee. Details of his early life in bondage are elusive. Trained as a carpenter and cabinetmaker, Singleton apparently had a history of defying slavery. He claimed that he had made nearly a

This essay originally appeared in Nina Mjagkij, ed., *Portraits of African American Life since 1865* (Wilmington, DE: Scholarly Resources, 2003), 15–33.

dozen attempts to escape his bondage before he finally made good on his bid for freedom in 1846. At the age of thirty-seven, Singleton escaped through Indiana to Detroit, Michigan. He never credited any individual or group with assisting his escape and in subsequent years recalled, "when the nostrils of the blood hounds were trailing at my heels" there was "no eye to pity or hand to deliver."[1] He made his way to Canada but returned to the United States within a year.

In Detroit, Singleton lived the hardscrabble life of a scavenger, constantly fearing his capture by fugitive slave catchers. The passage of the Fugitive Slave Law of 1850, which made it easier for slave catchers to apprehend fugitives as well as free blacks, further threatened Detroit's African American community. Singleton, like all fugitives, had to maintain a nondescript existence for his own safety. In later years, however, he claimed that he had labored as a member of the Underground Railroad, aiding fellow fugitives during the final leg of their journey across the border to Canada. Singleton undoubtedly contributed whatever aid he could and continued in this capacity until 1861, when the outbreak of the Civil War ended the fugitives' need to seek refuge in Canada. "There was a time," he later said, "when we could not see the clouds of heaven for the smoke of angry men until after it was settled, and the slaves could stare freedom in the face, and cry with a loud voice, 'We are free at last!' "[2] Singleton took advantage of the Union occupation of Nashville to return home, rebuild his life, and search for family and friends. Singleton apparently had children before he escaped to Canada. But since he remained illiterate and left no personal papers, little is known about his family.

Nashville occupied a unique position among southern cities. In February 1862, Confederate forces abandoned the city, and its citizens surrendered to the Union army with minimal resistance. As a result, Nashville avoided the widescale destruction other southern urban areas experienced, and its subsequent status as headquarters for Union troops kept money flowing into the region. Tennessee's state capital took on the characteristics of a frontier boomtown, attracting large numbers of black and white residents from the North and the South. Many freedpeople, particularly from the upper South, migrated to Nashville in search of economic opportunities.[3]

As the number of former slaves who flocked to the Union camps and shantytowns on the outskirts of Nashville grew, white legislators and city residents became alarmed and started to exclude African Americans from social and political life. In 1870, Tennessee enacted laws prohibiting interracial marriages, and it became the first southern state to adopt a poll tax, requiring prospective voters to pay for the privilege of voting. As a result, the majority of African Americans, who had limited financial resources, were virtually excluded from voting. In 1873, Tennessee segregated its school system, and two years later the state assembly gutted the federal Civil Rights Act of 1875, which sought to end racial discrimination in the selection of juries and in public accommodations. At the same time, Tennessee enacted contract labor and vagrancy laws, coercing African Americans to work for white planters and allowing for the incarceration of those who had no means of support. In the 1870s, Nashville became a focal point for antiblack sentiments, resulting in lynchings, black church burnings, and other manifestations of mob violence.[4]

Nashville's black residents recognized this ominous trend even before the state legislature passed the first of its exclusionary laws. In September 1869 a group of African Americans gathered in Nashville under the leadership of Randall Brown to discuss the possibility of relocating to the West. Brown, a former slave and Republican politician whom conservative Democrats had recently ousted from the city council, however, was more interested in reorganizing his own political base than in leading an emigration movement. While the meeting did not generate a black mass migration to the West, those who attended discussed the matter thoroughly. They understood that drastic changes were necessary to end black economic dependence on whites, which virtually ensured that African Americans remained second-class citizens in the South.[5]

Although there is no evidence that Benjamin Singleton ever collaborated with Brown, several of Singleton's associates had attended the 1869 convention. Singleton, aware of the deterioration of black economic, social, legal, and political conditions in the South, shared the meeting delegates' grim outlook for African Americans in the region.[6] Unlike Brown, however, Singleton eschewed politics. Distrustful of politicians, Singleton had nothing but contempt for those who used the black community to gain elective office and line their pockets. He had little patience with what he saw as the endless posturing of black leaders who talked without acting. In 1869, Singleton joined forces with Columbus M. Johnson and several other former slaves and began looking for ways to free African Americans from economic dependency by providing them with their own land.

The group, however, lacked the funds to purchase land and distribute it among the freedmen. Thus, the initial goal was to encourage blacks to seek out small farms that they could bargain for at favorable terms. Singleton and his associates had little immediate success and encountered stiff resistance from white landowners who either refused to sell land to former slaves or demanded an inflated price far above the fair market value of the property.[7] Johnson may have raised these issues when he served as a delegate to the 1872 Republican National Convention in Philadelphia and again at the party's 1876 convention in Cincinnati. A conservative resurgence, however, undermined the efforts of those in the Republican Party who sought to aid the former slaves and frustrated African American hopes for any federal assistance.[8]

Despite such discouragements, Singleton and his colleagues continued their efforts to find land for the freedmen in Tennessee, until the depression that followed the panic of 1873 ended Nashville's postwar economic boom. The depression had a severe impact on the city's African American population, as limited employment opportunities heightened the job competition between black and white workers.[9] Singleton realized that the economic crisis created potentially dangerous conditions for black residents. Singleton, who had worked as a coffin maker, had witnessed firsthand the horrifying results of lynchings. Given the racially explosive climate as well as the limited legal and political protection that the state provided for its black residents, Singleton feared that African Americans could no longer guarantee the safety of their families. It was at this point that he began to argue aggressively for black separatism. In September 1874 he and eight others organized the Edgefield Real Estate Association to assist former slaves living in the Nashville area in the acquisition of land.[10]

White opposition, however, remained a major obstacle to black land ownership in the South. Thus, Singleton and his partners began to explore the possibility of relocating African Americans to Kansas or other parts of the West. In May 1875 they became the leading participants in a black state convention that discussed the systematic resettlement of African Americans. Convention delegates agreed that black economic, political, legal, and social conditions had deteriorated, but they were initially split over the necessity of leaving Tennessee. It was not until the delegates considered the recent lynchings of David Jones, Joseph Reed, and schoolteacher Julia Hayden that those who advocated migration to the West finally forged a majority. Proclaiming that "prejudice is stronger than law," the convention concluded that the state was unable and unwilling to protect African Americans. Thus, the delegates declared, "as we desire . . . peace and prosperity, we deem it best for the negro to seek a place, where he can enjoy the privileges of mankind, where justice is too blind to discriminate on account of color."[11]

To implement their plan the delegates established a Board of Emigration Commissioners in Nashville and appointed recruiting agents for each county in Tennessee.[12] Local agents conducted emigration meetings and appointed subagents for each ward and civil district in the state. This communications network enabled Singleton's associates to spread their separatist message and generate statewide interest in black migration to the West. Furthermore, the commissioners directed Henry A. Napier to take a three-man scouting party to explore the Kansas plains in search of suitable land. The Napier team spent the summer of 1875 near Great Bend, Kansas. Returning to Nashville in August, Napier reported that he was pleased with the quality of the land. His report concluded, however, that given the limited resources of African Americans, black settlers would encounter more financial and environmental obstacles in Kansas than they could overcome. He calculated that each settler would need more than $1,000 to survive and warned that "it is not advisable for anyone to go to Kansas with a less amount than the above named sum at his command, with any hope of bettering his temporal condition."[13] Without sufficient funds to feed and clothe the migrants, Napier considered it folly to exchange one form of suffering for another. Not all of the commissioners agreed with Napier's blunt assessment. Another commissioner argued that $200 would be sufficient for the frugal settler who opted for a government homestead.[14]

Individual migration, however, was not what Singleton had in mind. He believed that black migrants could overcome the financial obstacles through mutual aid, cooperation, and, most important, racial solidarity. Singleton used the emigration commissioners' network of agents to encourage potential recruits to attend his real estate association's twice-weekly meetings in Edgefield and at the Second Baptist Church in Nashville. He also encouraged local ministers to spread word of his plans for a cooperative migration among their congregations.[15]

It took him a year, but by August 1876, Singleton had recruited between fifty and 100 African Americans who were willing to relocate to Kansas. Although his association had collected enough money to pay for most of the migrants' transportation expenses, the settlers had virtually no money to purchase land or support themselves after their arrival. Hence, Singleton sought an external source of aid. He asked Kansas governor Thomas A. Osborn if the state government would be willing to assist the colonists with land, work, or any type of relief that would help them get a start in the West. He assured Osborn that his followers were industrious workers and within a few years of getting settled would gladly repay any aid received. This was no idle request on Singleton's part, and he wanted the governor to understand the sense of urgency blacks felt about leaving Tennessee. "We are Bound to leve [*sic*] the State just as soon as we can get a way," he declared, "for Starvation is Staring us in the face."[16]

Osborn's staff never responded to the letter, but Singleton remained undeterred. In the late fall of 1876 he made a personal trip to Kansas to see if he could make other arrangements. Accompanied by Columbus Johnson, he visited Cherokee County in the southeastern part of the state. In December 1876 he may have reached a verbal understanding with agents of the Missouri River, Fort Scott and Gulf Railroad to reserve two thousand acres of ground north of the town of Baxter Springs.[17] Singleton returned to Nashville with the good news and during the summer of 1877 accompanied seventy-three settlers to Cherokee County. Reflecting his belief in black separatism, Singleton emphasized the importance of race unity to those leaving Nashville. Yet he also realized that because of the migrants' limited funds, temporary wage labor was an economic necessity. Thus, he encouraged his followers to "make their sustenance and their first gains by working for wages on the new farms of the more forehanded white settlers."[18]

The settlers who migrated to Cherokee County did so with every intention, as a local journalist observed, "of laying out a town, [and having] a post-office, newspaper and all the parapharnalia [*sic*] of an enterprising town."[19] Their dream was complete economic independence, but with the simultaneous development of lead mines in the nearby towns of Galena and Empire City the colony site rapidly increased in value. The black settlers had not made any down payments on the land before the mining boom, and when they arrived the railroad's land agents felt obliged to charge them seven dollars per acre with a 7 percent interest rate payable over ten years. The price was reasonable for the area but significantly more than Singleton's followers could afford. There were few employment opportunities for black unskilled laborers in the mines and towns, and without this source of income, on which the association had counted, the entire project collapsed. By 1878, African Americans in Cherokee County were appealing to the governor for aid to prevent starvation, and Singleton withdrew his support of the colony.[20]

Singleton was upset at having to abandon the Cherokee County colony but remained convinced that a separate economic existence was the only way for African Americans to succeed. Since land prices had defeated his first effort, Singleton turned his attention toward obtaining government homesteads. In 1878 the only government land still open to settlers in the eastern part of Kansas was along the Neosho River valley in Morris and parts of Lyon counties. This area had been part of the Kansa Indian Reservation, and the federal government had been selling the Kansa trust lands piecemeal since the removal of the tribe in 1873. Squatters and the railroads had long since claimed the best ground, but some marginal lands, selling for $1.25 and $2.00 per acre, near the village of Dunlap were still available. This area was where Singleton made his second effort, and between April 1878 and March 1879 his association directed almost two hundred settlers to the region. Most managed to make the initial down payment on a small claim in four distinct settlements in Dunlap and its vicinity, although they had nothing left for homes and had to live in dugouts or brush shelters. Nevertheless, their fortitude impressed the local postmaster, who commented, "they have got along better than the same class of whites would."[21] Within a year the settlers were building small houses from local stone, and it appeared as if Singleton's dream of a black separatist haven might come true. That is, until the Exodusters arrived.

Literally thousands of rural black southerners started arriving in Kansas when the Great Exodus began in the spring of 1879. Many whites, who had no understanding of the anxieties that stirred black people to leave the South, were initially surprised by the mass migration. They claimed that land sharks and other "unscrupulous men," who for their own profit shamelessly "deluded" impoverished African American people with false promises of free land in the West, were responsible for the Exodus. Only men with financial means, whites insisted, could overcome the hardships of prairie life, and they urged poor blacks to remain in the South. Assumptions of this sort angered Singleton, who countered, "it's because they are poor . . . that they want to get away, and ought to get away. If they had plenty, they wouldn't want to come. It's to better their condition that they are thinking of. That's what white men go to new countries for, isn't it? And do you tell them to stay back because they are poor?"[22] Members of Singleton's association in Topeka, including Columbus Johnson, immediately began organizing efforts to look after the welfare of the new settlers.[23]

Meanwhile, Singleton stopped conducting organized migrations from Tennessee so that he could remain in Kansas and act as an advocate for the largely voiceless Exodusters. In June 1879 he incorporated the Singleton Colony of Dunlap and accepted appointment as the "agent to procure aid for the destitute of the Colony." He had been calling himself the "Father of the Kansas emigration from Tennessee" since 1877 but now adopted the title "Father of the Kansas Exodus" to encourage racial unity and cooperation between blacks already settled in Kansas and those just arriving from other parts of the South.[24] Singleton rejoiced that African Americans were "now waked up to a sense of their duty," which was, as he saw it, to separate from the South and join together as a nation in the West. "The morning light has appeared to them," he proclaimed, "and they have got that light and are now traveling by it to the glory and promised land." Singleton's associates provided aid to the Exodusters while directing selected groups of new arrivals to the Dunlap colony. Singleton's resources, however, were limited and he hoped that African Americans throughout the nation would support the settlers. He urged black associations and churches to "come forward and contribute towards the relief of their brethren who are fleeing in their poverty."[25]

By spring many white Kansans had become worried about growing racial tensions in Topeka. Concerned individuals, under the leadership of Governor John P. St. John, realized that some form of assistance was necessary and organized the interracial Kansas Freedmen's Relief Association (KFRA). The KFRA helped relocate African American migrants to several colonies in Kansas, and a little more than 100 of them went to Dunlap in 1879. Unfortunately the influx was more than the struggling colony could bear. Although the original colonists had agreed to encourage migration and assist the newcomers, by the end of the year they were overwhelmed and had to appeal to the KFRA for help in meeting their fifteen-dollar annual land payments.[26] The KFRA provided some food, clothing, and shelter to those individuals it helped relocate, but to survive on their own the settlers needed land, money, and tools. The needed assistance came, but at the cost of the colony's independence.

In 1879 the Presbyterian Synod of North America appointed the Reverend John M. Snodgrass as missionary to blacks in Dunlap and to coordinate church relief efforts in the area. Snodgrass, in addition to helping with direct relief efforts, petitioned his church to sponsor construction of a literary and business school. In 1881, Snodgrass's labors resulted in the opening of the Freedmen's Academy of Dunlap, a primary school that also offered adult degrees in teaching, business, and vocal music as well as sewing classes for young women. Working with the Freedmen's Aid Association of Dunlap, the academy solicited land donations to distribute among the settlers in five- and ten-acre allotments. In 1882, Andrew Atchison, the academy's principal, declared the colony and school a success, although he admitted that farm crops remained "disheartening."[27] As a result of the Presbyterian Church's relief efforts, the Dunlap colony had become entirely dependent on donations from white philanthropists. When whites began to withdraw their support toward the end of the decade, the academy folded and the colony entered its final decline. Singleton's involvement with the Dunlap colony ended once the Presbyterian Church assumed relief efforts. Columbus Johnson and a few of his longtime associates remained in Dunlap to run the church-sponsored Freedmen's Aid Association, but Singleton could not subordinate himself to a white organization.[28]

Although Singleton ceased his formal association with the Dunlap colony, his advocacy on behalf of the Exodusters had earned him a measure of national prominence. In 1880, when the U.S. Senate convened an investigating committee to determine the causes of the Exodus, he received a subpoena to testify. The Senate investigation was sparked largely by concerns that the continued westward migration of African Americans threatened to deprive southern white landowners of their cheap agricultural workforce. With the exception of Republican William Windom of Minnesota, members of the investigating committee were hostile to the black migration. Singleton, determined to make a case for those still suffering in the South, refused to be intimidated by their hostility.[29] He admonished the senators to consider the plight of the majority of black southerners who were living in grinding poverty and without equal protection under the law. "I am a man," he insisted, "that will live in a country where I am going to cope with the white man, where the white man will lift himself to the level of justice; but when the white man will think that equal rights under the law to the colored man is a violation of his . . . dignity, I am going to leave." Singleton concluded that as long as the federal government shirked its responsibility of protecting African Americans, black separation was the only answer. Thus, he proclaimed that he would continue to encourage black people to migrate out of the South "if there ain't an alteration and signs of change."[30]

Traveling back to Kansas, Singleton continued to criticize the committee, particularly its Democratic chairman, Senator Daniel Voorhees. He attacked Voorhees in a speech, charging that the senator had manipulated the witness list to ensure that the committee would hear primarily from men "who were interested in keeping the colored people South." Singleton, who in the past had rejected politics as a viable means of fostering racial advancement, now encouraged his audience to vote against the Democratic ticket. Northern Democrats, declared Singleton, "say they are not like these Southern Democrats—they are as bad or worse—they are helping them, who boast of a solid South to carry out their purpose."[31]

Following his Washington testimony, Singleton realized that owning a parcel of land in the West was not enough to guarantee either black economic independence or racial equality. Rather than concentrating his efforts on encouraging blacks to leave the South, Singleton now started to focus his energy on uniting all African Americans into one national organization. Individual members of the race, he argued, had limited power to fight racial discrimination, but collectively they would have the strength "to be a great and prosperous people."[32] Singleton urged black ministers to help him disseminate his plans among their congregations while opening their churches as meeting halls "in the interest of consolidating my race."[33] Singleton envisioned an organization that would combine the financial resources of all African Americans to build black-owned factories, businesses, and trade schools. His efforts soon bore fruit.

On March 4, 1881, during an open-air rally in Topeka, Singleton launched a new organization designed to unite all African Americans in the struggle against racial discrimination. Those attending the rally acknowledged Singleton's charge that "as a race we have been since our enfranchisement, merely drifting along each pursuing his or her separate or private interests." This state of affairs had to end, and those attending proclaimed it was the "duty of every intelligent colored man to step forward and unite himself with his brethren in an earnest and unceasing effort to evolve a satisfactory solution" to the problem of racial discrimination in America. Addressing the rally, Singleton declared, "we the colored people form an organization to be known as the Colored United Links" (CUL).[34]

The CUL never gained the nationwide following Singleton envisioned. In Kansas, however, the organization became powerful enough to attract the attention of the Greenback-Labor Party. Both groups agreed to a joint convention in Topeka in August 1881. Singleton, who had shunned party politics in the past, hoped that the CUL's collaboration with the Greenback-Labor Party would secure social and political protection for blacks in an increasingly hostile and competitive job market.

The prospect of a fusion between the Links and the Greenbackers so frightened local white Republicans that they embarked on a campaign to destroy the CUL. Singleton criticized such Republican tactics, even though most African Americans believed that they owed their freedom to the party of Lincoln. Disappointed about the lack of support the Republican Party had extended to the former slaves, Singleton proclaimed that he felt no obligation to the Republicans: "I . . . say good bye to the party and sing a funeral dirge." For Singleton racial unity was more important than party loyalties, and he explained, "we are not on politics but on a sure platform, [so] step on board and do not fall asleep. No difference in the fare, one fare for all."[35]

While James B. Weaver of the Greenback-Labor Party highlighted the Topeka convention festivities, Alonzo D. DeFrantz, a longtime associate of Singleton, articulated the CUL's position. "We recollect," declared DeFrantz, "that the Constitution is a depository of every precious right of its citizens." He reminded the audience that blacks were entitled to the full privileges of citizenship, "and as we feel and know that our race has been deprived of those rights . . . we ask the sympathy of the Nation to enforce such laws as will secure our rights in common with other citizens." DeFrantz emphasized the CUL's continuing concern for African Americans in the South and stressed, "we want the freedom of speech, in the protection of life, liberty, and prosperity in the Southern States in the free exercise of the ballot inasmuch as the Constitution provides." In addition to these fundamental rights, he insisted that black people should have access to an "impartial trial by the juries of the country, and not the mob law that has taken possession of it." This message was the one the CUL wanted politicians of all parties to hear, and DeFrantz punctuated it with a final appeal to white northerners: "Dear people of the North, will you hear us cry for freedom, and suffer us to die! We don't believe that you will."[36]

Despite the apparent success of the August 1881 convention, the CUL never achieved the unity of effort for which Singleton had hoped. He felt that "the Spirit of the Lord" had instructed him "to call his people together to unite them from their divided condition," but his expectations never included a specific program beyond the vague promises of success through racial cooperation. Without any concrete agenda the CUL's membership dispersed after the August convention. The realization that the CUL was faltering struck Singleton particularly hard. "I have been slighted," he bemoaned, "all my work prevaileth nothing. I seek no more honor from man. I have got all the honor I want and what

I have got would not pay my burial expenses." At seventy-two years of age, Singleton was exhausted, but not quite ready to withdraw from public life.[37]

Singleton spent the next year contemplating the collapse of the CUL and by 1883 came to the conclusion that African Americans needed a "fresh start where the color line is not too rigid." Disillusioned with the entrenchment of segregation and the deterioration of race relations in the South, Singleton advised blacks to "never cast another vote in the south for it is just getting you all murdered up and slaughtered in a brutal manner." He was equally troubled by continued white efforts to prevent African Americans from achieving economic independence. "When we were delivered from slavery," he observed, "we were delivered with nothing and have been trying to rise up and be respected." Yet white southerners, he complained, "still try to hold us down but we can't stand to be treated in this manner." Singleton concluded that racial advancement was only possible if African Americans separated completely from the United States. His call captured the attention of Joseph Ware, a white businessman in St. Louis, who convinced Singleton that he should solicit the British government to open the Mediterranean island of Cyprus to black separatists.[38]

Singleton moved to St. Louis to work with Ware and John Williamson, an African American minister, on the formation of a "Chief League" for emigration to Cyprus. The project attracted little support, however, and fell apart in 1884 when Ware's business failed. The entire Cyprus debacle left Singleton embittered, and before returning to Topeka he unleashed a harsh epistle to the black community in St. Louis. His efforts to unite the race, he charged, had been undermined by members of the educated black urban elite, "some of the imported slippery chaps from Washington, Oberlin, [and] Chicago." Interested in safeguarding their own status in society, they had conspired and sent provocateurs in the form of "intriguing reverends, deputy doorkeepers, military darkeys or teachers; to go around the corrals, and see that not an appearance of a hole exists, through which the captives within can escape, or even see through."[39]

Although the Cyprus project never progressed beyond the planning stage, it gave Singleton a global perspective and pushed his separatism toward Pan-Africanism. He moved to Kansas City and in June 1885 organized his final venture, the United Transatlantic Society (UTS). The goals of the UTS were to colonize people of African descent in Africa and to "better the condition of the African race politically, socially and financially throughout the world." Like all of Singleton's projects, the UTS counted on African Americans to unite and donate their "assistance in labor of brain and finance to accomplish this great and grand purpose." The UTS served primarily as an outlet for the black collective rage that had been growing since the end of the Civil War. Black people had struggled in poverty for twenty years and, having received little assistance since emancipation, owed no allegiance to the United States. The officers of the UTS pointed out that whites' willingness to hire European immigrants, rather than African Americans, demonstrated that racial discrimination would always prevent blacks from attaining full equality. Singleton wholly condoned this line of reasoning and blamed immigrants for forcing African Americans to consider leaving the land of their birth. "We cannot feed, clothe, and school our children on starvation wages," lamented Singleton, "and when we have attained an education, of what use is it to them here? None whatever."[40]

Although the UTS held several conventions through 1887, and never compromised its declaration "that nothing short of a separate national existence will ever meet the wants and necessities of our people," it lacked the funds to send African Americans across the Atlantic. The organization collapsed in the summer of 1887, and Singleton returned to Topeka in October of that year to address a meeting of young civil rights activists who had united under the banner of the Afro-American League. This speech marked one of his last public appearances, and he closed his career with a formidable warning of dark days to come. Singleton told his youthful audience, "as the volcano bursts, with a louder explosion, when the combustible matter is confined within its bosom, so will a nation's revenge find vent the more their wrongs are repressed." He returned to Kansas City in ill health and made no further public appeals until 1889, when he raised his voice for the final time. Singleton had been observing the efforts of Edward P. McCabe and others who had been encouraging Congress to set aside part of the Oklahoma Territory for an all-black state. Singleton issued a brief statement of support and asked the railroads to give discounts to African Americans migrating to the region.[41] Following this appeal, he slipped into obscurity. Singleton died in St. Louis in 1892 at the age of eighty-three.

Historians have called Benjamin Singleton the Moses of the black Exodus, but this is a misnomer. He was first and foremost a nationalist who urged African Americans to seek a separate and dignified existence on the western plains of Kansas. His separatism failed, but he left an activist legacy in the West that placed him ideologically alongside Marcus Garvey and other advocates of a "race first" philosophy.

Notes

1. *Kansas City Gate City Press*, clipping, n.d., in Benjamin Singleton, Scrapbook, 53, Kansas State Historical Society, Topeka, Kansas (hereafter cited as Singleton, Scrapbook).

2. Ibid.

3. Howard N. Rabinowitz, *Race Relations in the Urban South, 1865–1890* (New York: Oxford University Press, 1978), 15.

4. Yollette Trigg Jones, "The Black Community, Politics, and Race Relations in the 'Iris City': Nashville, Tennessee, 1870–1954" (Ph.D. diss., Duke University, 1985), 58–59; and Rabinowitz, *Race Relations*, 52–53.

5. *Nashville Daily Press and Times*, September 21–28, 1869; *Nashville Union and American*, September 28, October 10, 1869; Rabinowitz, *Race Relations*, 250; Alrutheus Ambush Taylor, *The Negro in Tennessee, 1865–1880* (Washington, DC: The Associated Publishers, Inc., 1941), 108–10; May Alice Harris Ridley, "The Black Community of Nashville and Davidson County, 1860–1870" (Ph.D. diss., University of Pittsburgh, 1982), 83–84.

6. "The Negro Hegira," *Chicago Tribune*, March 27, 1879.

7. U.S. Senate, *Report and Testimony of the Select Committee of the United States Senate to Investigate the Causes of the Removal of the Negroes from the Southern States to the Northern States*, 46th Cong., 2d sess., 1880, S. R. 693, serial 1899 (Washington, DC: Government Printing Office, 1880), 389; *St. Louis Globe-Democrat*, April 21, 1879.

8. *Chicago Tribune*, March 27, 1879.

9. Rabinowitz, *Race Relations*, 24–25.

10. Charles N. Gibbs, Secretary of the State of Tennessee, Letter of Incorporation, Singleton Miscellaneous Collection, Kansas State Historical Society; U.S. Senate, *Report and Testimony of the Select Committee*, 387.

11. *Nashville Union and American*, May 20, 1875.

12. Ibid., May 21, 1875.

13. Ibid., May 25, 29, August 15, 1875.

14. Ibid., August 15, 1875.

15. "See What Colored Citizens Are Doing for Their Elevation," promotional handbill, Singleton, Scrapbook, 32.

16. Benjamin Singleton and W. A. Sizemore to Thomas A. Osborn, August 7, 1876, Correspondence, Thomas A. Osborn Administration, Records of the Governor's Office, Library and Archives Division, Kansas State Historical Society.

17. *Great Bend Inland Tribune*, December 23, 1876.

18. *Chicago Tribune*, March 27, 1879; and "Call for an Investigating Meeting," clipping, May 30, 1877, Singleton, Scrapbook, 50.

19. *Columbus Republican Courier* (Kansas), August 9, 1877.

20. Gary R. Entz, "Image and Reality on the Kansas Prairie: 'Pap' Singleton's Cherokee County Colony," *Kansas History* 19 (Summer 1996): 132–35.

21. Promotional handbills, Singleton, Scrapbook, 40, 52; Joseph V. Hickey, " 'Pap' Singleton's Dunlap Colony: Relief Agencies and the Failure of a Black Settlement in Eastern Kansas," *Great Plains Quarterly* 11 (Winter 1991): 24–26; London Harness, interview by Douglas Thompson and Arthur Finnell, February 6, 1974, Flint Hills Oral History Project, Emporia State University Archives, Emporia, Kansas; and *New York Daily Tribune*, May 20, 1879.

22. *St. Louis Globe-Democrat*, April 21, 1879.

23. "Kansas Colored State Emigration Board," *Topeka Colored Citizen*, May 24, 1879; "The Right Thing," *Topeka Commonwealth*, April 23, 1879; and "Kansas Colored State Emigration Bureau," *Topeka Commonwealth*, May 1, 1879.

24. "Certificate of Incorporation," June 1879; petition, Dunlap, Kansas, August 9, 1879, Singleton, Miscellaneous Collection, Kansas State Historical Society; and "To the Colored People of the United States," clipping, October 4, 1879, Singleton, Scrapbook, 28.

25. "A Prophecy," *Topeka Commonwealth*, July 31, 1879; and *Topeka Colored Citizen*, October 11, 1879.

26. Minutes of a meeting between the African American citizens of Dunlap, August 9, 1879, Singleton, Miscellaneous Collection; *Morris County Times*, December 19, 1879; and Hickey, " 'Pap' Singleton's Dunlap Colony," 29.

27. *Kansas Colored Literary & Business Academy* (Council Grove: Republican Print, 1881), in "Kansas Education Society" folder, Kansas State Historical Society; *Topeka Daily Capital*, October 19, 1882; and "Quarterly Report of the Freedmen's Aid Association of Dunlap, Kansas," 1882, Papers of the Freedmen's Aid Association of Dunlap, Kansas, Freedmen's Academy of Dunlap, Kansas State Historical Society.

28. *Topeka Daily Capital*, October 19, 1882.

29. *Topeka Herald of Kansas*, March 12, April 9, 1880; and clipping, n.d., Singleton, Scrapbook, 32.

30. U.S. Senate, *Report and Testimony of the Select Committee*, 381, 390.

31. Untitled notes from a Singleton speech, n.d., Singleton, Miscellaneous Collection.

32. "Declaration by Colored Citizens," clipping, n.d., Singleton, Scrapbook, 11.

33. Benjamin Singleton to Elder Merritt, February 12, 1881, Singleton, Miscellaneous Collection.

34. "Topeka, March 4th, 1881," "A Colored Conference," and "Convention of Colored Men," clippings, Singleton Scrapbook, 15, 8.

35. "The Convention of Links," *Topeka Commonwealth*, June 4, 1881; "The Colored Links," clipping, Colored United Links Convention Poster, Singleton, Scrapbook, 6, 20; and "A Few Words from Pap Singleton," *Topeka Daily Kansas State Journal*, July 22, 1881.

36. "Colored United Links," *Topeka Commonwealth*, August 2, 1881.

37. "From 'Pap Singleton,' " clipping; and "Pap Singleton Sees the Sign," *Topeka Daily Kansas State Journal*, September 1881, Singleton, Scrapbook, 39.

38. "To the Freed Slaves of the South," *North Topeka Times*, September 28, 1883; and "Negro Colonization," *Topeka Commonwealth*, October 21, 1883.

39. " 'Pap' Singleton. The Great Exoduster Arrives in the City—Off for Cyprus"; "A New Exodus"; and "Good Advice. Old 'Pap' Singleton Writes an Epistle to the Negroes of St. Louis," *St. Louis Post-Dispatch*, clippings, n.d., Singleton, Scrapbook, 32, 36, 54.

40. Handbill, "The United Trans-Atlantic Society," n.d.; and "Constitution of the United Transatlantic Society," Singleton, Scrapbook, 56, 61.

41. Clipping, n.d., Singleton, Scrapbook, 64, 56, 40; *North Topeka Benevolent Banner*, October 8, 1887; and *St. John Weekly News* (Kansas), October 11, 1889.

Suggested Readings

Benjamin Singleton was illiterate and left no writings. He did, however, maintain a scrapbook collection of newspaper articles about his activities. The Singleton Scrapbook is housed at the Kansas State Historical Society in Topeka and is available on microfilm. For Singleton's Senate testimony, see U.S. Senate, *Report and Testimony of the Select Committee of the United States Senate to Investigate the Causes of the Removal of the Negroes from the Southern States to the Northern States*, 3 vols., 46th Cong., 2d sess., S. Rep. 693 (Washington, DC: Government Printing Office, 1880). There is little information about Singleton's early life, but David M. Katzman, *Before the Ghetto: Black Detroit in the Nineteenth Century* (Urbana: University of Illinois Press, 1973), provides a good overview of Detroit's black community during the time of Singleton's residence. For race relations in 1870s Nashville and Singleton's activities in the black community, see Alrutheus Ambush Taylor, *The Negro in Tennessee, 1865–1880* (Washington, DC: The Associated Publishers, Inc., 1941); Howard N. Rabinowitz, *Race Relations in the Urban South, 1865–1890* (New York: Oxford University Press, 1978); and Bobby L. Lovett, *The African-American History of Nashville, Tennessee, 1780–1930* (Fayetteville: University of Arkansas Press, 1999). Singleton's involvement with the Exodusters in Kansas is covered in Nell Irvin Painter, *Exodusters: Black Migration to Kansas after Reconstruction* (Lawrence: University Press of Kansas, 1986), and Robert G. Athearn, *In Search of Canaan: Black Migration to Kansas, 1879–80* (Lawrence: The Regents Press of Kansas, 1978). For a well-written overview designed for younger readers, see Jim Haskins, *The Geography of Hope: Black Exodus from the South after Reconstruction* (Brookfield, CT: Twenty-First Century Books, 1999). Topeka's black community has been explored in Thomas C. Cox's *Blacks in Topeka, Kansas, 1865–1915: A Social History* (Baton Rouge: Louisiana State University Press, 1982). For studies of the two Singleton colonies, see Gary R. Entz, "Image and Reality on the Kansas Prairie: 'Pap' Singleton's Cherokee County Colony," *Kansas History* 19 (Summer 1996): 124–39; Joseph V. Hickey, " 'Pap' Singleton's Dunlap Colony: Relief Agencies and the Failure of a Black Settlement in Eastern Kansas," *Great Plains Quarterly* 11 (Winter 1991): 23–36; and Philip R. Beard, "The Kansas Colored Literary and Business Academy," *Kansas History* 24 (Autumn 2001): 200–217. Dated but still useful articles include Walter L. Fleming, " 'Pap' Singleton: The Moses of the Colored Exodus," *American Journal of Sociology* 15 (July 1909): 61–82; and Roy Garvin, "Benjamin, or 'Pap,' Singleton and his Followers," *Journal of Negro History* 33 (January 1948): 7–23.

3

Alexander R. Shepherd
The Haussmannization of Washington, DC

Alan Lessoff

The late nineteenth century witnessed the dramatic growth of cities, challenging local governments to provide everyday services and preserve the health of the citizenry. Rapid physical expansion and mushrooming populations strained existing urban infrastructure, resulting in an apparently limitless demand for more and better-built streets, bridges, sidewalks, streetlights, parks, and, in many instances, docks and beaches. In addition to the provision and maintenance of public works, city officials had to be concerned about public health and sanitation. In the new industrial age, a rising group of professionals provided technological solutions to these nettlesome urban problems, and city dwellers hailed the ability of municipal engineers and other experts to improve the quality of urban life. Rarely, however, were these achievements completely divorced from politics, as is clearly illustrated by the example of Washington, DC, under Alexander R. Shepherd. Chosen by President Ulysses Grant to head the city's Board of Public Works, "Boss" Shepherd presided over a program that vastly improved the capital, but at enormous expense. Investigations of Shepherd's methods eventually drove him from power, but, like many urban bosses, he had earned an ambiguous reputation for the triumphs and troubles he had wrought.

An associate professor of history at Illinois State University, Normal, Alan Lessoff received a Ph.D. degree from the Johns Hopkins University in 1990. He is the author of *The Nation and Its City: Politics, "Corruption," and Progress in Washington, DC, 1861–1902* (1994).

On June 23, 1874, the U.S. Senate put off adjourning for the summer to quarrel over the recent report of a House-Senate investigating committee. The 3,000 pages of documents and testimony concerned not familiar issues such as Reconstruction or railroads, but the profusion of paved, lighted, and tree-lined streets, parks and squares, and water and sewer lines constructed throughout Washington, DC,

This essay originally appeared in Roger Biles, ed., *The Human Tradition in Urban America* (Wilmington, DE: Scholarly Resources, 2002), 53–69.

since 1871. These projects formed the heart of a massive effort to end Washington's reputation as a "struggling, shabby, dirty little third-rate southern town" and to create a capital city "worthy of the nation," as the slogan of the time went.[1]

The bipartisan committee appreciated these accomplishments but could "not but condemn the methods by which this sudden and rapid transformation was secured."[2] The agency responsible, the Board of Public Works, had operated in a haphazard, unaccountable fashion. Influence peddling and conflict of interest pervaded the program. The Board had colluded with federal officials to shift costs for unauthorized projects to the United States. To hide spending of $18.9 million in a plan approved for $6.6 million, city officials had issued millions in vouchers and securities of dubious legality.

Days earlier, Congress had implemented the report's recommendation to abolish Washington's government at the time—the Territory of the District of Columbia—and replace it with an interim commission. In the session's final hours, the Senate now debated one of President U. S. Grant's nominees to this caretaker commission, Alexander Robey Shepherd. As vice president and de facto head of the Board of Public Works from 1871 to 1873 and then as territorial governor, Shepherd had devised and implemented the "Comprehensive Plan of Improvements" at the heart of the quarrel.

A handsome, charismatic man in his late thirties, six feet tall and 200 pounds, Shepherd inspired admiration in those who embraced the forceful, enterprising spirit of post–Civil War business and politics. Imperious, impetuous, and garish, he appalled those who condemned the willfulness and vulgarity of the era. While the hearings had uncovered no personal corruption on Shepherd's part, they had revealed much tolerance of others' impropriety in the cause of public works. Staunch supporters insisted that a program "to lift the city out of the mud and make it what it should be as the capital of the nation" faced so many obstacles that Shepherd's unorthodox, even unscrupulous methods were in order. Critics such as *The Nation* magazine countered that the turmoil and corruption surrounding the Shepherd program revealed the folly of entrusting complex tasks such as public works to boosterish amateurs: "What we must expect to find in every department of Government so long as a show of activity and energy is preferred to technical knowledge and administrative experience."[3]

Grant's insistence on his protégé Shepherd placed Senate Republicans in a bind. Party members who saw Washington's renovator as a hero would resent Senate rejection. Still, even long-standing allies were annoyed at Shepherd's ruses to force Congress to pay for projects it had never approved. Moreover, Democrats were gleeful to have a Republican city government embroiled in scandal, for this offset the recent exposure of New York's Democratic Tweed Ring. After a "stormy" debate, the Senate voted 36 to 6 against the nomination.[4] The 1874 rejection of Shepherd as District commissioner put a premature end to his political career. In 1880 the former governor, still youthful but now bankrupt, would move with his wife and seven children to Mexico's Sierra Madre mountains, where he would embark on a second remarkable career as a developer of silver mines. In his absence he came to be remembered not as the scoundrel or despot he was labeled at the time, but as "a household synonym for public benefaction,"[5] the leader who had sparked Washington's rise as an attractive capital indeed worthy of comparison to Paris or Berlin.

Shepherd's Comprehensive Plan was perhaps the most ambitious urban public works program in nineteenth-century America. Still, Washington was hardly alone in its scramble to upgrade its appearance and services. Cities throughout the Americas and Europe took on huge debts to improve streets, water supply, parks, and other services to keep up with unprecedented growth in population and social complexity. In the decade after the Civil War alone, the bonded debt of New York, Boston, and Chicago tripled, Cincinnati's debt rose five times, and Cleveland's increased 1,000 percent.

In an age of rapid governmental as well as industrial and commercial expansion, capital cities attracted special attention. Proponents of embellishing such disparate capitals as Washington and Buenos Aires often cited Paris's Georges Haussmann as inspiration. As prefect of the Seine in the 1850s and 1860s, Haussmann had driven magnificent boulevards through ancient, gnarled central Paris while also upgrading the French capital's parks, markets, water supply, sanitation, and transit. To describe this unprecedented program of urban renewal, contemporaries coined the term "haussmannization." Americans and other foreign admirers, moved by the grandeur and ingenuity of Haussmann's Paris, rarely tried to understand the tumultuous controversy that surrounded the prefect and his program. This controversy underscored the fact that public works are not arcane matters best left to engineers but vitally concern all urban dwellers because changes to infrastructure can reshape a city's economy and way of life. By driving boulevards through old quarters, lining these boulevards with fashionable apartments, and connecting the new thoroughfares to a ring of railroad stations, Haussmann secured Paris's position as France's political, business, and cultural center, but at the cost of displacing long-established neighborhoods of artisans, shopkeepers, and laborers. The political contentiousness of public works multiplies in capital cities, where urban politics intertwine with national affairs. Like Shepherd an imperious man intolerant of criticism, Haussmann adopted high-handed, irresponsible methods that finally prompted his removal in 1870. Within France, Haussmann came to symbolize the arrogance and venality of his patron, Emperor Napoleon III, whose regime survived Haussmann's ouster by less than a year.

Likewise, the Shepherd controversy concerned the direction of the American nation as well as official mismanagement and arrogance. The federal city's "ill-kept, noisome, and stinking" appearance seemed to Civil War-era patriots to symbolize the shortcomings of the antebellum Union.[6] A splendid Washington could provide symbolic reinforcement for American national loyalty. A modern Washington could serve as administrative center for the vigorous government that many Unionists hoped would result from a northern victory in the Civil War. In the course of remaking Washington physically, Shepherd and his allies intended to undermine the city's traditional, southern-oriented elite in favor of progressive, northern-minded leadership. Meanwhile, Shepherd's pro-development Republicans also struggled to distance themselves from local radical Republicans. The radicals believed that civil rights for Washington's black population should have equal priority with Shepherd's physical and economic improvements. In theory, the economic and civil rights agendas of Reconstruction-era Republicans were not in conflict: an enterprising, innovative society would be a more open, tolerant one and vice versa. Yet as occurred across the Reconstruction South, implacable white hostility toward black progress forced pro-enterprise Republicans to downplay civil rights to preserve their developmental goals. Shepherd worked to secure Washington as a dynamic, impressive capital even as the radical vision of Washington as avatar of democracy faltered.

Still another source of controversy stirred by Shepherd, Haussmann, and their counterparts stemmed from the sheer novelty of what they attempted. City officials knew how to build adequate, individual streets, water supplies, and sewers. No city, however, had yet devised effective methods for planning transportation, water, and drainage as systems coordinated with trends in business, population, and housing. The municipal engineers, planners, and health experts on whom city dwellers now rely for such tasks did not yet exist as distinct professions, even in France, which emphasized the training of engineers and civil servants. In the United States, with its cult of the self-made man, self-taught contractors such as Shepherd seemed as good as anyone else. The huge sums Shepherd wasted and the technical failure of his pavements and sewers helped to convince urban Americans that professionals should have direct control over infrastructure improvements, even if politicians retained the ultimate say. Even so, streets, water, sewers, and parks remain prolific sources of controversy, as in the days of Haussmann and Shepherd.

Born in 1835, Shepherd was the son of a lumber dealer in southwest Washington. This area had acquired the nickname "the Island" because it was isolated from the rest of the city by the Washington Canal, which stretched along the north side of the Mall where Constitution Avenue now runs. A putrid reminder of the failure of George Washington's dream of making his city a prosperous river port, the canal had degenerated by Shepherd's youth into a receptacle for garbage, street runoff, and sewage from federal buildings. One of the most applauded of Shepherd's extralegal acts while head of the Board of Public Works would be his diversion of an appropriation for dredging the canal to covering it and making it a main sewer.

Shepherd's father died when the boy was ten. After leaving school as a teenager, the young Shepherd was apprenticed to John W. Thompson, the District's largest plumbing and gas contractor. At a time when urban buildings were acquiring running water and gas lighting, plumbing was a new, booming business suitable for a youth interested in how cities were built. By his early thirties, Shepherd had bought Thompson out and was branching into other city-building enterprises. He invested in construction materials, a street railway, the Washington Market Company, and the *Evening Star* newspaper. His property investments by the early 1870s exceeded $250,000. Estimated to have developed as many as 1,500 houses within ten years, he played a noteworthy role in creating the fashionable neighborhoods of northwest Washington between present-day Farragut Square and Dupont Circle.

Shepherd relished displaying to his hometown that he had arrived. In the suburbs north of the current Florida Avenue, Shepherd and his wife, Mary, acquired a country house. Their townhouse overlooking Farragut Square became the site of lavish receptions. Although a native

Washingtonian from a Maryland family that had once owned slaves, Shepherd stood outside the southern-leaning elite, of whom he expressed resentment and who treated him as an upstart. His associates tended to be transplanted northerners or native Washingtonians with northern leanings who were engaged, as he was, in real estate, contracting, utilities, and other city-building enterprises.

With the old elite tainted by southern ties during the Civil War, Shepherd had a chance to rise as rapidly in politics as in business. After a brief Union enlistment in the spring of 1861, Shepherd won a seat on Washington's common council, becoming its president in 1862. Prominent in political offices and civic organizations throughout the 1860s, Shepherd gained a reputation as a dauntless champion of making "our city one of the most beautiful on the face of the globe," as he put the goal in an 1870 speech.[7]

While Washington had developed at a respectable rate, the capital had fallen far short of the expectations of the Founding Fathers. Galling evidence of this pervaded the city. The population leapt from 75,080 to 131,700 during the dramatic 1860s, but people were still scattered thinly over the grandiose plan made in the 1790s by French engineer Pierre Charles L'Enfant for a city with several times that number. L'Enfant's famous street system—his radiating 160-foot avenues imposed on a grid of 100-foot streets—had proved far too costly for Washington's taxpayers to maintain. In dry periods, dust from the broad, unpaved avenues covered everything and everyone. After rains, journalist Noah Brooks reported, the streets became "seas or canals of mud," whose "geographical features" were "conglomerations of garbage, refuse, and trash."

The Mall epitomized the city's disappointing condition. Fragmented into eight grounds under the control of separate federal agencies, landscaped piecemeal, encroached upon by railroads, and crowned by the half-finished Washington Monument (abandoned in its scaffolding for want of funds in 1855), the Mall offered, in the words of park designer Frederick Law Olmsted, "a standing reproach against the system of government."[8] Commercial and residential buildings matched the streets and Mall in decrepitude. Nearly all accounts concur with Mark Twain's characterization of the hotels, saloons, offices, and shops along Pennsylvania Avenue as "mean and cheap and dingy." "None of us are proud of this place," remarked Nevada Republican William Stewart in 1869, during a Senate debate over whether Washington should host the centennial exposition eventually held in Philadelphia in 1876.[9] Congress's dissatisfaction with Washington even reached the stage of discussing moving the capital to a midwestern city such as St. Louis.

Those most drawn to the goal of a "worthy" Washington were, like Shepherd, nationalistic, pro-development Republicans. This faction of the party coexisted uneasily with the Republicans' radical faction, whose agenda was to make Washington a model of post-emancipation race relations. During the 1860s, African Americans, mostly former slaves from the Chesapeake region, constituted the most rapidly increasing segment of the capital's population. By 1870 blacks were one-third of the population, long the largest black presence in a major American city. Between 1862 and 1869, Congress responded by passing measures to emancipate the city's remaining slaves, provide schools for black children, desegregrate streetcars, and extend the vote, jury service, and officeholding to blacks.

As much as possible, Shepherd and his allies kept their distance from the radicals. Though not a vehement racist, he shared the condescending views of blacks that prevailed in this former slave city. Shepherd's hesitancy to work with the radicals, however, resulted largely from nervousness that the capital's physical and economic development could be paralyzed by the visceral opposition to black rights displayed by the majority of white Washingtonians. An 1866 referendum in which Washington City voted 6,591 to 35 against black suffrage and Georgetown 712 to 1 dramatized the depth of this hostility. When Congress imposed black suffrage on Washington despite such expressions of opposition, the Shepherd group made a strategic alliance with the radicals. In this way, Shepherd's group hoped to persuade the powerful radical Republican faction in Congress to support federal appropriations for Washington's public works. In 1868, in a narrow election marred by violence, this alliance of newly enfranchised black voters, white radicals, and pro-business Republicans elected a white radical, Sayles J. Bowen, as Washington City mayor. Bowen pledged to expand both black rights and public works, but his administration became so mired in squabbling that, far from working to increase spending, the radicals in Congress distanced themselves. Securing federal appropriations would be impossible so long as Bowen remained mayor.

Shepherd switched tactics again. He became head of a Reform Republican movement that cooperated with old-line, mainly Democratic Washingtonians to oust Bowen in favor of a moderate Republican in the 1870 municipal elections. Meanwhile, the Shepherd Republicans lobbied Congress for a territorial government that would consolidate the ineffectual municipalities of Washington City and Georgetown with the outlying portions of the District known as Washington County. With a governor and legislative council appointed by the president and an elected house of delegates and delegate to Congress, this territorial format seemed to meet Congress's demand for more federal control over Washington as a price for federal underwriting of public works.

Congress passed the territorial bill on February 21, 1871, the day the city held a carnival—organized by the omnipresent Shepherd—to celebrate Pennsylvania Avenue's new wooden pavement. Along with the pending State, War, and Navy Building (now the Old Executive Office Building), the rebuilt Avenue signaled Congress's decision to rededicate itself to Washington and to ignore calls to move to the Midwest. President Grant bypassed Shepherd to appoint Henry D. Cooke, brother of financier Jay Cooke, as the first territorial governor. Grant instead placed Shepherd and several allies on the Board of Public Works. As governor, Cooke was ex-officio head of the Board, but he left its operation to Vice President Shepherd, who ran the Board of Public Works as a vehicle for his visions and ambitions "as though no one else were associated with him," investigators later remarked.[10]

Grant filled the Territory's other appointive offices with reliable Republicans. These appointments in effect handed Shepherd control of all contracts and patronage related to public works. The Shepherd Republicans used their patronage and the enthusiasm surrounding the new government to dominate elections for the house of delegates and congressional delegates. Superficial similarity to Tammany Hall's use of public works contracts and jobs to control New York elections led to the Washington leader's acquiring the nickname "Boss" Shepherd. While this epithet was useful to opponents who wished to tar Shepherd as a Republican William M. Tweed, Shepherd's movement differed from the machine politics then emerging in many American cities. Typical ward bosses were politicians by trade who delved into contracting or real estate as a way to make money through inside influence. Shepherd and his allies did not disdain such influence peddling, but they remained businessmen first and politicians second. Political machines, moreover, prided themselves on their ability to build loyal support in working-class and ethnic neighborhoods and to deliver votes reliably. Shepherd and his colleagues made little attempt to build constituencies at the precinct or ward level.

Indeed, the Shepherd group devised the Territory to insulate themselves from local voters. In racially tense Washington, nonradical Republicans such as Shepherd realized that they could not build a majority based upon white voters alone, but it would be politically fatal to rely too visibly on the black minority. The answer to Washington's public works quandary, it seemed, was to remove the issue from popular control. Black leaders responded with ambivalence to a government that, while not abandoning civil rights altogether, did treat their goals as problematic distractions. Shepherd's efforts to make Washington "an honor rather than a disgrace to the nation" deserved "earnest, active support," asserted the city's black newspaper, the *New National Era*, which nevertheless expressed "fear" that Shepherd meant "to relieve" Washington's Republican Party "of the influence of its radical element."[11]

Within three weeks after taking office in June 1871, the Board of Public Works submitted its Comprehensive Plan of Improvements. This program would not qualify as a "city plan" in the present-day sense of an integrated set of proposals based on estimates of housing, transportation, recreation, and other needs. Even so, the Shepherd plan embodied a more coherent sense of the intertwined character of streets, water, sewerage, parks, and public buildings than any American urban public works project to that time. In a departure from tradition, Shepherd and his associates proposed to finance two-thirds of the estimated $6.6 million cost of the plan through bond sales and only one-third through assessments on property adjacent to improvements. Until this time, American cities had usually assessed the entire cost of improvements to abutting property. Washington thus became one of the first American cities to accept that pavements or sewers were not simply of concern to the street or neighborhood through which they passed. Cities needed to treat public works as systems, because the condition of sections of a city affected the entire urban environment.

The scale and cost of the Comprehensive Plan prompted a rancorous split between Shepherd's pro-improvement Republicans and the Democratic elite with whom they had cooperated during the campaign for the Territory. Conservative Washingtonians objected that Shepherd's "ill-digested, incoherent, and blundering scheme" contained inadequate controls over the Board of Public Works and that contracts would go to "rings" of political cronies.[12] Supporters retorted that old-line critics were "rich people content with existing circumstances" who fought "progress and manifest destiny."[13] The quarrel over the Comprehensive

Plan reflected the division within Washington's business and civic elite over whether the city should weave itself into the northern commercial and cultural orbit or retain its customary orientation toward the Chesapeake and the South.

As soon as Shepherd had pushed the Comprehensive Plan through a compliant territorial legislature, the Board of Public Works contracted for projects throughout the city, but especially downtown and in fashionable areas of northwest Washington. In these areas, public works had the greatest potential for promoting growth by stimulating private investment. Not coincidentally, these were also areas where Shepherd's allies concentrated their own real estate operations. Given the period's penchant for romanticizing entrepreneurship, politically active businessmen such as the Shepherd group easily confused their public responsibilities with their private interests. Territorial leaders made only cursory efforts to avoid conflicts of interest and defended themselves forcefully when questioned, on the grounds that their public and private activities combined to advance the worthy cause of Washington's physical and economic progress. The costly scandals that ensued help to explain why laws and customs regarding conflict of interest have grown more stringent since the 1870s.

The obstructiveness and disdain of elite conservatives reinforced Shepherd's brusque manner of dealing with even well-meaning criticism. Shepherd alienated otherwise well-disposed Washingtonians with his grudging responses to pedestrians inconvenienced by torn-up streets, to neighborhoods bypassed by improvements, and to homeowners who sought compensation for rebuilt plumbing, stairs, and foundations necessitated by changes in street grades. The Board of Public Works did cancel improvement taxes imposed on two prominent senators who returned from a recess in late 1872 to find their houses on ledges ten feet above a regraded Massachusetts Avenue.

Two incidents in 1872 illustrate Shepherd's blunt approach. One Wednesday in early September, when stallkeepers at the Northern Liberty Market—dilapidated and slated for replacement—threatened legal action rather than relocate to temporary sheds, Shepherd invited the relevant judge to dinner at his country house. As stallholders cleaned up for the evening, workmen arrived to tear the hall down. In the confusion, two people died: a butcher and a young boy hunting rats with his dog. Shepherd never expressed remorse; the market was "necessarily sacrificed to the public good," he later wrote.[14] In November, when a railroad refused to remove tracks that ran right below the Capitol, Shepherd sent 200 workmen one night to tear them out. "I did that without authority of law," he recalled, "but it was the right thing to do, and the nuisance would not otherwise have been removed."[15]

Supporters from around the country cheered that Washington had found its "Baron Haussmann."[16] Especially given the city's backward reputation, Shepherd's accomplishments were indeed astonishing. By 1874 the Territory had overseen construction of 150 miles of paved roads, 120 miles of sewers, thirty miles of water mains, thirty-nine miles of gas lines, 208 miles of sidewalks, two new markets, and six new schools.

As enemies had predicted, the speed with which Shepherd pushed his program greatly inflated its cost. As an alternative to the time-consuming practice of putting contracts out for bids, the Board of Public Works hastily drew up a list of standard rates that enticed contractors with guaranteed profits. Rather than take pains to design, measure, and estimate work beforehand, Shepherd encouraged contractors to begin streets and sewers quickly. Shepherd then retroactively changed materials, specifications, and work sites. The huge profits ensured by such practices attracted contractors—reputable and otherwise—from around the country. Guaranteed profits also nurtured an unsavory level of brokering and lobbying in city contracts. The revelation that House Appropriations chairman James Garfield had accepted $5,000 to lobby Shepherd on behalf of a Chicago wooden paving firm damaged the reputation of the future president. As Garfield understood, in the absence of the checks provided by open bidding and careful planning, Shepherd could with little scrutiny channel lucrative work to contractors and building suppliers with political connections to the Republican Party.

By the spring of 1873 the Board of Public Works had already spent more than twice its original $6.6 million estimate. Nearly out of cash, the District began to issue floating securities to cover payrolls and keep projects going. Shepherd's allies even manipulated their control of the finances of the Freedman's Savings Bank to divert the hard-earned savings of former slaves to favored contractors. This callous chicanery contributed greatly to the bank's 1874 collapse.

Shepherd and his supporters defended themselves by insisting that much of the debt they incurred properly belonged to a negligent federal government. The Board of Public Works republished decades of statements by presidents, congressmen, and cabinet officers in favor of national underwriting of Washington's infrastructure on the grounds, as an 1835 Senate study had put it, that the L'Enfant Plan had been "calculated for the capital of the great nation" and was "from its very dimensions and arrangements" beyond local resources.[17] Between 1802 and 1871, Shepherd claimed, the United States spent as little as one-tenth what local taxpayers spent on improvements. In 1873 the federal government did spend $3.45 million to subsidize Shepherd's program. Investigators would conclude that this was too little, too late, and too random. Indeed, observers at the time and since suggested that Congress's dawdling prompted Shepherd's uncontrolled spending, because Congress would have to pay rather than let its capital default on its bonds. "I have been kicking my heels at the doors of Congress for five years to obtain appropriations," Shepherd told a House hearing in 1872, "and have invariably been met with the response: Why not do something for yourselves?" If residents "make the start," he insisted, Congress "cannot rid itself of responsibility."[18] One way that Shepherd acted on this threat was by colluding with Major Orville Babcock, the army engineer in charge of federal property in Washington and a close associate of President Grant, to bill the United States for work that Congress had never appropriated.

In 1872, Shepherd's opponents persuaded the House District of Columbia Committee to investigate the Territory. Chaired by one of Shepherd's political allies, the House committee meekly admonished that city officials had become "intoxicated with the spirit of improvement."[19] By the spring of 1873, Shepherd's political position was no longer so secure. A resurgent Democratic Party was making congressional Republicans anxious over scandals brewing around Grant associates such as Shepherd and Babcock. National newspapers disenchanted with Grant, such as the Republican *New York Daily Tribune*, began investigating the capital's finances and contracts. In April and May 1873 the *Tribune* published lengthy exposures of the "bankrupt and irresponsible" Board of Public Works.[20] The city's ability to survive on debt ended in September 1873 when the collapse of Jay Cooke and Company sparked the worst financial panic in decades and, incidentally, forced Henry Cooke to resign as territorial governor. Shepherd won confirmation as Cooke's replacement, despite the *Tribune*'s sneer that this was an "appointment not fit to be made."[21]

In early 1874, with worried Republican state officials pressuring national leaders to conduct a vigorous investigation, congressional Republicans agreed to a bipartisan House-Senate investigating committee. By late spring, copious evidence of loose administration, dubious financing, and influence peddling had the Territory reeling. Shepherd's fate was sealed when a disenchanted friend, Adolph Cluss, an architect who held the post of engineer to the Board of Public Works, provided details of Shepherd's autocratic governance and of ruses used to saddle the federal government with unauthorized costs. Meanwhile, the story hit the papers of a bizarre scheme to discredit one of Shepherd's upper-class enemies by framing him for the theft of evidence from the safe of a city attorney. This scheme, carried out by professional safecrackers commissioned by the U.S. Secret Service, was never solved. In such a charged atmosphere, only Shepherd's firmest supporters welcomed his nomination to the caretaker commission, though many Republicans continued to express admiration in private.

As passions cooled, the major players in the Washington improvement controversy gradually worked out accommodations on the issues they saw as fueling their quarrel. After gaining a majority in the House of Representatives in the 1874 elections, congressional Democrats reluctantly came to agree with Republicans on the need to complete the Shepherd improvements and to consolidate his debts into federally guaranteed bonds. Leaders from both parties also came to accept Shepherd's major point: that making large, regular federal appropriations was the only way to ensure Washington's steady development. In the government act passed in June 1878 to replace the caretaker commission, Congress promised to contribute 50 percent of the District's expenses in exchange for assuming direct control of the city's budget. This half-and-half plan would survive until eroded by new political and social circumstances early in the twentieth century. Satisfied in their chief demand, Republican business and civic leaders in turn accepted the controversial idea of abolishing local elections altogether and making the appointed commission format permanent. The republic's capital was destined to remain under the rule of appointed officials until the 1970s. Abolition of local self-government satisfied members of the southern-leaning elite, who had persuaded themselves that black suffrage was a root cause of the Shepherd mess. Over the next decades, federal and District officials and the northern-oriented faction within Washington's business community stood by as civil rights eroded in the voteless city and as Jim Crow laws took hold. Washington thus acquired the split personality that characterized it through much of the twentieth century: majestic capital of a great world power, but at the same time, a provincial city oppressive to minorities.

Within two years, Shepherd's impatient, improvisational approach showed in rotting wood pavements, crumbling asphalt, and ill-sealed sewers that ran uphill in places and that entered the Potomac below high tide. The cost in millions of dollars in additional expenditures to replace Shepherd's mistakes became a persuasive argument against placing self-taught contractors in charge of public works. Even Shepherd's close friends in the Army Corps of Engineers, which inherited oversight of the city's infrastructure, were scathing in their criticism of his commencing projects without "data or formulae" and of the "bad workmanship" and "worthless" materials that he had tolerated.[22]

Shepherd's mistakes were proportionate to his ambitions. In this early phase of the development of modern municipal engineering, all American and European cities experienced similar fiascos, though usually on a lesser scale. As cities recovered from their financial devastation following the 1873 Panic, they regained a taste for capital improvements. Yet even in cities where machine-style politics dominated, politicians came to accept the need for cautious financing and expert planning. Post-Shepherd Washington epitomized this trend toward expertise. By century's end, the capital would become a leader in the professionalization of public works, for example, by hiring famous experts on asphalt paving and sewer design and by publishing the 1902 McMillan Plan, the country's first modern, comprehensive plan. As was the case with Haussmann's tumultuous transformation of Paris, Shepherd's impetuous drive for a worthy Washington acquired an ambiguous reputation: a signal episode in the movement to create more inspiring capitals and more pleasant, healthful cities, but also an example of the dangers of reckless finance and imperious management.

Given the feeling that Shepherd's misdeeds had been motivated by excessive zeal for a worthy cause, politicians assumed that the youthful, charismatic former governor would remain a force in Washington for decades to come. In November 1876 news of his bankruptcy stunned the city. Associates insisted that Shepherd could easily revive his enterprises. Restless as ever, however, he became intrigued by promising silver mines in the Batopilas River Valley in Chihuahua, Mexico. Given the paucity of roads and rails in northern Mexico, these mines were nearly a month's travel—mostly by pack mule through the Sierra Madres—from Chihuahua city. After a scouting trip in 1879, Shepherd persuaded an investment group to underwrite a $3 million mining company. Five years of hard work, Shepherd assured his wife, "would ensure a fortune."[23]

In the twenty-two years that he spent running the Batopilas mines, Shepherd displayed his normal talent for overcoming obstacles that he had underestimated. He had power machinery carted into the mountains and added tunnels, dams, and reducing plants. Shepherd's imperious streak, energy, and paternalistic stance toward his Mexican workers won him friends among the pro-American technocrats known as *científicos* who surrounded the dictator Porfirio Díaz. While journalists portrayed the large Shepherd family living as Gilded Age aristocrats in a mountain duchy, their life was modest compared to their previous standards. Though nostalgic for Washington's bustle and for public attention, Shepherd returned to his hometown only a couple of times, the first in 1887, while recuperating from an infection contracted when his scalp was torn open against a rock in a tunnel. Old friends and former foes combined to organize an enormous parade along Pennsylvania Avenue, with fireworks, speeches, and a proclamation granting Shepherd, once driven from office amid rancorous conflict, the freedom of the city.

To the first generation to live in a dynamic, attractive Washington, Shepherd came to seem, as one former opponent put it, "a man of great energy, liberal views, and full of enthusiasm" whose plans "startle[d] the whole community," but who precipitated a necessary crisis that pushed the capital up the road of progress.[24] When he died in Mexico in 1902— of appendicitis that could not be treated quickly because of Batopilas's isolation—five teams of workmen carried his casket out of the mountains so that he could be buried in Washington's Rock Creek Cemetery. In 1909 civic leaders erected a statue in front of the new District Building on Pennsylvania Avenue. The statue stood there until 1979, when the District government, in a fit of historical negligence, removed it to an obscure location during a redevelopment project. From its pedestal on the country's main street, Shepherd's likeness could watch over the magnificent torn city he had indeed helped to shape. With his grand achievements and glaring faults, Shepherd remains a fitting symbol of his hometown.

Notes

1. *The Nation*, March 30, 1871.
2. *Affairs in the District of Columbia*, 43d Cong., 1st sess., S. Rept. 453, Report, vii.
3. *Washington Evening Star*, April 6, 1871; *The Nation*, June 25, 1874.
4. *Baltimore Sun*, June 24, 1874.

5. *Washington Critic*, September 28, 1881.

6. P. J. Staudenraus, *Mr. Lincoln's Washington: Selections from the Writings of Noah Brooks, Civil War Correspondent* (South Brunswick, NJ: Thomas Yoseloff, 1967), 344–45.

7. *Evening Star*, May 25, 1870.

8. Staudenraus, *Mr. Lincoln's Washington*, 116–17; Frederick Law Olmsted to Justin Morrill, draft letter, January 22, 1874, Olmsted Papers, Library of Congress, reel 14.

9. Mark Twain and Charles Dudley Warner, *The Gilded Age: A Tale of Today* (1873; reprint, New York: Penguin, 1994), 177; *Congressional Globe*, 41st Cong., 2d sess., December 22, 1869, 303–4.

10. *Affairs in the District of Columbia*, 43d Cong., 1st sess., S. Rept. 453, Report, xi.

11. *New National Era*, October 26, 1871 (second quote); December 12, 1872 (first quote).

12. *Washington Daily Patriot*, September 25, 1871.

13. *Evening Star*, June 30, 1871.

14. *Payment for Destruction of the Northern Liberty Market*, 54th Cong., 1st sess., May 12, 1896, S. Rept. 926.

15. *Washington Daily Chronicle*, February 26, 1876.

16. *Lippincott's Magazine*, March 1873.

17. Quoted in Howard Gillette Jr., *Between Beauty and Justice: Race, Planning, and the Failure of Urban Policy in Washington, DC* (Baltimore: Johns Hopkins University Press, 1995), 21.

18. *Affairs in the District of Columbia*, 42nd Cong., 2d sess., H. Rept. 52, 586–87.

19. Ibid., iv–v.

20. *New York Daily Tribune*, April 8, 1873.

21. Ibid., September 15, 1873.

22. District of Columbia Commissioners, *Annual Reports*, 1874, 162–65; 1875, 239–45.

23. Quoted in David M. Pletcher, *Rails, Mines, and Progress: Seven American Promoters in Mexico, 1867–1911* (Ithaca, NY: Cornell University Press, 1958), 191.

24. "Address of Ex-Mayor Berret," *Records of the Columbia Historical Society*, 52 vols. (Washington, DC: Columbia Historical Society, 1899), 2:15.

Suggested Readings

Three recent books analyze Shepherd's Washington within the context of the city's overall history and of nineteenth-century American urbanization: Carl Abbott, *Political Terrain: Washington, DC, from Tidewater Town to Global Metropolis* (Chapel Hill: University of North Carolina Press, 1999); Howard Gillette Jr., *Between Beauty and Justice: Race, Planning, and the Failure of Urban Policy in Washington, DC* (Baltimore: Johns Hopkins University Press, 1995); and Alan Lessoff, *The Nation and Its City: Politics, "Corruption," and Progress in Washington, DC, 1861–1902* (Baltimore: Johns Hopkins University Press, 1994). See also William M. Maury, *Alexander "Boss" Shepherd and the Board of Public Works* (Washington, DC: George Washington University Washington Studies, 1975); and James H. Whyte, *The Uncivil War: Washington during the Reconstruction* (New York: Twayne, 1958). On Shepherd's Mexican career, see David M. Pletcher, *Rails, Mines, and Progress: Seven American Promoters in Mexico, 1867–1911* (Ithaca, NY: Cornell University Press, 1958).

Works that place Shepherd's Comprehensive Plan within the development of urban public works include Jon C. Teaford, *The Unheralded Triumph: City Government in America, 1870–1900* (Baltimore: Johns Hopkins University Press, 1984); and Martin V. Melosi, *The Sanitary City: Urban Infrastructure in America from Colonial Times to the Present* (Baltimore: Johns Hopkins University Press, 2000). For a comparison of Washington to Paris, see David P. Jordan, *Transforming Paris: The Life and Labors of Baron Haussmann* (New York: Free Press, 1995).

4

Mary Lease and the
Sources of Populist Protest

Rebecca Edwards

Mary Lease faced more than her share of challenges. Her father died of dysentery in a Confederate prison when she was thirteen. She watched two of her own children die as infants and a grown son succumb to appendicitis. Her husband went bankrupt in the depression of the 1870s and failed again as a farmer in the 1880s. Lease was a central figure in the rise of Populist party power in Kansas yet suffered dismissal from office, sexual discrimination, and political abuse. At midlife she gained a divorce and started over again as a single woman in New York City, defying conventions of the time. Despite these setbacks, Mary Lease remained a fighter, refusing to compromise her ideals.

Rebecca Edwards, a historian of women and politics, devotes her chapter to this courageous and combative woman who became a symbol of the farmer protest on the Great Plains during the 1890s. Mary Lease's public career illustrates the range of political activities open to an energetic female before women could vote. She organized a female suffrage association, worked for the Woman's Christian Temperance Union, joined the local Knights of Labor, and spoke for the Kansas Farmers' Alliance, which sponsored the Populist political party. She campaigned for William Jennings Bryan, the Democratic candidate for president in 1896. She supported the birth control movement in New York City. But Lease will always be identified with Populism. As Professor Edwards shows, life on the Great Plains was hard generally, but it was harder for women and even more so for one who entered the male domain of politics and supported the underdogs.

Rebecca Edwards received her Ph.D. from the University of Virginia in 1995. She is the author of *Angels in the Machinery: Gender in American Party Politics from the Civil War to the Progressive Era* (1997). She is now working on a full-length biography of Mary Lease as well as a general history of the United States in the late nineteenth century, entitled *New Spirits: The Birth of Modern America*. She is associate professor of history at Vassar College and lives in Poughkeepsie, New York.

This essay originally appeared in Ballard C. Campbell, ed., *The Human Tradition in the Gilded Age and Progressive Era* (Wilmington, DE: Scholarly Resources, 2000), 53–68.

In the 1890s, Mary Lease was one of the most famous women in the United States, so well known that newspapers called her simply "Mrs. Lease of Kansas." The decade of her fame coincided with a deep economic depression, mass unemployment, and hundreds of strikes. By 1900, Americans were uneasily conscious of growing divisions between rich and poor. Lease won her fame by speaking to these issues with anger, humor, and eloquence. As a leader of the Populist Party, she helped shape a movement of farmers, workers, and reformers that challenged the political and economic status quo. Today, Lease is largely forgotten, receiving only an occasional mention as the woman who urged American farmers to "raise less corn and more hell."[1]

Historians have written a great deal about the Populists' ideas and identities. For the most part they have described populism as a movement of native-born, Protestant, Anglo-American farmers whose cause failed because of the fraud and intimidation practiced by southern Democrats and because the new party never won a following in the Midwest and Northeast. Yet although the Populist party disappeared in a few years, it left an important legacy. Much of its program won passage in the Progressive Era and New Deal, having been taken up by other reformers. Before Mary Lease died in 1933, she witnessed federal regulation of banks and railroads, government aid to farmers, direct election of U.S. senators, and a national progressive income tax, all of which the Populists had proposed.

The Populists, then, have not been forgotten, but Mary Lease has, perhaps because she remains an ambiguous figure. Her life contradicts much of what we think we know about populism. Born in Pennsylvania less than a year after her parents arrived from Ireland, Lease was heir to her father's legacy of agricultural poverty. A Catholic by birth and education, she had become an agnostic by 1900, contradicting historians' picture of populism as an evangelical Protestant crusade. Only briefly a farmer's wife, Lease gained an eclectic political education from the Woman's Christian Temperance Union, the women's suffrage movement, labor unions, and the Irish nationalist cause. A champion of "equal rights for all, special privileges for none," she nonetheless made anti-Semitic remarks and endorsed U.S. colonization of Latin America. When, in Lease's opinion, the Populists caved in to the Democratic party, she turned against them. She then divorced her husband, moved to New York City, and worked as a journalist, lawyer, and advocate of birth control.

Perhaps Lease was an oddity, a woman whose background and be-liefs lay outside the mainstream of her movement. If so, she was a very influential oddity. Her claim that she single-handedly brought the Kansas Populists to power was only a slight exaggeration. She sat in Populist inner councils, played a pivotal role in two national conventions, and conducted speaking tours across the nation from Georgia to Minnesota and Montana to New York. Her life tells us a great deal about the political and economic reshaping of the United States between the Civil War and the New Deal. It also tells us a great deal about how these changes affected women and how women themselves became agents of change. Lease was that much-feared figure, an angry woman. She helped build up populism, and then in bitter disillusionment she helped destroy it, exiling herself from history's ranks of Populist heroes. She remains, to-day, a complicated figure: courageous, ambitious, immensely talented, alternately petty and visionary, a woman of small prejudices and great dreams.

Mary Lease, born Mary Clyens, experienced poverty and loss from her earliest childhood. Her parents came to the United States in 1849 from County Monaghan, Ireland, during the devastating potato famine that reduced Ireland's population by 2.5 million through emigration, star-vation, and disease. Mary's two older sisters and one of her older broth-ers died in the famine, probably from cholera. Her father joined other tenant farmers in protesting British policies in Ireland; his absentee land-lord finally got rid of this "objectionable" tenant by paying the family's passage to America. Mary was born a year after the Clyenses' arrival in northwestern Pennsylvania. Her parents had barely scraped together enough money to buy a farm when her father and brother enlisted in the Civil War. Both died—her father of scurvy and dysentery in a Con-federate prison camp—and Mary's mother was forced to sell the land. Only through the help of family friends did Mary receive an education at St. Elizabeth's Academy in nearby Allegany, New York.

Twenty-year-old Mary Clyens, like many Americans of the postwar period, decided that a better future lay in the West. She had been an excellent student, and in 1871 the nuns at St. Elizabeth's arranged a teaching post for her at Osage Mission in eastern Kansas. Saying good-bye to her younger brother and sister and her widowed mother, Mary boarded the train and apparently never looked back. After three years teaching in Kansas, where the ratio of men to women was high, Mary fulfilled the contemporary prophecy that an unmarried woman, once west of the Mississippi, would soon write home as a bride. Surrounded by her new friends in Osage Mission, she married Charles Lease in January 1873.

Charles owned a successful drugstore, sat on the board of a local bank, and a year after the wedding became the mayor of Osage Mission. The Leases had many friends, and Mary seemed destined for respectable small-town prosperity until, in May 1874, her fortunes came crashing down with those of her new husband. In the wake of a severe financial panic, Charles Lease lost his store under circumstances that left him not only bankrupt but under a cloud of suspicion. When the scandal broke, Mary was four months pregnant with their first child. Embarrassed both financially and socially, the couple moved to Denison, Texas, where Charles found work as a pharmacy clerk. They stayed nine years.

For Mary, the poverty of these years was a sad repetition of her mother's troubles. She probably knew little of her husband's business affairs when they first married, but his financial ruin and the subsequent disgrace and social ostracism must have made a deep impression on her. She later asserted that the key source of women's oppression was economic dependence on their husbands—a conviction surely born of personal experience. Other shocks were in store. Less than a year after moving to Denison, she received news of her mother's death in Pennsylvania. After the birth of Charles, her first child, she became pregnant five more times and watched two of her children die in infancy—an event not uncommon at the time. On her husband's meager salary, Mary struggled to raise the surviving children, Charles, Louisa, Grace, and Ben. Like her own mother she valued education, and she took in other families' laundry in order to pay for her children's school clothes and books. Publicly, at least, she never expressed bitterness or anger toward her husband for the crisis into which they had plunged, but the couple grew increasingly distant.

By 1884 the Leases had saved enough money to move back to Kansas and pursue Charles's old dream of farming in the dry lands west of Wichita. During the post-Civil War years, frontier "boosters" offered glowing descriptions of the future prosperity of farms on the Great Plains. Fresh from Union victory, the nation abounded in optimistic editors, politicians, businesspeople, and railroad managers, the latter of whom needed to sell lands granted to them by Congress to finance a flurry of railroad construction in the largely unsettled West. Even scientists joined in, arguing that settlement would create more and more rainfall because the crops and trees planted by pioneers would attract atmospheric moisture. This prediction was not true, of course, but "rain follows the plow" became a Plains axiom. A settlers' guide commissioned by the Missouri Pacific Railroad, and published in the year Mary Lease first arrived in Osage Mission, made extravagant claims about Kansas's climate and the certainty of its economic growth. "Every year there has been a noted increase in the fall of rain," the guide reported, "unquestionably brought about by the cultivation of the soil, and planting of forest trees and orchards."[2]

The Leases, along with thousands of other settlers, were shocked by the actual conditions in western Kansas. Staking a claim in Kingman County, Charles and Mary took the government up on its offer, under the Homestead Act of 1862, to provide 160 free acres to anyone who lived on the land for three consecutive years. Because the policy encouraged settlement on lands of marginal quality, free land was not necessarily the road to prosperity. Like many others, the Leases found that rain did not follow the plow. A 160-acre farm could provide a good living in Pennsylvania, but it was not large enough to sustain a family on the Plains, especially during periods of drought. The Leases soon resettled in Wichita, little better off financially than at the start of their marriage. Charles found a job as a pharmacy clerk, and Mary continued to take in laundry.

Driven by her hardships, Mary began as early as 1880 to seek a public role in movements for political and economic change. While still in Texas she joined a local chapter of the Woman's Christian Temperance Union (WCTU), the most successful women's organization of the 1870s and 1880s. Though prohibition of liquor may today seem a quixotic or narrow-minded goal, the WCTU construed it broadly. Refusing to trivialize the costs of alcoholism, WCTU leaders argued that thousands of women and children suffered neglect and abuse at the hands of drinking husbands and fathers. For Mary Lease, as for many women, temperance was a way to begin speaking tentatively about women's rights. The WCTU also addressed economic injustice. By the 1890s the WCTU's charismatic national president, Frances Willard of Illinois, described herself as a Christian Socialist and cited poverty as the chief cause of alcoholism. Mary Lease's ideas developed along the same lines.

Lease became immersed in a host of reform organizations after moving to Wichita. First, she organized a women's study club, whose members sought to cultivate their intellectual talents. In 1886 she cofounded the Wichita Equal Suffrage Association (WESA), which asserted women's right to vote. Suffrage was a radical demand, and WESA was subject to immediate ridicule in the columns of Wichita newspapers, all of whose editors were men. When these men poked fun at the "pants-wearing" women who wanted to vote, Lease riposted with witty poems and letters. She learned, however, that suffrage was an uphill battle and its supporters had to bear public insults, including claims that they were aggressive, "unwomanly," and bad mothers to boot.

By the late 1880s, Lease's interests expanded in other directions. She reclaimed her Irish-American identity, which she seems to have downplayed or even hidden during her early quest for respectability. Wichita had a large working-class Irish community, many of whom had arrived to work in railroad construction. Invited to address Irish social and political clubs, Lease began to give stirring speeches advocating the end of British colonial rule in Ireland as well as fair treatment for Irish tenant farmers. Around the same time, not coincidentally, she joined a local assembly of the largest and most inclusive labor union in the United States, the Knights of Labor. In 1886 the Knights organized a massive strike against the Southwestern Railway System, operated by wealthy New York financier Jay Gould. At many points along Gould's railroads, including Wichita, local members of the Knights of Labor blocked trains and disabled engines. Though the governor of Kansas called in the National Guard to put down the strike, Lease had witnessed a vivid episode of collective protest against low wages, layoffs, and dangerous working conditions.

Three years later, well practiced in stump speaking and organizing, Lease also joined the Wichita branch of the Farmers' Alliance and Industrial Union, or "the Alliance," as it was widely known. At the time, the Alliance was sweeping across the South and the Great Plains in response to the problems of drought, low crop prices, and heavy farm debts. The Alliance sought allies among union members, including the Knights of Labor. These two groups saw themselves as sharing the same enemies, especially railroad owners such as Jay Gould, whom angry farmers accused of monopolizing key routes and overcharging farmers for the transport of crops to market. (Gould's Missouri Pacific, among others, had promised Kansans "rain would follow the plow.")

More broadly, Knights and Alliance members shared a common set of beliefs that historians have called "producerism." In the decades after the Civil War, railroads and large industrial corporations gained unprecedented power; farmers and laborers increasingly found their fate in the hands of faraway managers and shareholders. Influential thinkers such as Henry George, author of *Progress and Poverty*, identified the income from land rentals, bonds, and other investments as the cause of growing disparities between rich and poor. Lenders were growing rich on high interest rates, such thinkers argued, while borrowers were falling into hopeless debt. Thus, economic reformers began to draw a sharp distinction between bankers and bondholders on the one hand (viewed as parasites who lived on the labor of others) and farmers and the working class on the other. Both the Knights and the Alliance, along with organizations of international scope such as the Irish National League, spoke for the interests of "producers": men and women who did hard, physical work.

Lease's activities on behalf of temperance, women's suffrage, Irish nationalism, and farmers' and workers' rights thus were not as scattered as they might seem. The immigrant men and women who cheered Lease's speeches on behalf of Irish freedom were, in many cases, the same people she met in Knights of Labor meetings. They saw a connection between their parents' poverty in the Old World and labor exploitation in America. Many, like Lease, came from families experienced in protest, and they had emigrated from parts of Ireland where Ribbonmen and other secret societies organized to defend tenants' rights. In these movements, Irish women had long played an important role, so it was natural for Irish-American women to play prominent roles in both the Knights and Irish nationalist organizations.

In the meantime, many temperance leaders such as Frances Willard emphasized poverty and unemployment as causes of alcohol abuse, and the Knights and Farmers' Alliance promoted temperance among their members. Furthermore, male leaders of the Knights and the Alliance gave lectures, as Lease had done, to encourage women to join the movement. The strongest justification for women's entry into such public activities was the view, widespread at the time, that women were morally purer than men. Both the WCTU and many suffragists emphasized women's special role as mothers and wives, seeking to extend "housekeeping" and maternal love into the public sphere. Lease found this rhetoric to be powerful and applicable to the problems of poor laboring women and farm families. "After all our years of toil and privation, dangers and hardships upon the Western frontier," she told one WCTU audience, "monopoly is taking our homes from us by an infamous system of mortgage foreclosure. . . . Do you wonder the women are joining the Alliance? I wonder if there is a woman in all this broad land who can afford to stay out."[3]

Both the Knights and Farmers' Alliance were divided on the question of women's suffrage; conversely, not all WCTU members agreed on the importance of poverty and unemployment as causes of intemperance. In Wichita, however, Mary Lease found sympathetic allies on all sides, and many of her fellow organizers agreed on the need for a grand, unified movement that would work for economic and social reform. By the late 1880s, many activists were furiously debating whether a political party was the best vehicle for collective action. The WCTU had already helped to build up the Prohibitionist party, and its leaders were seeking alliances with other reform-minded groups. In 1888, at a Knights convention in Kansas City, Mary Lease argued vigorously that the union should make partisan endorsements and even run its own candidates. In the fall elections, like-minded Knights ran a fledgling campaign as the Kansas Union Labor party, on whose behalf Lease gave her first partisan speeches. By 1890 the Kansas Farmers' Alliance was also frustrated by the failure of its cooperative stores and other self-help measures, and its members declared their readiness for electoral politics. Thus, Kansas populism was born, and Mary Lease with her multiple affiliations and her experience as a speaker and organizer found herself on center stage.

From the start, Populists sought to remedy America's problems through electoral means, challenging Republicans and Democrats with a new program of government activism. Opposing Republicans' constriction of the money supply (a policy beneficial to lenders), Populists called for currency expansion to stimulate credit and ease the burdens of borrowers. They also demanded government regulation—if not outright ownership—of the railroads and telegraph, which made up the nation's basic infrastructure. At the local level, Populist editors and orators suggested a host of other measures to rescue farmers and industrial laborers from poverty and foreclosure. Like any movement embracing hundreds of thousands of people, populism contained tensions and contradictions; yet all Populists agreed that the "money power" (meaning Wall Street financiers and the politicians whose influence they bought) threatened the interests of hardworking Americans.

Populists' first testing ground was the Kansas election of 1890, a campaign in which Lease played a key role. Incensed at Republican senator John J. Ingalls—who ridiculed the Populists and told women their proper place was at home, not in politics—Lease went on the stump, giving an estimated 160 speeches in three months. Like her fellow Populists, Lease saw the new party as a movement not of farmers only but of all the producing classes. She excoriated bankers, corporate managers, and those who lived on income from their investments. In broader terms she spoke out against government and corporate policies that were rapidly making the rich richer while the poor stayed poor. "I hold to the theory," she said, "that if one man has not enough to eat three times a day and another man has $25 million, that last man has something that belongs to the first."[4]

Lease quickly emerged as one of her party's most effective orators. She had a low, powerful voice—described by listeners as resonant, masculine, or even hypnotic—along with a keen memory for statistics, a sense of humor, and the ability to think on her feet. In an era when political speeches were mass entertainment, she excelled at holding audiences' attention, often for two hours or more. "One of the best addresses, if not the best and most eloquent address I ever heard from a woman," a Nevada newspaperman wrote in his diary after hearing her speak. "Splendid style, voice and elocution." "She is the greatest natural orator of the female sex (or of either sex) that has appeared on earth," wrote another admirer.[5] Lease laced her speeches with quotations from Shakespeare and the Bible, and she learned to handle hecklers with scathing sarcasm or disarming wit.

Hailing "Our Queen Mary," the upstart Kansas Populists won five of the state's seven congressional districts and a majority of seats in the legislature. Because state legislatures elected U.S. senators until the Seventeenth Amendment, ratified in 1913, the new legislature promptly unseated John Ingalls and chose William Peffer as the nation's first Populist senator. It was a stunning victory. The events of 1890 in Kansas brought national fame to the new party and to Lease, and they persuaded Alliance members and Knights in other parts of the country that electoral politics was worth a try.

Thus, there was hardly time to celebrate the Kansas victory as organizers hastened to build the movement nationwide. A proven orator, Lease spent little time in Kansas over the next two years. Leaving her four teenage children in Wichita with their father, she represented the party all over the nation. In February 1892 her speech in St. Louis provoked wild enthusiasm from a gathering of thousands. The following June, as the lone woman in the Kansas delegation, Lease participated in the Omaha convention that established a national People's party. She helped craft parts of the platform in committee, and she gave the seconding speech for James B. Weaver, the party's presidential nominee. In the famous Omaha Platform, the new party presented a bold program for

reform. "The conditions which surround us best justify our cooperation," argued the platform's preamble.

> The fruits of the toil of millions are boldly stolen to build up colossal for-
> tunes for a few, unprecedented in the history of mankind; and the possessors
> of these, in turn, despise the republic and endanger liberty. . . . We believe
> that the powers of government—in other words, of the people—should be
> expanded . . . as rapidly and as far as the good sense of an intelligent people
> and the teachings of experience shall justify, to the end that oppression, in-
> justice, and poverty shall eventually cease in the land.[6]

The 1892 campaign was, in retrospect, the height of populism and
of Mary Lease's fame. By this time a member of the party's top inner
circle, she accompanied Weaver and his wife on grueling campaign tours
around the country. In August they spoke to huge audiences in the West
with Lease making as many as eight speeches in a day. "A mortgaged
home, an empty stomach and a ragged back know no party," she told a
San Francisco audience, urging it to make the "nonpartisan" choice and
vote for populism. "We will live to write the epitaphs of the old parties:
'Died of general debility, old age and chronic falsehoods.' "[7]

Populists' greatest difficulty lay, however, in capturing support beyond the West. This they failed to do. Though a Populist coalition
emerged in Chicago, most urban workers in the Midwest and Northeast did not respond to appeals from a movement depicted as a "farmers' revolt." Eastern newspapers alternately ridiculed the party and
warned that its leaders were anarchists and Communists. Both Republicans and Democrats, wherever they were entrenched at the state and
local levels, commanded vastly greater funds and patronage than did
the upstart party and were not averse to using it. Lease herself apparently received offers of bribes to work for the Republicans. Many North-
easterners apparently stayed loyal to the Grand Old Party (GOP) for
other reasons: Republicans still took credit for preserving the Union in
the Civil War, and they argued that their protective tariff policies shel-
tered workers in the textile and other industries from low-wage com-
petitors overseas.

The South was the site of populism's most tragic failures. Before
1892, thousands of southern farmers had built a strong Farmers' Alliance ranging from North Carolina to Texas, including a segregated but
active Colored Farmers' Alliance. Yet this activism never translated into
Populist strength. Black Southerners' voting rights were increasingly
restricted through poll taxes and disfranchisement laws, and white farmers were reluctant to abandon the Democrats, who pronounced them-

selves the champions of (white) "home rule" for the South and of resistance to federal intrusion. Those Southerners who became Populists often did so at great risk. Weaver and Lease vividly experienced southern Democrats' fear and hatred when they arrived in Georgia in September 1892. In Macon, only a few miles from the place where Lease's father had died in a Confederate prison camp, she and Weaver were hooted down and pelted with rotten vegetables and eggs. At Albany, the speakers and their entourage hid in their hotel, unsure for hours whether the angry crowd outside intended to lynch them. Within a week Weaver and Lease had canceled the rest of their southern tour. In November, Democrats retained control of almost every southern state—by persuading Populist voters where they could and, where necessary, by using overt violence and fraud.

Weaver's defeat—though he won more than a million votes—was only the beginning of Mary Lease's troubles. Though Kansas Populists won many offices in 1892, including the governorship, they did so through ticket-splitting (or "fusion") arrangements with Democrats. To Lease, who spent less and less of her time in Kansas, such an alliance was a betrayal of populism. Democrats were the men she had encountered in Georgia, many of whom were former Confederates, and in her view they were responsible for killing her father.

Furthermore, Democrats in Kansas and elsewhere were staunch opponents of women's suffrage and prohibition, and Populists had to give up these goals in order to appease their new friends. For some Populists this apparent compromise was not a problem, since they had never supported such measures in the first place. But many others, Lease included, wanted the party to articulate a much broader vision. Outside the former Confederacy, in almost every state where they had held a convention in the early 1890s, Populists had adopted women's suffrage planks. Some had also made favorable mention of prohibition. Yet at the 1892 National Populist Convention these planks had been dropped, largely in deference to the party's more conservative southern wing. Lease observed the same Populist-Democratic fusion in her home state of Kansas: the men in power dismissed women's suffrage and prohibition as side issues at best or even as extremist, illegitimate demands. Small wonder that some Kansas Populists began bitterly denouncing the fusionists, claiming they were no longer Populists at all. Those who favored fusion responded, with some justification, that unless the new party allied itself with Democrats, it could not win; with fusion, it had elected a Populist governor.

For Lease, the biggest affront was the division of appointments after the 1892 state campaign. She let it be known that she was interested in Kansas's second U.S. Senate seat, which the new legislature would fill. Lease's candidacy created a nationwide sensation: in only two states (Wyoming and Colorado) were women allowed to vote for national offices, and the idea of a woman senator was entirely new. To many progressive-minded onlookers, this issue was a test of the party's true colors. Women's suffrage leader Susan B. Anthony offered a public endorsement. James Weaver and other Populists also wrote letters of support, stating that the Constitution clearly allowed women to serve in Congress. But Kansas's new governor and legislators had no desire to appoint either a woman or a "mid-roader," a Populist who avoided fusion with either the Democrats or the Republicans. Their victory had been at best a shaky one, and they calculated that Lease's strongest supporters among the citizenry of Kansas were Alliance women, who had no future votes with which to retaliate if they were displeased. Lease was shunted aside and offered a lesser appointment as state superintendent of charities. No American woman had ever held such a prominent office, and the new governor, Lorenzo Lewelling, no doubt thought he was making a suitable offer. Lease, who rightly considered herself one of her party's most valuable assets, took a different view.

She nonetheless accepted the post Lewelling offered and for a year oversaw the state's asylums for orphans, the mentally retarded, and elderly veterans. With little experience in such work, Lease attended national conferences and listened to the advice of experts, but at the same time she continued to jockey for power within the Kansas party. When Lewelling tried to appoint two Democrats to the Board of Charities as part of the new fusion agreement, Lease protested vigorously and even criticized the governor in her interviews with reporters. Populists who supported Lewelling began to criticize her for disloyalty; many mid-roaders hailed her as a hero. Facing division within Populist ranks, Lewelling dismissed Lease from her post in December 1893. Lease fought an expensive legal battle for reinstatement, but she lost.

By 1895, Lease was also worn down by opponents' attacks. As a woman who spoke for new, radical ideas, she was an outsider to the world of politics, and from the first she received treatment as such. Republican and Democratic editors and politicians branded her as ugly, loud, aggressive, and "unwomanly"—terms of abuse that activist women of all political persuasions have faced. After Kansas's 1892 inauguration ceremony, *Harper's Weekly* ignored Lease's speech for the occasion, reporting instead that she was too flat-chested to wear a ballgown. Some opposition newspapers hinted that Lease "prostituted" her talents; one snidely remarked that her voice was the only thing marketable about her. As Kansas Populists split between fusionists and mid-roaders, some Populists joined in such attacks. Lease claimed in 1894 that Governor Lewelling, when Lease had begun to expose corruption in his administration, had threatened to buy evidence purporting to prove that she and James Weaver had slept together during their 1892 campaign tour. As a poor woman, Lease was particularly vulnerable to such charges, in part because her use of words such as "hell" (even though she was quoting from the Bible) shocked many a respectable citizen.

Angry and isolated, Lease found herself cut off from many former allies as the Populist party fell apart. She first tried to reestablish her influence by publishing a book, *The Problem of Civilization Solved*, which appeared in 1895. It was a rambling work that foreshadowed the logic of the most extreme imperialists in the next decade. Lease argued that European-American farmers needed new land and resources in order to prosper; their future lay in Central and South America, and "enterprising white men from the North" should "colonize the valley of the Amazon and the tropical plateaux."[8] How they would acquire this land remained unclear; Lease repeatedly denounced war and helped found the National Peace Society. In contrast, she praised the U.S. Army for its wars against the Sioux and Cheyenne on the northern plains, and she later gave her wholehearted endorsement to imperialism. With her muddled thinking and overt racial condescension, Lease was lucky that her book was largely ignored.

In 1896 she recommitted herself to stump-speaking tours in one of the most important presidential elections in U.S. history. Democrats nominated William Jennings Bryan for president on a platform that borrowed a few planks from the Populists, most notably in advocating currency expansion. Despite strenuous objections from Lease and others, the Populist national convention seconded Bryan's nomination, adopting a fusion strategy again. Lease spent most of the autumn in New York and Minnesota, speaking for Bryan but noting in an occasional aside that Bryan's platform offered only the barest of reform measures. By the time the Republican candidate, William McKinley, won the White House in November, Lease was declaring herself a Socialist. She was one of the first prominent Populists to do so, and many other Populists (including Eugene Debs, later a famous Socialist candidate for the U.S. presidency) soon followed her lead.

In the wake of McKinley's election the Populist party fragmented and fell into decline. Bitter about the effects of fusion, Lease probably also agreed with former Colorado governor Davis Waite, another Populist who had exhausted himself for the cause. "I have done traveling 1000 miles to make a single speech," Waite wrote Ignatius Donnelly in 1896, "or attempting to fill spasmodic appointments with spasmodic speeches. I want some organization, to make a regular daily series of appointments, provide halls & pay actual living & travel expenses from day to day."[9] The Populist leadership, presiding over a shrinking party, could not offer even these shreds of support.

At the age of forty-eight, so financially desperate that on one occasion her luggage was repossessed, Lease decided to leave Kansas and start a new life. She secured an amicable divorce from Charles and moved with her children to New York City. Having studied law and passed the bar in Wichita during the 1880s, she established a part-time legal practice on New York's Lower East Side, largely serving the immigrant poor. She also taught evening classes on history and literature for the New York Board of Education, and she lectured occasionally on literary, economic, and political topics. In the 1910s she joined a group of reformers working for women's reproductive rights—no doubt recollecting her harsh experiences as a frontier wife and mother. At the end of her life, looking back, Lease considered her efforts on behalf of the National Birth Control League, headquartered in New York, among her most important works of public service.

After 1900, Lease never quite found another political home. As early as 1896 she had identified herself as a Socialist, and she became a friend of American Socialist party leader Eugene Debs, for whose ideas and candidacies she spoke on many occasions. At the same time, Lease was painfully aware of the difficult position of third parties, which had meager campaign funds and no patronage posts to distribute and whose enemies increasingly sought to exclude them from the ballot altogether. Lease retained a fierce hatred of Democrats, based on her father's death and her own touring experiences in Georgia, and she remained hopeful that Republicans would take up new reforms. She admired Theodore Roosevelt, and when he made his Progressive party presidential bid in 1912, she made a series of speeches on his behalf. In a typical move, she afterward sued the campaign for not paying her as much as they had promised—reminding male party leaders, as always, that they could not take her services for granted.

In 1905, Lease suffered another personal tragedy when her beloved oldest son, Charles, died suddenly of appendicitis. In her last years, however, she found the financial security she had sought for so long and proudly watched her three surviving children graduate from college, fulfilling the dream of her own mother, Mary Clyens, that her American grandchildren be well educated. Louisa, Grace, and Ben settled comfortably in Brooklyn. Ben, ironically, became a stockbroker; Louisa married a writer; and Grace followed her mother into politics, becoming a district organizer for the Republicans. In 1932, Mary Lease purchased a farm in Sullivan County, New York, along the Delaware River, where she spent the final year of her life.

Before she died, Lease witnessed the implementation of many policies she had espoused even though Progressive Era economic reforms fell far short of what Populists had dreamed of, leaving the "money power" more entrenched than reformers had hoped. Lease lived to see national women's suffrage, and she watched a one-time Populist ally, Rebecca Felton, become the first woman to sit in the U.S. Senate, albeit if only briefly to serve out her deceased husband's term.

Lease died in 1933 at the age of eighty-three. William Allen White, an old foe who had grown more sympathetic to some of Lease's views, wrote upon her death that "as a voice calling the people to action she has never had a superior in Kansas politics. . . . She was an honest, competent woman who felt deeply and wielded great power unselfishly."[10] Lease did, indeed, seek public solutions to private problems, impoverishing herself in the 1890s by working for measures that would aid millions of Americans rather than only herself. In her long life she experienced many reversals of fortune. Poverty and the deaths of three children were griefs she shared with millions of women; other sufferings—including the countless attacks on her as a public speaker, in which she heard herself called everything from a harlot to a harpy—she shared with only a few. Her restless search for reform continued despite it all.

In her private life, Lease continually reinvented herself. She remained open to new ideas and willing to start again from scratch in the face of bankruptcy, a failed marriage, public scorn, and the loss of those close to her, from the death of her father when she was thirteen to that of her oldest son when she was fifty-five. In her public life she displayed the same willingness to start over when the causes she worked for crumbled to dust and had to be resurrected or reshaped under new names. "Keep your eye fixed upon the mark," she once remarked, "and don't flinch when you pull the trigger."[11] Not all her views were admirable, but they were bold and often ahead of her time, and throughout her career she kept a sustained focus on inequities of class and gender. Her eloquence moved tens of thousands of listeners to share—whether for a few moments, a few years, or a lifetime—a vision of a future America in which citizens would demand that their government guarantee equality to women and justice to the poor.

Notes

1. Lease once told a reporter that she never made this comment but that she "let it stand, because she thought it was a right good piece of advice." O. Gene Clanton, "Intolerant Populist? The Disaffection of Mary Elizabeth Lease," *Kansas Historical Quarterly* 34 (1968): 190, n. 2.

2. *Facts and Figures about Kansas: An Emigrants' and Settlers' Guide* (Lawrence, KS: Blackburn, 1870), 24–25.

3. Joan Jensen, ed., *With These Hands* (Old Westbury, NY: Feminist Press, 1981), 158–59.

4. Dorothy Rose Blumberg, "Mary Elizabeth Lease, Populist Orator: A Profile," *Kansas History* 1 (1978): 14.

5. Walter Van Tilburg Clark, ed., *The Journals of Alfred Doten, 1849–1903*, 3 vols. (Reno: University of Nevada Press, 1973), 3:1825; Ignatius Donnelly, *Representative*, September 8, 1897.

6. John D. Hicks, *The Populist Revolt: A History of the Farmers' Alliance and the People's Party* (Minneapolis: University of Minnesota Press, 1931), 439–41.

7. Blumberg, "Mary Elizabeth Lease," 14.

8. Mary Elizabeth Lease, *The Problem of Civilization Solved* (Chicago: Laird and Lee, 1895), 176, 178.

9. Davis Waite to Ignatius Donnelly, August 20, 1900, Donnelly Papers, Minnesota Historical Society, Minneapolis.

10. William Allen White, *Forty Years on Main Street* (New York: Farrar and Rinehart, 1937), 227.

11. *Wichita Independent*, March 23, 1889.

Suggested Readings

Robert McMath's *American Populism: A Social History* (New York: Hill and Wang, 1993) is an excellent account of populism's origins, platforms, and fate. In his introduction, McMath reviews four influential works on populism that are very much worth reading in their own right: John Hicks's classic *The Populist Revolt* (Minneapolis: University of Minnesota Press, 1931); C. Vann Woodward's *Tom Watson, Agrarian Rebel* (New York: Oxford University Press, 1938); Richard Hofstadter's *The Age of Reform* (New York: Knopf, 1955), which is highly critical of populism; and Lawrence Goodwyn's *Democratic Promises:*

The Populist Moment in America (New York: Oxford University Press, 1976), a controversial account of the Populists' "movement culture." McMath also analyzes producerism as espoused by the Knights of Labor, Farmers' Alliance, and other movements for economic reform, and he provides a good bibliography. Michael Lewis Goldberg's *An Army of Women: Gender in Kansas Politics* (Baltimore: Johns Hopkins University Press, 1997) places Mary Lease in state and gender contexts.

For broader overviews of women in politics see Mary Jo Buhle, *Women and American Socialism* (Urbana: University of Illinois Press, 1981); Ruth Bordin, *Woman and Temperance* (Philadelphia: Temple University Press, 1981); and Rebecca Edwards, *Angels in the Machinery: Gender in American Party Politics from the Civil War to the Progressive Era* (New York: Oxford University Press, 1997). The views of representative farm women who joined Lease's crusade appear in Marion K. Barthelme, ed., *Women in the Texas Populist Movement: Letters to the Southern Mercury* (College Station, TX: Texas A&M University Press, 1997).

On the settlement of western Kansas see Craig Miner's *West of Wichita* (Lawrence: University Press of Kansas, 1986). For women's experiences on the Great Plains see Glenda Riley, *The Female Frontier* (Lawrence: University Press of Kansas, 1988); and Joanna L. Stratton, ed., *Pioneer Women: Voices from the Kansas Frontier* (New York: Simon and Schuster, 1981).

5

Clelia Duel Mosher and the Change in Women's Sexuality

Kathleen R. Parker

Attitudes toward sex in the Victorian era were restrictive and biased against women. Conventional understanding about the physiology of female sexuality during the latter decades of the nineteenth century had little scientific foundation and relied heavily on rigid stereotypes of how nature programmed gender roles. Women were understood to be innately passive and emotional; men were presumed to be naturally assertive and cerebral. Clelia Duel Mosher challenged these myths and helped to lay the groundwork for systematic research into women's sexuality.

Kathleen Parker traces the career of this educator and reformer who dedicated her life to combating misconceptions that limited women's activities. Mosher worked to overcome the presumption that women were unsuited for advanced education and that menstruation was a sickness requiring bed rest. Her interest in female sexuality led her to question the attitudes and marital practices of middle-class women between 1892 and 1920. Her findings from this pioneering survey rebutted the belief that women engaged in sexual relations only for reproduction. Mosher also found that although new views about marital intimacy had emerged, women still retained older, idealized images about marriage. Professor Parker sees Mosher's own bittersweet life as mirroring this subtle mixture of tradition and modernity in middle-class marriages.

Kathleen R. Parker holds a Ph.D. in American studies from Michigan State University and teaches at Indiana University of Pennsylvania. Her research focuses on sexuality in America and comparatively in a global context.

In the years 1880 to 1920, urban middle-class women campaigned for the vote, worked in settlement houses, called for temperance laws, stood in picket lines with their working-class sisters, and lobbied to raise the age of consent regarding cases of statutory rape. Confronting

This essay originally appeared in Ballard C. Campbell, ed., *The Human Tradition in the Gilded Age and Progressive Era* (Wilmington, DE: Scholarly Resources, 2000), 119–35.

the human troubles that marked an industrializing and urbanizing society, they employed various styles of voluntary activism that demonstrated new avenues of personal choice and social commitment for women outside the traditional domestic sphere. Among these "new women," a small but growing number established themselves in the professions. One of these women was Clelia Duel Mosher, who sought in her lifelong work as a physician, scientist, and educator to dismantle the biological and sexual beliefs that limited women's achievements. Her studies to prove the constricting effects of Victorian clothing and disprove the common perception that menstruation was disabling contributed to a new stream of scholarship that questioned women's assumed physical weaknesses. The unique aspect of her work was her survey of sexual attitudes and practices administered to forty-five married middle-class women during the years 1892 to 1920. Although the survey itself was not published in her lifetime, her challenge to existing gender definitions accompanied rising expectations for women and men in higher education, family mobility, consumerism, and reform.

Clelia Mosher was born on December 16, 1863, in Albany, New York, into a family for which medicine was a traditional occupation. Her father, four uncles, and a distant cousin, Eliza Mosher, were all physicians. Clelia hoped to study medicine too, a goal that was possible only for daughters whose families believed in women's education. Her father had supported her early schooling at Albany Female Academy, but he worried that the demands of college life would threaten her health. Her only sister, Esther, had died, and Clelia had been weakened by childhood tuberculosis. To compensate for discouraging her educational ambitions, her father converted the small family greenhouse into a laboratory, financed her lessons in botany and horticulture, and built a small store from which she could sell her flowers. Clelia's floral business became the means to obtain the education she desired. Within a few years, she saved two thousand dollars, a sum sufficient to pay her way through college. At the age of twenty-five, she announced to her parents her intention to enroll at Wellesley College in Massachusetts. Her father accepted her decision and helped his independent daughter prepare for college by letting her study medicine with him.

Clelia arrived at Wellesley in 1889, when 36 percent of college students were women. The first year of study left her near physical collapse from overwork but it led her to an important decision. Inspired by Wellesley professor Mary Roberts Smith, Mosher committed her life to the women's movement. For her this resolve would mean using medical science to free women from culture-driven health limitations. Mosher followed Smith first to the University of Wisconsin in her junior year and then to Stanford University, where she graduated with a biology major in 1893.

As a student, Mosher questioned prevailing assumptions about women's health. Male physicians had relied on their observations of unhealthy women to make conclusions about all women. What seemed rather peculiar to Mosher, for example, was the common belief that women breathed costally (only with the upper chest) and men breathed diaphragmatically (a deeper breathing that involves the entire diaphragm). Upheld in all the nineteenth-century textbooks, women's shallow breathing was assumed to be an innate characteristic that served to justify their "natural" incapacity for heavy exertion. Such an idea seemed preposterous in light of the physical tasks performed by ordinary women in their households and by poorer women in industry, agriculture, and domestic service. Acting on Smith's suggestion to study healthy women, Mosher determined to expose the myth behind the so-called scientific truth of women's costal breathing.

Upon graduation Mosher accepted a position at Stanford as an assistant in the girls' gymnasium. She began examining the breathing of female students and pregnant girls at the nearby Pacific Rescue Home. Using an elaborate measuring device of her own making, she measured the upper-body circumferences of eighty-eight subjects, male and female, at three sites: under the arms, at the ninth rib, and at the waist. Each site was measured at repose, at expansion in quiet breathing, at fullest expiration, and at fullest inspiration. The process took several hours for each subject, evidence of her precise and thorough research methods. In all cases, she found that the presence of clothing decreased the measure of chest expansion. By 1894, she was able to offer her findings for her master's degree. What she had learned was corroborated two years later at Harvard University, namely, that women's more shallow breathing was not due to any inherent sex differences but rather to the societally imposed requirement that women wear a corset. As a constrictive undergarment, the corset altered the bone structure of a woman's rib cage and confined her lung capacity to a small portion of the natural chest cavity.

From these findings, Mosher came to suspect that the incapacitating "sickness" routinely associated with menstruation—referred to then as "functional periodicity"—was at least partly a result of fashion. Corsets and voluminous skirts put downward pressure on all the abdominal organs and hindered their functioning. She measured the clothing of ninety-eight Stanford women students enrolled in her physical culture classes and found that the average circumference of their skirts was 13.5 feet. More impassioned than others who were making similar arguments, Mosher urged her students to abandon their corsets and heavy skirts. If they would wear sensible clothing, they could eliminate their monthly seven-day confinements in bed. Mosher's own dress reflected her belief in functional simplicity. As fashions came and went, she was well known among colleagues and students for her unchanging attire: a loose black shirtwaist dress, starched collar, four-in-hand tie, and untrimmed round hat. She was, noted one student, "quite a sight."[1]

Mosher's interest in debunking the assumed disability menstruation imposed on women is better understood given the ideas that shaped contemporary thinking. As women sought new opportunities to participate in the commercializing world of the late nineteenth century, keepers of tradition warned them against violating the dictates of their biology. Doctors and psychologists believed that a woman's uterus controlled both her physical and mental life, making her naturally weak, submissive, uncreative, emotional, intuitive, and inferior in comparison to men. The implications of this view, as one-time Harvard physician Dr. Edward Clarke had argued in his 1873 book *Sex Education; or, a Fair Chance for Girls*, were that women should not expend their energies on education. Mental exertion would impair the proper functioning of their reproductive organs. Clarke's ideas were buttressed in the 1870s by a dominant strain of Darwinian thinking, holding that orderly evolution toward advanced civilization depended on the proper maintenance of sex differences. In 1871, Charles Darwin had written in *The Descent of Man* that men could attain higher eminence than women in anything requiring "deep thought, reason, or imagination." Women's "greater tenderness" was characteristic of a "lower state of civilization." Noted British economist Herbert Spencer agreed with Darwin but saw women's "intuitive capacity to empathize" in positive terms; it made them "especially well fitted for their parenting role."[2] In support of these ideas, Clarke University's G. Stanley Hall believed that male strength must be preserved to ensure optimum evolution of the human race. Hall feared that coeducation would lead girls to assimilate boys' ways and boys to assimilate girls' ways, threatening boys' understanding of a thoroughly masculine identity. By the 1890s, ideas about men and women were polarized: men were believed to be competitive, adventurous, and predisposed to excitement and to exhibit "mental variability"; women were assumed to be nurturing, passive, uncreative, tranquil, and lacking in sustained mental application.[3] It was this view of sex differences that Clarke, Hall, and others feared would be lost if women became educated.

Mosher's theory regarding "functional periodicity" challenged this kind of biological determinism. By 1896, her study had led her to examine 400 women and keep records of 3,350 menstrual cycles. Twenty years earlier, Dr. Mary Putnam Jacobi's award-winning book *The Question of Rest for Women during Menstruation* had concluded that there was no need for bed rest during menstruation. Mosher believed her study would result in similar conclusions that would carry more scientific weight, since Jacobi had based her observations on 286 responses obtained from a mail-in questionnaire. By contrast, Mosher interviewed her subjects personally and conducted follow-up discussions with them over a longer period.

As the extent of her study expanded, she decided to pursue her dream of medical training in order to properly interpret her data. With characteristic self-confidence, she applied only to Johns Hopkins School of Medicine, believing it offered the best medical training in the country. The school had been open for just three years and was prepared to admit both male and female students because a group of local women benefactors had raised an endowment of $500,000 on the condition that the school be open to women. Dr. Jacobi hailed this enrollment policy as an important precedent. Nineteen women's medical colleges had been established between 1850 and 1895, but Johns Hopkins was the first of its academic standing to admit both male and female students. After she completed the precondition of an additional course in physics, Mosher enrolled in 1899 as one of thirteen women in a class of forty-one students. Later she would write that at Johns Hopkins, she found a climate of support for women students and for her interest in women's physiology.

Mosher was fortunate to study under Dr. Howard Atwood Kelly, a leading figure in gynecological surgical methods and, by all accounts, an "extraordinary operator." When Mosher graduated in 1900, Kelly offered her a one-year position as a gynecological assistant in his sanatorium, which she accepted. She believed her work had come to Dr. Kelly's notice because of the attention it was getting from Dr. George Englemann, a noted Boston gynecologist. Englemann had collected records on menstruation from college and university teachers around the country. He had earlier sought access to Mosher's records while she was still a senior at Stanford, and now he pressured Kelly to "put the screws on Miss Mosher and see that she is heard from—and send me her data." When Kelly passed Englemann's letter on to Mosher, she chose to protect her research and did not respond. Englemann persisted by contacting her directly, allowing that if she wanted to utilize her records for "any especial purpose," she should at least give him the "general results." In a carefully worded letter of response, Mosher told Englemann that she was extending her Stanford studies, implying that her results were not yet complete. Privately, she wrote with indignation, "For what purpose would one spend all one's leisure and all the money to pay expenses of an extensive investigation of a subject if it was not to be used?" Very soon after this incident, in 1901, her research was published as her own work in the *Johns Hopkins Medical Bulletin*. Her findings contradicted those of Englemann, who believed that education and labor had caused "great harm to the female nervous system."[4]

Kelly was apparently pleased with Mosher's performance as his assistant. At the end of the one-year appointment, he offered to train her as a gynecological surgeon, adding the warning that no male physician would likely be willing to work under her. Apparently she declined his offer not for this reason but because she preferred to work independently. She returned to California to begin a private practice in Palo Alto. There she would also be near her friend, Mary Roberts Smith. This decision proved to be an important turning point in her life. Her private practice was never more than a meager success. Her clients were mostly the chronic patients referred to her by established physicians, and her income was never adequate in this period to meet her needs. Records of her own medicinal recipes and her visits with patients suggest she devoted a good deal of attention to the science of healing. When she was offered in 1910 a chance to teach personal hygiene at Stanford and serve as medical adviser to women students, she eagerly accepted. From this position, she would be able to resume her research on menstruation. This work, she believed, would "make a great difference in women's lives . . . helping to give every woman her birthright of health."[5]

During these years she pursued her research and developed a series of exercises designed to strengthen abdominal muscles and "equalize circulation" among all the organs. These exercises, known through her several published articles as "moshers," were adopted by "physical culture" departments in other schools to prevent the kind of "congestion" that Mosher believed contributed to menstrual discomfort. In test studies, students who carried out the prescribed exercises reported experiencing less menstrual pain than had been customary for them before. Such testimony provided a valuable basis for challenging the restrictions of tradition. In a 1915 speech before a national officers' convention of the Young Women's Christian Association (YWCA), Mosher urged women to appreciate their physiological capabilities. Published as a small book, *The Relation of Health to the Woman Movement,* her speech concluded: "What we need are women no less fine and womanly, but with beautiful, perfect bodies, a suitable receptacle for their equally beautiful souls, who look sanely out on life with steady nerves and clear vision."[6]

Clelia Mosher gained national prominence in her lifetime for her work on breathing and menstruation, especially for her abdominal exercises. It is her survey on sexual attitudes and practices, however, that has uniquely captured the interest of historians, offering in a treasury of private, subjective responses a fascinating glimpse of marital intimacy, childbirth, and the psychosexual health concerns of women at the turn of the century. The story behind the survey begins in 1892, while Clelia Mosher was still a twenty-eight-year-old biology student at the University of Wisconsin. Her mentor, Mary Roberts Smith, asked her to speak to the Mothers Club, made up mostly of the wives of university faculty, in Madison. Smith and Mosher collaborated in formulating a series of twenty-five health- and sex-related questions, to which Mosher initially compiled the responses of seven club women (one of whom was Smith herself). Over the next twenty-eight years (until 1920), a total of forty-five women responded to the survey. Their responses, which Mosher recorded in her own hand, constitute the only late-nineteenth- to early-twentieth-century document we have that was designed from the outset to elicit personal sexual information in a systematic way.

The limitations of the survey's historical value are that the respondents were few in number and did not represent a balanced cross section of women. All the respondents were white, married, well educated, and existing economically and culturally within a middle- to upper-middle-class frame of reference. It appears not to have been within the realm of appropriateness or possibility for Mosher to conduct the study otherwise. At the time only 2 percent of women graduated from college, and 40 to 60 percent of women college graduates did not marry. Thirty-four of Mosher's respondents had attended college or normal school (at Vassar, Smith, Cornell, Stanford, Indiana, Iowa State, and the University of California), twenty-seven had worked as teachers prior to marriage, and all were married to men who held college degrees. Moreover, at a time when major cities were teeming with immigrants, all of the respondents were born in the United States. All of them lived and went to school in the North or in California; not one was from the South.

In spite of these limitations, both the nature of the survey questions and the responses to them, collectively and individually, teach us much about turn-of-the-century normative sexual expectations. Each survey respondent was first asked general questions about her family history, her years of marriage, and her health. Then she was asked more specific questions about the condition and duration of her menstrual flow, how much she had known about sexual physiology before marriage, whether she slept with her husband and why, and how many times she had conceived and whether conception had been by choice. The most intimate questions came last. Each respondent was asked to describe her sex life with her husband: habits of sexual intercourse, whether she experienced orgasm, what she believed the purposes of intercourse to be, whether she used any means of birth control, and what she considered an ideal habit of intercourse to be.

Particularly significant to this era are the questions pertaining to sexual intercourse. They explore the distinction between intercourse for reproduction and intercourse for pleasure, both for the man and for the woman. Throughout much of the nineteenth century, the popular assumption was that men's desires for sex were boundless but that respectable women were "passionless." Thus, sexual intercourse for a woman was understood as a matter of duty, endured to please one's husband and to produce children. This survey posed the possibility that intercourse might be "agreeable" for the woman, which suggests that a less proscribed view of women's sexuality existed. By asking whether women "always" had a "venereal orgasm," Mosher conveyed the presumption that they would have them at least some of the time and that it was acceptable for them to admit it.

Late-nineteenth-century medical opinion was divided on the question of women's ability to experience sexual passion. From 1857 until its last printing in 1894, William Acton's widely quoted book *The Functions and Disorders of the Reproductive Organs* argued that women were "not troubled with sexual feelings of any kind." Their indifference to sex was "pre-ordained." In contrast, Orson S. Fowler, a phrenologist, wrote in 1870: "That female passion exists is as obvious as that the sun shines." The practice of coitus interruptus as a form of contraception, wrote Henry Chevasse, should be discouraged because it is "attended with disastrous consequences, most particularly to the female, whose nervous system suffers from ungratified excitement."[7]

The leader among those who believed that women were capable of sexual feelings was Dr. George Napheys, whose *Physical Life of Woman: Advice to the Maiden, Wife, and Mother* was published in 1869. With much scientific authority, Napheys proposed that women were divided into three groups: the first and smallest was made up of women who had no passion, the second and larger group was made up of those who had strong passion, and the third and largest group consisted of "the vast majority of women, in whom the sexual appetite is as moderate as all other appetites." The popularity of Napheys's work (there were sixty thousand copies in print in two years) suggests that it resonated well with the experiences of the literate middle-class women who constituted his readership.[8] They likely identified with those of moderate appetite. Poorer women, by contrast, were assumed to be promiscuous.

Remarkably, some doctors were so committed to an ideology of women's passionlessness that they performed clitoridectomies, or castrations, on their women patients to "cure" them of their feelings of sexual arousal. Intended to check a "growing incidence of female masturbation," these medical reactions were evidence that even respectable women had a natural sexual appetite.[9] Experts' more general acceptance of women's sexual capacity did not occur until after 1900. As early as 1912, William Robinson asserted in *Sex Problems of Today* that "every case of divorce has for its basis lack of sexual satisfaction." Charging men with the responsibility of arousing their wives' natural passions, Dr. Walter Robie wrote in 1921, "The husband should not rest easy, nor should his wife allow him to, until they have discovered the methods and positions which give her greatest pleasure and completest orgasm." Metaphorically, he added, "As dough is prepared for baking, so must a woman be prepared for sexual intercourse." The new premise, for both men and women, was that sex was to be playful and was to be mutually enjoyed by both parties.[10]

Among Mosher's earliest respondents, however, reluctance about intercourse seems to have outweighed enthusiasm for it. The women interviewed before 1900 were more likely to report that sex was not a necessity, especially for women; after 1900, the women were more accepting of the belief that sex was necessary for both men and women. One of these interviewees wrote that the "highest devotion is based upon it. . . . It is a very beautiful thing, and I am glad nature gave it to us."

Representative of the thirty-four respondents who reported experiencing orgasm were admissions that the "absence of orgasm" is "disastrous, nerve wracking, and unbalancing"; the presence of orgasm "produces physical harmony."[11]

Mosher's later interviewees demonstrated this shift toward greater sexual pleasure for women, yet the qualifiers they offered suggest where the boundaries of such pleasure lay. One woman who found intercourse "agreeable" and "very nearly always" had an orgasm nonetheless wrote with some ambivalence that "the pleasure is sufficient to warrant it, provided people are extremely moderate and do not allow it to injure their health and degrade their best feelings toward each other." Her words imply that too frequent intercourse would be a detriment to well-being and might compromise the moral basis of the marital sexual relationship. Arguing for mutuality in the marital relation, respondents valued spirituality and a sense of affection in sexual intercourse over any reported physical arousal. One interviewee indicated that intercourse was "one of the highest manifestations of love, granted us by our Creator." Another stated that any "necessity" for intercourse was not physical, as with food and drink, but spiritual. She further elaborated, "My husband and I . . . believe in intercourse for its own sake . . . and spiritually miss it . . . when it does not occur because it is the highest, most sacred expression of our oneness."

Their desire for moderation, together with their insistence on the spiritual quality of intercourse, suggests that women wanted the intimacy of this relation to be treated with propriety. One woman interviewed in 1913 stated that although intercourse was a necessity to man and woman and served the purposes of both pleasure and reproduction, it could nonetheless be "loathsome" if a "pure woman [was] treated by her husband as he has treated the prostitute he had been to before marriage." Self-identified as a "pure woman" of middle-class social standing, she did not condone what she understood to be the more fluid sexual arrangements of the lower classes of women, especially prostitutes. Prostitution did indeed thrive in the nineteenth and early twentieth centuries—a result of the lack of viable employment opportunities for women and the double standard requiring "respectable" women to be completely chaste and excusing men their uncontrollable sexual urges.

A middle-class wife who in 1913 saw herself as a "pure woman" may have fully understood the economic and social realities that separated her from the prostitutes of the "red-light districts." She may have had sympathy for girls and women who had turned to prostitution.

Nonetheless, she felt vulnerable because of the possibility of an unfaithful husband and the risks of venereal disease and the destruction of her family. Prince Morrow, a prominent New York physician, had powerfully articulated these apprehensions when he stated in 1899, "There is more venereal infection among virtuous wives than among professional prostitutes."[12] Doctors' concern over prostitution turned to alarm when gonorrhea was discovered in the 1890s to cause insanity among its carriers and blindness in infants born to infected mothers. Mosher would surely have been privy to intense discussions on these findings while at Johns Hopkins. Long thought to be little more serious than a common cold, gonorrhea (which was far more prevalent than syphilis) was now regarded as a deadly menace to society.

Campaigns to prevent premature sexual experience in adolescent girls, in the belief that it would lead to prostitution, brought on a flurry of state laws to raise the age of consent regarding statutory rape. By the early years of the twentieth century, psychiatrists had invented the category of the "hypersexual," providing a scientific justification for confining sexually active adolescent girls in state-funded "industrial schools." In the hysteria over ending prostitution, doctors gave up their campaign to "regulate" it, and social-purity reformers abandoned their opposition to sex education in the schools. Finally, the federal government enacted the Mann Act in 1911 for the prosecution of anyone who transported a white woman across state lines for purposes of prostitution. With such a fearful atmosphere of protection and condemnation separating respectable wives from women who were sexually active outside of marriage, it should not be surprising that Mosher's respondents, well into the twentieth century, distanced themselves from sexual excess and looked with favor on husbands who were neither sexually aggressive nor cavalier. Like women of her class, Mosher was repelled by public displays of affection. She held that women should be free to experience pleasure in sexual intercourse and believed that their ignorance of sexual matters before marriage was a prelude to sexual maladjustment in marriage. Nonetheless, like her respondents, she believed that sexual fulfillment should not be separated from morals.

Although early-twentieth-century thinking offered greater sexual autonomy to women, the belief that sexual anarchy was at hand contributed to a context in which later survey respondents idealized sex in spiritual terms. This idealization emerged as a new norm at the turn of the century and became a necessary condition of making a "pure" woman's enjoyment of sex morally acceptable, both to her and to society. It distinguished middle-class sexual experience from the alleged coarseness of sexual activity among the lower classes and prostitutes. A married middle-class woman could more readily admit to experiencing orgasms by the early twentieth century, but she would also believe that her physical pleasure was less important than the overall sense of metaphysical connection she shared with her husband. Imbuing sexual pleasure with piety, in other words, was a way to preserve the nineteenth-century ideal of women's moral superiority in a modern twentieth-century context.

The very real sexual pleasure reported by Mosher's respondents was nonetheless suffused with anxiety. Whereas their actual practice of intercourse was reported to be about one to two times a week, their reported "ideal habit" was considerably less often—about once a month. In short, they feared pregnancy. One woman articulated best what others hinted: "I heartily wish there were no accidental conceptions. I believe the world would take a most gigantic stride toward high ethical conditions if every child brought into the world were the product of pure love and conscious choice." This wish was no idle musing. In numerous heartfelt stories, respondents revealed the physical trauma and risk of death, either to themselves or to the infant, that pregnancy and childbirth occasioned. Even if the mother and newborn survived the birth process, the mother could sustain severe vaginal or urinary tract injuries that if surgery could not repair, left her an invalid for the rest of her life. Children's path to adulthood was fraught with health risks that today are mostly a dim memory: rickets from measles; diphtheria, scarlet fever, and tuberculosis; infections that never healed—and infants died from *cholera infantum*, spinal meningitis, prolonged labor, and intolerance to milk. In addition to health problems, numerous pregnancies brought financial strain. As families increasingly sought their livelihoods in urban environments, their children became less the economic asset they might have been on a farm and more of an economic burden, especially if they were to be educated. New ideas of child development required that parents give more attention to fewer children.

In spite of these compelling reasons to limit family size, suspicion of legalized birth control was widespread. Mainstream Americans feared it would give women an independence that would threaten the authority of men in the family. Feminists feared that birth control would free men to indulge their sexual passions both within and outside marriage. They called for a single standard that would hold men to the same high moral sexual ideal as women. Child-labor reformers derided the naïveté of birth control advocate Margaret Sanger, who argued that birth control would eliminate the exploitation of children. Doctors argued that legalizing contraceptive practice in the face of perceived working-class sexual promiscuity would bring about race suicide among the better classes. In the belief that reproduction was the only true purpose of intercourse, social-purity reformers aimed to protect for all women the high ideal of motherhood. They successfully pressured federal and state lawmakers to make illegal the printing, mailing, and disseminating of any "obscene material," including contraceptive devices or information. With the Comstock Law in 1873, the U.S. Post Office was empowered to intercept contraceptive devices and related information sent in the mail.

The irony was that the repression of birth control was a reaction against behavior patterns already in place. The average number of births among white women had dropped from 7.04 in 1800 to 3.56 in 1900, indicating that couples had long been exercising control over their fertility.[13] That two-thirds of Mosher's respondents confessed to using a variety of contraceptive methods and devices further illustrates this trend. Still, the societal suppression of birth control inhibited contraceptive practices. This suppression is apparent in the respondents' inconsistent use of unreliable methods, such as early withdrawal (which gave women no contraceptive power) and postcoital douching with hot, cold, or tepid water, alcohol, and sulfate of zinc (all of which were generally ineffective). One early interviewee, who reported that all three of her children were accidentally conceived, admitted to having used a douche only once. Another woman, married for twenty-seven years, reported having tried "a period of immunity" that "did not work." After giving birth to six children, only two of whom survived past childhood, she and her husband eventually resorted to sleeping in separate beds, by several accounts the most common way to sustain a habit of abstinence. A 1912 respondent recounted the sequencing of her five accidental conceptions (with one miscarriage); she and her husband tried unsuccessfully to limit their intercourse to the "two weeks [that are] supposed to be safe." The woman lamented that she "did not mean to have children for five years in order to study." These women and their husbands used birth control, but with much more restraint than the desire of both parties suggests would have been appropriate. Their contraceptive practice was reflective of societal misgivings about separating reproduction from intercourse.

In her introductory comments to the survey, Mosher wrote that the reported experiences of her respondents had given her "a priceless knowledge" that enabled her "to avoid prejudice in her work with women" as a physician and educator. She claimed that the "pressure of other routine work" prevented her from "arranging the work for publication." Since the number of survey participants was tiny relative to the sample size used in her studies of breathing and menstruation, it is likely she never intended to publish this work.[14] She received hundreds of letters from women who wrote of the positive effects of her abdominal exercises, but she would never know how readers might have benefited from the survey. Much of what Mosher's survey revealed would be corroborated in 1918 by Katherine Bement Davis. As was true for Mosher's later interviewees, Davis found that most of her 2,200 participants believed that love justified intercourse, that the use of contraceptives was acceptable, and that prior instruction in sexual matters would lead to a better adjustment in marriage for women. Davis's survey was more exploratory than Mosher's, asking about attitudes toward homosexuality, for instance. The Davis study would be followed in 1931 by Robert Latou Dickinson's book *A Thousand Marriages*. As a gynecologist who long advocated birth control, Dickinson wrote from his meticulous case records of 5,200 former patients. Alfred Kinsey's work would follow soon after World War II. Thus, in spite of its limitations, the Mosher survey stands as a lone pioneer in what would soon become a vital area of medical and social scientific investigation.

In her early life, Clelia Duel Mosher made important independent choices. Her decisions to get a college education, become a physician, and pursue and protect her research even as others attempted to take over her data are evidence of her intense claim to self-definition. Having chosen this course and having achieved so much, however, she later found herself searching for an involvement apart from the intellectual fulfillment of her work. In 1917, at the age of fifty-three, she initiated through an acquaintance a connection with the Red Cross in order to serve as a physician in France during World War I. In her journal she wrote that everything in her "cried out to do its part in this world catastrophe." From January 1918 through January 1919, she served as medical investigator for the Children's Bureau. Her assignment was to evacuate children from Paris. This experience left her profoundly moved by the devastation and human suffering she witnessed. She wrote to her mother, "It wrings this heart to see what the war has done to the people—especially the children—the helpless children and women! It makes me wish we could speed up the arrival of our American Army and bring this war to a victorious close."[15] She also came back from the war impressed with the competence of French women in replacing their men in all avenues of labor, even those requiring muscular strength. From these observations, she declared, albeit too broadly, that women were physically just as strong as men. She would present these ideas in 1924 at the International Conference of Women Physicians in England.

After the war, she seems to have gone through a period of personal difficulty. There were quarrels with the new Stanford administration, and her mother, who had come to live with her in California, was not well. She longed to give more time to her garden and to her failing mother, but resolved: "I must reap my intellectual harvest. I have something to contribute . . . something to give to the question of woman."[16] What followed was the publication in 1923 of her second book, *Woman's Physical Freedom*. This book achieved wider popularity than any of her previous writings. Within five years, it was in its sixth printing. In it, Mosher assured middle-aged women that any difficulties they might experience in menopause were due more to the social changes that accompany midlife than to the mental or emotional imbalance they supposed was to blame. She urged women whose children were now grown to fill their time with political, church, and community service. Such advice, so popular with women her age, belied her own solitary ways.

Mosher's uniqueness as a woman of great intellectual intensity isolated her from most of her contemporaries. At Stanford, she was one of only three women to become tenured before World War II. Her only close friend, Mary Roberts Smith, had left Stanford for San Francisco in 1904, remarried in 1906, and went on to teach at Mills College. Mosher was keenly aware of what she had missed in not marrying or having children. Her journal entries from 1915 to the mid-1920s make frequent mention of her loneliness, especially after the death of her mother in 1920. In 1915, after teaching at Stanford for five years, she conveyed in exquisitely delicate phrases the sensuous inner world within which her heart found expression. She looked out at her garden and wrote to an imaginary friend, "As I ate my breakfast in my booklined study I looked past the half opened daffodils and the violets, past your empty chair, through the open door to the miracle of beauty and awakening life which we call spring—realized suddenly why I have cared for you as no other friend. . . . I could see you with your hands full of the tiny golden poppies. . . . I know you will understand me when I say that the beauty of this perfect California spring almost hurts—I long for you to share the beauty of the spring with me—it would be too perfect."[17]

Mosher's unfulfilled longing for a close friend was in part a result of her own habit of mind. Whenever the possibility of collaboration presented itself, Mosher nearly always chose a path of singular action. She turned down the opportunity to work with Dr. Kelly at Johns Hopkins. While practicing medicine in California, she refused membership in the Women's Medical Club of the Pacific and did not join other women physicians in creating and serving the Children's Hospital. She declined an offer to join the prestigious Medical Women's Association, whose membership included better-known female physicians in the country, explaining that she had retired three years earlier.

Highly analytical and deeply introspective, she wrote at the age of fifty-two: "I am finding out gradually why I am so lonely. The only things I care about are things which use my brain. The women I meet are not much interested and I do not meet many men, so there is an intellectual solitude which is like the solitude of the desert—dangerous to one's sanity." Later she wrote, "Dear Friend who never was: I have given up ever finding you. I have tried out all my friends and they have not measured up to my dreams. . . . But I keep normal and wholesome by going ever alone in my land of dreams." She added, with a hint of intellectual disdain, "It would not take long to be as drab as most of my contemporaries were it not for this land of my dreams."[18] Aloof and single-minded, she seems to have felt that anyone who embodied less than the ideal of her imagination would disappoint her. She had closed many emotional doors in pursuit of scholarship, even those that would have connected her with other professional women. Perhaps such women, whose similarly marginal positions had led them to form networks of support, reminded her of the kind of feminine vulnerability and dependency she had rejected. Claiming her research was her first priority, she seems to have used it to establish distance from a social arena in which she felt profoundly uncomfortable. For someone who so encouraged women's self-determination, this isolation was surely a high price to pay.

By her own account, her final years were happier. In her retirement she moved into a "dream house" of her own design and wrote of looking forward to her "solitary future, rich in the beauty of my surroundings."[19] Here she was able to draw on her relationships with former students, to whom she had always been devoted. They had once regarded her as an amusing oddity on campus. Now many of them visited her frequently, thanking her for her advice on "good citizenship, honesty in all situations, sensibility in dress and lifestyle, unselfishness, and the need for regular exercise."[20] In 1932 she began an autobiography entitled *The Autobiography of a Happy Old Woman*, which she dedicated "to my father, who believed in women when most men classified them with children and imbeciles."

Clelia Mosher's life in medicine, research, and teaching was the product of her feminism. When she died in 1940, she left behind a legacy of scholarship that challenged Victorian prescriptions for women. She proved that a woman's reproductive biology did not impose limits on her mental, physical, and sexual potential.

Notes

1. Kathryn Allamong Jacob, "The Mosher Report: The Sexual Habits of American Women, Examined Half a Century before Kinsey," *American Heritage* 32 (1981): 59; Elizabeth Brownlee Griego, "A Part and Yet Apart: Clelia Duel Mosher and Professional Women at the Turn-of-the-Century" (Ph.D. diss., University of California, Berkeley, 1983), 161–63.

2. Griego, "A Part and Yet Apart," 47–49.

3. Rosalind Rosenberg, *Beyond Separate Spheres: Intellectual Roots of Modern Feminism* (New Haven, CT: Yale University Press, 1982), 42, 60–62, 68–72.

4. Griego, "A Part and Yet Apart," 130–31; Jacob, "The Mosher Report," 58.

5. Griego, "A Part and Yet Apart," 148.

6. Jacob, "The Mosher Report," 60.

7. Griego, "A Part and Yet Apart," 276–77.

8. Carl Degler, "What Ought to Be and What Was: Women's Sexuality in the Nineteenth Century," in *The American Family in Social Historical Perspective*, ed. Michael Gordon (New York: St. Martin's Press, 1978), 404–5.

9. G. J. Barker-Benfield, *The Horrors of the Half-Known Life: Male Attitudes toward Women and Sexuality in the Nineteenth Century* (New York: Harper and Row, 1976), 120–22.

10. Peter Laipson, " 'Kiss without Shame, for She Desires It': Sexual Foreplay in American Marital Advice Literature, 1900–1925," *Journal of Social History* 29 (Spring 1996): 507–26.

11. All of the quotations attributable to the survey respondents are taken from Clelia Duel Mosher, *The Mosher Survey: Sexual Attitudes of Forty-Five Victorian Women*, ed. James MaHood and Kristine Wenburg (New York: Arno Press, 1980).

12. Allan F. Brandt, *No Magic Bullet: A Social History of Venereal Disease in the United States since 1880* (New York: Oxford University Press, 1984), 14–18.

13. James Reed, *From Private Vice to Public Virtue: The Birth Control Movement and American Society since 1830* (New York: Basic Books, 1978), 3–5.

14. Mosher, *The Mosher Survey*, 3.

15. Griego, "A Part and Yet Apart," 217–18.

16. Jacob, "The Mosher Report," 60.

17. Griego, "A Part and Yet Apart," 345.

18. Jacob, "The Mosher Report," 64.

19. Ibid.

20. Griego, "A Part and Yet Apart," 152.

Suggested Readings

Analyses of the Mosher survey are found in Carl Degler, "What Ought to Be and What Was: Women's Sexuality in the Nineteenth Century," in *The American Family in Social Historical Perspective*, ed. Michael Gordon (New York: St. Martin's Press, 1978), 403–25; Kathryn Allamong Jacob, "The Mosher Report: The Sexual Habits of American Women, Examined Half a Century before Kinsey," *American Heritage* 32 (1981): 59; Carroll Smith-Rosenberg, "A Richer and Gentler Sex," *Social Research* 53, no. 2 (Summer 1986): 283–309. Rosalind Rosenberg discusses the influence of Darwin in *Beyond Separate Spheres: Intellectual Roots of Modern Feminism* (New Haven, CT: Yale University Press, 1982).

On the social-purity movement, see David Pivar, *Purity Crusade: Sexual Morality and Social Control, 1868–1900* (Westport, CT: Greenwood Press, 1973). On prostitution, see John C. Burnham, "The Progressive Era Revolution in American Attitudes toward Sex," *Journal of American History* 59, no. 4 (March 1973): 885–908. John D'Emilio and Estelle Freedman, *Intimate Matters: A History of Sexuality in America* (New York: Harper and Row, 1988), is a solid history of sexuality. On public responses to sexual change, see Barbara Epstein, "Family, Sexual Morality, and Popular Movements in Turn-of-the-Century America," in *Powers of Desire: The Politics of Sexuality*, ed. Ann Snitow, Christine Stansell, and Sharon Thompson (New York: Monthly Review Press, 1983), 117–30. Sheila M. Rothman, *Woman's Proper Place: A History of Changing Ideals and Practices, 1870 to the Present* (New York: Basic Books, 1978), offers an excellent overview of women in this period.

6

Black Zack and Uncle Amon

Paul K. Conkin

After the end of the Civil War, former slaves began to fashion a new world built on the ruins of the old and on different foundations as well. But such attempts did not come easily. Violence, segregation, peonage, and more all represented attempts to control that change. The struggle continued for decades after the war had ended. Not all areas of the South had sizable black populations, however. The Appalachian mountain region had long been stereotyped as a place where few blacks lived, an image that, as this essay demonstrates, had much to support it.

Historian Paul Conkin tells a very personal narrative about one Appalachian community. He talks to the reader directly about two people who held special memories for him. While the nicknames suggest the racial mores of that time, the lives of Zachariah Bennett and Amon Hays show, once more, how difficult it is to stereotype a region and those who reside there.

Paul K. Conkin has published widely on a variety of topics, including *The New Deal* (1967), *Big Daddy from the Pedernales: Lyndon Baines Johnson* (1987), *The Southern Agrarians* (1988), *Cane Ridge: America's Pentecost* (1991), and *When All the Gods Trembled: Darwinism, Scopes, and American Intellectuals* (1998). A former president of the Southern Historical Association, he currently is Distinguished Professor of History Emeritus at Vanderbilt University in Nashville, Tennessee.

I have two stories to tell. They are as truthful as scanty sources and my own memories from childhood and youth allow. I have tried to minimize any historical interpretations. I have avoided analysis like the plague. The stories involve two black men—Zachariah Bennett and Amon Hays. For much of their lives they represented the only two black families in my home village or anywhere else in a radius of at least five miles. They were thus blacks in an all-white world. I find their stories fascinating.

The setting for the first story is a small farm community in northern Greene County, in upper East Tennessee. It was located between the

This essay will also appear in James C. Klotter, ed., *The Human Tradition in the New South* from Scholarly Resources, forthcoming.

county seat, Greeneville, and Kingsport, in Sullivan County, both seventeen miles away and both with small black populations. The closest town, at fourteen miles, was tiny Jonesborough, the state's oldest town and the county seat of Washington County, and also the home of a small black community. My village, confusingly, has three names. A walk-in post office in the late nineteenth century was called Cedar Lane, a name still on some maps. The one church, Cumberland Presbyterian, adopted the Biblical name Bethesda at its 1834 founding. Later the county school would be named Bethesda (the name I will use). But almost no one locally refers to the village as Bethesda, but as Green Shed, or just the Shed. This name derives from the preaching stand at a well-developed antebellum camp-meeting site. The village, in the early twentieth century, had the church, a two-room school, a blacksmith shop, a water-powered gristmill and sawmill, and usually at least one all-purpose store.

Otherwise quite similar to other communities in a rather prosperous farming county, Bethesda had one clear distinction after 1900. It had, as residents, the only black families still remaining anywhere in this northern part of Greene County. After 1910 it also had a quite visible landmark—Zack's Monument, as we all called it. It was on a hill back of the church, and visible for over a mile from the highway that leads into the valley and by the church. In the 1930s it was surrounded by a hay field or an occasional tobacco patch. The road to my grandparents passed within thirty feet of this obelisk, which is over twenty feet high. I read the inscription and often asked questions about the well-to-do black man buried beneath it. Only much later, when the monument gained more widespread attention and newspaper coverage, did we learn that it was the second largest monument in Greene County, exceeded in size, but not necessarily in height, only by the tomb of President Andrew Johnson in Greeneville.

How did such a monument get to this unlikely site? Zachariah Bennett was born a slave about 1847 on a large farm, or the nearest approach to a plantation anywhere close to our home, about twelve miles north of Bethesda. This was in western Sullivan County, in the midst of the only large pocket of Confederate supporters in upper East Tennessee. This valley farm bordered what is now called Horse Creek, which probably gained its name from the farm. It was noted for the horses it bred. All the legends about Zachariah Bennett, or Black Zack as he was called locally, note that as a slave youth he became an expert horse trainer. I cannot confirm this. Note that he was only eighteen at emancipation.

But his later life did involve horses, and he was obviously skilled in training the best of riding stock.

I know nothing about his immediate postemancipation years. Possibly he remained on this farm and continued to work with horses. He first appeared in the Bethesda community records in the census of 1880. By then he was a hired hand on a local farm. As far as anyone knows, he never married. He had no children, at death no known relatives. From 1880 to 1892 he must have worked hard and saved his money. In the latter year he bought a farm, the second downstream from what later became our family farm. The recorded deed makes clear that he paid $1,000 cash for 100 acres, an average-to-above-average-sized farm in our area (my father later owned only 51 acres). One thousand dollars in cash in 1892, albeit a year before the crash of 1893, was a lot of money, comparable to a small fortune today. The land he bought for $10 an acre now sells for $2,000; my first cousin owns it. At a multiple of only 100, Zack's $1,000 in 1892 would be worth $100,000 today. I doubt that any other landowner in our community had ever bought such a large farm without a mortgage or promissory note. I do not know how Zack, working as a hired hand, accumulated so much money. I suspect he bought, trained, possibly bred, and sold horses.

Little is known of Bennett's life in Bethesda. Did he join the Bethesda Church? (No records survive, but he would have been welcome as a member.) He certainly clearly identified with the church and later became its benefactor. My father was ten when Bennett died and retained only hazy memories of him. The image that has remained is of a very ambitious man, driven by a desire to make money. He was a cagey horse trader, frugal and stingy, and was reputed to lend money to his white neighbors at the highest interest the market would bear. This money-lending image is borne out by the probate of his will, when his assets included three outstanding loans. Two of the notes bore the name of a next-door neighbor of our family and my distant cousin. The trustees collected not only the $455 of principal but also $178 in interest due. Around 1900, Bennett built a very nice farmhouse and apparently lived in it alone. He died in 1910, leaving behind an estate valued at $4,950, again, a lot of money for the time. His unusual deathbed will is signed with an "x," but I suspect he was literate. He obviously knew his numbers, since in effect he ran a local lending bank.

In his will, Bennett requested that his three named trustees, all prosperous local white farmers, distribute his assets as follows: first, they were to erect at his grave a nice monument, costing no less than $1,000.

Then they were to place the remainder of his estate in a perpetual trust, with the principal never to be spent, but 25 percent of its annual earnings going to the Bethesda Church and 75 percent to be used by the trustees and their successors to maintain his monument and the grounds around it. He also specified that he be buried in the cemetery of the Bethesda Church and that all his property be sold at public auction. Clearly he was very much concerned about his own tomb, and at the end of the will made careful provisions for the succession of trustees, all in order "to have my grave cared for as long as time lasts."

The trustees did much of what Zack wanted. For reasons unclear, they did not set up a continuing trust. After costs of his tomb and other expenses, they still had $3,318 left. Instead of giving the church one-fourth of the earnings of a trust, they simply gave it one-fourth of the remaining estate, or $830 after taxes, surely the largest gift the congregation had ever received up until that time. At the time of the gift the average collection on Sunday was often less than a dollar. Children brought a penny, adults nickels or dimes. I am sure the then-indebted congregation preferred the instant cash to future interest payments and therefore did not protest the failure to set up a trust. It may have conspired to block the trust.

Within the next three years the trustees finished their work and turned over an unspent $1,786, in escheat, to the state, leaving no money to care for Zack's monument or the cemetery. This failure to follow Zack's will had to be approved, or possibly mandated, by the probate judge. When, a few years ago, I made these facts available to the church session, some elders were shocked that the state took the money. They even talked, unrealistically, about legal action to get back their stolen cemetery fund, which, with interest of 6 percent compounded annually, would be now worth over $500,000.

During the three years the trustees managed the estate, apparently with full knowledge that the state would get any remainder, they sought every opportunity to spend money, including ample fees for themselves. Everyone who contributed any labor to the monument received full pay. In the final settlement the trustees also charged the estate $500 for their services. They had worked hard. I suspect no impropriety, but rather a pushing against the limits, getting as much as they legally could out of Zack's estate. Did his race influence the disposition of his estate? I have no way to know. I doubt it. I might note that in none of the probate proceedings, and on none of the deeds, is there any mention of Bennett's race.

The trustees' great achievement was Zack's monument. He would have been pleased. They mounted it on the land owned by the church, but not really in the cemetery, which was then grown up in weeds and full of graves. Instead they placed it on the opposite side of the church, at the highest point on the lot. The old cemetery, almost hidden down in the valley, was not a good place for Zack's monument. Burials had practically ceased at this old cemetery. We think some of the illegible tombs were those of former slaves. But it is possible that some local families did not want a black man buried among their relatives and that they influenced the choice of the site. In retrospect the trustees made the best possible choice.

The trustees had to travel to Morristown, forty miles away toward Knoxville, to find anyone who could order a tombstone costing as much as $1,000 (a very good gravestone cost no more than $30 or $40). They paid $1,085 to the Morristown Marble Company. They hauled the heavy monument on wagons to the site. They must have dug a deep foundation. They poured on top of it a thick, 18-by-24-foot concrete platform. Into this concrete they embedded an encircling steel fence. The concrete work and the fence cost around $150. After ninety years the concrete platform is still as solid as ever, with only one small, almost invisible crack. Despite its weight the tomb shows no signs of settling in any direction. And the fine granite obelisk shows no water damage and no moss, unlike all the other older tombs in the cemetery. About thirteen local men did all the work. Only one of these was black—the Amon Hays of my next story. He collected over $12, probably as payment for about twelve days of labor. In total, hundreds of hours of work were involved. The total cost of the mounted monument was about $1,400 or just over half the sale price of Zack's 100-acre farm, house, and barn.

The farm auction revealed a great deal about Bennett. All his personal property, save the outstanding notes, sold for just under $1,600. Household and kitchen items sold at what would seem a giveaway price today, with few items from the house selling for as much as a dollar. (His silverware sold for twenty-five cents, his dinner plates for the same amount, chairs for ten cents, the best table for $1.55, a cast-iron outdoor kettle for $1.75, and only a shotgun for as much as $3.50.) Farm tools did not do much better, with a wagon leading at $8.50, a corn planter at $5.10, plows for around $2.00. In total, over 150 household and farm items sold for less than $150. I might note that two paternal uncles and my grandfather bid on different items. His was a representative inventory of a well-stocked, turn-of-the-century farm.

What sold well in Zack's auction was the farm inventory and livestock. The corn, wheat, hay, and straw sold for $235, more than for all the household goods and farm implements combined. The livestock sold for $1,236, or over three-fourths of the value of the total sale, excluding the farm itself. Local farmers paid $381 for thirteen cows and steers, $61 for six hogs, and $23 for 199 chickens (a larger than average inventory for a local farm). But the big items were five horses. One, a male draft horse, sold for only $61, or the going price for draft horses. But one breeding mare, named Mary, sold for a then-astonishing $230; a second, named Nina, for $160. They went to the two wealthiest farmers in the area. Two yearling mares sold for $177 and $130. These prices give a clue as to how Zack made his money. He had continued to breed the best of riding stock, perhaps what he learned to do well as a slave. He was getting as much as $300 a year from the sale of his colts, more than the total gross income of most local farmers. He improved upon his income by the sale of steers, pork, and eggs, and by interest earned from the money lent to other farmers. By all measurements, the tomb inscription is correct—he was well-to-do; I suspect, the most affluent black man in the county. He must have relished being able to lend money to less prudent white farmers, and have gained enormous satisfaction from his dream of a great monument that would be ten times more expensive, and thus more imposing, than that of any white man in any rural cemetery that he had ever seen.

The subsequent story of Zack's monument is checkered. An indebted congregation sold the land containing Zack's monument in 1917, an act of betrayal to one who had been so generous to the church. The new owner respected the monument, but plowing and erosion lowered the surrounding ground level. The local farm economy almost came to an end after 1945. Bethesda became a bedroom community for people who worked in Kingsport. The church became more prosperous, repurchased the land surrounding Zack's monument in the fifties, and by 1980 had incorporated it into an expanding cemetery. As one elder said, they reintegrated Black Zack. The civil rights movement changed racial views. Some church members, including my mother, welcomed the Civil Rights Acts and admired Martin Luther King. Suddenly, local people recognized that Zack's monument was a village asset. Young ministers, some just out of seminary who came to presbytery when it met at Bethesda, were fascinated with the monument and tried to find information about old Zack. Newspapers ran articles. A man and wife, now deceased, former friends of mine, worked for weeks clearing the honeysuckle from the monument and sanding and repainting the rusted steel fence. As the cemetery committee plotted new grave sites, they left plenty of room around Zack's monument and built a paved street up the hill by it. Finally, as Zack tried to ensure by his will, his tomb is now well cared for, although I cannot assure it will be so as long as time lasts.

I turn now to Amon Hays and a less dramatic story, but a story of a much more complex and less conventional man than a focused Zachariah Bennett. I have one advantage: Hays lived on until after World War II. I knew him reasonably well. His background is also clearer. His father, Jackson Hays, was born in 1837, at the end of the popular Jackson administration. He was a slave on the farm of a Captain George Hays, who may have gained his military title in Jackson's Florida campaign. The Scotch-Irish Hays family had been one of the first to settle in our part of Greene County, in the 1790s moving down from the Shenandoah Valley of Virginia. George Hays was probably the only slaveowner in the village or, at the very least, the only one to own several slaves. Hays had a very large farm, possibly four hundred acres. But it scarcely qualified as a plantation. When George Hays died (circumstantial evidence suggests this was in 1877 or 1878), he apparently willed a part of his farm to Jackson Hays. This is what everyone locally believed when I was a boy, and I have no reason to doubt it. Jackson took the Hays name at emancipation and remained a worker on the George Hays farm. The gift of a farm, when land prices were very low, was a type of belated payment for his loyalty and work. One might suspect, in a case like this, that Captain George was the father of Jackson Hays. But the very dark complexion of Amon Hays (I have no description of Jackson Hays), although not conclusive, makes this blood relationship less likely. In any case, the black and white Hays families remained intimate friends. They would join at one home or another for Sunday dinners. The relationship must have been paternalistic on one side, deferential on the other, but by the time I knew both families, it seemed to be a relationship of social equals.

Jackson Hays married a Peggy Swinney, and they had at least four children. Two of the four, a twin boy and girl, died young. Amon Hays, born in 1868, was the oldest child and the only surviving male when Jackson Hays died in 1892, leaving only Amon and his younger sister, Esther, locally always pronounced Easter. For the rest of his long life, Amon operated what had been his father's farm. Esther lived with him until her death, five years before Amon. Amon delayed marriage until he must have been over forty. Before his marriage, according to well-substantiated local gossip, he briefly kept company with a white widow in the community, a liaison that sullied her already tarnished reputation. When he finally married, he traveled to Jonesborough to get his bride. I suspect some of Jackson Hays's family had also moved there, creating a link back to the farm. I know almost nothing about Oliveve, the wife. She died when I was young. At her death, Amon buried her back in Jonesborough, but he did not join her there at his death. They had no children. My first cousin, who now owns the Zack Bennett farm, often worked on Amon's farm as a youth and tells me that she was a superb cook. He enjoyed the dinners she prepared for the field hands.

The Amon Hays farm was about the size of our own, around fifty acres. Eventually, Amon built a modest new home, a much better home than I lived in during the first ten years of my life. The only black man in an all-white community, he seemed to blend in well. I doubt that most whites, whatever the stereotypes they had of blacks in general, ever applied them to Amon. My father noted that a near-middle-aged Amon was still very strong and loved to wrestle (a game in which each wrestler tried to get the other off his feet and to the ground). When younger, rather wild country boys challenged Amon, he almost always threw them. He somehow had the personality to do this without offense, or without exciting racial resentments. In his dealings with neighbors, he always seemed to me to be direct and businesslike, without any special deference or clear role-playing.

Amon was, by the verdict of my mother and the most pious church members, anything but a role model for youth. He joined with a white neighbor to run a still in the twenties and made money. He loved music and led in the formation of a local hillbilly band. He played the instrument whose proper English name was "fiddle," although ignorant people sometimes refer to it by a foreign, Italian name. Throughout the twenties he hosted periodic Saturday evening square dances, using his large living room for the dancing. Although most young men and women, and this includes my father, attended these dances, a few proper families kept their daughters home. My mother was not allowed to attend and had perhaps exaggerated images of the sinfulness that prevailed. My father attests that nothing untoward happened. Most of the band members were older men, one a church elder. Most who came were church members. And, of course, Oliveve and Esther were there, the only black folk save Amon. It is possible that young men moved outside the house to drink moonshine whiskey. Some hot "sparking" probably took place as couples walked home, but this was also what happened after church every Sunday night.

Amon was a good but in no way exceptional farmer. He grew burley tobacco and later sold grade B milk. He exchanged labor with white neighbors. When too old to farm, he rented his farm to white share-croppers. He did well economically but had none of the driving ambi-tion of Zachariah Bennett, a near neighbor until Zack's death in 1910. Amon was genial and had a wide array of friends. He enjoyed the repu-tation of growing excellent watermelons. My father recounted how a group of white boys stole many of his melons during a summer night, probably around 1925. Stealing watermelons was a near rite of passage for young men. It is not clear that they picked on Amon, at least not because he was black. Boys stole everyone's melons. But Daddy swore Amon usually had the best. Amon, like most farmers, had to smile and profess his willingness to share his melons with anyone who asked. But getting them that way would have spoiled all the fun. I often wondered if his race, his visible minority status, forced him to be more careful in reacting to this thievery, and if to some extent he had to assume care-fully outfitted roles.

I knew Amon only when he was old. I can remember visiting his home only once, with Daddy, and this to buy sweet potato plants. Al-though unschooled, he was quite literate and well informed. When the man who held the mortgage on our farm seemed, unintentionally, to overcharge on interest, my mother turned to Amon Hays to mediate. He was the local expert on figuring interest. Unfortunately, as he aged his eyesight weakened. In his last five years, after Esther died, he was totally blind. Even my mother forgave his earlier transgressions. One day, feeling the side of the pavement with a cane, Amon walked by our house on the way to the store, probably to buy groceries. Usually some-one gave him a ride before he walked the half-mile to our house, but not this day. Always, at the store, he could depend on someone to drive him home. Daddy went out to greet him and invited him to the house to rest and to talk. They loved to visit and tell stories. My mother prob-ably served him a piece of cake. On this day, as Daddy guided Amon through the yard, my mother turned to me and said I should always respect this elderly man, and that out of respect I should always address him as Uncle Amon. I was in high school and did not need such in-struction. By then everyone called him Uncle Amon.

Amon Hays was never a member of Bethesda Church or of the almost equally close Pleasant Hill Church, where he was buried. In fact, many considered him a lost sinner. I remember seeing him in church only once. It was during a summer revival. The minister went to get a nearly blind Amon, and he came. He was the center of attention, as everyone almost fawned over him. Now very old, he loved the singing and seemed affected by the hotter than usual preaching. I now suspect he knew another religious style from visiting his relatives in Jonesborough and did not feel comfortable with our Presbyterian services. This experience may have revealed an unknown side of Amon. Some Sundays his yard would fill with cars of visiting relatives from Jonesborough. Even at a distance one could hear the laughter and singing. In these interludes white neighbors sensed an alien culture, one that excluded them. But Amon's main life was among whites. When he died in 1952, black relatives attended his funeral, but all the pallbearers were white neighbors, and he was buried in the Jackson Hays plot, amidst white people in a white cemetery. His cousins in Jonesborough inherited and promptly sold his farm.

Amon had kept his ties to the white Hays family. Childless, he knew that he would be the last black in Bethesda. Marion Hays, the grandson of Captain George and the last owner of the old Hays home place, also had no children. Amon and Marion died within a year of each other. Thus, this branch of the Hays family, black and white, is now gone from Bethesda. After Amon died, a very close friend of my family, and for years my Sunday school teacher, Haven Middleton, bought his farm. Like Zachariah Bennett, he paid cash. He had lived for thirty years on a farm that adjoined Amon's. I did not realize it as a child, but Marion Hays owned this land, and Haven was a sharecropper—a sharecropper with tenure. Haven owned his own horses and tools; he owned cows and sold milk in town. In fact, he probably had more money in the bank than any of his immediate neighbors, including my father. He was a very close friend of the owner, in every way a social equal in the perspective of the church and community. Most people thought Marion Hays, when he died in 1951, would will the farm to Haven. He did not but did give him a small bequest. My cousin bought some of the land and added it to the old Zack Bennett farm. Haven had only a year to evacuate his long-term house, and thus, he bought Amon's old house and moved next door, still on the ancestral lands of the Hays family. His wife died within five years of breast cancer, and Haven lived on, alone, for eighteen years. He was found dead in the Amon Hays house in 1979. His heirs split up the farm and sold Amon's house to outsiders that no one locally ever knew. The vacant house eventually burned, with the empty shell only removed recently. Old-timers still refer to the Amon Hays place. But soon no one will remember the last black person to live in Bethesda. No blacks live anywhere even near the community today. Zack's monument remains the only tangible but still impressive symbol of what had once been an unusual biracial community.

My two stories are complete. I do not know what they mean. I have many unanswered questions. I know that Black Zack and Uncle Amon were exceptional men, black or white. In no wise were they saints. Against great odds, they made a good life for themselves. I can only wonder how, in private moments, they saw the world around them, what they really thought of their white neighbors. I have always wondered if they were active politically, if they voted (the county automatically collected the poll tax with land taxes, so they were eligible, and undoubtedly would have followed over 90 percent of the local whites in voting Republican). I have also wondered what would have happened had they had children. Where would they have gone to school? I suspect—I cannot prove—that in no other southern village were local black farmers as successful, or as respected by white neighbors, as Black Zack and Uncle Amon. I am all but sure that no rural black farmer, anywhere in the South, left funds for a monument as large or impressive as Zack's.

Suggested Readings

For general studies of the region in this timeframe, see Richard B. Drake, *A History of Appalachia* (Lexington: University Press of Kentucky, 2001); John Alexander Williams, *Appalachia: A History* (Chapel Hill: University of North Carolina Press, 2002); Ronald D. Eller, *Miners, Millhands, and Mountaineers: Industrialization of the Appalachian South, 1880–1930* (Knoxville: University of Tennessee Press, 1982); and Mary Beth Pudup, Dwight B. Billings, and Altina Waller, eds., *Appalachia in the Making: The Mountain South in the Nineteenth Century* (Chapel Hill: University of North Carolina Press, 1995). Dealing with the idea of the image of the area and race are: Henry Shapiro, *Appalachia on Our Mind: The Southern Mountaineers in the American Consciousness* (Chapel Hill: University of North Carolina Press, 1978), and James C. Klotter, "The Black South and White Appalachia," *Journal of American History* 66 (1980): 832–49. Dealing even more specifically with race in the region are: William H. Turner and Edward J. Cabell, eds., *Blacks in Appalachia* (Lexington: University Press of Kentucky, 1985), and John C. Inscoe, ed., *Appalachians and Race: The Mountain South from Slavery to Segregation* (Lexington: University Press of Kentucky, 2001).

7

Ma Rainey
Mother of the Blues

S. Spencer Davis

Americans have often been accused of contributing little to general culture and of taking most of their cultural cues from others, especially from Europe. In blues and jazz, however, they have made new and exciting contributions, most of which have been exported throughout the world.

"Ma" Rainey is often described as the first blues singer and certainly one of the greatest. She represents the enduring popular culture of rural African Americans in the time of the Harlem Renaissance, which was largely an urban movement. Her work was taken by whites, most often without acknowledgment, and at the time of her death she was almost alone and forgotten. Ma Rainey was a complex character—exuberant, lusty, and, in her later years, religious. She lived in a period when the two worlds of blacks and whites were more carefully defined than they are today.

Spencer Davis, a professor of history at Peru State College in Nebraska, is a specialist in African-American intellectual and cultural history. His degrees are from Brown University and the University of Nebraska-Lincoln, with a Ph.D. from the University of Toronto. Professor Davis is a member of the Nebraska Humanities Committee Speakers Bureau.

Gertrude "Ma" Rainey is remembered today as second only to Bessie Smith among blues vocalists—a judgment that is at once accurate in the minor sense and yet inadequate as a full understanding of Rainey's career. She was the first professional singer to incorporate blues numbers into her act, and as an entertainer she was the greatest crowd-pleaser of the women singing blues. But even these substantial "firsts" are not the full measure of her achievements.

Gertrude Pridgett was born in Columbus, Georgia, in 1886, the second of the five children of Thomas and Ella Pridgett. Columbus was a town of 7,000. With its industry and location on the Chattahoochee River, it had attracted Thomas and Ella to migrate from their native Alabama.[1]

This essay originally appeared in Donald W. Whisenhunt, ed., *The Human Tradition in America between the Wars, 1920–1945* (Wilmington, DE: Scholarly Resources, 2002), 47–58.

No evidence beyond a baptism record describes Gertrude's youth, but undoubtedly she was singing at church and school events. At fourteen she sang in a local group called "The Bunch of Blackberries." Soon afterward, she must have begun to sing professionally. At eighteen she married William "Pa" Rainey, the manager and a performer in the Rabbit Foot Minstrels. They immediately worked together in the show as "Pa" and "Ma" Rainey, with an act combining comedy, singing, and dancing. Since Pa Rainey was substantially older than his eighteen-year-old bride, the match must have been as much professional as romantic.[2]

The situation of black entertainers in the first years of the last century was complex. A life of constant travel brought them into collision with the absurdities and indignities of segregation. Within the black community many religious believers frowned on secular music and looked on entertainers as Satan's assistants. The tangled cultural life of the nation put black entertainers in the dilemma of seeing their culture derided by Anglo-Saxon supremacists while their works were being adopted—or stolen—by white performers.[3]

Charles Dudley Warner, Mark Twain's coauthor of *The Gilded Age*, toured the South in 1888 and recorded his impressions in *On Horseback: A Tour in Virginia, North Carolina, and Tennessee*. In Asheville, North Carolina, Warner and a crowd of both races were entertained by Happy John. Once a slave of Wade Hampton, one of the largest and most famous slaveowners, and now appearing in Uncle Sam costume and black-face make-up, Happy John sang and told stories. According to Warner, Happy John received the biggest response, from blacks in the audience as well as from whites, when his jokes were at the expense of his race. Warner, perhaps momentarily troubled by the situation, reached a conclusion that did not entirely disguise his anxiety. "I presume none of them analyzed the nature of his infectious gayety, nor thought of the pathos that lay so close to it, in the fact of his recent slavery, and the distinction of being one of Wade Hampton's [slaves], and the melancholy mirth of this light-hearted race's burlesque of itself."[4] The possibility of double-meaning in this stereotyped humor did not occur to Warner.

Happy John may not have been performing in the minstrel format, but there were similarities. The minstrel show is a strange American creation. White minstrel shows first appeared in the 1840s and created a sensation among white audiences. Most of them focused on plantation life, and many or most of them purported to depict "authentic" slave life. How white Americans could believe that is difficult to understand, given the fact that the actors were white people using burnt cork to blacken their faces. Their exaggerated physical movements helped to establish stereotypes that have persisted to this day.

By the middle of the 1850s black actors began to appear as minstrels, and they became firmly established as a part of the show business tradition by the 1870s. Showmen such as Charles Callender and J. H. Haverly were instrumental in making minstrels an integral part of show business. Black-owned companies also formed in the 1860s. Among the more important ones were the Brooker and Clayton Georgia Minstrels, a group that was very popular in the Northeast. Minstrels succeeded partly because they appealed to an essentially illiterate society, but their popularity was not limited to the unlettered. Prominent people, including Abraham Lincoln, reportedly found them very entertaining.

By the 1870s a separation occurred between black and white minstrels. Because black minstrels had the aura of authenticity, especially with "real Negroes," white shows moved away from portrayals of "realistic" plantation and black life to more lavish productions. They became more professional as well but continued to use African American culture as a major focus. Black minstrels flourished in the later decades of the nineteenth century and the first few decades of the twentieth.[5]

Thomas L. Riis, in his study of jazz, suggests a plausible explanation for the popularity of minstrels among whites and blacks alike. People have wondered why blacks would participate in and attend minstrel shows when portrayals were racist, degrading, and grotesque. He suggests that the actors and audiences of the day may not have seen them in the way that contemporary society does. In fact, he explains the low educational level of the country at the time and the importance of oral-cultural entertainments. In an oral culture, he believes, exaggeration and grotesque portrayals are necessary and are common in most nonliterate or semiliterate cultures. The exaggerations are needed to deliver the message, and the audience does not see the performances as degrading.[6]

Such was the minstrel tradition that Ma Rainey joined when she became a performer. Whether she was conscious of the subtleties of its historical and cultural significance is a moot point. She was essentially illiterate herself; and, if one accepts Riis's conjecture, she might not have seen it as degrading at all. Perhaps the Rabbit Foot Minstrels had no such figure as Happy John in their cast in 1904 when Ma Rainey joined the troupe, but minstrel shows, though they typically had black casts by that time, retained their stereotypes and the indignity of black-face. In the 1870s black minstrel shows and white minstrel shows had begun to diverge; the black entertainers included spirituals as well as stereo-types.[7] To play within yet rise above the stereotypes was a difficult feat.

The Rabbit Foot Minstrels played only in the South, traveling in their own railroad car and playing one-nighters in their gigantic tent. The program included acrobats and a contortionist; eventually Ma Rainey was the star of the show. The Rabbit Foot Minstrels usually spent the winter in New Orleans, which gave her the chance to perform with some of the greats of New Orleans music such as Joe Oliver, Louis Armstrong, Sidney Bechet, and Kid Ory. In 1914, 1915, and 1916 she toured with Tolliver's Circus and Musical Extravaganza with the billing of "Rainey and Rainey, Assassinators of the Blues." In 1917 she created her own traveling show, Ma Rainey and Her Georgia Smart Set.

There is a fairly detailed account of that show. Rainey was short and heavy-set; she had diamonds in her hair, gold-capped teeth, and heavy jewelry. In order to lighten the tone of her skin she used a great deal of skin cream and powder. Her humor, warm smile, and open sexu-ality compensated for her lack of classic features. Rainey played to all-black, segregated, and all-white audiences. If the audience was segregated, whites were seated on one side of the tent and blacks on the other side. Her show began with a band number followed by several numbers by male and female dancers. Next came two skits of ethnic humor, the first portraying a Japanese character and the second a black man stealing chickens. A fast number featuring the soubrette and the dancers was followed by another comedy routine. Then Ma Rainey came on stage, began with some comedy, sang half a dozen numbers including "Mem-phis Blues" and "Jelly Roll Blues," and ended with her specialty, "See See Rider Blues." The show closed with all the cast on stage for the finale.[8]

By this time, Rainey had been singing blues in her performances for a decade and was the preeminent female blues artist. She claimed that while she was working a tent show in Missouri in 1902, she overheard a young woman singing a strange lament about the man who left her. Taken by the unique sound, she learned the song and put it in her act. When asked what kind of song it was, she replied "the blues" and thus named the genre. It is unlikely that Rainey was in Missouri before 1904 and, therefore, equally unlikely that, in a moment of inspiration, she invented the label. But as an explanation of how Rainey became the first professional singer to put blues in a minstrel show, the story is more credible.[9]

The first sheet music with "blues" in the title was published in 1914 by a white band leader from Oklahoma, but the blues genre began almost certainly in the 1890s, almost certainly in the Mississippi Delta, and quite certainly among rural blacks. Defining the blues is more difficult. Blues began in the 1890s (or perhaps a little earlier) in the Delta— the heart of share-cropping, cotton-producing, rural Mississippi. The typical blues artist was a man singing and playing the guitar. The typical blues form was a twelve-bar, three-line stanza with the second line repeating the first (AAB) and the third line ending with the rhyme word. Blues singers drew on familiar lines from earlier songs, added their own, and used filler words or moans to complete lines. Blues numbers could change from one rendition to the next as lines were changed, or formulas from other numbers were added, or new stanzas were improvised. Blues lyrics focused on personal problems such as unfaithful lovers, whiskey, debts, and trouble with the law. The leading study of these original down-home blues finds surprisingly little social protest in them.[10]

Down-home blues were sung at picnics, on the porch, at the depot, and outside the barbershop. But to fit into the structure of the minstrel and tent shows, changes had to be made. Instrumental soloists could improvise, but too much improvising by vocalists would upset the band.[11] Rainey had to standardize the lyrics, but accompaniments had to be worked out for the band or small group.

In the late 1910s, Rainey's act changed. Pa Rainey, always a dim figure, dropped out of the picture. Ma Rainey was then a singles act. She may have spent a year in Mexico, but that is not confirmed. Within a year, however, she was back, entertaining southern black audiences. In 1922 and 1923 she worked with a pianist, usually Troy Snapp, accompanying her.[12] By this time the first recorded blues, Mamie Smith's "Crazy Blues," had appeared, and no doubt Rainey changed to keep up with the popularity of recorded blues—keep up, but never totally imitate. She remained closer to down-home blues than any of the other women recording classic (or vaudeville) blues in the 1920s.

On her own, Ma Rainey performed with many others, but she also befriended and assisted struggling entertainers. One of the most famous was Bessie Smith, who would overshadow Rainey in fame and popularity. In the beginning, however, Rainey gave her a start in the business. Their relationship may have been more than that. Smith later was well known for her bisexuality, and Rainey may have been bisexual as well. *Completely Queer* indicates that Rainey was a lesbian and that she introduced Bessie Smith to lesbian love. "Rainey was one of a number of legendary women singers associated with the Harlem Renaissance who were known to prefer women over men." This reference work also indicates that her nickname, Ma, referred to "the affection and nurturing she lavished on those around her."[13] Whatever her personal affairs may have been, her career flourished in the 1920s.

In 1920, Mamie Smith recorded "Crazy Blues" for Okeh Records. Its success persuaded record companies that there were profits to be made in "race records." Other vaudeville singers who had the clear tone and distinct pronunciation of Mamie Smith were rushed into studios to record blues. In 1921 about fifty race records were released; by 1927 the number had soared to five hundred.[14] These blues—classic or vaudeville blues—were neither the down-home kind nor the blues of tent show veterans such as Ma Rainey and Bessie Smith. But, in 1923, both Smith and Rainey were recorded.

The phenomenal growth of radio in the 1920s created a crisis for the music industry. Record sales continued to decline throughout the decade. Since music could now be disseminated even to the most rural and unsophisticated audiences, record companies began to look for other entertainers who performed less well-known "folk" music. Company scouts fanned out across the country, especially the South, to find singers who would sound good on wax and whose talents could be promoted. One of the pioneers in this development was Ralph Peer, the man who first recorded Mamie Smith in 1920, but he became better known because he soon focused on recording country singers, including Jimmie Rodgers.

Mamie Smith's records for Okeh were successful and offered a potential new market for black singers—African Americans themselves who preferred to hear people of their own race perform music from their own culture.[15] Several recording companies created separate listings for songs designed for other races—meaning, almost always, African Americans. These became known as "race records." The term "race" in the 1920s was a badge of pride in the black community. "Although race records included spirituals, instrumentals, comedy, sermons, and even occasional classical arias, the biggest money was in the blues."[16] Okeh, Columbia, and Paramount set the pace for race records in the 1920s. Paramount had a black talent scout and recording director, J. Mayo Williams, who aggressively recruited black entertainers.[17]

In December 1923, at age thirty-seven, Rainey went to Chicago to record eight songs at Paramount Records. Despite its array of talent, Paramount was limited when compared to Columbia Records. Paramount recorded Rainey acoustically, "a crude process in which she sang into an enormous horn," and the results were primitive and disappointing.[18] That first session produced one hit, "Moonshine Blues." Rainey did most of her recording for Paramount in Chicago, where she kept an apartment, but in 1924 she had two Paramount recording sessions in New York. The back-up musicians were among the stars of the jazz world: Fletcher Henderson, a leading New York band leader, on piano; Charlie Green on trombone; and, for the second session, Louis Armstrong on cornet. Of these six tracks, "See See Rider Blues" was the most important.[19]

With recording success came the opportunity to move from tent shows to the stages of the Theater Owners' Booking Agency (TOBA), the black vaudeville circuit. TOBA had been around since about 1907, but it really came into its own in the 1920s. The shows were targeted to black audiences, but on Thursday nights a separate performance was given for whites. The "Midnight Ramble" was a standard—a late show featuring the blues—unlike the regular performances, which were more like white vaudeville in that various types of entertainment were provided. The typical TOBA show might include "comedy, circus acts, dramatic scenes, and pure vaudeville hokum as well as singing and dancing."[20] While TOBA stood for Theater Owners' Booking Agency, the performers often referred to it as "Tough on Black Artists," or, in more crude moments, "Tough on Black Asses." Even so, and despite low pay, hard work, and poor working conditions, TOBA offered regular employment for hundreds of black entertainers who would have had a difficult time arranging bookings for themselves.[21]

For her TOBA act, Rainey worked with Tommy Dorsey, a prominent musician in years to come, as pianist and music director. He put together and rehearsed a five-piece group, the Wildcats Jazz Band.[22] Evidently "jazz," like "blues," was an elastic and even indefinite term. The publicity photo of Rainey, Dorsey, and the rest of the Wildcats put them in awkward poses that nevertheless captured some of Rainey's energy.

Dorsey defined the connection between jazz and blues in several ways that help place Ma Rainey's music. He described jazz as music played at the better clubs; blues was played in Chicago in the back of saloons, at rent parties (held to raise funds to pay rent), and at buffet flats (unlicensed clubs set up in apartments and patronized by working-class people). Jazz was blues speeded up, a faster and flashier music; blues maintained a slower tempo to fit its sad mood.[23] Dorsey also described slowing down or dragging out popular tunes of the day to suit the taste of couples who wanted to "slow drag" or "shimmy" late at night.[24] Rainey's power over the audience is given in Dorsey's words:

> When she started singing, the gold in her teeth would sparkle. She was in the spotlight. She possessed her listeners; they swayed, they rocked, they moaned and groaned, as they felt the blues with her. A woman swooned who had lost her man. Men groaned who had given their week's pay to some woman who promised to be nice, but slipped away and couldn't be found at the appointed time. By this time she was just about at the end of her song. She was "in her sins" as she bellowed out. The bass drum rolled like thunder and the stage lights flickered like forked lightning. . . . As the song ends, she feels an understanding with her audience. Their applause is a rich reward. She is in her glory. The house is hot. . . . By this time everybody is excited and enthusiastic. The applause thunders for one more number. Some woman screams out with a shrill cry of agony as the blues recalls sorrow because some man trifled with her and wounded her to the bone. [Ma Rainey] is ready now to take the encore as her closing song. Here she is, tired, sweaty, swaying from side to side, fatigued, but happy.[25]

Rainey's record sales and TOBA bookings were very successful through 1928, but at the end of that year conditions changed abruptly. Paramount decided not to renew her recording contract. The competition from sound movies, introduced in 1927, had sent the TOBA theaters into a steep decline, and in May 1929, Rainey quit the circuit with wages owed her. Thereafter came a series of desperate moves to keep her career going, but the Great Depression took its toll on her as it had on many other black performers. Still she persevered, taking whatever engagements she could find. She toured with some of the tent repertory companies, but the depression was destroying more prestigious careers than hers. Paramount Records went bankrupt in the early 1930s, black vaudeville died, and Ma Rainey quit the business.

In 1935 she returned to Georgia to her hometown of Columbus after the death of her sister Malissa; her mother died during the same year. Rainey purchased two theaters in Rome. During this time, she joined the Friendship Baptist Church where her brother, Thomas Pridgett, was a deacon. Her life in Georgia is not well known today, but clearly she dropped out of entertainment except for owning the theaters, and she essentially was forgotten in blues circles.

Rainey died on December 22, 1939, and was buried in Porterdale Cemetery in Columbus. She was only fifty-three years old; the cause of death was reported to be heart disease—not unexpected considering her lifestyle and weight. Her death went entirely unnoticed by the black press or by any other news medium. It seems especially ironic that her death certificate listed her occupation as housekeeping. One wonders if her neighbors were aware of her career in entertainment.[26]

Ma Rainey was a black woman and a professional entertainer. She played minstrel shows, tent shows, circuses, carnivals, clubs, theaters, and even a Texas cattle show. Wherever engagements were offered, she took them until, in the Great Depression, there were none. When wealthy white folks in Jackson, Mississippi, hired her, she serenaded at their homes. When black sharecroppers in Alabama were flooded out, she organized a fund-raising concert. She sang blues, popular tunes, and comedy numbers; she danced; she told jokes, often at her own expense and often ribald; she worked with partners in comedy routines. At times, she managed her road shows. She composed about one-third of the numbers she recorded, or, more accurately, she was listed on the copyright forms as composer or co-composer. She paid her musicians on time, treated them well, and never missed an engagement.

For all her versatility, Ma Rainey was most successful singing traditional blues—that is, songs employing many of the formulas and the loose organization of down-home blues but performed by a vocalist and small group as were vaudeville blues. In his poem celebrating the power of Ma Rainey over her audience, Sterling A. Brown tells how her rendition of "Backwater Blues" so perfectly expressed the tribulations of the audience that heads bowed and tears flowed.[27] Brown explained her appeal: "Ma Rainey was a tremendous figure. She wouldn't have to sing any words; she would moan, and the audience would moan with her." She dominated the stage. "She had them in the palm of her hand. I heard Bessie Smith also, but Ma Rainey was the greatest mistress of an audience."[28]

Her commanding presence was also reported by Jack Dupree: "She was really an ugly woman, but when she opened her mouth—that was it! You forgot everything. She knew how to sing those blues, and she got right into your heart. What a personality she had. One of the greatest of all singers."[29] Almost everyone who saw her perform agreed that she was a "blues queen" who, like so many others, acted the part. Strong, unpredictable, and "volcanic," she spoke her mind. She was "soft-hearted and generous; but she was a tigress when roused."[30]

In her recorded blues, Rainey touched upon all the causes of heartache and anguish—unfaithful lovers, violent men, poverty, debt, jail time, alcoholism—of women abandoned, betrayed, or overpowered by life's problems. But in some of her numbers she portrayed aggressive, violent, lustful women—those sinning rather than those sinned against. Thus, in "Bared Home Blues," written by Louie Austin, Rainey's "Mama" matches "Papa," vice for unblushing vice.[31] In "Black Dust Blues," she is a woman who has stolen another one's man but pays the price through the effect of the voodoo potion placed in her house.[32]

In his path-breaking analysis of French folk tales, Robert Darnton discovered a world of constant poverty, death, hunger, starvation, injustice, and cruelty. The poor survived only by tricking others; in such a world the eradication of personal and social problems was inconceivable.[33] Reading the lyrics to Ma Rainey's blues can create the same sense of global despair. But when we turn from the lyrics on the printed page to the recordings, the power of her voice and the gusto in her delivery come into play. The sadness and hurt do not disappear but undergo a transformation. The sheer waste and inwardness of suffering are overcome; artistry gives meaning to the pain of a world we must take as we find it. For Ralph Ellison this was the outrageous, inexplicable truth of African American culture.[34] Many artists represent Ellison's insight as well as Ma Rainey, but none represents it better.

Notes

1. Hattie Jones, *Big Star Fallin' Mama*, rev. ed. (New York, 1995), 19–21.

2. Sandra Lieb, *Mother of the Blues* (Amherst, MA, 1981), 4–5.

3. W. C. Handy, *Father of the Blues* (New York, 1969). Chapters 1–4 describe the conflict between religion and secular music.

4. Quoted in Alton Hornsby Jr., ed., *In the Cage: Eyewitness Accounts of the Freed Negro in Southern Society, 1877–1929* (Chicago, 1971), 140–42; quote on 142.

5. Lieb, *Mother of the Blues*, 4–7; Thomas L. Riis, *Just before Jazz: Black Musical Theater in New York, 1890–1915* (Washington, DC, 1989), 4–5.

6. Riis, *Just before Jazz*, 5–7.

7. Lieb, *Mother of the Blues*, xiii, 5.

8. Ibid., 10–13.

9. Ibid., 3–5.

10. Jeff Todd Titon, *Early Downhome Blues*, rev. ed. (Chapel Hill, NC, 1994).

11. For the problems created by an improvising soloist in Mahara's Minstrel Show see Handy, *Father of the Blues*, 40–41.

12. Lieb, *Mother of the Blues*, 18–25.

13. Steve Hogan and Lee Hudson, *Completely Queer: The Gay and Lesbian Encyclopedia* (New York, 1998), 471.

14. Titon, *Early Downhome Blues*, 200.

15. Bill C. Malone, *Country Music U.S.A.*, rev. ed. (Austin, TX, 1985), 34–35.

16. Lieb, *Mother of the Blues*, 21.

17. Ibid.

18. Ibid., 22.

19. Ibid., 10, 26, 178.

20. Ibid., 27.

21. Ibid., 26–27.

22. Paramount Records talent man J. Mayo "Ink" Williams paired Dorsey with Rainey. Lieb, *Mother of the Blues*, 29; Michael W. Harris, *The Rise of Gospel Blues* (New York, 1992), 86–87.

23. Harris, *Rise of Gospel Blues*, 53.

24. Ibid., 59.

25. Ibid., 89–90.

26. Darlene Clark Hine, ed., *Black Women in America: An Historical Encyclopedia*, 2 vols. (Brooklyn, NY, 1993), 960; John A. Garraty and Mark C. Carnes, eds., *American National Biography* 18 (New York, 1999), 80.

27. Sterling A. Brown, "Ma Rainey," in *The Collected Poems of Sterling A. Brown*, ed. Michael S. Harper (Evanston, IL, 1980), 62–63.

28. Quoted in Derrick Stewart-Baxter, *Ma Rainey and the Classic Blues Singers* (New York, 1970), 42.

29. Ibid.

30. Ibid.

31. Angela Y. Davis, *Blues Legacies and Black Feminism* (New York, 1998), 200–201. Davis provides the words to all the songs of Rainey and Bessie Smith, a tremendous aid to scholars, but the interpretive section of her book is another matter.

32. Ibid., 203.

33. Robert Darnton, *The Great Cat Massacre* (New York, 1984), chap. 1.

34. Ralph Elllison, in *Collected Essays*, ed. John Callahan (New York, 1995).

Suggested Readings

Albertson, Charles. *Bessie*. New York, 1982.

Armstrong, Louis. *Satchmo*. New York, 1986.

Cohn, Lawrence, et al. *Nothing But the Blues*. New York, 1993.

Davis, Angela Y. *Blues Legacies and Black Feminism*. New York, 1998.

Falkenburg, Carole van, and Christine Dall. *Wild Women Don't Have the Blues*. San Francisco: California Newsreel, 1989, videorecording.

Floyd, Samuel A., Jr. *The Power of Black Music*. New York, 1995.

Handy, W. C. *Father of the Blues*. New York, 1969.

Lieb, Sandra. *Mother of the Blues*. Amherst, MA, 1981.

Malone, Bill C. *Country Music U.S.A.* Rev. ed. Austin, TX, 1985.

Morgan, Thomas L., and William Barlow. *From Cakewalks to Concert Halls*. Washington, DC, 1992.

Oliver, Paul. *The Story of the Blues*. Boston, 1997.

Oliver, Paul, et al. *The New Grove Gospel, Blues and Jazz*. New York, 1986.

Riis, Thomas L. *Just before Jazz*. Washington, DC, 1989.

Southern, Eileen. *The Music of Black Americans*. 3d ed. New York, 1997.

Stewart-Baxter, Derrick. *Ma Rainey and the Classic Blues Singers*. New York, 1970.

Titon, Jeff Todd. *Early Downhome Blues*. Rev. ed. Chapel Hill, NC, 1994.

8

Pauline Newman
Immigration, Jewish Radicalism, and Gender

Annelise Orleck

Industrialization wrought a profound change in the life of American workers. Small shops employing artisans or skilled workers increasingly gave way to large mechanized factories using unskilled labor. The wage system came to dominate the workplace, and workers found themselves reduced from independence to dependence. The history of labor in the twentieth century was largely the history of workers seeking to gain lost power through organization. Pauline Newman devoted her long life to that struggle. A Jewish immigrant from Lithuania, Newman went to work in New York City's garment district at an early age. Appalled by the conditions there, she soon began to speak and write against inhumane employers. Her fervent advocacy won the attention of reformers in New York's Democratic Party, and she became an effective lobbyist for workers' interests. She was also an ardent supporter of women's rights, both within the labor movement and in society at large. By dint of her own example and through personal encouragement, she nurtured a new generation of women labor leaders.

Annelise Orleck received her Ph.D. in history from New York University in 1989 and currently teaches at Dartmouth College. Her publications include *Common Sense and a Little Fire: Women and Working-class Politics in the United States, 1900–1965* (1995) and *The Soviet Jewish Americans* (2001).

Pauline Newman was a diehard union loyalist. In an era when the idea of unionism was, for most labor leaders, synonymous with notions of brotherhood and masculine bonding, the tough Lithuanian Jewish immigrant was described by a male colleague as "capable of smoking a cigar with the best of them." In 1909, when she was not yet out of her teens, Newman became the first woman paid to organize by the International Ladies' Garment Workers' Union (ILGWU). Often a thorn in the side of male union officers for her insistence that they organize women as well as men, black workers as well as whites, immigrants as

This essay will also appear in Eric Arnesen, ed., *The Human Tradition in American Labor History* from Scholarly Resources, forthcoming.

well as native born, Newman came to be admired both by leaders and the rank and file as a living embodiment of the union's history. Despite conflicts and disappointments, Newman remained an ILGWU employee for more than seventy years, almost the entire lifespan of the union. At first the young militant served in the field: as a strike organizer, a riveting speaker, and a highly successful fundraiser. In later years she worked out of union headquarters as a labor journalist, a health educator, and a liaison between the union and government officials. Newman played an essential role in galvanizing the early twentieth-century tenant, labor, socialist, and working-class suffrage movements. She also left an important legacy through her writings as one of the few working-class women of her generation to chronicle the struggles of other immigrant working women.[1]

A witty, acerbic woman with unorthodox tastes that ran to slicked-back hair and tailored tweed jackets, Newman was sensitive, emotional, and complicated. Concerned equally with class and gender discrimination, she dedicated herself to two very different causes: the male-dominated labor movement and the cross-class women's reform movement. A union member from her childhood, Newman referred to the ILGWU as her family. She believed that it was, for all its flaws, the best hope for women garment workers. Through the union, Newman sustained her connections to the world of Jewish Socialists. Though run by men who were ambivalent toward women workers, dismissive of women's activism, and often hostile to the idea of incorporating women's issues into their vision of the labor movement, the ILGWU was a deeply familiar environment for Newman, harkening back to her childhood in Lithuania. She shared with the Jewish immigrant men who held power in that union the Yiddish language and the particular mix of Marxist and Old Testament imagery that characterized their brand of working-class organizing. And so, despite years of conflicts with the ILGWU leadership, she could never bring herself to leave what she called "the Jewish movement."

Still, Newman was a pragmatic feminist who understood that most male union leaders were only marginally interested in the concerns of working women. So, along with her union work, she campaigned throughout her life for legislation to protect women workers and forged alliances with progressives of all classes. Newman was drawn in particular to cross-class women's alliances. There she found the warmth and collegiality that was too often missing from her connections with men in the labor movement. In the large and varied women's reform community that flourished in pre-World War II New York City, Newman found her closest friendships and her strongest professional relationships. For all of those reasons, she devoted herself for decades to the major women's labor federations of the early twentieth century, the New York and national Women's Trade Union Leagues (WTUL), organizing for the Leagues and serving as an officer from the 1910s through the 1940s.

Her career was a delicate balancing act. Torn between the male-dominated Jewish Socialist milieu of the ILGWU and the more nurturing woman-centered WTUL, Newman chose, for personal as well as political reasons, to remain loyal to both throughout her long life. In the WTUL she was part of a community of women that sustained her, providing essential support for a working-class immigrant who had chosen to forgo the traditional protections of marriage and family. Theirs was a multiethnic and cross-class circle. It included Irish-Catholic labor activists Maud Swartz and Leonora O'Reilly; Jewish immigrant garment organizer Rose Schneiderman; and affluent native-born Protestant reformers, among them Eleanor Roosevelt and Newman's partner of fifty-six years, Wisconsin-born labor economist Frieda Miller. (Miller served in the 1930s as Industrial Commissioner for New York State and in the 1940s as director of the U.S. Women's Bureau.) This circle played a vital role in the women's labor uprisings of the early twentieth century and also helped to shape the new government agencies and labor laws that guaranteed a minimum wage and minimum standards of safety for all American workers. Running for eight decades in two very different worlds, Newman forged a political career that addressed her complex identity as a Jewish working-class woman. Her choices and her life illuminate the tensions between gender, class, and ethnicity that both powered and fractured alliances within the labor and women's movements during the first half of the twentieth century.

Pauline Newman was born to deeply religious parents in Kovno, Lithuania, sometime in the early 1890s. (The exact date of her birth was lost when her family emigrated.) She was the youngest of four children, three girls and a boy. Her father taught the Talmud to the sons of wealthy townsmen. Her mother supported the family by buying fruit from peasants in the countryside and selling it in the Kovno marketplace.

Pauline's activist career began when, as a child, she fought for the right to an education. Her first experience with exclusion highlighted her class and ethnicity: the Kovno public school refused her admission because her family was Jewish and poor. She soon realized that her sex was also a hindrance. Newman was rebuffed when she asked her rabbi to let her attend her town's all-boy *heder* (religious school). Already a gifted negotiator, she kept wheedling until she won his permission to attend Sunday school classes, where she learned to read and write Yiddish and Hebrew. Still the rabbi would not allow her to study religious texts. Undaunted, she begged her father to let her sit in on the Talmud class. He agreed, shrugging off scandalized whispers among his neighbors.

To her father's chagrin, the bright little girl began to challenge local religious customs. She demanded to know "why the synagogue had two sections—one for men, the other for women—since they all came to worship the same God." Unsatisfied by any of the answers she was given, the young Newman became aware for the first time that gender affected her life opportunities as powerfully as did her ethnicity and her class. "In later years," she wrote, "I often wondered whether this observation conditioned me to resent and to fight all discriminations based on sex. I think it did."[2] Not yet ten years old, she began to fashion the integrated political vision that would guide her career.

Newman's mother decided to take her three daughters to New York City in 1901 after the sudden death of her husband. Her son had already settled there, and Mrs. Newman hoped that he could provide some opportunities for his younger sisters. The Newmans were part of a vast wave of immigrants, most of them from Europe, who arrived on U.S. shores between 1870 and 1920. Twenty-six million people—Slavs, Poles, Greeks, Italians, English, Irish, and smaller numbers of Chinese, Japanese, Mexicans, and Latin Americans—migrated to the United States during those years, most of them settling in crowded slum neighborhoods in the nation's largest cities. Among these were more than two million East European Jews, driven from Russia, Poland, and the Hapsburg empire by the economic hardships that accompanied industrialization as well as by successive waves of anti-Semitic violence, peasant unrest, wars, and revolutions. Like most new arrivals in that era, the Newmans passed through Ellis Island in New York Harbor and settled on Manhattan's Lower East Side, the largest community of East European Jews in the United States.

The reality of life in New York's notorious immigrant ghetto proved different from anything that Newman had envisioned when she fantasized about leaving Lithuania. At the turn of the twentieth century, the Lower East Side was the most densely populated square mile on Earth, with the possible exception of some neighborhoods in Beijing. Entire villages of Jews from Eastern Europe shared adjoining neighborhoods with Chinese from the southern provinces, southern Italians, and Irish immigrants. Most of them lived cheek by jowl in blocks of walk-up tenement buildings with toilets in the halls, bathtubs in the kitchen, and long, skinny airshafts providing a minimum of light and even less fresh air. Despite the grim conditions, many young immigrants found city life exciting. In New York they came to know people from widely differing backgrounds, radical politics served up by streetcorner speakers, and a greater degree of freedom from parental supervision than they had ever known in their now-distant homelands.

Young Jewish women, like other émigrés from small, tradition-bound towns, were powerfully drawn to the diversions that the big city offered: libraries, theaters, music halls and later movie theaters, amusement parks, and dance halls. But they found themselves with little time and even less money to spend on such pleasures. Most were soon working long hours to help support their families. For Jewish and Italian women and girls, a job most likely meant a place in one of New York's myriad garment shops, stitching shirtwaists (blouses), dresses, undergarments, or caps and hats. Pauline Newman quickly found her place among them.

For a girl whose dream of America had been filled with visions of herself attending high school and college, maybe even graduate school, the reality of daily life on the Lower East Side was a profound disappointment. Newman began to work at the tender age of nine, assembling bristles in a hairbrush factory. Her story was not unusual. In 1901, when Newman joined the wage labor force, nearly one in five U.S. children between the ages of ten and fifteen had to help support families who were just barely subsisting. Anxious to assist her widowed mother, the eleven-year-old Newman jumped at the chance in 1903 to begin working at one of the city's most modern, best-paying garment shops, the Triangle Shirtwaist Factory.

Employed in the factory's "kindergarten," she and other child workers trimmed threads from nearly finished blouses. On the rare occasions when government labor inspectors appeared, she and the other children would hide in barrels and simply disappear. Like other children raised in miserable conditions, Newman and her co-workers found ways to have fun. They sang, made games of their work, and told stories to pass the time. Still, Newman would recall that she frequently felt overwhelmed by depression at the dreary conditions on the Lower East Side. Walking home from her job, having worked from dawn to dark, she passed children playing in piles of garbage. She noted the uniformly "tired and drab" expressions on the faces of working men and women shuffling home. One night she whispered to herself sadly, "Dear God, will this ever be any different?"[3]

Newman fought depression by recording what she saw, filling notebooks with her detailed descriptions. As an adolescent she found solace in the workers' poetry she read in the Socialist Yiddish press. She later turned her own hand to poetry, even publishing a few poems before she was out of her teens. Creating an identity for herself as a chronicler kept her from feeling that she had been reduced to the status of a machine. She later explained her passion for reading and writing in this way: "The desire to get out of the shop, to learn, to understand became the dominant force in my life."[4]

The young Newman was drawn to the ideals of socialist trade unionism. That was to be her way out. Like so many Jewish immigrants of her era, her first education in the fundamentals of socialism came through the Yiddish-language newspaper, the *Jewish Daily Forward*. Its pages introduced her to the works of popular socialist journalist Abraham Cahan and to the Yiddish labor poets. Newman soon began to write for the *Forward* and other papers, describing the conditions under which she and her friends labored. Her transition from reader to writer was unusual, but her devotion to the *Forward* was not. Most Jewish immigrant New Yorkers of her day were nourished on the same diet of socialist fundamentals. In the Jewish socialism of the time there was a cross-fertilization of Biblical and Marxist imagery that made even men and women from religious homes feel comfortable with socialist ideas and activism. Jewish socialists liked to use allusions from the Book of Isaiah, with its warnings to the rich and haughty, said former organizer Sidney Jonas, to appeal to "Jewish workers who were deeply imbued with an Old Testament sense of social justice."[5]

Newman's growing sense of political commitment was rooted in that rich mixture of Marx and Isaiah, but it was nourished primarily by anger at the filthy and dangerous conditions under which she was forced to work. It was sustained by affection for and loyalty to her fellow workers, and it was guided by the tutelage of more seasoned political hands—especially older workers, many of whom were already members of the Socialist Party. For the young women, it was a cruel accident of class that they had to spend their girlhood at loud, dangerous sewing machines instead of in school. They were capable of greater things, they insisted. That belief was at the core of their activism. Newman would later describe the visceral, pragmatic nature of the politics of her generation of women workers: "We of the 1909 vintage knew nothing about the economics of . . . industry or for that matter about economics in general. All we knew was the bitter fact that, after working seventy or eighty hours in a seven-day week, we did not earn enough to keep body and soul together."[6]

Always anxious to improve themselves, Newman and her friends perfected their reading and writing skills during evening study groups. "We took turns reading poetry in English to improve our understanding of the language," she recalled. A member of the Socialist Literary Society, Newman chose their texts with an eye toward developing political consciousness. Contemptuous of the popular romances that appealed to many girls her age, she shared with her friends and co-workers the social realist literature that she had come to love. It "appealed to us," she later noted, "because it was a time when we were ready to rise." As often as she could, Newman hosted her fellow workers from the Triangle factory in the room she shared with her mother and sisters. "We read Dickens, Eliot, the poets. I remember when we first heard Thomas Hood's 'Song of the Shirt' I figured that it was written for us, you know, because it told the long hours of stitch, stitch, stitch. . . . It had an impact on us."[7]

Among her co-workers, Newman found hundreds like herself whose desire for an education—for a life that included art, poetry, theater, and the chance to escape city life now and then—drew them to trade unionism. The cultural dimension of this vision of rebellion would distinguish the "girls' uprising" of the 1910s from both the bread-and-butter unionism of the American Federation of Labor and the stark black-and-white vision of class struggle expressed in the rhetoric of many immigrant socialists. Newman's close friend, Polish capmaker Rose Schneiderman, would famously sum up the difference. "The woman worker must have bread," she noted in 1911, "but she must have roses too."[8]

From her first foray into large-scale organizing, Newman built on women's networks both in and out of the shops. The close relationships forged by young women in the shops provided the solidarity that they needed to launch effective campaigns for improved working and living conditions. Parallel to the young women's shop-floor networks were those developed on neighborhood streetcorners by their mothers and older sisters. In the rent strike of 1908, Newman made use of both of those networks to point out the ways that the language of trade unionism also applied to issues of food and shelter. The previous summer, with New York City in the grip of a depression and thousands facing eviction, the 16-year-old Newman took a group of "self-supporting women" to camp on the Palisades above the Hudson River. There they planned an assault on what they called "the high cost of living." Through the following autumn, 400 women workers canvassed nearly every apartment in Lower Manhattan. On New Year's Day in 1908, 10,000 families refused to pay their rent. It was the largest rent strike that New York City had ever seen as well as one of the first successful campaigns in what would become a decades-long tenant movement eventually leading to the establishment of rent controls.

The strike received a great deal of attention across the city. The *New York Times* dubbed Newman the "East Side Joan of Arc," and the teenage immigrant girl became an unlikely working-class heroine. At the age of seventeen, she won the New York State Socialist Party nomination for secretary of state. Newman proudly rode the famous "Red Special" campaign train, standing beside the larger-than-life Socialist Party leader, Eugene Victor Debs. It was a heady political education for a young immigrant girl and she made the most of it.

Since women did not yet have the vote in New York, the ever practical Newman used her 1908 campaign as an opportunity to stump for woman suffrage. For the next twelve years she echoed the arguments that she had made from the back of the Red Special. Arguing both with middle-class women who, she felt, saw the vote as a panacea, and socialist men who decried the woman suffrage movement as "a paltry reform," Newman insisted that the suffrage struggle was an integral part of the working-class campaign for political and economic empowerment. "Woman suffrage should not be regarded as an end in itself," she wrote. "It is only a means to an end." Women workers, she believed, needed the political power of the ballot to back up the economic power they had won by joining unions. Using the two together, they would help the working class "slowly but surely achieve the end—economic freedom."[9]

Newman's campaigns for the vote were always conducted in the context of organizing women workers. For almost two years after the great rent strike, Newman and other immigrant garment workers—capmaker Rose Schneiderman, shirtmaker Leonora O'Reilly, and dressmakers Clara Lemlich and Fannia Cohn, among others—went shop to shop in Lower Manhattan organizing young women who were growing increasingly discontented with steady speedups in the production rate, with being charged for thread and electricity, and with having their pay docked whenever they made mistakes. After a series of small strikes, Newman and others began to plan a general strike to improve wages and conditions in the shirtwaist and dress trades. Virtually every male labor leader they knew warned them that such a strike would not succeed. It was foolhardy, impossible. The majority of workers in these trades were little more than girls.

On November 22, 1909, striking workers from the Triangle factory and two other shops called a general meeting at Cooper Union. After AFL president Samuel Gompers and a number of other labor leaders cautioned against taking precipitous action, 23-year-old Clara Lemlich took the stage and insisted that only the "working girls" themselves could make such a decision. When she called for a general strike, the crowd roared its approval. In the weeks and months that followed, more than 40,000 young women workers in New York left their sewing machines. It was the largest strike by American women up to that time, and Pauline Newman was a whirlwind at its core. She seemed to be everywhere at once: planning strategy at strike headquarters, stirring crowds to action on the streets of the Lower East Side, and sitting teacup in hand in the parlors of some of New York's wealthiest women, explaining the horrific conditions under which shirtwaists were manufactured and persuading the daughters of the elite to contribute to the dressmakers' strike fund. Drawing on her readings of English literature to come up with images that these affluent women could relate to, Newman won the sympathy of some of the city's most powerful socialites—women with names like Morgan and Belmont. A group of socially prominent New York women even joined the young, immigrant garment workers on the picket line. They were soon dubbed the "mink brigade" by the New York press. Their mere presence dramatically cut down police brutality against the strikers. After weeks of forceful arrests, during which the young female strikers sustained broken noses and cracked ribs, city officials sternly warned patrolmen not to club anyone on the Social Register.

The shirtwaist "uprising" dragged on into the bitter winter of 1910. Some workers went back to their jobs before the New Year, while others remained out of work until March 1910. With hundreds of small and larger shops engaged in negotiation, the union was able to win only partial settlements in some of the larger shops. Still, the strike resulted overall in better wages, shorter hours, and improved conditions for many of the immigrant girls and women who labored on garments in New York City. Perhaps more important, it also sparked a wave of garment strikes across the United States. By decade's end these uprisings had brought 40 percent of all women garment workers into unions—a remarkably high percentage of unionized workers and one that belied male labor leaders' insistence that "girls" could not be organized. Important compromises were made in negotiations, however, that would come back to haunt the 1909 strikers. Most devastating was the male union leaders' decision to bargain away the workers' demand for improved safety conditions at the Triangle Shirtwaist Factory. When the factory burned in a terrible fire a year later, killing many of Newman's friends, the young organizer blamed herself.

For a time after the strike Newman was riding high. In recognition of her key role in organizing and sustaining the 1909 uprising, she was appointed the first woman general organizer for the International Ladies' Garment Workers' Union. From 1909 to 1913 she organized garment strikes in Philadelphia, Cleveland, Boston, and Kalamazoo, Michigan. She stumped for the Socialist Party in the gritty, grey steel towns of Pennsylvania and the freezing, bleak coal-mining camps of southern Illinois. And wherever she went, she campaigned for woman suffrage. Moving far beyond the Jewish immigrant milieu of her youth, she worked with native-born Protestant women as well as Slavic, Irish, Polish, and Italian Catholic immigrants. She had no real home for four years, living instead in hotel rooms and boardinghouses and sleeping on the couches and floors of grateful strikers. It was a profound education. Newman later likened it to graduate school, saying that she had received her undergraduate degree at Triangle.

During her years on the road, Newman developed a sophisticated understanding of the complex ethnic mix that made up the American working class, which forced a change in her strategy for organizing. She now believed that the only way to bridge ethnic, linguistic, and religious divisions was to nurture labor leaders from within each ethnic, national, and religious group. The wave of strikes that Newman left behind her proved the success of her strategy. Still, it was a lonely and frustrating few years for her. She began to feel that the union leadership had little interest in organizing women, that her work was undervalued and undermined at every turn. Demoralized, she became increasingly sensitive to slights and condescension by middle-class and affluent women who cast themselves as friends of the working class, and she began to wonder whether it was indeed possible, given limited resources and low self-esteem, to build a lasting movement of women workers.

Her anger, fears, and doubts sank her into deep depression following the Triangle Shirtwaist Factory fire of March 25, 1911. One hundred and forty-six young workers lost their lives on that warm spring afternoon, most of them leaping to their deaths from eight and nine stories up as thousands of horrified New Yorkers watched. Most of the dead were young immigrant women, Jews and Italians who had arrived in the United States during the preceding decade. Newman had worked at the factory for seven years. Many of the fire's victims had helped her to organize the 1909 "uprising," had walked picket lines with her, and had confided to her their hopes, fears, and romantic secrets. Crippled by an overwhelming sense of grief, she decided that she had to give up her weeks on the road and return to New York to be with her friends. At night she lay heartbroken and tried to think of strategies that might prevent such disasters in the future.

The answer both to her personal and political needs seemed to come in the following year, when New York State established the Factory Investigating Commission (FIC). An investigative body with real powers of enforcement, the FIC brought government into the shops to guarantee worker safety. Newman was offered a post as one of the FIC's first inspectors. She happily accepted. Through this job, she met Frances Perkins, later to become Franklin D. Roosevelt's secretary of labor and the first woman to serve in a cabinet post. Perkins was then employed by the National Consumers League, a largely middle-class women's organization committed to using the strength of consumers to investigate, publicize, and improve industrial working conditions. Perkins, whose Greenwich Village apartment was around the corner from the Triangle Factory, had watched in helpless horror as scores of young girls jumped to their deaths. That traumatic afternoon seared Perkins's conscience. She vowed that she would do what it took to legislate improvements in the hours, wages, and conditions of American laborers.

Working together on the FIC, Perkins and Newman built a strong friendship based largely on their shared commitment to educating political officials who had the authority to transform state policy toward factory workers. Together they befriended two powerful allies: the leaders of the New York State Assembly and Senate, future New York governor Alfred E. Smith and future U.S. senator Robert Wagner. Newman and Perkins took the two politicians on tours of the worst factories in the state. The four climbed through ice-covered fire exits and crouched on the freezing floors of cannery "pens" where children sat for twelve hours at a time husking vegetables. Her years on the FIC marked the beginning of a new career path for Newman that would end her days as a street-level organizer. Largely as a result of her ability to speak with equal effectiveness to workers, government officials, labor leaders, and educated women reformers, Newman had become a liaison between the labor movement and government. By the end of World War I, she had gained the respect of key figures in the New York Democratic Party. They would call on her for advice many times over the next half-century.

The Triangle fire had moved Newman from a strict focus on organizing to a new and lasting interest in legislating change. The idea of working with a benevolent state was seductive. Organizing women into unions was a slow and painstaking process, and the gains were never assured. Union memberships rose and fell. Contracts with employers were only as good as the strength of the union to enforce them. But with the stroke of a pen, one law could improve the wages, hours, or safety standards for millions of women. In the aftermath of the Triangle tragedy, Newman, Perkins, and many others considered it deeply irresponsible to make women workers wait for change when quick and wide-ranging improvements could be won by lobbying for legislative action.

Forging bonds with sympathetic women of other classes and with male politicians such as Smith, Wagner, and, later, Franklin Roosevelt also gave Newman and the other working-class women of the Women's Trade Union League a sense of power that they did not have in the male-dominated labor movement. To their amazement, they found that it was easier for working-class women to articulate and win entitlements from an expanding state than from male colleagues in their own unions. It was ironic. As big labor moved closer to government in the 1930s, these women's access to key figures in the Democratic Party would give them more clout with male union leaders than anything they had done as organizers.

The careers of Pauline Newman and WTUL president Rose Schneiderman also illustrate the problems raised by working-class women's enthusiasm for the U.S. welfare state. What the state gives in times of working-class strength, it can take away when the political climate is less sympathetic. Newman lived to see such retrenchments in the 1920s and again in the 1950s. In addition, labor laws that looked good on paper did not necessarily translate in reality to improvements for all workers. Employers found ways to get around such laws, as Newman found out graphically when negotiating minimum wage codes in New York State during the 1930s. Minimum wage and maximum hour legislation often resulted in speedups, mass layoffs, or both. Safety regulations were meaningful only to the extent that they built in a budget and mechanisms for enforcement. In the absence of regular inspections and the fining or prosecution of violators, employers who wished to evade labor regulations found it relatively easy to do so. Newman was keenly aware of all of these problems because she worked frequently during the 1920s, 1930s, and 1940s as a consultant for government agencies negotiating directly with business leaders. Still, the limitations of legislated improvements in wages, hours, and working conditions did not ultimately change her mind about the need for a partnership between labor and government. The image of the Triangle dead remained too vivid throughout her life to allow her to question the efficacy of such a strategy. Instead, she challenged labor to step up its efforts. Labor laws, she insisted, were best enforced by a unionized work force.

Personally and professionally, Newman's life was forever changed by her entry into the world of lobbying and legislative politics. In 1917 the WTUL dispatched her to Philadelphia to build a new branch of the League and to lobby the Pennsylvania legislature for progressive labor codes. There she met a young Bryn Mawr College economics instructor, Frieda Miller. Chafing at the constraints of academic life, Miller gladly left her post to help Newman with her political work. Within the year, the two were living together. It was the beginning of a turbulent, though mutually satisfying, partnership that would last until Miller's death in 1974. During the early years of that partnership, Miller had a brief encounter with a married male friend and in 1923 gave birth to a daughter whom she named Elisabeth. We will never know just what conversations the two women had about Miller's romance, but in the end they decided to raise the child together. In the same year they moved to New York's Greenwich Village, where they would maintain a home for the next half-century.

They were drawn to the Village in part by the lure of a bohemian environment where they could live openly as a "nontraditional" family. West 12th Street, where the two set up housekeeping, was home to a community of female couples who shared Newman and Miller's commitment to progressive and labor politics. Democratic Party activists Nancy Cook and Marion Dickerman as well as Molly Dewson and Polly Porter soon became friends as well as neighbors. Through these women, Newman and Miller met Eleanor Roosevelt, an influential political wife who was becoming one of the state's most savvy and successful lobbyists on behalf of women workers.

Although the idea of lesbian families was not openly discussed during the 1920s, Miller's daughter Elisabeth Burger recalled of her childhood that "from time to time I had the sense that my situation was different but only from time to time." She did not encounter prejudice either in her school or among neighbors. "People didn't stereotype," Burger said of the Village community in which they lived. At the Little Red School, the now-venerable alternative elementary school that she attended, "conventional ways of living were not stressed." In later years, she acknowledged the courage that Newman and Miller had displayed more than a half-century before gay liberation: "Just as Pauline was a pioneer in her role as an organizer of women in sweatshops and factories," Burger noted, "the home that I grew up in was in some respects a harbinger of things to come—a female-headed household made up of two employed women and a child."[10]

What is perhaps more interesting and surprising is that Newman's unconventional domestic life seems to have been equally well received beyond the women's world of the West Village. Letters to Newman from government and union colleagues asked about Frieda and Elisabeth. The family was invited to official functions together. Indeed, according to ILGWU colleague Leon Stein, men in the union respected Newman's courage and determination in creating a family: "She had a life outside the union. She had Frieda and Elisabeth. The union wasn't her family. She could go home at the end of the day." Stein and other ILGWU men found Newman's mix of the political and the personal more comprehensible than, say, the life of another ILGWU pioneer, Fannia Cohn, who seemed to live and breathe only for the union. It was her night as well as her day. Newman at least had a partner, Stein recalled. She had a child. Whether that made her more womanly or more one of the boys, either way her male comrades felt at ease with her.[11]

With a child to raise, Newman could no longer lead the peripatetic life of an organizer. Instead, she chose work that allowed her to stay closer to New York City. Since her appointment to the Joint Board of Sanitary Control, a labor/business factory inspection system created in 1913, Newman had been one of the key players in the emergence of union-sponsored health care for workers. The ILGWU's vision of health care drew on the same sources as the movement for worker education. Young garment strikers in the 1910s argued that they were entitled to a decent quality of life. They were keenly aware of the physical strain on eyes, ears, hands, and psyche that accompanied years of drudgery in loud, mechanized industrial shops. They wanted affordable health care, health education, and prevention. In her columns for the *Ladies Garment Worker*, Newman stressed the importance of exercise, recreation, and relaxation. In 1923 the ILGWU created the Union Health Center, the first union-based comprehensive medical program for workers. Its director, George Price, who knew Newman from the Joint Board, asked her if she would coordinate educational and public relations programs. She accepted the post of educational director and retained that position for sixty years, using it to promote health care, adult education, and greater visibility for women in the union.

From the late 1920s on, Newman also did a great deal of investigative work and policy analysis for women in the WTUL circle who had been appointed to executive positions in state and federal government. Her partner, Frieda Miller, served as director of New York State's Division of Women in Industry, becoming industrial commissioner in 1938 and director of the U.S. Women's Bureau in 1944. Newman's closest friend, Rose Schneiderman, was appointed secretary of labor for New York State in 1937. Both women made abundant use of Newman's long experience with factory conditions to help shape new government agencies charged with the task of improving conditions for women workers.

Newman developed a staggering knowledge of the details of wages, hours, and working conditions in virtually every major industry in which American women were employed. She negotiated state minimum wage and factory safety codes during the 1930s and 1940s that exceeded federal standards. She served on the U.S. Women's Bureau's Labor Advisory Board. After World War II, she and Miller, as appointees to the United Nations Subcommittee on the Status of Women and the International Labor Organization's Subcommittee on the Status of Domestic Laborers, investigated conditions in occupied Germany. During the Truman years, Newman addressed the White House Conference on the Child and served as a regular consultant to the U.S. Public Health Service on matters of child labor and industrial hygiene.

Newman's access to the federal government had come first through her connection to Eleanor Roosevelt. Newman and Miller were among the circle of progressive women who spent time at Val-Kill, the cottage that Franklin Roosevelt had built for Eleanor near the family mansion at Hyde Park. Eleanor's influence also opened doors at the White House, where Newman was a regular visitor throughout FDR's presidency. Her most publicized visit to the White House came in 1936, when, during the national WTUL conference, Newman led a delegation of women garment and textile workers invited by the Roosevelts to be their guests for seven nights. Eleanor breakfasted with the young women daily. FDR greeted them in his bathrobe. (Newman claimed that her job was to ensure that no one misbehaved. They didn't.) One star-struck dressmaker who had just spent the night in the Lincoln Bedroom gushed to the *New York Times* that this was an historic moment. No president had ever invited factory workers to sleep and dine for a week in the White House. "Imagine me," the young Jewish garment worker exclaimed, "Feigele Shapiro, sleeping in Lincoln's bed!"[12]

The visit, like much that FDR did for workers, was little more than a symbolic gesture. And yet it had great meaning for Newman and for the young workers who were so easily won over by the Roosevelts' warmth and graciousness. The sense that they were being listened to by a sitting president was a powerful inducement to become part of the new Democratic Party coalition. The once-cynical Newman seemed unable to resist. She had never planned to become primarily a negotiator or a government functionary. Organizing remained her passion, and she continued to work at it through the 1930s. Still, she took satisfaction in her liaison role. If she could build bridges that working women could walk across to an easier life on the other side, then she was accomplishing the goal to which she had dedicated her life.

Beneath the unruffled surface of Newman's letters and diary entries, however, one can sense a gnawing, if unspoken, discontentment as well. Educated middle-class members of her circle such as Frances Perkins and Frieda Miller were appointed to executive state and federal positions. Fellow working-class organizers Maud Swartz and Rose Schneiderman received high-level, if not policy making, appointments, but Newman was always a consultant, an investigator, or a committee member, never a political appointee. She never complained. Lacking an undergraduate degree, she understood that there were limits to her career trajectory within state or federal government. And yet, others with limited education had official recognition. Perhaps it was Newman's outspokenness or her sometimes gruff demeanor that held her back, or even her butch appearance. Her short hair, tweed jackets, and knickers distinguished her from the more conventionally dressed members of the WTUL circle. Whatever the reasons, she turned back with a fury to organizing in the mid-1930s.

As if in a burst of renewed youthful energy, Newman poured herself into organizing and strike support work both through the ILGWU and the WTUL. While WTUL president Schneiderman served in Washington as the only woman on FDR's National Labor Advisory Board and then in Albany as New York's secretary of labor, Newman redoubled the League's organizing efforts. With the passage of federal labor legislation guaranteeing workers' right to organize, the nation saw a dramatic rise in strikes and union activity. Women workers struck canning, textile, and garment factories across the country. Increasing numbers of women were concentrated in service sector jobs by the 1930s, and they too were swept up in the strike fever. Waitresses, hotel maids, and laundry workers all walked out in the 1930s, demanding not only that their employers enforce New Deal regulations but also that they recognize their right to belong to unions. Finally, working-class housewives, many of them members of union auxiliaries, began to organize around their power as consumers, leading rent strikes and boycotts of high-priced staples such as meat, bread, and milk, walking picket lines, and lobbying in Washington. Newman was exhilarated by this resurgence of working-class activity.

As she had during her years on the road for the ILGWU before World War I, Newman made a point of reaching out to ethnic constituencies who had been ignored or explicitly shut out of established trade unions. She worked to build a laundry union in New York, brought the League into textile strikes in Tennessee, and tried to nurture the growth of a domestic workers' union that would regulate their wages, hours, and working conditions. In each of these cases, Newman and the WTUL brought African American women into previously all-white labor unions. Through the massive dressmakers' strikes of 1933 and afterward, Newman and other ILGWU organizers, including Rose Pesotta, enlisted sizeable numbers of Mexican American, African American, and Afro-Caribbean women into the ILGWU.

One who rose to prominence by the 1940s was Panamanian-born Maida Springer, who became the first black labor unionist to be appointed to a senior position in the American Federation of Labor. When later interviewed about her own career, Springer cited Newman as "one of my mentors, . . . one of the giants, determined, articulate, volatile about workers' dignity." Springer admiringly described Newman, her ILGWU colleague Fannia Cohn, and the WTUL's Schneiderman as "rambunctious, tenacious women who made themselves heard." As a young dressmaker, Springer recalled that she was determined to become like them. And even as an accomplished labor veteran, she still looked back at the "1909 generation" with respect and awe.[13]

Mentorship may have been Newman's major contribution to the women's labor struggle in the later years of her long career. She continued to work for the ILGWU until 1983 by writing, lecturing, and advising younger women organizers. During her seventy-plus years with the union, she waged a constant struggle to convince male leaders to acknowledge the needs and talents of women workers. By nurturing younger women in the ILGWU and in the WTUL, Newman helped to forge human links between generations in the labor movement. Esther Peterson, who rose through the ranks of the AFL-CIO to direct the U.S. Women's Bureau under John F. Kennedy and the Consumer Affairs Office under Jimmy Carter, wrote in 1978 to the 87-year-old Newman: "I think of you so often and especially of all the help that you and Frieda gave me. . . . I am trying to carry on in the same tradition and help other women as they come along."[14]

With the revival of the feminist movement in the 1970s and with the emergence of women's labor history as a growing field, the elderly Newman found herself in a flattering but uncomfortable position, that of feminist heroine. In 1974 the Coalition of Labor Union Women honored her as a foremother of the women's liberation movement. In years to follow, she would be called on repeatedly to play the role of living witness to the sweatshop conditions that had prevailed during the early part of the twentieth century. She spoke regularly to historians and reporters and to groups of young women workers, her heavily wrinkled face and time-worn voice telling as much as her words about the decades of struggle on behalf of the labor movement. Newman wanted younger workers to appreciate the fact that the benefits they currently enjoyed were hard won, but she understood that many continued to labor in substandard conditions. She spoke on behalf of striking southern textile workers in the 1980s. She cheered the Chinese women workers in New York's Chinatown who led their own "Uprising of the 20,000" in 1982. As resurgent immigration brought sweatshop labor back to New York in the last years of Newman's life, she once again urged her union not to ignore the new immigrants, many of them women, who made up the late twentieth-century garment workforce.

Near the end of Pauline Newman's almost century-long life, she allowed me to visit her. She had misgivings even before I arrived and, within moments, she seemed ready to end our discussion. "About myself I will not speak," she said immediately, peering at me intently through watery grey eyes. Uncertain about the motives of these young historians who suddenly seemed so interested in her, she feared we would distort her legacy. She planned to write her own autobiography, she told me; "no one else would get it right." I did not doubt her ability to do so. From 1909 to 1913, Newman was a regular contributor to the *New York Daily Call, Progressive Woman*, and the WTUL publication, *Life and Labor*. From 1913 to 1918 she had a regular column in the

Ladies Garment Worker entitled "Our Women Workers." She continued to write for WTUL publications until 1950 and for the ILGWU's *Justice* through the 1960s. The stories, columns, and reportage that she left behind form an important part of her legacy.

Nevertheless, there I was, sitting before her in 1984 and asking her to help me sum up the meaning of her career. It was probably an impossible question. She replied modestly but tersely, "I did my share. That's all." She was uneasy at being cast as a heroine. There were so many others, she said, who had done at least as much as she, and still others who had given far more. In her last years, recalls Elisabeth Burger, Newman liked to tell the story of a young Philadelphia waistmaker who, during the strike of 1910, walked the raw, rainy streets night after night to distribute leaflets in support of her fellow strikers. The woman contracted pneumonia and died. Nearly eighty years later, Newman lamented, no one remembers the young garment worker's name. Perhaps that haunting memory was part of the reason that Newman decided ultimately to donate to the Arthur and Elizabeth Schlesinger Library at Radcliffe College—the nation's premier women's history archive—a collection of published and unpublished writings about both the personal and public struggles of politicized working women of her generation.

If she had nothing further to say about herself, I asked, would she talk about her friends in the movement? She looked at me appraisingly, silent for a few moments. And then the 95-year-old labor veteran began to reminisce. Her voice broke as she remembered the women who were her friends, partners, and comrades in the Women's Trade Union League through decades of struggle. Their social and professional network provided an emotionally fulfilling alternative world for women who had chosen lives of political activism outside the confines of traditional heterosexual marriage. This women's circle sustained its members over nearly half a century. Through long careers in the public eye, these women offered each other personal support, sage advice, and the release of countless evenings playing penny-a-point poker.

The last survivor of the group, Pauline Newman, felt an obligation to write about her friends and to sketch them as vividly as she could. That day, with tears flowing, she told me about the passionate devotion of Leonora O'Reilly to the cause of peace and about conversations with Maud Swartz as they worked together in the garden of Newman's West Redding, Connecticut, country home. Memories of the bonds she shared with other women in the labor movement were woven into every one of her assessments of her eighty-year career. Newman's life and the lives of her friends—-the remarkable group of activist women who did so much to recast the relationship between the U.S. government and the people who spend their lives engaged in wage labor—illuminate the complex linkages between personal ties and political change.[15]

Pauline Newman died in 1986 at the home of her adopted daughter, Elisabeth Burger. She was about ninety-six years old. Newman's death evoked a deep sense of loss in the ILGWU and among women trade unionists. She had carved out a niche for herself in the rocky gap between two worlds. Standing with one foot in the male-dominated labor movement and the other in the cross-class group of women reformers, she influenced a great many people. Her contributions as an organizer, a legislative expert, a writer, and a mentor to younger women activists were profound and wide-ranging. Indeed, her historical significance far exceeds any official title she had.

Notes

1. Author's interview with Leon Stein, Cranbury, New Jersey, October 19, 1988.

2. Pauline Newman, "Letters to Hugh and Michael" (1951–1969), Box 1, Folder 3, Pauline Newman Papers, Arthur and Elizabeth Schlesinger Library, Radcliffe College, Cambridge, Massachusetts.

3. ibid..

4. Pauline Newman, "Fragments," 1958–1961, Box 1, Pauline Newman Papers.

5. Author's interview with Sidney Jonas, Brooklyn, New York, August 10, 1980.

6. Newman, "Letters to Hugh and Michael."

7. Interview with Pauline Newman in Joan Morrison and Charlotte Fox Zabrisky, eds., *American Mosaic* (New York: E. P. Dutton, 1982).

8. "Miss Rose Schneiderman, Gifted Young Lecturer," Handbill of the American Suffragettes, 1914, Rose Schneiderman Collection, Tamiment Institute Library, New York University, New York City.

9. Pauline Newman, *New York Call*, May 2, 1914.

10. Author's interview with Elisabeth Burger, New York City, December 15, 1987; "Bid Farewell to Pauline," *Justice*, July 1986.

11. Leon Stein interview.

12. *New York Times*, May 1, 5, 6, 7, 1936; Charlotte Baum, Paula Hyman, and Sonya Michel, *The Jewish Woman in America* (New York: New American Library, 1977), 160.

13. Elizabeth Balanoff, "Interview with Maida Springer Kemp," in *The Black Woman Oral History Project*, ed. Ruth Edmonds Hill, 10 vols. (Westport: Meckler Press, 1990), 7:45–157. Quote is from 7:73.

14. Esther Peterson to Pauline M. Newman, November 30, 1978, Box 9, Pauline Newman Papers.

15. Author's interview with Pauline Newman, New York City, February 9, 1984.

Suggested Readings

For a fuller treatment of Pauline Newman's life, see Annelise Orleck, *Common Sense and a Little Fire: Women and Working-Class Politics in the United States, 1900–1965* (Chapel Hill: University of North Carolina Press, 1995). Ann Schofield has done an insightful short sketch of Newman's life in *"To Do and To Be": Portraits of Four Women Activists, 1893–1986* (Boston: Northeastern University Press, 1997). An early and important article including information about Newman is Alice Kessler-Harris, "Organizing the Unorganizable: Three Jewish Women and Their Union," *Labor History* 17, no. 1 (Winter 1976): 5–25. A brief interview about Newman's childhood is one of the oral histories contained in Joan Morrison and Charlotte Fox Zabrisky, eds., *American Mosaic* (New York: E. P. Dutton, 1982).

For a look at the era of the garment strikes and the lives of young women garment workers during the early twentieth century see Orleck, *Common Sense*; Elizabeth Ewen, *Immigrant Women in the Land of Dollars: Life and Culture on the Lower East Side, 1890–1925* (New York: Monthly Review Press, 1982); Susan Glenn, *Daughters of the Shtetl: Work and Unionism in the Immigrant Generation* (Ithaca: Cornell University Press, 1990); and Nan Enstadt, *Ladies of Labor, Girls of Adventure: Working Women, Popular Culture, and Labor Politics at the Turn of the Twentieth Century* (New York: Columbia University Press, 1999).

For the Women's Trade Union League see Orleck, *Common Sense*; Nancy Schrom Dye, *As Equals and Sisters: Feminism, Unionism, and the Women's Trade Union League of New York* (Columbia: University of Missouri Press, 1980); Robin Miller Jacoby, "The Women's Trade Union League and American Feminism," *Feminist Studies* 3, nos. 1 and 2 (Fall 1975): 126–40; and "The Women's Trade Union League School for Women Organizers," in Joyce Kornbluh and Mary Frederickson, eds., *Sisterhood and Solidarity: Worker's Education for Women, 1914–1984* (Philadelphia: Temple University Press, 1984).

9

Gerald L. K. Smith
Political Activist, Candidate, and Preacher of Hate

Cynthia Clark Northrup

The United States has a long tradition of supporting evangelists, from George Whitefield during the Great Awakening of the eighteenth century to the televangelists of today. Some of these revivalist ministers, especially in the twentieth century, have found the lure of politics so irresistible that they have tried to use religion to influence political change. Today, leaders of the religious right are the most successful in this long line of activists.

Gerald L. K. Smith was a pioneer who helped to pave the way for the contemporary politically active religious leaders, even though most of them probably would have rejected his basic philosophy, especially his anti-Semitism and his opposition to the rights of African Americans. Even so, Smith was an important religious, and then political, leader in the period between the world wars. He was an opportunist who attached himself to people— such as Huey Long—who agreed with him and were willing to tolerate his involvement. Before long, however, most political conservatives rejected him, and he found himself isolated. Near the end of his life he abandoned his political views and returned to religion.

Cynthia Northrup, a history faculty member at the University of Texas at Arlington, chronicles Smith's importance in this essay. A specialist in modern American history, she holds a Ph.D. in history from Texas Christian University. She is coeditor of *Tariffs and Trade in U.S. History: An Encyclopedia* (2003).

Americans have gravitated traditionally toward strong, dynamic individuals who exude an air of self-confidence, especially during tumultuous times. The common-man qualities of Andrew Jackson persuaded many newly enfranchised voters to vault him into the presidency in 1828 as the nation adapted to the market revolution. The rugged individualism and fortitude of Theodore Roosevelt inspired patriotism

This essay originally appeared in Donald W. Whisenhunt, ed., *The Human Tradition in America between the Wars, 1920–1945* (Wilmington, DE: Scholarly Resources, 2002), 153–68.

in the public as the president enthusiastically led a reluctant and uncertain United States into an era of world domination. The poise and resolve of Ronald Reagan restored the spirit of the country after the Iranian hostage crisis, a prerequisite for the steadfast confrontation of communism that ended the Cold War.

Other effective communicators have enthralled the masses with their rhetoric, with some leaving a lasting impression on the nation's consciousness. Charles Finney sparked a revival movement that altered religion in America by calmly depicting, in vivid detail, the horrific consequences in store for the sinner who failed to repent. William Jennings Bryan took up many causes with his oratory to preserve traditional American values. Dr. Martin Luther King Jr. embued a generation of African Americans with the hope that his dream of equality could be achieved even as the nation struggled to deal with the assassination of President John F. Kennedy and America's continued involvement in the Vietnam conflict.

Just two months before the Spanish-American War, another great orator entered this world. Gerald Lyman Kenneth Smith, born in Pardeeville, Wisconsin, on the bright Sunday morning of February 27, 1898, followed in the footsteps of his father but exhibited a speaking talent far greater than Lyman Smith ever possessed. With a family steeped in the tradition of the Republican Party, as a youth Smith attended church regularly wherever congregations gathered to listen to his father, a third-generation fundamentalist preacher, proclaim the word of God. At the age of seven, Smith was baptized; and five years later he informed his family that preaching would be his chosen profession, a decision that pleased all of his loved ones. Although his family was poor and his father frequently ill, Smith remained in school while working odd jobs to help support the household. During these early years he displayed an eloquence evident through his participation in school debates and plays. For one particular oratory competition, Smith recited Bryan's "Cross of Gold" speech to the roaring applause of the audience.[1]

Before entering the ministry, Smith decided to further his education. In the spring of 1918 he graduated from Valparaiso University, a school for indigents in Indiana, and started applying to graduate schools where he hoped to earn his master's degree in theology. During the summer he contracted nephritis, a severe kidney infection, and his plans to attend school in the fall faded as he was forced to move back to his parents' house in Viroqua. After a lengthy recovery that lasted almost a year, Smith accepted his first ministerial position as a temporary pastor in Soldier's Grove, Wisconsin. In the pulpit he found his calling. While at the Christian Church, he found that his oratory skills drew new congregants and so inspired original members that within a few months he raised enough money to pay off the $4,000 mortgage on the building.[2]

Smith's ambition, dedication, and brilliant speaking brought him recognition and success in the ministry. Shortly before marrying Elna Sorenson, Smith accepted a pastorate at the church in Beloit, Wisconsin, where he stayed for more than three years before his compulsive working led to a breakdown. After a three-month recovery he immediately accepted the responsibility of leading a larger church in Kansas, Illinois, and two years later became the minister of the Seventh Christian Church in Indianapolis, where he organized youth groups, attended night classes to earn his degree in theology, and increased the size of the congregation to 2,000 members after preaching his "Come to Jesus" sermon. Always searching for a bigger challenge, Smith agreed to work with a small group of college students meeting at the University Place Christian Church, helping them to develop and implement a twenty-five-year plan to build and finance a new sanctuary. In one year his dynamic sermons drew 1,600 new converts to his flock. In 1929, Elna contracted tuberculosis. Smith, after consulting specialists and inquiring about the best area for recovering patients, resigned his pulpit and moved with his wife to the pine hills of northwestern Louisiana, where his diligence and persuasive sermons helped increase the membership at King's Highway Christian Church by 356 people within the first two years. Despite the stock market crash in 1929 and the onset of the Great Depression, Smith continued to raise more contributions than ever. His exceptional oratorical skills brought him a significant number of invitations to speak at local clubs, civic meetings, and church groups, including the Chamber of Commerce, Rotary Club, Boy Scouts, YMCA, and area revivals. His charismatic personality attracted the praise of clergy from other faiths as well as of E. H. Williams of the American Federation of Labor and wealthy businessmen such as W. K. Henderson, who contributed to Huey Long's organization.[3]

Gradually, Smith shifted his focus from salvation to social reform, leading many of his parishioners to question his motives and his commitment to the church. The first sign of trouble appeared when Henderson financed the broadcast of Smith's radio sermons during which he voiced opposition to the corrupt practices of Standard Oil. By 1932 he had accepted an invitation to address the United States Olympic Committee in Los Angeles and also headed the local Community Chest fund. Members of the church objected to the amount of time that Smith spent on nonpastoral activities, especially after their minister began devoting a minimum amount of time and thought to the development of his homilies. Dedicated to assisting his parishioners, Smith found himself in the role of intermediary when several members asked for his help to save their homes from foreclosure by the Mutual Building Association, a company owned by other church members and a Jew named Philip Lieber. Smith called on Lieber, who refused to consider an extension of the notes until after Smith contacted Huey Long, the U.S. senator who controlled Louisiana politics. After receiving a call from Long, the banker cancelled the mortgage. While some of the church members thanked Smith for his involvement, others criticized him for interfering in private business matters, an area they deemed outside the purview of his position as the head of the church. Criticism over Smith's actions in this matter led the young crusader to resign.[4]

Smith and Long crossed paths again a few months later. Smith had decided to focus on humanitarian causes after leaving the ministry, and Long provided the opportunity for him to link his need and desire for recognition to a noble cause. In the midst of the Great Depression, Long devised a plan to help the poor masses who made up his power base, but he needed an organizer and spokesman to promote the idea. Smith, whose religious background disarmed many of Long's opponents and critics, formed the Share Our Wealth Society nationwide, calling for a maximum yearly individual earning of $1 million and an amassed fortune of no more than $5 million per person. Under the plan any excess amounts would be confiscated and redistributed; every family would receive a guaranteed income of $2,000 to $3,000 per year, free college tuition for qualified students, bonuses for veterans, and pensions for the elderly. Long spoke before many crowds, persuading them to support his program; those who backed him had their names placed on a mailing list. Smith spoke if Long had a scheduling conflict or was too exhausted to address the people himself. The positive response by the crowds to Smith's showmanship and dynamic appeal convinced Long to employ Smith's gift of persuasion more frequently. Using a combination of mellow, reassuring tones with sudden shifts to violent, emotional pitches, Smith spoke to more than one million people throughout the South in 1934. Just four weeks after he assumed responsibility for communicating the message to the public, membership in the Share Our Wealth Society increased by 207,000 members. By January 1935, one year later, he had recruited 4.5 million Americans, and by July of that year the numbers had swelled to 7 million. With sweat soaking his shirt and running down his face, with his strong masculine presence dominating the audiences, and with the conviction of a hellfire-and-brimstone preacher, Smith persuaded the poor and the masses to support Huey Long, who would save the American people from their deep despair and uncertain future.[5]

At the height of his popularity as the right-hand man of a powerful and influential politician, Gerald Smith's world vaporized with the flash of a gun. In September 1935 an assassin murdered Long in the Louisiana capitol in Baton Rouge. After eulogizing his mentor, Smith attempted to assume leadership over the slain senator's followers, but the political contributors, particularly Seymour Weiss and Robert Maestri, reached a compromise with Franklin D. Roosevelt, agreeing to support the president's reelection bid in exchange for federal aid for Louisiana. Once the deal was concluded, Smith, who received word that his services were no longer required, attempted to obtain a copy of Long's mailing list to start his own organization. When he discovered that Weiss and Maestri had destroyed the names and addresses, he sought out other Long employees who might have the list, particularly Earle Christenberry, who had gone to work for Dr. Francis E. Townsend, another depression-era demagogue with a cure for the nation's problems.[6]

During the difficult economic times of the 1930s, Americans accepted the demagoguery and radicalism of a number of charismatic leaders with the hope that their ideas and programs would resolve the ever-deepening crisis. Smith joined the ranks of these nationally recognized personalities to find a replacement presidential candidate for his beloved Huey Long. In late 1935 he backed Eugene Talmadge, who supported the rights of the poor while accepting money from rich conservatives such as Pierre S. du Pont and Alfred P. Sloan, chairman of General Motors. Talmadge organized a convention to announce his intentions to run for the presidency and invited Smith to speak. When Smith received more applause from the crowds than he did, Talmadge severed the relationship and later withdrew altogether from the campaign.

Never discouraged, Smith located Christenberry at the headquarters of Dr. Townsend and within a matter of weeks worked himself into a position as adviser to the aging physician. Townsend advocated an "Old Age Revolving Pension" that guaranteed retirees over the age of sixty a monthly income of $200 from the government on condition that they spend the entire amount before the next month, thereby stimulating the economy; supporting earlier retirement that opened jobs for young workers; and increasing revenue for the government through a

2 percent sales tax. Smith persuaded Townsend to change the name of the program to the "Townsend Recovery Plan" and generated support for the idea. At the same time, Smith contacted Father Charles E. Coughlin, a popular Catholic priest in Royal Oak, Michigan, who reached millions of listeners each week through his radio programs. Coughlin, who received thousands of letters and calls weekly, opposed the financial policies of Roosevelt; he particularly disagreed with the president on the use of silver to back U.S. currency, favoring the use of the white metal to inflate the currency.[7]

The triumvirate of Smith, Townsend, and Coughlin formed a new political party to oppose the reelection of Roosevelt in 1936. The Union Party chose Congressman William Lemke of North Dakota as its candidate and defined the party's platform as opposing inflation, assisting farmers, supporting a high protective tariff, and pursuing an isolationist foreign policy. The Townsend Recovery Plan formed the basis of the party's attitude concerning senior citizens. Coughlin's insistence on the use of silver dictated the economic policies of the organization, while Smith influenced social aspects such as free education for the poor and liberal labor policies. Although Smith and Coughlin employed their formidable speaking skills to arouse their supporters, they failed to develop a strong grassroots organization that would sustain the election. The Union Party candidate appeared on the ballot in only fourteen states, with an additional six states allowing for the candidate on a write-in basis.[8]

Weeks before the November election, Smith alienated himself from both the candidate and the other members of the triumvirate and ensured the failure of the party. On October 22, 1936, he announced that he personally would lead a group of more than 10 million followers against an "international plot to collectivize" the United States. Comparing Smith's strong nationalism to an American version of Nazism, Lemke, Townsend, and Coughlin severed all ties to Smith. Although Lemke received 891,858 votes, the disunity among the leaders, the lack of a strong labor base, and a reliance on anti-Roosevelt sentiment resulted in the dissolution of the Union Party in 1938.[9]

After the 1936 defeat, Smith experienced a political transformation. He moved to New York City where he formed an anti-Communist and anti-New Deal organization that he called the Committee of Ten Thousand, later to be known as the Committee of One Million. Members devoted their energies to investigating all Communist meetings and groups in an effort to preserve the right of private property, defend the Christian faith, and uphold the Constitution and democratic principles of the United States. Instead of poor people and the masses providing the financial support for the group, most of the funds originated from wealthy businessmen such as William Brown Bell of American Cyanamid, Charles Costa of Costa Trucking, members of the Pew family of Sun Oil, and Horace Dodge, the automobile magnate.[10]

When President Roosevelt announced his intention to seek an unprecedented third term, Smith devoted his energy to opposing FDR. In 1940, Smith chose Ohio's Governor John W. Bricker as the candidate whom he would support, but Bricker failed to win the Republican nomination. Then Smith decided to back Wendell Willkie, the Republican candidate, during the presidential campaign. After losing the election, Willkie toured the country promoting the idea that the United States should join a world organization, a concept that Smith adamantly opposed. Afterward, he determined to challenge any attempt by Willkie to seek the Republican nomination again in 1944.[11]

Just as Smith appeared to be settling down into a comfortable life based on his own popularity instead of relying on the fate of others, accusations concerning his motives and extremism derailed his movement once again. The first problem arose when Smith and Pat Powers, one of the partners of the Committee of One Million, disagreed over the direction of the group. Powers had been involved with its finances, and his separation from Smith negatively influenced fundraising efforts. Then a March of Time newsreel on Smith entitled "The Lunatic Fringe" portrayed him as a self-promoter concerned only with his own fame instead of with the plight of others. The documentary showed Smith practicing his speeches before a mirror, which led the producers to question whether he was a "man of destiny or merely a political windbag." The political fallout from the newsreel ended Smith's effectiveness in New York.[12]

In 1939, after moving to several towns in the Midwest, Smith and his wife settled in Detroit, where financial supporters such as Dodge breathed new life into his dying career. In addition to numerous offers to speak to local groups, Smith also obtained the financial backing necessary to produce a program carried on the forty-eight radio stations across the country that had previously aired Father Coughlin's sermons and speeches. Within a matter of months, Smith received more speaking invitations than he could accept, collected more than 250,000 names for his own mailing list, initiated a direct-mail program to address local issues, and offered a number of books to his followers. To promote his organization, he recruited volunteers, including such high-level government officials as Senator Robert R. Reynolds of North Carolina, Senator Arthur H. Vandenberg of Michigan, and Senator Burton K. Wheeler of Montana. In 1940, Smith reached 40 million listeners weekly who sent in contributions totaling $1,800 per week. By 1944 he was receiving more than $5,000 per week in donations.[13]

Instead of attacking the rich as he had done with Huey Long, Smith vilified Communists, labor unions, and Jews. According to Smith, labor unions acted as an instrument of the Communist Party in influencing workers to pursue a socialistic society. He particularly hated Walter Reuther of the United Auto Workers and his brother Vic who, according to Smith, had received instructions directly from Communist leaders during a visit to Moscow. His close ties with automobile moguls such as Dodge and Henry Ford distorted his views of labor.

Ford's distrust of Jews also influenced Smith, especially after he read Ford's book, *The International Jew*, which condemned Jewish bankers for the financial problems associated with the depression. Memories of another banker named Lieber from Shreveport convinced Smith that America should distance itself from Jewish financiers. Smith, who always blamed FDR for the assassination of Huey Long, argued that the president relied on too many Jews who filled the top positions in his administration—among them Bernard Baruch, Samuel Rosenman, and Supreme Court Justice Felix Frankfurter. Smith advocated a constitutional amendment that guaranteed the right of the American people to recall the president for unpatriotic acts such as filling cabinet positions with Jews.[14]

In 1942, Smith campaigned for a Senate seat from Michigan, but his failure as a political candidate altered his future once again. Campaigning with all the energy and heart that he could muster, he spoke to every group that extended an invitation. Broadcasting over loudspeakers mounted on trucks, he reached as many constituents as possible while his opponents in the Republican primary rarely made an appearance. His unsuccessful attempt to secure the Republican nomination devastated him, and the defeat was compounded by the unwillingness of the convention organizers to let him address the party members. His initial reaction—to run as a third-party candidate—turned to cynicism when his political backers pulled out. After several unsuccessful attempts to win an election by either supporting another candidate or by running for office himself, Smith turned his back on the political system.[15]

Between 1938 and 1942 he pursued an isolationist policy encouraging Congress and the American people to resist the temptation of fighting a war for the Jews and for the British empire. In July 1940 he delivered a petition to Congress calling for the government to outlaw communism and continue America's policy of neutrality. He argued against the Lend-Lease program, suggesting that the obvious benefits for the British would eventually draw the United States into the conflict. The antiwar rhetoric ended with the Japanese attack on Pearl Harbor in December 1941, and thereafter Smith, along with other isolationists, believed that the United States must defend its territory and honor.[16]

When Willkie opted not to run for president in 1944, Smith, more determined than ever to fight against a fourth term for FDR, searched for a suitable Republican candidate and threatened to back a third-party candidate under his America First Party if a conservative nominee was not selected at the Republican convention. His choices included the famous transatlantic pilot Charles A. Lindbergh, World War I flying hero Captain Eddie Rickenbacker, Senator Gerald P. Nye of North Dakota, *Chicago Tribune* publisher Colonel Robert McCormick, General Douglas MacArthur, now-retired Senator Reynolds, and Governor Thomas E. Dewey of New York. One by one he issued statements concerning the desirability of the men, but every one of them spurned Smith's support. Dewey stated that "the Gerald L. K. Smiths and their ilk must not for one moment be permitted to pollute the stream of American political life." Reacting to Dewey's comments after he received the Republican nomination, Smith called for a national convention in Detroit to select the America First candidate. On August 30 the delegates met and, not surprisingly, chose Smith to represent their party.[17]

The 1944 America First Party's platform reflected Smith's personal ideology; in fact, he had published the various planks in an issue of *The Cross and the Flag* prior to the convention. One of the important issues involved providing food for American citizens at home before sending supplies overseas to the French. Moreover, Smith argued that the time was right to "absorb Canada, buy Greenland, and accept strategic islands in the Pacific in lieu of payment of the allies' war debts." He also suggested that British and French territory be used for the creation of a homeland in Africa for American blacks, while some members of the party went so far as to propose that Jews in the United States be forced to leave the country. If some Jews could give a compelling reason why they should stay, then they would be automatically sterilized. Smith opposed this last measure and tabled the idea permanently. On election day he received a mere 1,781 votes. Although frustrated and disappointed, Smith rebounded quickly. Over the next several years he continued to look for a viable candidate to run in 1948.[18]

After World War II, Smith reverted to his isolationist position. He argued against joining the United Nations unless legislators insisted on ratifying the treaty along with the Connally Resolution, which reserved the right of Congress to confirm any foreign policy commitments made under the new organization. Smith also promoted the America First Party with the argument that Americans should place their interests before those of the rest of the world.[19]

During the immediate postwar years, Smith underwent several personal changes. In 1947 he and his family moved from Detroit to St. Louis and then to Tulsa, Oklahoma, where they purchased a house. In 1953 he toured California, where he resolved to establish his headquarters. Throughout his career, Smith had relied on his gift of oral communication, but for the rest of his life he focused on disseminating his ideas through the distribution of written literature, especially after the spread of television, a medium he always feared. As early as 1942 he published *The Cross and the Flag* for his followers who believed in the importance of both Christianity and the United States.[20]

As the election of 1948 approached, Smith actively involved himself in the selection of the Republican nominee once again. He was convinced that General Douglas MacArthur offered the best chance of defeating the incumbent, Harry S. Truman, who had assumed the office after FDR's death in 1945. At the Democratic convention many of the delegates, opposed to the position of the president on civil rights, walked out and later nominated their own candidate in Birmingham, Alabama. Smith attended the Dixiecrat convention and offered his support to J. Strom Thurmond, who promptly rejected Smith's endorsement. Angry over the rebuff, Smith announced that his own party, the Christian Nationalist Party, would meet in St. Louis on August 20. The delegates unanimously nominated Smith as their candidate and accepted a platform that was even more radical than the earlier one. The Christian Nationalists called for the deportation of blacks and Jews and the establishment of ghettoes for those who refused to leave; their homes would be confiscated and redistributed to returning veterans. All international agreements reached by FDR without open discussion would be rescinded. The Christian Nationalists won few votes, partly because Smith had spent four months of the campaign recovering from food poisoning and partly because he had alienated too many voters with his extreme positions and rhetoric.[21]

Throughout the 1950s, Americans accepted a societal conformity based on a distrust of communism, a strong faith in religion, an emphasis on family bonds, and an aversion to people and ideas that represented any deviation from the norm. Smith believed in the same values but to an extreme, especially as he grew older. During the congressional hearings on Un-American Activities, Smith supported investigations into the background of government officials and Hollywood actors, although he believed that congressmen such as Richard M. Nixon failed to conduct a thorough examination of Communists within the United States. He defended Senator Joseph McCarthy for his stand against Communists even after his censure, although two of McCarthy's aides of Jewish descent disliked Smith for his anti-Semitic views. Smith believed, as did many Americans, that Jews remained a problem in this country. He traced their negative impact back to the Civil War when the Rothschilds supposedly assassinated Abraham Lincoln after he refused to borrow money from their banking house to finance the war. Twice, Smith led a movement to preserve Christianity in America in 1933 and 1942. He particularly distrusted Roosevelt and his cabinet, who, he believed, fought World War II primarily to establish the state of Israel. Smith's attitude toward civil rights remained consistent with his bigotry. He regarded blacks as inferior and claimed that those who refused to accept a dominant white society, such as Martin Luther King Jr., deceived their people into believing that they could achieve equality. Moral impropriety of any sort drew attacks by Smith, especially homosexuality and the sexual content of Hollywood films. Women who wore immodest clothing, such as miniskirts, and who advocated abortion felt the sting of his criticism. He vehemently disapproved of the use of tobacco, alcohol, and drugs. The number of groups and actions that Smith publicly condemned earned him the title of "preacher of hate."[22]

Defeated again in 1952, Smith continued to write tracts and literature and to plan for the next presidential campaign. In 1956 he ran again as the Christian Nationalist Party candidate against President Dwight D. Eisenhower, whom he referred to as a Swedish Jew. Still passionately anti-Communist and anti-Semitic, Smith emphasized his desire to maintain a society dominated by white Anglo-Saxon Protestants. He spoke out against the Supreme Court's decision in *Brown v. Board of Education*, often referring to the judicial branch as a "nine-headed tyrant" after the appointment of Chief Justice Earl Warren, when rulings against school prayer and in favor of pornography and civil rights threatened his core beliefs. To preserve American independence he continually resisted efforts to strengthen the United Nations and encouraged legislators to restrict immigration. Although he received the nomination, Smith's name did not appear on any of the state ballots since he either missed the filing deadline or failed to meet other requirements.[23]

During the 1960s, Smith continued to support a number of candidates, but each time his endorsements were spurned or his choice lost. In 1960, Nixon alienated Smith by commenting "that there was no place for Gerald Smith and his followers in the Republican Party." Smith hated President Kennedy even more since the former Massachusetts senator espoused liberal views on social and political issues. In 1964, Smith initially backed George Wallace and then Barry Goldwater as the Republican nominee against Lyndon B. Johnson, who had assumed the presidency upon Kennedy's assassination. In 1968 his passionate dislike of the Kennedys forced him into campaigning against the nomination of Robert Kennedy. After Nixon won the election, Smith gradually accepted the president's foreign policy as the most realistic course to follow. The Soviet Union and Communist China had developed into formidable countries, and the appropriate method of dealing with them was not confrontation but through trade and negotiation. Nixon never sought Smith's approval nor did he recognize Smith as an influencing factor during his presidency. Smith continually supported losers or individuals who rejected his endorsements since "he claimed to uphold principle, but his stance can be more accurately described as inflexible stubbornness. He never admitted that he could misjudge candidates and issues like other politicians and journalists." Smith pursued the presidency personally or through others "out of his own egotism and his neurosis, not because he could realistically appraise men and issues."[24]

Smith's popularity declined after the late 1940s for a number of reasons. The Jewish community realized that the most effective way of silencing him was to ignore him. Pressure placed on local newspapers, television, and radio stations restricted the amount of publicity given to Smith and his rallies. Protesters vanished, and the meetings were conducted with little fanfare. The less controversial that Smith appeared, the fewer the number of people who showed up. The strategy worked. In addition, television increased in popularity during the late 1950s and 1960s. Smith refused to adapt to the new technology and lost some of his audience as a result. During that same period his message grew stale. Times had changed, but Smith had not altered his message or his method.[25]

As Gerald Smith reached his sixty-fifth birthday, he reflected on his long career and contemplated a memorial suitable to leave the American people as his legacy. He toyed with the idea of erecting a traditional homestead site complete with log cabin but scuttled the idea when a genuine log house could not be purchased. In 1964 his business manager stumbled across an old Victorian home in the Ozarks called Penn Castle. The beautiful hand-carved, four-story stone structure contained fourteen rooms that Smith and his wife filled with antiques and keepsakes that they had collected during their travels. Situated in Eureka Springs, Arkansas, Penn Castle provided the Smiths with a quiet place to live in their retirement.[26]

Before long, Smith's boundless energy and continued need to promote a cause led the former minister to come full circle and once again devote his life to religious matters. Looking up from his home to the top of Magnetic Mountain, he envisioned a lasting shrine that would bear witness to his faith. He arranged for the purchase of the property, hired an architect, and raised the money for the construction of a seventy-foot-high statue called "the Christ of the Ozarks," which was dedicated on June 15, 1966. Within the next year, Smith added an amphitheater on the 167-acre complex where actors performed a Passion play depicting the last days of Christ for the edification of visiting pilgrims. In 1971, under the direction of the Smith Foundation, two additional structures, the Christ Only Art Gallery and the Bible Museum, completed the project.[27]

During his later years, Smith experienced health problems that ultimately led to his death. In 1971 a virus caused severe pain in his neck. Three years later a blockage in his left nostril restricted his breathing. That same year he endured a bad case of influenza. In April 1975 he contracted phlebitis, which affected his ability to walk. In the fall he and his wife flew to California where he had another bout of the flu that led to pneumonia. In a weakened condition, Smith drew his last breath on April 15, 1976, after suffering a heart attack.[28]

Gerald Smith dedicated his entire life to communicating his beliefs to others and to leaving his mark on American society. While he professed his Christian faith, he attacked those in opposition to him. His anti-Semitism and racial bigotry encouraged many Americans to resist change during the early civil rights movement. His anticommunism and anti-New Deal rhetoric fueled the movements of other demagogues such as Senator McCarthy, Father Coughlin, and Dr. Townsend. He declared his hatred of President Roosevelt because of his "socialist" policies and because FDR placed Jews in top positions within his administration.

While some historians argue that Smith's fundamentalist background had a direct bearing on his extremism, a closer look reveals that his hatred began to flourish after the assassination of Huey Long. Turning his back on the ministry, he justified his actions by attending to the needy masses through the Share Our Wealth Society. After his humanitarian efforts ended with Long's death, Smith failed to find another cause worthy enough to keep a sense of guilt from developing. Throughout the majority of his life he fought against the evils that he believed threatened Christianity and the United States while waging a spiritual battle internally. At the end of his life he focused on Christ once again and appeared more at peace. The passionate hatred seemed to have subsided within both Gerald L. K. Smith and American society.

Notes

1. Glen Jeansonne, *Gerald L. K. Smith: Minister of Hate* (New Haven, CT, 1988), 11–19; Elna M. Smith and Charles F. Robertson, eds., *Besieged Patriot: Autobiographical Episodes Exposing Communism, Traitorism, and Zionism from the Life of Gerald L. K. Smith* (Eureka Springs, AR, 1978), 4, 5, 37, 74, 96, 114, 225, 255, 258, 291; Leo P. Ribuffo, *The Old Christian Right: The Protestant Far Right from the Great Depression to the Cold War* (Philadelphia, 1983), 128–30.

2. Ribuffo, *Christian Right*, 130; Jeansonne, *Smith*, 16–21.

3. Jeansonne, *Smith*, 19–28; Smith and Robertson, *Patriot*, 144–45; Ribuffo, *Christian Right*, 133–35; *Boston Globe*, September 20, 1935; Harriett T. Kane, *Louisiana Hayride: The American Rehearsal for Dictatorship, 1928–1936* (Gretna, LA, 1971), 151; David H. Bennett, *Demagogues in the Depression: American Radicals and the Union Party, 1932–1936* (New Brunswick, NJ, 1969), 115.

4. Jeansonne, *Smith*, 19–28; Ribuffo, *Christian Right*, 133–35.

5. Jeansonne, *Smith*, 33–41; Ribuffo, *Christian Right*, 135–40; Smith and Robertson, *Patriot*, 225.

6. Ribuffo, *Christian Right*, 140–44; Jeansonne, *Smith*, 41–54; Kane, *Louisiana Hayride*, 154–55, 180–99.

7. Ribuffo, *Christian Right*, 144–47; Jeansonne, *Smith*, 46–51; *New York Times*, January 27, 1936; Arthur M. Schlesinger Jr., *The Politics of Upheaval* (Boston, 1950), 521–22; *Detroit Free Press*, February 5, 1936; Bennett, *Demagogues*, 138; Abraham Holtzman, *The Townsend Movement: A Political Study* (New York, 1963), 171–72.

8. Ribuffo, *Christian Right*, 144–47; Jeansonne, *Smith*, 46–51.

9. Jeansonne, *Smith*, 51–63; Schlesinger, *Politics of Upheaval*, 526–58, 607–27; Alan Brinkley, *Voices of Protest: Huey Long, Father Coughlin, and the Great Depression* (New York, 1982), 91–94.

10. Jeansonne, *Smith*, 65; Ribuffo, *Christian Right*, 147–48; Smith and Robertson, *Patriot*, 36.

11. Ribuffo, *Christian Right*, 156–57; Jeansonne, *Smith*, 66–90.

12. Jeansonne, *Smith*, 66–67; Ribuffo, *Christian Right*, 145–46; Smith and Robertson, *Patriot*, 74–75; *New York Times*, March 19, 1939.

13. Ribuffo, *Christian Right*, 148–49; Smith and Robertson, *Patriot*, 36, 59, 107–8, 136; Jeansonne, *Smith*, 67–69; *Detroit News*, November 2, 1937.

14. Jeansonne, *Smith*, 70–76; Smith and Robertson, *Patriot*, 26, 48, 160–62; Nathaniel Weyl, *The Jew in American Politics* (New Rochelle, NY, 1968), 103; Ribuffo, *Christian Right*, 149–57.

15. Ribuffo, *Christian Right*, 159–62; *Detroit News*, September 13, 1942; Smith and Robertson, *Patriot*, 153–54.

16. Jeansonne, *Smith*, 80–100; Ribuffo, *Christian Right*, 159–66.

17. Jeansonne, *Smith*, 152–59; Smith and Robertson, *Patriot*, 157–58; *New York Post*, June 26, 1944.

18. Jeansonne, *Smith*, 152–59.

19. Ibid., 90–100; Smith and Robertson, *Patriot*, 316.

20. Jeansonne, *Smith*, 98–100.

21. Ibid., 92–100, 157–59; Smith and Robertson, *Patriot*, 37.

22. Jeansonne, *Smith*, 101–14; Smith and Robertson, *Patriot*, 178; Ribuffo, *Christian Right*, 165–70.

23. Ribuffo, *Christian Right*, 165–77; Jeansonne, *Smith*, 115–29.

24. Smith and Robertson, *Patriot*, 92; Jeansonne, *Smith*, 165–70.

25. Jeansonne, *Smith*, 206–8.

26. Ibid., 188–89.

27. Ibid., 188–213; John R. Starr, "Gerald L. K. Smith: From Politics to Passion," *Tulsa Daily World*, November 7, 1971.

28. Jeansonne, *Smith*, 309.

Suggested Readings

Bennett, David H. *Demagogues in the Depression: American Radicals and the Union Party, 1932–1936.* New Brunswick, NJ, 1969.

Brinkley, Alan. *Voices of Protest: Huey Long, Father Coughlin, and the Great Depression.* New York, 1982.

Holtzman, Abraham. *The Townsend Movement: A Political Study.* New York, 1963.

Jeansonne, Glen. *Gerald L. K. Smith: Minister of Hate.* New Haven, CT, 1988.

Kane, Harriett T. *Louisiana Hayride: The American Rehearsal for Dictatorship, 1928–1936.* Gretna, LA, 1971.

Ribuffo, Leo P. *The Old Christian Right: The Protestant Far Right from the Great Depression to the Cold War.* Philadelphia, 1983.

Schlesinger, Arthur M., Jr. *The Age of Roosevelt*, vol. 3, *The Politics of Upheaval.* Boston, 1950.

Smith, Elna M., and Charles F. Robertson, eds. *Besieged Patriot: Autobiographical Episodes Exposing Communism, Traitorism, and Zionism from the Life of Gerald L. K. Smith.* Eureka Springs, AR, 1978.

Weyl, Nathaniel. *The Jew in American Politics.* New Rochelle, NY, 1968.

10

The Hara Family
The Story of a Nisei Couple

Thomas Hara

At the beginning of World War II, in one of the grimmest episodes in American history, Japanese Americans living on the West Coast were evicted from their homes and placed in internment camps in desolate areas. Given the hard feelings engendered by the Pearl Harbor attack, some isolated injustices against Japanese Americans might have been expected, although not condoned. Harder to explain was the stance taken by the U.S. government against some of its citizens solely because of their ancestral background. The order for the evacuation of Japanese Americans was signed by President Roosevelt, endorsed by Congress, and upheld by the Supreme Court. Many of them were allowed only forty-eight hours to dispose of their homes and belongings. Ultimately, 110,000 Japanese Americans, of whom two-thirds were U.S. citizens, were dispossessed; the government never filed charges against them.

Among those who suffered in the darkest single chapter of America's World War II record were members of the Hara family. Thomas Hara, a graduate of Austin Peay State University in Clarksville, Tennessee, persuaded his parents, Rose and Benji, to record their story. Thomas Hara served in the U.S. Army as both an enlisted man and an officer. After retiring from the army, he worked as a tactical adviser to the Royal Saudi Land Force and as a munitions disposal expert. He currently serves as the Fort Campbell Area Combined Federal Campaign Coordinator.

U ntil recently, one of the least publicized episodes in American history was the forced removal and detention of more than 110,000 Japanese American citizens who lived on the West Coast at the outbreak of World War II. This is not one of the greatest moments in the American past, and many who were victimized by that experience would not talk about their years as prisoners of their own government. Unfairly stigmatized by accusations of disloyalty by virtue of their physical appearance, they could not find the voice within themselves to tell others what they had experienced. For Rose and Benji Hara this silence

This essay originally appeared in Malcolm Muir Jr., ed., *The Human Tradition in the World War II Era* (Wilmington, DE: Scholarly Resources, 2001), 45–64.

lasted for more than forty years. This chapter is not, of course, a definitive history of the Japanese American internment. Taken from Rose and
Benji's written and spoken accounts, it presents in human, personal,
and ethical terms the experience of two American citizens.

The Japanese attack on the U.S. naval base at Pearl Harbor on December 7, 1941, triggered a series of events on the West Coast of the
United States that culminated in one of the most extraordinary epi-
sodes in the history of this country—the establishment of relocation
camps in America for the express purpose of interning American citizens. On February 17, 1942, President Franklin D. Roosevelt signed
Executive Order 9066, which made Japanese Americans on the West
Coast subject to military edict. Executive Order 9066 also appointed
Lt. Gen. John L. DeWitt commander of the relocation. Lieutenant
General DeWitt and California State Attorney General Earl Warren (later
Chief Justice of the U.S. Supreme Court) went on record as backing a
policy of mass exclusion. DeWitt stated: "The very fact that no sabotage has taken place to date is a disturbing and confirming indication
that such action will be taken."[1] Warren supported DeWitt's argument
before a congressional committee in February 1942, saying that to believe the absence of sabotage by the Japanese population was proof of
loyalty was "simply to live in a fool's paradise." Warren saw the absence
of sabotage to that point as an "ominous sign" that "the fifth column
activities that we are to get are timed just like Pearl Harbor was timed."[2]

DeWitt also testified before a congressional committee: "A Jap's a
Jap. They are a dangerous element. . . . There is no way to determine
their loyalty. . . . You can't change him by giving him a piece of paper."[3]
Thus, under the guise of military necessity, American citizens were herded
into relocation camps. Eugene V. Rostow described the situation: "One
hundred thousand persons were sent to concentration camps on a record
which wouldn't support a conviction for stealing a dog."[4]

Ten relocation camps were erected in remote areas in the country's
interior. These were not the death camps of Nazi Europe, but they were
characterized by barbed-wire fences, guard towers, searchlights, and
armed military guards. The relocation camps were specifically built to
imprison civilians, none of whom was ever charged with any crime.
Eventually, the camps housed men, women, children, infants, the elderly, and even the infirm.

Most of the incarcerated, some 77,000 out of 120,000, were U.S.
citizens, born and raised in this country.[5] These second-generation Japanese Americans were known as Nisei, a subset of whom were known as

Kibei: Nisei who had returned to Japan for schooling. Others were resident aliens, known as Issei. These people were first-generation immigrants who had come to the United States more than fifty years earlier. However, unlike their European counterparts, the Issei were denied the right to become naturalized citizens by federal immigration laws.

The government's exclusion policy was based on an incredible notion that this particular group of people, because of their ancestry, had to be regarded as inherently disloyal to the United States. They were presumed to be a racial nest of spies and saboteurs because of their physical appearance. They had no individual recourse at all.

The internment of the Japanese Americans was an episode unparalleled in the history of the United States. A group of American citizens and their alien parents became the victims of a racist policy that ignored all the protections of individual rights that are intrinsic to the principles of our constitutional government. However, in that time of national crisis, panic, emotion, greed, and political expediency prevailed, and the Constitution was grossly violated. All three branches of our government failed the trust and mission given to them by assuming a policy that included prejudice and racist overtones. The exclusion and internment of Japanese Americans during World War II was an injustice felt at the deepest personal level by those who experienced it, and it is only now that some of those who lived through those times have recovered and are strong and courageous enough to be silent no more.

Representative of the human costs of the relocation was the experience of approximately five hundred fishing families who lived and worked on Terminal Island in Los Angeles Harbor, near a navy installation. On February 14, 1942, by authority of the president and the attorney general, the navy posted signs on the island ordering the Japanese to evacuate by March 14. However, on February 25, only eleven days later, the navy posted a second notice that superseded the first, ordering the Japanese Americans to evacuate by February 27. That notice gave those on Terminal Island only forty-eight hours to leave their homes. The navy made no provision for heads of families already incarcerated or for bank accounts that were frozen. Church groups, particularly the Quakers, tried to get the navy to extend the deadline with no success.

The chaos that resulted is unimaginable. The scene on Terminal Island on February 26, 1942, the day before the deadline, was described as follows:

> The narrow streets between the little shacks were jammed with trucks and milling women and children. Secondhand dealers, "descending like wolves

to prey on the helpless," flocked in to take the things people could not carry with them. They were reported to be giving a nickel on the dollar. A Nisei volunteer wrote later, "The women cried awful. . . . Some of them smashed their stuff, broke it up, right before the buyers' eyes because they offered such ridiculous prices . . . the beautiful wedding tea sets, saved for better homes, lying smashed to pieces on the floors of cottages."[6]

Benji and Rose Hara were two residents of Terminal Island who were relocated. In 1985, while working on my undergraduate degree at Austin Peay State University in Clarksville, Tennessee, I persuaded my parents to record their experiences during World War II. What follows is in their own words.

Rose's Story

My name is Rose Hara. I was born Fusako Ikeda in the town of Fort Lupton, Colorado. My parents' family name was Ikeda. After both my parents died during the World War I flu epidemic, I was adopted by the Kawagishi family of Denver, Colorado, when I was an infant. My adopted parents owned a barbershop and pool hall.

As was the custom of many alien Japanese parents in those days, my stepsister and I, when I was seven, were sent to live with my grandparents in a small, provincial village in the southern part of the main island of Japan. After finishing grammar school, I attended a girls' school from which I graduated in 1935 and returned to the United States.

Two other sisters and two brothers were also sent to Japan after I was. They remained in Japan and married there. They did not return to the United States until after World War II. After I spent a short period [of time] in Denver, Colorado, I returned to California and lived on Terminal Island. I worked in the fish canneries until December 1941. On September 27, 1940, I married Benji Hara, who was a radio operator on a tuna boat.

After Pearl Harbor, Benji was held in the San Diego jail without charges for three weeks. When the Federal Bureau of Investigation (FBI) came to Terminal Island on February 25, 1942, we didn't know what to think. We were so young, we didn't realize what was going on. We were so confused and afraid. They took all the Issei and Kibei men away and put guards on the drawbridge so no one could leave or enter the island. My father was one of those who were taken. He was imprisoned in Bismarck, North Dakota (in a prisoner of war camp), for a year before he was moved to a relocation camp.

Some newspapers started saying we were spies and accused us of all sorts of ridiculous things. Then they started demanding that we all be moved away from the coast. In California, most of those accusations and demands were made by the Hearst newspapers. The navy arrived and tacked up the first evacuation poster. We were told the island had been condemned and we had thirty days to vacate. We packed up a few of our household goods and sent them to relatives in Colorado. We intended to follow, but then we began to hear that other people had been beaten up on the road and we were afraid to make the trip. Benji had been out of work for quite awhile too, so we really didn't have any money to travel that far and there wasn't anyplace else for us to go.

About two weeks before the day we were supposed to leave our home, the government issued a new evacuation notice that said we had to get off the island in two days. It was just terrible. People came over from the mainland in trucks, buying our things for little or nothing because they knew we had to get rid of them or leave them behind. They were buying stoves and sofas for $5 or $10. We could take only what we could carry in one duffel bag. We had no choice but to take what we could get, however pitiful it was. We didn't know what was going to happen to us. Many people ended up leaving most of their belongings behind to be looted. Some people, in frustration, smashed their things because they were offered such ridiculous prices. We lived in several places under restriction and curfew after leaving Terminal Island. One of those places was the basement of the Quaker church. We slept on cots they had set up for us.

In 1942 we were sent to an internment camp in Poston, Arizona. We traveled to Poston by train. The blinds were drawn over the train windows all the way to Arizona, so we couldn't see where we were going. There was a whole list of things we weren't allowed to take, like cameras, scissors, or a kitchen knife. Benji had his typewriter in the bottom of the duffel bag and they even took that away. The Quakers were able to find the typewriter, and later when it had been declassified as a security risk, they sent it to him.

Poston was a big concentration camp in the middle of the desert. There were rows after rows of army barracks and armed guards in towers. A tag— bearing our camp identification number—was tied to each person's coat. Each of us quickly memorized our number because it became like our name.

We were given mattress covers and told to fill them with straw. We shared a small barracks room that had no furniture with other people.

Army cots were provided for our straw-filled mattress covers. The showers, bathrooms, and mess halls were located far away from our barracks, which was really hard on some families, especially those with little children and the elderly.

The first summer was terrible. Dust storms would blow up out of nowhere. It was awful if you got caught in one because you couldn't see the next barracks. The sand would blow into the barracks through the cracks between the floorboards. At first, the barracks had double roofs, but eventually the top layer of shingles blew off during the dust storms.

Because it was so hot in the daytime, we would wet down the floorboards and the edges of the spreads that covered our cots. Then we would crawl under the cots and lie there until about 2 P.M. After that, it was so hot, it didn't matter where you were. Many of the old people, especially those from northern California, died during those first six months.

We organized ourselves into blocks and elected our own government. We had to organize because the federal government hadn't provided any educational facilities for the children. Benji took a job teaching algebra.

Every day in the winter the children filled lard buckets with charcoal that the old people had made from mesquite, which grew in the desert. The charcoal provided the only heat we had that first winter, and the cold in the winter was as bad as the heat in the summer. By the second winter, we had enough handmade adobe bricks to build a proper school building.

Poston was a horrible place when we arrived there, but we made it beautiful. We made furniture out of scraps of wood. We covered the walls with paintings and partitioned the barracks to give privacy to families. We planted Japanese gardens and built gateways and pools. By the next summer, with all the grass and plants, we found that the dust storms didn't come through as often.

On February 9, 1943, my first son, Lawrence, was born in Poston by caesarean section in the makeshift camp hospital. There was no doctor. In late 1943, Benji was allowed to leave camp to look for a job in the east. Because I was Kibei, I was blacklisted and more suspect, so I remained in camp with our son.

About a year later, I was able to join my husband, who had found a job in Long Island City, New York, as a radio engineer. The government paid my train fare only to Cleveland, Ohio; from Cleveland to New York City I paid my own way. In New York City, we lived in a "railroad flat," a common housing facility during the war. It had one bedroom and community kitchen and bath facilities. It was in the Columbia University area. When Columbia bought the apartment building for student housing, we moved to a two-bedroom apartment in the City College area. We lived there until we moved to Florida in 1971.

On June 25, 1951, our second son was born in New York City. Benji read a lot of American history in those days, so we named our son Thomas after Thomas Jefferson and Thomas Paine. Both our sons have college educations. Larry is a biochemist for General Foods Corporation and has a master's degree. Tom, a captain in the U.S. Army, is an Airborne, Ranger, and Special Forces soldier. In spite of everything that happened to us, my husband and I were able to make a good living, and our sons were able to get college educations, become good citizens, and contribute to our country.

I often wonder if students are taught of the wartime internment of Japanese Americans. Although time has passed, I still wonder why we were prisoners in our own country. We were American citizens by birth and upbringing. We committed no crime, and yet we were dislocated from our homes and livelihoods and were herded into relocation camps. I wonder if people know that our civil rights were violated.

Despite what has happened to us, I still think that America is a good country. Where else would we have been able to do so well?

Benji's Story

My name is Benji Hara. My father, an immigrant who arrived in this country in 1898, worked with maintenance gangs on the tracks of the Santa Fe Railroad in California. As was common among the early immigrants, a marriage was arranged for him. My mother, a "picture bride," came to the United States in 1914 to marry him. At the time of my birth in 1915 in San Diego, California, my father was employed as a house servant in the home of a bank president. Between the time of his arrival in the United States and his employment in San Diego, he had worked as a railroad gang member, strawberry farmer, and pool hall owner. He had managed to attend a language school and learned to speak, write, and read English. He was one of the few in his circle of friends that took advantage of this opportunity.

I was about three years old when my father decided to enter into the fishing business and moved to East San Pedro, a manmade island in Los Angeles Harbor. This fishing town later was named Terminal Island.

My father became a commercial fisherman when the industry was in its infancy. I remember seeing the bright blue arcs of the radio-telegraph transmitting station visible through an open door as we went by a fenced area of a World War I wireless station. Perhaps this fascinating sight and a story in a Horatio Alger book my father had given me, *Mark Mason's Victory, or the Story of a Telegraph Boy*, were subconscious influences in my becoming involved in radio and electronics as my profession.

My early education was obtained at the East San Pedro grammar school. In later years, there were several hundred children born of immigrant parents attending this school. Because most of these parents did not attend American schools, they were not well versed in the English language; therefore, the children became bilingual to some degree. My mother never learned to speak English and I never mastered the Japanese language, so communication with her was limited to everyday casual conversations pertaining to things in and around the home. My father did speak and write English, so communication with him was easier. He was the one who gave me spelling lessons so I excelled in that subject in grammar school.

When I graduated from high school in 1934, I was given a job as a crew member on my father's fishing boat. I remember the cold, miserable winter nights hauling the net for sardine. I decided fishing was not what I wanted to do for a living, and I quit the job after one year. I had made enough money to enroll in a technical school in Los Angeles to study radio engineering. In 1937, I graduated from technical school, but there were no engineering job opportunities for Orientals, so I took a job as a radio operator on a tuna clipper, maintaining Morse code communication between ships and shore stations. The tuna fishing grounds covered the offshore areas of Mexico, Central America, and down to the Galapagos Islands on the equator and as far west as 400 miles to the outlying islands and reefs in the Pacific Ocean. The tuna catch was sold by contract to the various canneries in San Diego and Los Angeles. I worked on three different tuna clippers between 1937 and December 1941. The last trip lasted ninety-one days and unfortunately, we arrived in San Diego the day after Pearl Harbor, December 8, 1941. Our boat crew consisted of resident alien Japanese and Japanese Americans born in the United States. When we heard the news on the radio, I anticipated that we would have some problems because of it, but I never dreamed of the hardships and indignities that we were to experience.

Upon our arrival at San Diego Harbor, sailors from a navy patrol boat boarded our tuna clipper. Several of the patrol crew carried submachine guns. Our boat was searched from stem to stern and one rifle and one shotgun, which we used for shooting sharks, and all kitchen knives and scissors used for mending nets were confiscated. Crew members were herded to the bow deck at the point of the machine guns. An armed guard was stationed in the engine room to watch the engineer. I was on the bridge with the fishing captain with another guard watching us. We were ordered to proceed to the cannery dock. Customs and immigration authorities boarded us there. We were told that everyone was to be taken to the Immigration Station to check on our status. I remained on the boat with the engineer until we could hire another engineer to take care of the refrigeration machine for the frozen tuna in the hold of the boat. All other crew members were taken away.

That evening, after we were able to hire an outside engineer, the boat's engineer and I started to pack our little ditty bag with toilet articles and a change of underwear since we thought it would be at least an overnight stay. The agent said, "Oh, you're going to be out right away and you won't need that," so we did not take them. The only thing I took was my adrenaline chloride vaporizer for inhalation to alleviate my asthmatic condition, which always troubled me when I returned from the warm southern climate to the cooler California weather. I thought we were going to the Immigration Station but when we got out of the car, we found ourselves in front of the county jail.

We entered and were put into a holding tank to await processing. After a mug shot and several sets of my fingerprints were taken, I was led through a door, told to pick up two blankets from a pile on the floor, and was led up two flights of open stairwell. It was about 10 P.M. by this time. On every landing, there was a large solid steel door, and never having been in a jail before, I wondered what a commercial refrigerator might be used for in a jail! I did not know that each of these doors was an entrance to cellblocks. Upon a signal from the guard who led me up the stairs, the electrically controlled door opened and a regular inmate trusty let me in. Thus, I was "thrown" into the third-floor cell block of the San Diego County Jail for being a citizen of Japanese ancestry. The floor of the cell was full of sleeping men. They were other alien Japanese and Japanese Americans possibly from other boats and the city of San Diego. After the first night of sleeping on the concrete floor, my asthmatic condition got worse and on the following day I had to convince the jail authorities to give me a bunk in one of the cells.

During the following weeks, other alien Japanese fishermen were brought into the cell block. None of my shipmates was in the same cell block, and the only person I knew was Captain Takahashi, a tuna boat skipper. Eventually, all the alien Japanese were removed from the jail and (we were to learn later) were taken to another facility in the Los Angeles area and subsequently sent to POW camps in Montana and North Dakota. During this incarceration period, we were not allowed to contact anyone on the outside. A series of questioning sessions began, and those of us remaining were called singly on certain days to report to the main downstairs office. During these sessions, which were conducted by the FBI, agents asked us questions pertaining to birthplace, schools attended, who we knew, and so on. After several of these sessions my records seemed to consist of written information several inches thick.

Daily life in the cell was very boring. Everyone was issued a tin cup and a tablespoon, which we carried hooked to our belts; if we laid them down, they were stolen and hammered into a souvenir. Meals consisted of four slices of bread and coffee for breakfast, no lunch, and supper consisting of, if I remember correctly, an entree, vegetable, and bread and coffee. Any money that we had when we were first brought into the jail was held in the office but later could be used to order cornflakes, sugar, and milk to supplement the furnished food. A radio and a hot plate were available in the cell block. Each of us saved two slices of our breakfast bread and with the sugar and milk we were able to order, we made a sort of porridge on the hot plate with an empty gallon can. We ate this porridge for lunch.

After I had spent three weeks in jail, my name was called on the public address system for what I thought was going to be another session of questioning by the FBI. When I got downstairs to the office, an FBI agent said, "You're okay, you can go." I asked if I was going to get any documents showing that I had been investigated and released. The agent replied, "No, we don't give out anything like that." He then asked if I had any way of getting back home. I replied that I could call my wife and have someone drive down to pick me up. The agent said that I had better do that because if I tried to take a bus or train, someone would try to turn me back in. So after three weeks of incarceration in the San Diego County Jail without any charges against me, I was released.

As I stepped out of the front entrance, a convoy of trucks filled with GIs passed by. When the GIs who saw me yelled, "There's a Jap!" I immediately scooted back into the jail building. After they had gone by,

I walked to our ship's broker about a mile away and called home. I walked back to the jail building and waited many hours for my wife, who hadn't seen me for 120 days, to come and get me.

I arrived home about three days before New Year's Day 1942 to find that my father-in-law had been taken away. He was eventually interned in a POW camp in North Dakota. No specific information regarding the status of aliens and citizens of Japanese ancestry was furnished to us; we only knew what was published in the newspapers. According to one report, California would be divided into a military and nonmilitary zone, and we would all have to move away from the coastal military zone. Another rumor was that we were to be relocated to detention camps. As we were nervously waiting for the next step, a mass raid was made on all the homes of Terminal Island in February 1942. The men were either FBI or deputized FBI agents and the homes were searched without warrants. During this raid, all components of my amateur radio station equipment were confiscated after they asked me what the components were. I was not given a receipt.

The next news we received was that we would be allowed to travel inland to relocate to other states. I decided we would go to Denver where my wife's relatives lived, so we shipped some clothing and bedroom articles there. Rumors of all kinds were floating around. When we heard that some people who had moved inland were getting beat up, we became afraid and canceled our trip to Denver, so we stayed on Terminal Island.

One night we were startled by the sound of heavy guns. We ran out and saw beams of searchlights scanning the skies while the guns were being fired from military bases in Long Beach and San Pedro. We did not see any target picked up by the searchlights, which were scanning haphazardly across the sky. The next day, the newspapers reported that an unidentified aircraft was flying over the area. The navy immediately announced that all persons of Japanese ancestry must leave their homes within forty-eight hours. We and other people who were sympathetic to our problem believed that the incident on the previous night had been staged to justify an immediate move.

At the time, we were living in a cottage rented from one of the canneries. My household consisted of my wife, my wife's sister, and my brother. The Quaker Society had established a hostel in Los Angeles for families that had nowhere else to go. We stayed at the hostel until President Roosevelt's Executive Order 9066 was issued on February 19, 1942. The order required that all persons of Japanese ancestry must report and register for evacuation to government internment camps, which we later learned had been built secretly in the early months of the war. People evacuated from Terminal Island were scheduled to be sent to a camp in Manzanar, California, in the desert. Having previously heard of the desert dust storms, I became apprehensive about how the climate would affect my asthma, so I requested to be sent to an internment camp in a nondesert area.

We were sent to Poston, Arizona. With one suitcase and a duffel bag per person, we were taken by railroad from Los Angeles through the Mojave Desert and into Parker Dam, Arizona. After a bus trip of five or ten miles south, we reached the internment camp of Poston I. Poston was the only camp that contained more than one section. Poston I, II, and III were each one mile apart. The three camps eventually housed 20,000 persons. My cousin was one of the early volunteers to go into this camp to make final preparations for receiving the thousands of internees. When we reached the camp, we were assigned to a room in one of the barracks and each of us was given a mattress cover, which we had to fill with straw to use as bedding. Army cots were provided for each person in the household group. We were assigned a room with another family, a widowed mother with two young daughters. My cousin was waiting for us. With a garden hose attached to the single faucet located at one end of each barracks, he hosed down all the sand and dust that had accumulated on the edges of each rafter and the floor. Water on the floor was no problem since the floorboards had quarter-inch gaps between each board, and the hot weather quickly dried out the boards.

After the dust and commotion and confusion of the first few days had subsided, we began to try to adjust to our new circumstances. We held block meetings during the first weeks to select a manager and volunteer cooks. One room in each barracks was assigned as the block manager's office where all complaints, requests, and other matters were handled. One barracks in each block contained the cooking facilities and the mess hall with tables and benches.

At many block meetings, complaints were aired about the food. Initially, the government published a list of daily menus, but the supplies required were not available to the cooks. Months afterward, it was discovered that the food supplies shipped into the camps were being pilfered by the Caucasian supply managers and sold to the outside black market. Later, many of the fresh vegetables we ate were grown in the camps by internee farmers who had come from the Imperial Valley and San Joaquin Valley. Our fish diet consisted of barrels of salted cod from the East Coast, which was an unfamiliar fish to West Coast Japanese and not too appetizing, especially when salted. Meat consisted mostly of frankfurters. For breakfast we had toast and apple butter. Although not always appetizing, the food was nourishing, if you ate it!

My next problem was how to make our living quarters more comfortable. The only furniture supplied were an army cot and the straw-filled mattress. We stored our clothing and bedding in the suitcase and duffel bag we had brought. The scrap lumber left over after the barracks were built became the source of wood for the construction of stools and benches for our rooms.

When summer came, the daytime temperature was over 100 degrees in the shade most of the time. Everyone began to build desert coolers, which consisted of a screen made with excelsior or woodshavings, as the outside part of a housing containing a large 16-inch fan blade and motor. The screen was kept moist by a water supply that dripped along the top edge of the screen. The internal fan pulled in the outside air through the wet screen and lowered the air temperature. Because there was no running water in the rooms, the water was held in a wooden box above the screen. The box was filled at regular intervals with buckets of water from the faucet located at one end of the barracks. In my younger days, I had watched my fisherman father build many wooden rowboats and skiffs; now this knowledge came in handy, for I had learned how to make leakproof wooden boxes for the desert coolers. The fan blade and motor were ordered from Denver through the mail from the Montgomery Ward catalog. That company must have had a booming business filling orders from the many camps located in the desert. The government provided an allowance of four dollars per month for clothing; and with the accumulation of several months of allotments, we purchased whatever became necessary.

Before we made the desert coolers, we tried to stay cool by wetting down the entire floor and the overhanging sides of the bedspread on our cots. Then we crawled under the cot. Any breeze that came up through the spaces in the wet floorboards and the open door and windows provided some cooling. But early in the afternoon, this technique did not work because the temperature was too high. Some people dug deep holes in the sandy ground under the crawl space of the barracks and tried to keep cool. A stop was put to this practice because of the possibility of cave-ins.

Because of the summer heat, the barracks in our camp were built with double roofs. The top roof was about one foot above the lower one with open air space in between. During dust storms, many of the top roofs were torn off by the wind, and repairs were delayed for weeks. An approaching dust storm could be seen before it hit camp, and whatever one was doing outside at the time was stopped and everyone ran for the shelter of the barracks. The dust and sand became so heavy during these storms that adjacent barracks became blotted from view. Then the dust came up through the gaps between the floorboards and covered everything in the room. Fortunately, these desert storms did not cause me to have asthma attacks. I may have overcome them and become cured by then. Cleaning up after every dust storm became a standard chore. To protect our clothing from these dust storms, we obtained portable closets from Montgomery Ward.

Seven thousand people now lived in Poston, and facilities and services for a town of this size became necessary: rubbish collection, road maintenance, building maintenance, teachers, and administrative office workers. The government wages for this work were from twelve dollars per month to sixteen dollars per month.

In Poston, accreditation for the school system that was established in camp was obtained from the California Board of Education. The volunteer teachers were mostly professionals who were interned. I was accepted as a volunteer teacher. I taught high school algebra and was an assistant teacher of electricity. Grammar school and high school classes began in the fall of 1942. One or two rooms in a barracks on certain blocks were allocated as classrooms. One school building was constructed entirely of adobe bricks handmade by a volunteer corps of workers.

We had no direct outside news except through newspapers, which were occasionally available in the sparsely stocked canteen. Radios were prohibited in camp. Because of my amateur radio interests and my commercial radio operator's experience, I was proficient in Morse code. Since some of my electrical students showed interest in ham radio, I started a class in Morse code. The audio tone oscillator was made from salvaged pieces of a broken car radio. The first day of class caused quite a commotion because the sound of Morse code coming out of the speaker carried across the firebreak to the administration building. Soon a Jeep carrying the camp manager and two armed MPs came racing to the classroom wanting to know what I was doing. I explained the activity and assured them that it was not an actual on-the-air radio transmission. They were satisfied with my explanation, and my students and I had great fun during subsequent classes.

In my plans to be "marketable" when I was released, I obtained civil service ratings as a radio instructor in the Air Corps and a radio instructor in the Signal Corps. But as soon as those services found that I was an internee, I could not get an appointment.

Sometime during 1943 the government announced plans for relocating internees from the camps to the Midwest or the East Coast. I decided to try to get work in the field of my interest: radio. I made inquiries to the War Relocation Authority (WRA) office in Philadelphia. I knew that Philco was in Philadelphia and RCA was in nearby Camden, New Jersey, so I applied for relocation just for myself. My plan was to have my wife and first son, who had been born in the camp, follow me later. My request was approved and I was given tickets to Philadelphia and fifty dollars in cash. At this point, I did not have any savings and all my possessions were in household furniture, most of which we had lost prior to internment. So on the day after Columbus Day, October 13, 1943, I "set sail" out into the world.

The relocation group consisted of one trainload of Japanese Americans, most of whom were going to either Chicago or New York. I was the only one going to Philadelphia. When I arrived in Philadelphia, I reported to the WRA office. Many families that were sympathetic to our plight offered temporary housing to relocated internees. I became a guest with a family in the Chestnut Hill area in north Philadelphia.

When I started to look for a job, I found that it was impossible to get work in electronics because the entire industry was engaged in classified wartime production. A couple of weeks later, I was offered a temporary three-hour-per-day job as gardener in the western suburbs of Philadelphia in Wallingford, near Swarthmore College. I was given room and board in exchange for my work. The owner of the house was a member of the Quaker Society and he was in charge of the establishment of the hostel for the relocatees around the country.

After finishing my chores every day, I rode the suburban train into the city seeking work without success. In the evenings, to pass the time, I attended lectures given by visiting professors at Swarthmore College. Eventually, I decided to move back to the city and rented a room in a home owned by a Quaker family close to Temple University. They were most gracious and kind.

After trying practically every electrical and electronic plant, including broadcast stations, without success, I finally found a warehouse job with the Nicholson File Company, which made all kinds of files from fingernail files to large 18-inch machine files. I was given the job of packing prepackaged files into wooden crates, and later I replaced the shipping clerk when he was drafted. After a couple of weeks they offered to train me to do office work but I thanked them and declined. I was planning to return to the internment camp and try to relocate in the Chicago area, this time with my family.

In March 1944 I decided that since I was so close to New York, I would see the city before going back to Arizona. On the day of my visit to New York City, I reported to the WRA office and was told that an electronics company, Radio Engineering Labs (REL), in Long Island City was looking for workers. I went to the plant and was immediately given a job. The president of the company sent me to a building where they were manufacturing LORAN systems, which were classified secret at the time. The engineer in charge asked me if I had a navy clearance. Of course, it was not possible for me to get such a clearance. I returned to the main plant and was assigned to test unclassified equipment made for the Signal Corps. I tested the units on a go/no-go basis per test procedure but was not allowed to see any schematic diagrams. After a week or so, the foreman decided I was trustworthy, and he gave me the schematics for the modules I was testing. Having the schematic made it possible for me to make repairs on defective units on the test line rather than sending them to the repair department. Later I was promoted to final inspector of overall equipment. When the production of this Signal Corps equipment was completed, I worked as a technician on portable backpack radio equipment made for the Marine Corps.

About four months after I started at REL, my wife received permission to join me with our son. Because my wife was a Kibei (a U.S. citizen educated in Japan), the government funded transportation only from Arizona to Cleveland, Ohio. I had to pay the transportation from there to New York City. By this time, my draft status had changed from 4-F to 1-A; during the internment, we were disfranchised citizens. Now my employer at REL said that I could apply for draft exemption because I was in a war industry. How ironic!

When the war ended, I was promoted to a position in the lab and my practical education in FM technology began. I participated in the design of the first postwar commercial FM receiver, early FM broadcast, and point-to-point transmitter links. I also designed some modulator equipment and installed the first experimental FM stereo transmitter in New York City. Later I became a specialty designer for all the FM Tropospheric Scatter system radios produced by REL. Equipment was furnished by REL to a chain of stations starting in the Aleutians, across Alaska, the Canadian Arctic Circle to Greenland, and then to Iceland and England. The chain of stations continued through Spain, Italy, and Greece and terminated in Turkey. This was a U.S. Air Force and NATO communication system. By this time the company was sold and became a part of a holding company, Dynamics Corporation of America. I worked for REL for twenty-seven years in New York and moved with the company to Florida in 1971 when Dynamics decided to combine REL and another division in Florida. I retired from REL in April 1985, after forty-one years of employment. I still do some consulting work for the company.

My life has not been a Horatio Alger rag-to-riches story but I have been fortunate to have made a living in the profession of my choice. My sons have grown to become good citizens who contribute their talents to industry and our country. I hope their lives will become even better in the years to come.

I have been a member of the U.S. Power Squadron and have contributed whatever I could as an instructor. Since 1971 I have been a member of the U.S. Coast Guard Auxiliary and have held both elected and appointed offices in the Delray Beach–Boynton Beach Flotilla. My contribution includes serving as instructor in the Public Education Safe Boating Courses.

Regarding the evacuation and internment of Japanese Americans, legal scholars, organizations, churches, newspapers, and many other groups have expressed their opinions on the gross violations of our constitutional rights and the injustices we suffered. These findings have been recorded in volumes of publications of all kinds. The congressional committee formed to study the evacuation and internment has recommended compensation on a per-person basis and a governmental public apology. A majority of the members of Congress and the administration have not yet supported the redress bills reintroduced each year. The committee report recommends compensation to all living former internees. A large percentage of the internees are now deceased, and if each succeeding Congress delays long enough, we shall all be dead and payments will not be made. As for me, I am waiting for a public apology from my government, which may never come.

In spite of everything that happened to us, I was able to make a good living and provide for a college education for both of my sons. I'm grateful to my country for that opportunity. Heck, I've even forgotten my tag number.

Postscript

In 1992, Benji and Rose Hara received the following note:

> The White House
> Washington, D.C.
>
> A monetary sum and words cannot restore lost years or erase painful memories; neither can they fully convey our Nation's resolve to rectify injustice and to uphold the rights of individuals. We can never fully right the wrongs of the past. But we can take a clear stand for justice and recognize that serious injustices were done to Japanese Americans during World War II.
>
> In enacting a law calling for restitution and offering a sincere apology, your fellow Americans have, in a very real sense, renewed their traditional commitment to the ideals of freedom, equality, and justice. You and your family have our best wishes for the future.
>
> Sincerely,
> s/George Bush
> President of the United States
> October 1990

This letter came with the Haras' $20,000 restitution payments. Their payments went into a trust fund for their grandchildren. Their older son, Lawrence, received the same note and his payment in 1993. (Reparations were issued to internees according to age, which accounts for the time lapse.)

Benji Hara was seventy-nine years old when he died on December 24, 1994. At the time of Benji's death, Lawrence was a biochemist for General Foods Corporation. I was preparing to retire from the U.S. Army after twenty years of service. Both of us had master's degrees and were married. Lawrence has two sons who knew Benji as Grandpa.

Benji served more than twenty years in the Coast Guard Auxiliary during his retirement. In the auxiliary, he showed his love of the sea by donating not only his time but also his experience in electronics. The Coast Guard Auxiliary buried Benji's ashes at sea, where he "set sail" again into the world. In 1995 the Boynton Beach, Florida, Coast Guard Auxiliary radio room was named in his memory.

Rose Hara lives in Florida but is preparing to move back to California to be with her sisters. She is grandmother to Lawrence's two sons and daughter. Rose Hara still has Benji's Horatio Alger book.

Notes

1. John Tateishi, *And Justice for All* (New York: Random House, 1984), xv.

2. Ibid., xv–xvi; Bill Hosokawa, *Nisei: The Quiet Americans* (New York: William Morrow, 1969), 288–89.

3. Hosokawa, *Nisei*, 260.

4. Michi Weglyn, *Years of Infamy* (New York: William Morrow, 1976), 53.

5. Tateishi, *And Justice for All*, xiii. Although 110,000 people were involved in the West Coast evacuation, 120,000 ethnic Japanese eventually came under the War Relocation Authority's custody. This number included 1,275 institutionalized individuals transferred to the centers; 1,118 citizens and aliens evacuated from Hawaii; 219 voluntary residents; and 5,981 who were born in the camps. WRA Statistic Section.

6. Audrie Girdner and Anne Loftis, *The Great Betrayal* (New York: Macmillan, 1969), 101. After the war my parents received some reparation for all their possessions lost or taken during relocation. They settled for ten cents on the dollar, which was about all that any of the internees got.

Suggested Readings

Bosworth, Allan R. *America's Concentration Camps*. New York, 1968.

Brimmer, Larry D. *Voices from the Camps: Japanese Americans during World War II*. Danbury, CT, 1994.

Crost, Lyn. *Honor by Fire: Japanese Americans at War in Europe and the Pacific*. Novato, CA, 1996.

Daniels, Roger. *Concentration Camps: North American Japanese in the United States and Canada during World War II*. Melbourne, FL, 1993.

Grodzins, Morton. *Americans Betrayed: Politics and the Japanese Evacuation*. Chicago, 1949.

Hosokawa, Bill. *Nisei: The Quiet Americans*. New York, 1969.

Sone, Monica. *Nisei Daughter*. Boston, 1953.

Weglyn, Michi. *Years of Infamy*. New York, 1976.

11

Daisy Bates
The Struggle for Racial Equality

David L. Anderson

Daisy Bates was a journalist and president of the Arkansas State Conference of the National Association for the Advancement of Colored People when she was thrust into the center of one of the pivotal events of the civil rights revolution. She became a symbol of black hope and a target of segregationist hatred as a mentor to the first black students to integrate Little Rock's all-white Central High School, an action that required President Dwight Eisenhower to order U.S. Army troops to escort the students to class. From her living room, she advised the nine black teenagers before and after school on how to face the taunting mobs. Ernest Green, one of the students, who later became an investment banker, has said that Bates is on the same plateau of civil rights leaders with Martin Luther King Jr., Sojourner Truth, and Frederick Douglass. Her story illustrates the worst and best of America in the twentieth century. She personally experienced some of the most extreme forms of racism, yet she also was an example of the personal courage and collective conviction of the civil rights movement that upheld some of America's most cherished principles of freedom and equality.

A professor of history, David L. Anderson is dean of the College of Arts and Sciences at the University of Indianapolis in Indiana. He received the Ph.D. degree from the University of Virginia, Charlottesville. His books on America since 1945 include *The Human Tradition in the Vietnam Era* (2000) and *The Columbia Guide to the Vietnam War* (2002).

On the evening of August 22, 1957, Daisy Bates had just come in from walking her dog, Skippy, and was reading the newspaper when a rock came crashing through the picture window of her house in Little Rock, Arkansas. Tied to the missile was a scrawled note: "STONE THIS TIME. DYNAMITE NEXT."[1] The circumstances that made her a target of death threats and segregationists' hatred were a combination of the remarkable fortitude of this woman, the racially divided culture

This essay also appears in David L. Anderson, ed., *The Human Tradition in America since 1945* (Wilmington, DE: Scholarly Resources, 2003), 151–69.

of America in the 1950s, and some dramatically changing constitutional guarantees of civil rights protection. The life of Daisy Bates illustrates the courage and persistence of thousands of African Americans who, through their efforts and sacrifices, helped produce the profound transformation in race relations that occurred in the 1950s and 1960s. Along the way of her personal journey from victim of discrimination to respected community leader, she played a pivotal role in one of the most decisive moments in the civil rights revolution—the use of the U.S. Army to prevent violent white resistance to the integration of Little Rock's Central High School in September 1957.

Daisy Lee Gatson was born on November 11, 1914, in Huttig, Arkansas, a tiny company-owned sawmill town deep in the woods near the Louisiana state line. As was typical of the region, the little village was clearly segregated with a "Negra Town" of weather-beaten houses, two poorly maintained church buildings, and a badly equipped two-room school, and a "White Town" of painted homes, steepled churches, and a spacious school. Daisy's parents protected her from the harsh realities of discrimination until she was about seven, but from encounters with white shopkeepers she began to learn a hard lesson that blacks had no rights that whites were bound to respect. At age eight, she learned another terrible fact from her older cousin. Her loving parents, in fact, were not her birth parents. When she was a baby, her biological mother had been murdered by a drunken white man while resisting his sexual assault, and her father had been forced to leave Huttig immediately afterward rather than press charges. He left Daisy in the care of the couple whom she had always known as her parents. There was no arrest of the suspected murderer.

As a child growing up, Daisy harbored bitterness toward white people because of what had happened to her mother and because of the frustration she saw in her strong and proud adoptive parents. She anguished over the humiliations they endured. When she was a teenager, her father became gravely ill. As he lay dying, he counseled Daisy on how to direct the hatred she felt. He instructed her not to hate white people but instead to hate their insults and discrimination and to focus her anger on doing something to change it. She took his advice to heart.

Not long after her father's death, Daisy married L. C. Bates. He was thirteen years older than Daisy and had been a good friend to her father and to the whole family. She first met him when she was fifteen and he had come to their house to sell her father an insurance policy. Born in Mississippi, L. C. was educated at Alcorn A & M College and then at

Wilberforce College in Ohio. He had worked for newspapers in the West and South for a few years before turning to selling insurance to make a living during the Great Depression. After their marriage, he and Daisy settled in Little Rock. Although L. C. had success in the insurance business, his true desire was to run his own newspaper. He yearned for the independence of being his own boss, and he and Daisy shared a common passion "to carry on the fight for Negro rights."[2] They invested their savings in the lease of an old printing plant and established the *Arkansas State Press*. The first issue of this weekly appeared on May 9, 1941, and it was destined to become the most influential black-owned newspaper in the state.

The newspaper was a great financial risk for L. C. and Daisy. Their hard-hitting stories—about police brutality against blacks, the shameful treatment of black soldiers and of black veterans returning from service in World War II, slum housing conditions, and the prejudiced judicial system—made it difficult, if not impossible, to sell advertising to the principal businesses in Little Rock. The paper's crusading style, however, attracted a large readership that many advertisers, especially small businesses that served the African American community, could not ignore. Circulation reached 20,000, and revenues enabled the Bateses to purchase a new and modern newspaper plant. Daisy took courses at Shorter College and Philander Smith College to help develop her skills as a journalist, and she wrote some of the paper's most critical reports of local discrimination. One of her stories that sharply criticized a powerful judge briefly placed Daisy and L. C. in jail for contempt of court, a judgment overturned by the state supreme court.

Daisy and L. C. were members of the Little Rock chapter of the National Association for the Advancement of Colored People (NAACP) from the time they arrived in the city. Formally organized in 1910, the NAACP was the leading civil rights organization in the country. Although it operated primarily through local chapters, its national strategy was to find ways to promote the idea of federal responsibility for racial justice in America. Absolutely essential to this approach was to seek a reversal of the doctrine of "separate but equal" that had been declared by the U.S. Supreme Court in the 1896 case of *Plessy v. Ferguson*. This judicial standard was the legal defense for state and local ordinances that segregated the races in schools, public transportation and accommodations, and almost every aspect of public life. Using the Roosevelt administration's New Deal rhetoric of equal opportunity rather than integration, NAACP lawyers made some headway in the 1930s and 1940s in breaking racial barriers in graduate and law schools. The end of World War II, however, opened the door for a direct legal assault on *Plessy*. The public's horror at revelations of the Nazis' barbarity toward racial minorities together with postwar prosperity that eased working-class job fears and black veterans who expected and sometimes demanded acknowledgment of their patriotic service combined to make discrimination less tolerable.

Through their participation in the NAACP and in the pages of the *Arkansas State Press*, Daisy and L. C. endorsed the legal challenges to segregation, and they became civil rights leaders in Arkansas. Their paper backed candidates for governor who challenged segregationist politicians, and in 1952 they supported former governor Francis Cherry, who defeated Orval Faubus. Also in 1952, Daisy was serving as co-chair of the NAACP State Conference's Committee for Fair Employment Practices when she was invited to run for president of the Arkansas State Conference. She was elected without opposition. Although the NAACP was a national organization that could provide legal assistance to local efforts, it was in many respects grassroots in nature. In Little Rock there were only a few hundred members and most were inactive. For practical purposes, the NAACP in the city was only the local executive committee composed of the Bateses, three black attorneys, a couple of other African Americans, and two white faculty members from Philander Smith College. Much of the work to advance civil rights in Little Rock, therefore, fell directly on the shoulders of Daisy Bates.

As Daisy assumed the leadership of the Arkansas State Conference, the NAACP's direct assault on *Plessy* had reached the U.S. Supreme Court. Coordinated by attorney Thurgood Marshall, the NAACP brought five cases to the high court in which African American parents were suing segregated public school systems to admit their children to currently all-white schools. The specific grounds of these suits was that separate schools were not equal and denied black students the equal protection of the law guaranteed by the Constitution. Collectively, these cases were known by their shortened title, *Brown v. Board of Education*. On May 17, 1954, speaking for a unanimous court, Chief Justice Earl Warren unequivocally declared segregated public schools to be unconstitutional. In plain language he explained: "We conclude that in the field of public education the doctrine of 'separate but equal' has no place. Separate educational facilities are inherently unequal."[3] Having stated the constitutional principle, the Court did not address the complex process of integration, and in a subsequent decision on May 31, 1955, it remanded the cases to the federal district courts with the vague instruction to implement integration "with all deliberate speed."[4]

In a pattern that would occur repeatedly in the civil rights struggles in many states over the next decade, the Negro citizens of Arkansas responded to these momentous rulings with calls for immediate integration, but many white politicians and racists openly defied the law and demanded that they wait. Although Governor Cherry said after the *Brown* decision that "Arkansas would obey the law," his opponent for governor in 1954, Orval Faubus, took a position widely held by white voters. Faubus declared, "It is evident to me that Arkansas is not ready for a complete and sudden mixing of the races in the public schools and that any attempt to solve this problem by pressure or mandatory methods will jeopardize, in many communities, the good relations which exist between whites and Negroes."[5] Faubus was clearly exploiting racial prejudice to help his election effort, and his ploy succeeded, for he defeated Cherry and took office in January 1955.

Civil rights activists such as Daisy Bates hoped that the federal government would step in to enforce its courts' rulings, but President Dwight Eisenhower maintained a careful silence on the *Brown* decision. He declined to endorse it publicly, and privately he told staff members that "it's all very well to talk about school integration, . . . [but] the fellow who tries to tell me that you can do these things by *force* is just plain *nuts*."[6] In the view of the sole African American on Eisenhower's White House staff, E. Frederick Morrow, the president and his closest aides did not understand "how deeply aggrieved black Americans felt."[7]

With no real pressure from federal or state officials, most school boards in Arkansas made little or no movement to implement the Supreme Court guidelines. Virgil T. Blossom, the superintendent of the Little Rock schools, talked for two years about a gradual plan for integration in the city's schools starting with the higher grades, possibly in 1957. After months of such talk, African American parents concluded that Blossom was stalling and asked Bates and the State Conference to seek a court order to mandate immediate integration in all grades. The suit was filed in the spring of 1956. The Eighth Circuit Court of Appeals upheld the district court's ruling that Blossom's gradual plan was a good-faith effort and could be followed, but it also made clear that the school district was under federal court order to begin the plan in September 1957.

In August 1957 racial tension escalated dramatically in anticipation of the start of the school year. Although definitely a segregated city, Little Rock had more of a reputation for racial harmony than some other cities in the old Confederacy. During that summer, however, the Ku Klux Klan, the White Citizens Council, and various other local and outside segregationist firebrands boldly denounced the planned integration of Central High School and openly called for violent mob action if necessary to prevent it. It was after a rally filled with hate speeches that the first rock had sailed through the Bateses' window on August 22.

Daisy had one courteous but fruitless meeting with Faubus before that incident to try to persuade him to curtail the extremists, but the governor had allowed the hateful rhetoric to continue. In fact, when a white parent filed suit in the local court to stop the integration plan because allegedly there would be armed gangs of both races in the school, Faubus testified in support of the suit. The local judge issued the requested order to block integration on August 29, and the gleeful segregationist drove past the Bates home that evening shouting, "Daisy! Daisy! Did you hear the news? The coons won't be going to Central!"[8] The next day, however, a local NAACP attorney and Thurgood Marshall appeared before Judge Ronald N. Davies, who was on temporary assignment from North Dakota to the federal district court, and obtained an order overruling the local court and mandating immediate implementation of the integration plan. With school scheduled to start on September 3, the battle lines were about to shift from the courts to Central High School.

Headed into the front lines of that battle were nine African American teenagers—Carlotta Walls, Jefferson Thomas, Elizabeth Eckford, Thelma Mothershed, Melba Pattillo, Ernest Green, Terrance Roberts, Gloria Ray, and Minnijean Brown—who had been carefully selected by the school authorities out of an original group of eighty. They all had good records in the segregated school system, and they and their parents had agreed to be the vanguard in what was known as the Blossom Plan for integration. They soon became known as the Little Rock Nine, but as school began they and their families had no internal organization of their own. They looked to and came to rely entirely upon Daisy Bates for leadership, mentoring, counseling, and support through the difficult weeks ahead.

As the nine young people and their families prepared themselves on the evening of September 2 for the opening day of a new era, Faubus shocked them, the city, and the nation by surrounding Central High

School with troops from the Arkansas National Guard. In a broadcast address, the governor declared that his purpose was to keep order against mob violence, but it was also clear that the guard had orders to prevent the African American students from entering the school and thus to block the court-ordered integration. The pro-segregation extremists who had vowed to do whatever it took to prevent black and white students from attending classes together had received exactly what they wanted from the state's chief executive.

The nine students did not attempt to go to the school on September 3. In part, Faubus's move confused the legal issues, and also some of their frightened parents interpreted the governor's speech—including a line that predicted that "blood will run in the streets"—as a reminder of the lynchings of blacks in Little Rock back in the 1920s. NAACP attorneys met with Judge Davies, and Bates and the parents met with Superintendent Blossom. In both meetings the integration plan was reaffirmed and assurances were given that the nine young people would be protected. Daisy remained very concerned about the danger, however, and sent out a request for local ministers to escort the black pupils into the high school the next morning. She also arranged for a time and place for the students to meet to go in together, although she was unable to reach Elizabeth Eckford's family because they did not have a phone. Exhausted, she fell asleep about 3:00 A.M. and was at the prearranged meeting place at 8:15. When she got there, she remembered that she had never notified Elizabeth of the plan.

The morning of September 4 was filled with tension. Two white and two black ministers attempted to cross the National Guard line with the students, but the students and their escorts were turned away. Daisy and L. C. then drove the children to Blossom's office, but he was out. They next went to the office of the U.S. Attorney, who had the FBI take a statement but who took no other action. It was clear to Daisy that neither the State of Arkansas nor the U.S. Department of Justice was going to take any action to implement the integration plan in the face of the public opposition against it.

While Daisy and eight of the students were finding that the political system was determined to resist and not to enforce the court-ordered integration, 15-year-old Elizabeth Eckford was facing alone a mob of over 500 ranting segregationists outside Central High School. She had gotten up early that morning and pressed the new dress she had made for school. Her family heard news reports of a large crowd at the high school, but with the trust of youth she reassured her parents that the National Guard would protect her. She got off a city bus and walked a block to the front entrance of the towering school building. With the angry, jeering protestors behind her, she faced the guardsmen lined up shoulder to shoulder. Still believing they were there to look out for her, she tried to squeeze between them to enter the school. Instead, the soldiers blocked her path with their bayoneted rifles and glared menacingly at her.

Suddenly aware of her predicament, Elizabeth was gripped by fear and retreated to the bus stop with the unruly crowd following her. She made it to the bench at the bus stop and sat there in tears while the mob continued to yell, "Lynch her! Lynch her!" "No nigger bitch is going to get in our school. Get out of here!" "Drag her over to this tree! Let's take care of the nigger." Benjamin Fine, the education editor of the *New York Times* who was there to cover the story, and Grace Lorch, the wife of a Philander Smith faculty member, stayed with Elizabeth until the bus arrived. They encouraged her to keep her head up and not to let the mob see her cry. These two compassionate white people also became targets of invectives. To them, Mrs. Lorch was "another nigger-lover" and Dr. Fine was "a dirty New York Jew."[9] The guardsmen did nothing to protect the three and, at one point, even threatened to arrest Fine for inciting a riot. News photographs of the hate-filled faces screaming at the little girl, wearing her new dress and clutching her school-books, appeared in papers across the country. She became a heroic symbol, but Daisy anguished over the trauma Elizabeth had suffered. She was able to regain Elizabeth's trust only gradually over time.

As Virgil Blossom later wrote, the school year had opened with "the triumph of mob rule, abetted by the Arkansas National Guard under orders of Governor Faubus."[10] Local officials such as Superintendent Blossom and Mayor Woodrow Mann deeply resented the loss of control of their own streets to the protestors, many of whom had poured into the city from elsewhere in Arkansas and the South. These city leaders also deplored the damage being done to Little Rock's reputation as a community of racial harmony by the governor's opportunistic racism that was encouraging the hoodlum extremists. The guardsmen in battle dress continued to surround Central High School to seal it off from nine children while the segregationist crowds outside daily celebrated their victory by singing renditions of "Dixie" and waving the Confederate flag. For the time being, Daisy Bates and the parents kept the nine students away from the school while the scene shifted to the federal courts and the Eisenhower administration.

The NAACP attorneys had no difficulty in getting orders from Judge Davies rejecting all requests for delays of the integration plan. The angry judge also directed the FBI to begin an investigation of all persons, including the governor, who were interfering with the court's previous directives, and he set a hearing for September 20 at which the governor and the National Guard's commanders would be required to show why they should not be found in contempt of court. Despite the outrageous behavior of the mob, Faubus made the incredible rejoinder that it was Judge Davies who was taking an "extreme stand," and the governor sought a personal meeting with Eisenhower to seek approval of his claim that he intended only to exercise his state power to maintain order.[11] It was his contention that the nine children and NAACP leaders such as Daisy Bates were the threat to public safety, not the hate-mongering mob. In view of the Eisenhower administration's previous hands-off approach to federal enforcement of the *Brown* decision, Faubus's effort to turn to Eisenhower for sanction had its own logic.

On September 14 the governor traveled to Newport, Rhode Island, where the president was on a golfing vacation. The two leaders met privately for about fifteen minutes and then were joined, for a longer discussion, by Congressman Brooks Hays of Arkansas, U.S. Attorney General Herbert Brownell, and White House Press Secretary James Hagerty. Personally, Eisenhower was sympathetic to the idea of not pressuring white southerners to move quickly to accept school integration, but he also held the firm conviction that he, as president, was duty bound to enforce the U.S. Constitution as interpreted by the U.S. Supreme Court. When the meeting ended, Eisenhower believed that he had Faubus's agreement to change the National Guard's orders to keep the peace while the nine students began attending classes at Central High School. This outcome would not challenge the governor's authority to deploy the guard, but it would preserve the Court-approved gradual integration plan. Upon his return to Little Rock, however, Faubus did not change the orders. On Friday, September 20, his lawyers walked out of the contempt hearing in federal court, and Judge Davies proceeded with his threatened action. He issued an injunction prohibiting the governor from any further interference with the integration plan. That evening, in a broadcasted speech, Faubus announced that he was complying with the injunction by withdrawing the National Guard from the school grounds. He then departed the city for a governors' conference, leaving Daisy Bates and the local police to find a way to get the nine children past the mob and into the school safely.

On Monday, September 23, the potential for violence changed into terrible reality. At 8:00 A.M. the Little Rock Nine arrived at the Bates home with their parents. Also at the house were white and African American journalists from the national, regional, and local press. Coordinating their plans with Assistant Chief of Police Gene Smith, Daisy and NAACP field secretary Frank Smith left about 8:30 in two cars that were carrying the children by an indirect route to the campus. The reporters left separately at the same time. When the students' automobiles arrived at a side entrance to Central High School, the out-of-control crowd of over 1,000 segregationists was rushing toward the front of the building. The nine ran for the side door and entered just as someone in the throng screamed, "They're in! The niggers are in!"[12] The raging mass then tried to converge on Daisy and her companions, but they were able to get in the cars and speed away. Despite news flashes that the children were being attacked outside the school, Daisy reassured the parents that they had made it safely inside.

The diversion of the mob that had enabled the nine students to enter the side door and the reports of attacks outside the school were the results of the arrival at the front door of five black journalists who had driven from Daisy's house. They got out of their car about five minutes before Daisy brought the pupils. With cries of "Here they come!" and "Get the niggers!" the horde pounced on the reporters and began beating and kicking them.[13] They were on the verge of being gravely injured or worse when the scream of "They're in!" sent the mob to the side, where Daisy and the others were getting back into their cars. Now aware that the black students were, in fact, inside Central High School, the enraged throng began to advance on the police officers guarding the doors. Knowing that his small force could not stop the mob if it rushed them, Chief Smith escorted the nine out of the building through a service entrance and delivered them safely to their homes in police cars. Frustrated by the escape of their targets, some of the protestors assaulted the *Life* magazine photographers and reporters on the scene. There were also random acts of violence during the day against a few black men and women on the streets of Little Rock.

Daisy and L. C. Bates did not sleep that night. A city police car remained outside their house, and cars were also posted at the homes of each of the nine students. L. C., a neighbor who was a dentist, and a fellow black journalist sat through the night in the Bateses' living room with loaded shotguns. During the night, the police intercepted a caravan of about 100 cars, carrying dynamite, guns, clubs, and other weapons, headed toward the Bateses' home. The houses of some other black families in the city were targets of rock throwing and harassment. As long as this reign of terror continued, Daisy and the parents had no intention of sending the children back to the school. Their caution was well placed because the next morning again brought the chanting, threatening mob to Central High School.

Although some journalists reported that Daisy Bates had requested that federal troops be sent to Little Rock, her actual statement to reporters on Monday afternoon was that the children would remain out of the school until the president could guarantee their protection. The formal request to President Eisenhower for U.S. Army assistance came from Mayor Mann, who telegraphed the White House on Tuesday that the mob was armed and out of control. The president was outraged by what he considered to be Faubus's conspicuous failure to implement the gentlemen's agreement the governor had made at Newport. More fundamentally, Eisenhower—the soldier-statesman who valued order and his sworn duty to uphold the Constitution above all else—absolutely would not allow a violent street mob to defy the constitutional authority of the federal courts. On Tuesday afternoon he issued an Executive Order placing all 10,000 members of the Arkansas National Guard under federal authority. Telling his aides that he did not want to place brother against brother in the streets of Little Rock, Eisenhower also deployed to the beleaguered Arkansas capital about 1,000 troops of the regular army's 101st Airborne Division from Fort Campbell, Kentucky.

In a national radio and television address that evening, the president declared: "Mob rule cannot be allowed to override the decisions of the courts. Let me make it very clear that federal troops are not being used to relieve local and state authorities of their primary duty to preserve the peace and order of the community. Nor are the troops there for the purpose of taking over the responsibility of the School Board. . . . The troops are there pursuant to law solely for the purpose of preventing interference with the orders of the court." With the Cold War never far from the minds of national leaders in the 1950s, Eisenhower also added another concern about the chaos in Little Rock: "At a time when we face a grave situation abroad because of the hatred that communism bears toward a system of government based on human rights, it would be difficult to exaggerate the harm that is being done to the prestige and influence, and indeed to the safety, of our nation and the world."[14]

Daisy welcomed the president's actions, but she was saddened to think that it required the U.S. Army to make it possible for black children and white children to attend school together. She wondered if such a dramatic course would be required in other school districts. She was also concerned about the next steps in Little Rock. Despite the announcements out of Washington, she heard nothing from Superintendent Blossom all day on Tuesday. When he called her after midnight, she told him that she had arranged with the parents to keep the children home on Wednesday because she had no other instructions. He implored her to have them come to her house in the morning because Washington had ordered the troops to take them in without further delay. Since the families did not answer their phones late at night because of threatening calls, Daisy went in the company of the principals from two black schools to each house during the early morning hours to spread the word.

On the morning of September 25, the paratroopers of the 101st Airborne Division—the Screaming Eagles—carried out their mission with military directness. To assist Major General Edwin A. Walker, who commanded the Arkansas military district, the Pentagon sent Major General Earle G. (Bus) Wheeler, who was then assistant deputy chief of staff for Military Operations and who would later be chairman of the Joint Chiefs of Staff during the Vietnam War. Wheeler informed Blossom, "We don't want to hurt anybody, but those Negro students are going into that school."[15] At about 9:00 A.M. an army station wagon arrived at the Bateses' home accompanied by a detachment of armed soldiers in jeeps. As the officer in charge came to the front door, Minnijean Brown declared, "For the first time in my life, I feel like an American citizen."[16] With tears in their eyes, Daisy and the parents watched the young people depart in the station wagon. In front of the school other soldiers cleared from the street at bayonet point a small group of segregationists who refused an order to disperse. With 350 paratroopers surrounding the building, the escort detachment led the nine students into Central High School at 9:22 A.M.

The soldiers returned the Little Rock Nine to the Bateses' house after school. As would become the daily routine for the school year, Daisy debriefed them on how the day had gone. Their reception inside had been mixed, with some students helpful, most indifferent, and a few openly hostile. The emotions of the group were also ambiguous. They had a feeling of satisfaction finally to be in Central High School, but they were saddened that their attendance had required a military escort. In fact, as momentous as the day had been, the Battle of Little Rock was just beginning.

The segregationists had lost a round but were not ready to concede the fight. Daisy Bates was a principal target of their continuing attack. In October the Little Rock City Council passed an ordinance requiring local NAACP leaders to disclose information about members. Viewing this move as an attempt to intimidate the NAACP, Daisy and other officers refused to comply and were arrested. In contrast, local authorities made no arrests of any of the individuals who had beaten the black journalist or had committed other blatantly criminal acts. The Arkansas Supreme Court upheld the fines imposed on Daisy and the others who had been arrested, but the U.S. Supreme Court eventually overturned these rulings. Even more frightening was the violence directed at the Bateses. Their house became the target of rocks, bricks, and gunshots, and even fiery crosses in their yard. L. C. and other men in the neighborhood armed themselves with shotguns and pistols and kept watch every night because the local police made no move the stop the nightly harassment. Because the local community tolerated the terrorist tactics of a minority of segregationists, the danger of physical harm persisted not only for adult leaders such as Daisy but also for the nine students.

At the end of September, when the 101st Airborne withdrew from inside the school, the physical and mental torment of the Little Rock Nine began almost immediately. The African American students were subjected to daily name calling, hitting, pushing, kicking, and other forms of abuse. The federalized National Guardsmen, who had replaced the regular army troops, looked the other way or watched approvingly. Teachers and school administrators who witnessed overt acts of violence usually intervened to stop them, but the punishments of the perpetrators were often minimal. After one such attack left Jefferson Thomas unconscious from a blow on the head, Daisy Bates confronted the superintendent about the lack of protection. Blossom at first was defensive, but policies did change. As Daisy wrote to Roy Wilkins, the national director of the NAACP,

> We also pointed out that the treatment of the children had been getting steadily worse for the last two weeks in the form of kicking, spitting, and general abuse. As a result of our visit, stronger measures are being taken against the white students who are guilty of committing these offenses. For instance, a boy who had been suspended for two weeks, flunked both six-weeks tests, and on his return to school, the first day he knocked Gloria Ray into her locker. As a result of our visit, he was given an indefinite suspension.[17]

Daisy also prevailed upon General Walker to place army guards back inside the building with soldiers assigned to protect individual students.

Tensions did not end inside Central High School, but eight of the nine black students did manage to make it through the year. School officials expelled Minnijean Brown after several incidents in which she retaliated against her harassers verbally and with actions that included dumping a bowl of hot chili on a white boy. Daisy arranged for her to go to New York City, where she lived with the family of a professor at City University of New York. She graduated from high school there in 1959. In the spring of 1958 and despite various maneuvers to try to prevent his graduation, Ernest Green, who had entered Central High School as a senior, was granted his diploma and became the school's first African American graduate. He went on to a successful career as an investment banker in Washington, DC. Also, at the end of the 1957–58 school year, the Little Rock Nine traveled with Daisy to Chicago and New York City, where they received civil rights awards and recognition from civic leaders.

In the long-term struggle for Negro rights in America, what Daisy Bates, the nine students, and a handful of other black and white citizens of Little Rock had accomplished in 1957–58 was of enormous significance. Their courage and perseverance had produced a situation in which the Eisenhower administration had little choice but to exercise federal protection of constitutional rights identified by the federal judiciary. They helped establish important legal precedents. The injustices that they suffered were broadly reported, and this knowledge advanced the education of many Americans who had been oblivious to how hateful and destructive racial discrimination and intimidation could be. Within Little Rock itself and throughout the South, however, much effort and sacrifice remained before real integration would become a reality.

When the school year ended in Little Rock in the spring of 1958, the integration battle returned to the courts. In June the federal district court under a new judge granted a petition from the school board to delay integration in Little Rock for three years and thus to deny the return of black students to Central High School in the fall. In July, Faubus easily won renomination for governor, which assured his reelection in the fall. He immediately sought and obtained state legislation that empowered the governor to close any school in order to maintain the peace. Thus, in September, when the U.S. Supreme Court ruled that the lower court erred and that integration in Little Rock must proceed immediately, Faubus responded by closing all the public high schools in Little Rock. He allowed a private, segregated school to re-open supported by donations. This time, no federal troops appeared to take control.

Not only was the governor's legal maneuvering a setback for integration, but his demagoguery also encouraged the hoodlum element of the segregationists who remained determined to silence Daisy Bates. She, her friends, and the parents of the black pupils became targets of continuous attacks. Dynamite was exploded in her front yard. Her car was rammed, and the white teenagers in the other vehicle threatened to drag her out of hers. Daisy, L. C., and some of their black supporters obtained permits for handguns and armed themselves for protection, but they were still arrested for carrying weapons by men claiming to be plain-clothes state police officers. Some of the parents of the students lost their jobs when segregationist extremists threatened their employers. The most personally devastating blow to Daisy and L. C., however, was the loss of the *Arkansas State Press*. An organized campaign by the white supremacists intimidated large and small advertisers alike to withdraw their accounts from the paper. After eighteen years of courageous reporting, the Bateses shut down the presses of the newspaper that they had built with their own hard work and that had been a voice advocating social and economic justice in Arkansas.

In the fall of 1958, after Faubus closed the public high schools, the school board resigned en masse, and Blossom departed. Within months the various attempts at private schools were bankrupt, and education for all students was in a shambles. In the fall of 1959, after further legal wrangling and more acts of violence and threats, Little Rock reopened Central High School and other schools. Although the system was nominally integrated, very few black students attended classes with white students and tensions remained high.

Having lost their livelihood with the demise of the *State Press*, Daisy and L. C. had to make some changes. In 1960 he began working as NAACP field director for Arkansas and served in that job until he retired in 1971. She went to New York City to work on a memoir of her experiences, and the book, *The Long Shadow of Little Rock*, was published in 1962. Former First Lady Eleanor Roosevelt, a champion of human rights, wrote the foreword. Daisy then worked in Washington, DC, for the Democratic National Committee and for the Johnson administration's antipoverty programs. During the March on Washington on August 28, 1963, when Martin Luther King Jr. delivered his famous "I Have a Dream" speech, Daisy Bates was the only woman to be one of the principal speakers that day. Historians John Hope Franklin

and Alfred A. Moss Jr. list her as one of that group of black women—
Ella Baker, Fannie Lou Hamer, Jo Ann Robinson, Angela Davis, and
others—who "emerged as catalysts of the Black Revolution" and who
were "major contributors to the struggle for black equality."[18]

In 1965 a stroke incapacitated Daisy, and she returned to Arkansas.
She regained the ability to work, however, and moved to Mitchellville
in 1968 to seek community improvements for black residents. As director of the city's Office of Economic Opportunity Self-Help Project, she
helped the town obtain improved water and sewer systems, more paved
streets, and a community center with a swimming pool. She retired from
that position in 1974, and the next year the state legislature approved a
resolution recognizing her outstanding service to Arkansas.

In 1980, L. C. Bates died without having realized his and Daisy's
dream of restarting the *State Press*. In 1984, however, she was able to
assemble enough financing to make the dream come true. She had two-
thirds ownership, and, ironically, one of her partners in the enterprise
was the then-superintendent of Little Rock schools, Dr. H. Benjamin
Williams. The paper was almost an instant community and commercial
success. Ernest Green was its national marketing director. In keeping
with the times, Daisy had the writers use the term "Afro American" in
place of "black." Also, in 1984, the University of Arkansas awarded Daisy
an honorary Doctor of Laws degree, and the University of Arkansas
Press reissued her book. This new release of *The Long Shadow of Little
Rock* received an American Book Award, a first for a reprint edition. In
1987 she sold the newspaper.

She continued to make public appearances in support of social justice and to accept additional honors. An elementary school in Little
Rock was named after her. Wheelchair bound, she carried the Olympic
torch as part of the opening ceremonies of the 1996 Summer Games in
Atlanta. In 1997 at the fortieth-anniversary observance of the integration of Central High School, President Bill Clinton once again recognized her achievements as a leader in the civil rights movement. When
she died on November 4, 1999, Governor Mike Huckabee issued the
following statement:

> Arkansas and the nation have lost a courageous soldier for righteousness and
> justice with the passing of Mrs. Daisy Bates. She placed herself in harm's way
> to open doors for others regardless of whether they were doors to a school,
> doors to a theater, or doors to a café. She was small in stature but large in
> legacy. Every citizen who believes America ought to be a land where justice
> and freedom are for all and not just a privileged few should take a moment
> and say a prayer of thanks for the life of Daisy Bates. . . . I have ordered that

the flags of our state Capitol be lowered to half-staff on the day of her funeral to show our respect and appreciation for her service to God and others.[19]

The life of Daisy Lee Gatson Bates covered almost the entire journey of the African American quest for equality in the twentieth century. When she was a small child, her mother's murderer had gone unpunished because her parents had no rights that the white authorities in her town respected. With a steely resolve, she built respect for herself and her race. As Virgil Blossom described her, "Mrs. Bates . . . was a woman of great energy with an aggressive, crusading spirit. . . . She was not a person about whom others were indifferent. They either approved of her activities or they were highly antagonistic to her, and she was constantly under intense fire of the segregationists. This did not in any way slow her down and sometimes it seemed merely to spur her to greater efforts."[20]

The challenges and personal dangers that she faced were formidable. The contrast between the facts of her life and the initial reluctance of the Eisenhower administration to intercede in school integration revealed the obvious lack of knowledge among officials in Washington of the burdens that African Americans endured. In some ways, the leadership that Daisy provided in the fight for civil rights was conservative. Her preferred weapons were not violent confrontation but the power of the press, the courts, and, finally in the 1960s, the Johnson administration's social reform programs. There was nothing restrained, however, about her intense hatred for discrimination—a hatred that she channeled into constructive action as her dying father had urged her to do. The life of Daisy Bates that leaders such as President Clinton and Governor Huckabee honored was emblematic of a transformation in racial understanding in America at large and of the truth that one person can make a difference.

Notes

1. Daisy Bates, *The Long Shadow of Little Rock* (Fayetteville: University Press of Arkansas, 1987), 4.

2. Bates, *Long Shadow*, 34.

3. John Hope Franklin and Alfred A. Moss Jr., *From Slavery to Freedom: A History of African Americans*, 7th ed. (New York: McGraw-Hill, 1994), 622.

4. Robert Weisbrot, *Freedom Bound: A History of America's Civil Rights Movement* (New York: Plume, 1991), 12.

5. Bates, *Long Shadow*, 48–49.

6. Chester J. Pach and Elmo Richardson, *The Presidency of Dwight D. Eisenhower*, rev. ed. (Lawrence: University Press of Kansas, 1991), 143.

7. Ibid., 144.

8. Bates, *Long Shadow*, 57.

9. Ibid., 70–75.

10. Virgil T. Blossom, *It Has Happened Here* (New York: Harper and Brothers, 1959), 85.

11. Robert F. Burk, *The Eisenhower Administration and Black Civil Rights* (Knoxville: University of Tennessee Press, 1984), 178.

12. Bates, *Long Shadow*, 90.

13. Ibid., 91.

14. Blossom, *It Has Happened Here*, 116.

15. Ibid., 115–16.

16. Bates, *Long Shadow*, 104.

17. Daisy Bates to Roy Wilkins, December 17, 1957 [archive on-line] (Library of Congress); available from http://lcweb.loc.gov/exhibits/odyssey/archive/09/0918001r.jpg; accessed December 31, 2001.

18. Franklin and Moss, *From Slavery to Freedom*, 497.

19. Governor Huckabee's Press Release, November 4, 1999 [archive on-line] (State of Arkansas); available from http://www.state.ar.us/governor/press/110499-3.html; accessed December 31, 2001.

20. Blossom, *It Has Happened Here*, 27.

Suggested Readings

On the events at Little Rock specifically and on the civil rights movement generally, the works cited in the notes are an excellent place to begin. For a somewhat technical legal discussion see Tony Freyer, *The Little Rock Crisis: A Constitutional Interpretation* (Westport, CT: Greenwood Press, 1984), and for a favorable view of Eisenhower's policies see Herbert Brownell with John P. Burk, *Advising Ike: The Memoirs of Attorney General Herbert Brownell* (Lawrence: University Press of Kansas, 1993). Good studies of women's contributions to the civil rights movement are Vicki L. Crawford et al., eds., *Women in the Civil Rights Movement: Trailblazers and Torchbearers, 1941–1965* (Bloomington: Indiana University Press, 1994), and Lynne Olson, *Freedom's Daughters: The Unsung Heroines of the Civil Rights Movement from 1830 to 1970* (New York: Simon and Schuster, 2001). A helpful work on legal battles is Jack Greenberg, *Crusaders in the Courts: How a Dedicated Band of Lawyers Fought for the Civil Rights Revolution* (New York: Basic Books, 1994).

12

Walter Reuther
The Promise of Modern America

Kevin Boyle

In many ways the midtwentieth century marked the high tide of the organized labor movement in the United States. Under legal protections passed by the federal government during the New Deal, unions enjoyed a healthy growth and emerged as effective representatives of workers in their continuing struggles with the managers of the factories that had come to dominate the American economy. Moreover, unions loomed large in the nation's politics, and their leaders played highly visible and influential political roles, especially in the Democratic Party. One of the most powerful of these leaders was Walter Reuther. Although Reuther initially imbibed socialist precepts from his father and from a sojourn in the Soviet Union, he turned away from political radicalism and joined the United Automobile Workers (UAW) as a more effective means to promote workers' well-being. He rose quickly in the union's ranks and became an important voice for labor within the Democratic Party. He also brought the UAW's power to bear on behalf of the civil rights movement and President Lyndon Johnson's War on Poverty in the 1960s. But differences over the Vietnam War exacerbated increasing tensions among American workers, and Reuther's effort to exploit the rising protest culture to further labor's cause was cut short by his death in 1970.

Kevin Boyle received his Ph.D. in history from the University of Michigan in 1990 and currently is associate professor of history at the Ohio State University. He is the author of *The UAW and the Heyday of American Liberalism, 1945–1968* (1995).

O n May 2, 1936, twenty-nine-year-old Walter Reuther sat down to write to his younger brothers, Roy and Victor. He was bursting with news. The previous autumn, determined to become a political activist, Walter had moved to Detroit. He quickly made contact with radicals like himself, who were then working to unionize the city's autoworkers. He threw himself into the campaign, crisscrossing Detroit

This essay will also appear in Eric Arnesen, ed., *The Human Tradition in American Labor History* from Scholarly Resources, forthcoming, to speak at political meetings, attend planning sessions, and organize union locals. His efforts won him notice. In April 1936 he was elected to a high-ranking position in the United Automobile Workers (UAW), which the Congress of Industrial Organizations (CIO) hoped would bring unionization to the auto industry. "Is this not speed?" he wrote in triumph a few days later. "Yes, this is a remarkable age. The zep[pelin] crossed the Atlantic in 49 hours, nothing is impossible. It seems I have caught the spirit of the age."[1]

He would never surrender that belief. Walter Reuther was a product of the modern period, a time when engineers, scientists, and businessmen employed new machines, new systems, and new ideas to reshape the United States. As a young man, he embraced the promises of the modern world—that poverty could give way to abundance, that conflict could give way to order, that exploitation could give way to justice. For thirty-four years—from the spring day in 1936 when he joined the union's upper echelon to his death in 1970—Reuther used the UAW to demand that America fulfill those promises. He had his victories. But despite a lifetime of effort he could not make the modern world into what he wanted it to be.

The United States had been undergoing industrialization since the early nineteenth century. In the last quarter of that century, the pace of change accelerated dramatically. Rail and telegraph lines connected cities, towns, and farms from coast to coast. Determined to exploit the new national market, businessmen expanded their operations. Industrialists developed new techniques to produce consumer goods on a mass scale and adopted new business practices to maximize their companies' efficiency. Powerful bankers, meanwhile, promoted a merger movement that created corporations of unprecedented size. By the 1900s, huge firms such as U.S. Steel and Standard Oil dominated industry after industry.

These changes improved life for many Americans. The mass market helped to break down the isolation and deprivation that had afflicted many farm families. Rural and city folks alike wanted the factory-made goods that filled their stores. But the industrial order also created terrible burdens. To produce the flood of goods, industrialists pushed their workers relentlessly; to increase profits, they paid their workers as little as possible. Working people thus lived under a cloud of insecurity. They struggled constantly to make ends meet. Even the smallest setback—an accident in the factory or a downturn in the economy—pushed families into desperate poverty.

Working people did not simply accept these burdens as the price of progress. Throughout the late nineteenth and early twentieth centuries, many strove to find responses to the new world in which they labored. Often they tried to organize, building a bewildering array of unions and political organizations. These groups had no single goal. Some working-class organizations hoped to stop the march of industrialization; others sought to win workers the best deal possible within the new order; still others tried to transform the new order. Whatever their purpose, the organizations faced staggering odds. Most corporate officials despised unions and were more than willing to use their awesome power to keep them out of their factories. By 1900, only 3 percent of American workers were unionized.

Walter Reuther grew up in the midst of this new industrial world. He was born in 1907 in Wheeling, West Virginia, a factory town on the edge of the industrial heartland. His father, Valentine, drove a wagon for a local brewery; his mother, Anna, cared for the couple's five children, of whom Walter was the second oldest. Walter's father was also a passionate Socialist, a devotee of Eugene Debs, whose ringing denunciations of capitalism won him a large following in the early twentieth century. Like Debs, Valentine believed that capitalists reduced workers to "wage slavery." Socialism offered workers the hope of a new life in a more just economic order. But no one would construct a socialist America for working people. They had to do that for themselves, building their own political party and their own unions. Valentine took these ideas seriously. He traveled the state on behalf of Debs's presidential campaigns. He worked hard for his union, the Brewery Workers. And he trained his sons to carry the fight into the next generation.

Walter and his younger brothers, Roy and Victor, learned their father's lessons well. They were intense, high-minded young men who believed, as Victor wrote in his high-school yearbook, "the needs of humanity are more important."[2] For his part, Walter coupled his idealism with a driving ambition. He quit school at sixteen to accept an apprenticeship in a machine shop, where he trained to be a tool and die maker. Tool and die workers made the complicated machine tools and fixtures upon which mass production depended. To do their job, they had to be able to puzzle through complex problems; they had to understand how to use technology to solve those problems; and they had to be utterly precise in putting their solutions into practice. Tool and die makers, in other words, had to have the rational mindset that the industrial world most prized. Walter proved perfectly suited to such demands.

Having completed three years of his four-year apprenticeship, he decided he had learned all he could. On February 27, 1927, nineteen-year-old Walter Reuther left Wheeling for Detroit, the workshop of modern America.

Detroit had been just another midsized American city at the turn of the century. Then a group of visionary businessmen began to produce automobiles there. The automakers ran their industry according to the newest standards. By the mid-1910s, automobile factories were marvels of integrated production, giant plants filled with complex machinery carefully arranged along assembly lines designed to maximize productivity. The production system worked: in the mid-1920s, four million autos rolled off assembly lines every year. Such staggering productivity made the auto industry the engine of the American economy. It was an ideal place for a man of Walter's skills. The auto companies relied on tool and die workers to keep the machinery up to date and were willing to pay top dollar for their services. Weeks after arriving in Detroit, Walter secured one of the most highly prized jobs available to a working man: earning $1.05 per hour as a diemaker in the Ford Motor Company tool room.

The automakers were much less generous with most of their workers. About 400,000 men and women labored in auto plants in the late 1920s. Most of them had no special skills. Drawn to Detroit and other auto towns from the American countryside or from abroad by the promise of a steady paycheck, they staffed the assembly lines, stoked the furnaces, and hauled the parts. It was demanding labor in the best of times. Workers had to keep pace with the assembly line, endure the foreman's prodding for more production, and risk injury from the presses, stamps, and belts they operated. On their own, they had virtually no ability to improve their conditions. The automakers were fiercely opposed to unions; any worker who dared even to whisper about organizing was summarily fired.

The best of times, moreover, proved shortlived. Just two years after Reuther arrived in Detroit, the economy plummeted into the Great Depression. When auto sales collapsed, automakers responded by laying off the unskilled in massive numbers. By 1931, Detroit's unemployment rate had skyrocketed to 30 percent. Hundreds of families were evicted from their homes every month, while one Detroit hospital reported treating four cases of starvation per day. "I have never confronted such misery as on the zero day of my arrival in Detroit," a social worker recorded in 1930.[3]

As a skilled worker, Walter was protected from the depression's fury. Not only did he keep his job, but his wages actually increased. The economic collapse nevertheless affected him deeply. The depression seemed to confirm what his father had taught him. Capitalism could not provide ordinary people with justice; in the dark days of the early 1930s, in fact, capitalism seemed incapable of providing for them at all. Across industrial America, radicals were agitating for fundamental change in the economic order. Victor joined Walter in Detroit in 1930, and together the brothers threw themselves into the city's socialist movement. That decision proved to be transforming. Detroit's leftwing community was a hothouse of ideas, discussions, and debates. As he rushed from meeting to meeting, Walter could complete the political education he had cut short in Wheeling years before.

It is impossible to pinpoint when Walter's thinking crystallized. But sometime in this period he settled on the ideas that would remain central to his politics for the rest of his life. He took his inspiration from the iconoclastic social theorist, Thorstein Veblen. In his 1921 book, *The Engineers and the Price System,* Veblen argued that technology gave Americans the ability to enjoy permanent prosperity. But businessmen refused to unleash technology's extraordinary capacity, Veblen said. Instead, they manipulated the price system to create scarcity and to maximize their profits. The key to prosperity, then, was to take control of the industrial system from businessmen and give it to experts who would make it serve the public interest. Here was a political vision perfectly suited to Walter's passions. It was socialist in its goals but technocratic in its execution. Experts—problemsolvers like himself—would apply technical solutions to the nation's ills and thereby unleash the great potential of the machines Reuther knew so well. The modern world, the world Walter had embraced, could be made just.

For the next few years, Walter and Victor looked for realistic ways to put their ideas into practice. Walter finally lost his job in late 1932 when, he said, Ford caught wind of his socialist activities and fired him. The next year, he and Victor began a two-and-one-half year tour to "study the economic and social conditions of the world."[4] The brothers spent eighteen months of that time as skilled workers in the Soviet Union, where they were impressed by the Communist government's social and economic engineering. They returned to Detroit in mid-1935 determined to bring similarly sweeping changes to the United States.

They came back to a nation different from the one they had left. In 1932 voters had elected Democrat Franklin D. Roosevelt as president of the United States. The next year, FDR launched his New Deal, an ambitious attempt to end the depression by reforming American capitalism. One of the most important parts of the New Deal was the government's support of workers' right to form unions without employer interference. FDR and Congress had guaranteed that right in two pieces of legislation: the 1933 National Industrial Recovery Act, and the 1935 National Labor Relations Act. These bills had triggered a series of strikes, many of them led by radical organizers. But no mainstream labor union had taken control of the inchoate union movement. The leaders of the nation's foremost labor organization, the American Federation of Labor (AFL), had talked about the need to bring unionization to major industries such as steel and auto making but had taken virtually no action. Just as the Reuthers were returning to the United States, matters changed. John L. Lewis, the president of the United Mine Workers, formed a new labor association, the Congress of Industrial Organizations, dedicated to unionizing the millions of men and women who worked for the great corporations of industrial America. Lewis began planning for a confrontation with the corporations, sending scores of organizers to factory towns to prepare for the strikes that would force industrialists to recognize their workers' rights.

In Detroit, CIO partisans took control of the United Automobile Workers, a union the AFL had created to organize autoworkers but had never used. Walter's brother, Roy, was already working as a UAW organizer in nearby Flint, Michigan. Almost immediately after their return to Detroit, Walter and Victor joined him, seeing in the UAW a vehicle for advancing the radical program they had embraced. Throughout late 1935 and early 1936, Walter and Victor built their connections to the UAW's radicals and volunteered their time as organizers in Detroit. Amid the rush of activities, the course of Walter's life began to take shape. He fell in love with a fellow socialist, May Wolf; the couple married on March 13, 1936. A month later, he was elected to the UAW's Executive Board, his first official post in the union.

As exhilarating as it was to be a union officer, Reuther's position had more promise than power. In mid-1936 the UAW still had virtually no members. Walter and his fellow organizers set out to change that. Throughout the balance of 1936, Walter and Victor strove to unionize the men and women who worked in the auto parts plants that dotted Detroit's west side. In December, Walter led his first strike, a two-week confrontation with the Kelsey-Hayes Company. The strike was immediately overshadowed, however, by a dramatic turn of events in Flint.

On December 31, 1936, the workers at a Chevrolet plant in that city occupied the factory and refused to leave until Chevrolet's parent company, General Motors (GM), recognized their right to join the UAW. GM was an immensely powerful company—the largest manufacturing firm in the world—and its officials had no intention of giving in to the strikers. So the sit-downers stayed in the plant, week after week, as GM's operations ground to a halt. Finally, on February 11, 1937, the corporation agreed to the strikers' demands. The extraordinary victory transformed the UAW. Two months later, the nation's third-largest automaker, the Chrysler Corporation, recognized its workers' right to join the UAW. A host of smaller companies followed suit. By year's end, the UAW had 400,000 members, who together had the ability to shutter the foremost industry in the country. And Walter Reuther, all of thirty years old, was one of its leading figures.

Reuther was far from the stereotypical cigar-chomping union boss. Typically dressed in a three-piece suit, fit, trim, and almost ascetic in his personal habits—he neither drank nor smoked—he looked more like a junior executive than a labor activist. He and May built a thoroughly conventional family life, raising their daughters, Linda and Lisa, in the same serious, high-minded manner in which Valentine had brought up his sons. But for all his conservatism in personal matters, Reuther proved to be tenacious in his determination to confront corporate power. From 1937 to 1946 he served as director of the UAW's General Motors Department, where he was responsible for negotiating with the giant automaker. Reuther was a tenacious bargainer, determined to wring every last penny out of contract talks. When talks failed, he did not hesitate to lead the rank and file out on strike. In 1939 and again in 1945 he shut down GM to force concessions.

Reuther had not joined the UAW, however, simply to win autoworkers higher wages and better benefits. From the start, he saw the union as a platform from which to advance his vision of a restructured economy. He believed that increasing wages served that goal, since it redistributed corporate wealth from the executive suite to the factory floor. True to Veblen, he also believed that the modern economy would never achieve its extraordinary potential until corporate officials no longer had absolute control over such basic decisions as product pricing and investment strategy. He tried to use collective bargaining to win the UAW a say in those decisions. When the UAW struck General Motors in 1945, he demanded that the union participate in setting the price of cars. GM officials were willing to concede UAW members higher wages, but they insisted that only corporate officials, not unions, had the right to make basic business decisions. The two sides struggled over the principle for 113 days before Reuther abandoned the demand.

By that time, Reuther had also taken his agenda to the highest levels of American public life. From the moment the UAW won its victory in Flint, Walter began building his political reputation. He resigned from the Socialist Party in 1938 and joined the Democratic Party. By the 1940 presidential election, he had become a vigorous supporter of Franklin Roosevelt. He also had become the leading opponent of the UAW's communist faction. That turn was a surprising one. Reuther had been impressed by the Soviet Union during his time there and had been more than willing to work with communists to organize the UAW. Once the union had been established, however, Walter and the communists began jockeying for power. At first, the conflict was largely a matter of union infighting, but then it became entangled with profoundly important questions of unionists' loyalty to the United States, labor's responsibility to promote national defense, and the extent to which communism threatened the UAW's standing in public life. For his part, Reuther insisted that a democratic union could not tolerate communist members, whom he condemned as beholden to a totalitarian state. His actions won him widespread support. By the early 1940s, the UAW's various anticommunist factions had begun to consolidate behind him.

Walter used his new credentials as a Democrat to push his ideas in Washington, DC. He first won attention in 1940, when the Roosevelt administration was struggling to convince American manufacturers to convert their plants to making desperately needed armaments. The United States had the ability to produce 500 military planes per day, Reuther insisted, but corporate officials were refusing to meet the nation's wartime needs. The federal government therefore ought to take aircraft production out of private hands and put it under the control of a government board whose membership would be divided evenly between representatives of business, government, and labor. The proposal—perfectly in keeping with Veblen's ideas—died a quick death when corporate officials refused to consider it. But it put Reuther's core principles into public debate and made the young labor leader well known inside the Roosevelt administration.

His reputation grew over the next few years as he participated in wartime government agencies, offered more plans to democratize corporate decision making, and campaigned for the Democrats. "I was very taken with him," New Dealer Joseph Rauh recalled. "Reuther was a person who understood the social forces in America, how you work with them to make a better America."[5] Rauh was not alone in his opinion. By the end of World War II, Reuther had become a darling of the liberal elite. Eleanor Roosevelt considered him to be a friend, as did such up-and-coming figures as Hubert Humphrey and Arthur Schlesinger Jr. Finally, in 1946, Reuther put his rising stature to the test and ran for the UAW presidency. He was not a beloved figure among autoworkers, many of whom viewed him as a self-promoter, but they appreciated his skill and tenacity and they enjoyed his celebrity. Reuther "worked hard, fought well, deserved much credit," a union activist said, "and saw that he got it."[6] The UAW election in 1946 was a bitter contest, with Reuther barely edging out the UAW's communists and their allies for control. As soon as the returns were in, Walter began consolidating his power. He traded on the mounting Cold War hysteria to attack his communist opponents. It was a brutal affair. Many of the communists were UAW stalwarts who had risked much to build the union in the 1930s. But Reuther and his supporters portrayed them as Soviet lackeys who had to be purged from the union's ranks. At the same time, Walter built a political machine of his own, so well oiled that the opposition never stood a chance against it. Reuther's leftwing opponents "sat glum and silent" when he ran for reelection at the 1947 UAW convention, *Newsweek* reported, "while Reuther's anti-Communist steamroller clanked over them."[7] Ten years after Flint's autoworkers had transformed him from a radical organizer into a trade union official, Reuther had become the undisputed leader of the most powerful union in the United States.

"We are the vanguard in America," he proclaimed as he accepted his victory. "We are the architects of the future, and we are going to fashion the weapons with which we will work and fight and build."[8] In that moment, he revealed his greatest hopes. The UAW—Reuther's UAW—could shape the nation's future. And it could do so as an architect would, with the plans only an expert could prepare, with the precision only a craftsman could provide. Bit by bit, the UAW would build a new America, better than the old. His union would make the promise of modern America a reality.

Reuther certainly made the UAW into a model modern union. The early CIO had been a mixed bag. Some of its largest affiliates had been top-down bureaucratic organizations, while others had grown from the grassroots. The UAW was in the latter group. Its members were famous for walking off the job when they thought their rights were violated and for ignoring union directives when they saw fit. Reuther shifted union power upward, centralizing decision making in the union headquarters. He moved the UAW into a sleek office block along the Detroit River. He filled the most important staff positions with men and women like himself—working-class intellectuals, many of them former socialists, who read widely, traveled regularly, and understood the intricacies of economic policy and political process. His chief adviser, Jack Conway, was a plumber's son who held both a B.A. and an M.A. from the University of Chicago; his leading "idea man" was a high-school dropout who had earned a B.A. at night from New York University. Roy and Victor also took up important positions, the former as head of the UAW's political arm, the latter as director of its international department.

This team used their skills to push the boundaries of collective bargaining. From the start, they were determined that autoworkers would share in the nation's abundance. So they did. Not only did the UAW win for its members regular wage increases, but it also forced the auto manufacturers to write cost-of-living adjustments and profit-sharing programs into their contracts. The typical autoworker earned $1.50 per hour, excluding overtime, when Reuther assumed the union's leadership. By the time of his death in 1970, the typical wage stood at $4.23 per hour, an increase of almost 300 percent. The UAW also won for its members an impressive array of fringe benefits. Between 1946 and 1970 autoworkers secured pension plans, medical insurance, paid vacations, and even wage protection during layoffs. Together, these gains made autoworkers some of the highest-paid industrial workers in the nation.

Reuther also presided over the consolidation of the American labor movement. Since 1935, organized labor had been divided into two hostile camps: one led by the AFL, the other by the CIO. When Reuther was elected president of the latter organization in 1953, he set out to heal the rift. For two years, he and AFL president George Meany conducted delicate merger negotiations. They completed the process in 1955 by creating the AFL-CIO, fifteen million members strong. Reuther saw great hope in the new federation. The merger, he said, "is part of that . . . dream that mankind can fashion a world in which . . . the great power of creation which God gave us can be used by man to create a better world."[9]

Walter also made the UAW into a major force in national politics. It mounted highly effective get-out-the-vote drives each election year, union officials held high positions in Michigan's Democratic Party, and the UAW sent more members to the national Democratic conventions than any other union. Walter used the union's position to support many progressive causes, from nuclear disarmament to civil rights. He also continued to promote his vision of fundamental economic change. Repeatedly insisting that the federal government and unions be given a say in corporate decision making, he fashioned proposal after proposal to accomplish that goal. A public agency could harness technology to mass-produce housing, he said in 1949. A public agency could rationalize military production, he declared during the Korean War. A public agency should establish national economic planning, he insisted in the early 1960s, setting guidelines and standards for corporations to follow.

It proved much easier to call for fundamental change, however, than to put those changes into place. Time after time, Reuther found himself checked by the institutions to which he had committed himself. He and his advisers feared that their success at the bargaining table made UAW members satisfied with the existing economic order. "The union helps [its members'] economic interests, until they can have a front porch," a staffer wrote, "and for that they become capitalists."[10] Reuther also became bitterly disappointed with the AFL-CIO. The federation's president, George Meany, had no interest in spearheading a union campaign to rebuild America, and he had no time for those, like Reuther, who harbored such hopes. "Those who miss labor's crusading spirit should go back to the days when their daily bread and beer came from . . . anemic union payrolls," Meany said after Reuther made one of his typical appeals for social change.[11] "We don't have a labor movement," Reuther fumed in response. "We have a club. It's a very exclusive club; stays in the best hotels, in the finest resorts in the western hemisphere. But it isn't doing the job."[12] Democratic Party politicians, meanwhile, were pleased to accept the UAW's largesse but showed no interest in the sweeping reforms that Reuther envisioned; his proposals received a flurry of publicity, then faded away. Corporate officials thus maintained an iron grip on production and investment decisions and therefore on the American economy. These defeats took their toll on the UAW leadership. By the early 1960s, Reuther and his supporters seemed to have settled into an uncomfortable middle age. Reuther "seems a little obsolete," columnist Murray Kempton wrote, his union "little more than a nursing home" for tired activists.[13] Just as the great hopes of the 1930s and 1940s began to fade, however, public life took a sudden turn. The promise of modern America brightened once again.

The transformation of American politics began far from the UAW's center of power. In the spring of 1963 southern civil rights activists launched a frontal assault against the region's system of apartheid. They centered their campaign in Birmingham, Alabama, a hard-edged steel town where segregationists ruled with an iron fist. When peaceful black protesters took to Birmingham's streets, city officials responded with wanton violence. The carnage made civil rights the dominant issue in American life as church groups, union members, college students, and liberal activists rallied in support of the southern movement. The pressure forced President John F. Kennedy to propose a sweeping civil rights bill designed to outlaw legal segregation in most of its forms.

Reuther put the UAW's full force behind the surging movement. He provided $60,000 in bail money to the Birmingham protesters and put the UAW's highly effective Washington lobbyists to work on behalf of the civil rights bill. Moreover, he helped to underwrite the August 1963 March on Washington, the greatest civil rights demonstration the capital had ever seen. And he was the only white labor leader to speak at the event. Although he took these actions because he believed in racial equality, he also supported the movement because he saw in it a way to force policymakers to address the fundamental question of economic inequality. Even as they demanded an end to Jim Crow, therefore, UAW spokesmen insisted that racial justice had to be linked to economic justice. "Equality before the law becomes a mockery for the unemployed worker or the hopeless occupant of a slum tenement, whatever the color of his skin," Victor Reuther declared in late 1963. "The coalition of Negroes, many churches, a large segment of the labor movement, and the liberals . . . must channel its full energies into the fight for full employment. For without jobs, even the essential protection of a strong civil rights law will prove to be, for millions of Negroes, little more than ashes in the mouth."[14]

This was grand political strategy, the veteran labor leader trying to use the civil rights movement—so grounded in the black communities of the South, so infused with the power of Christian witness, so gloriously irrational in its courage—to advance his vision of rational, technocratic social change. Throughout most of 1963, Reuther's strategy made little headway. Then, on November 22, John Kennedy was assassinated. Determined to prove he was not the southern conservative many liberals feared him to be, the new president, Lyndon B. Johnson, committed himself to an extraordinary reform agenda. His administration would support the pending civil rights bill, LBJ announced. But civil rights was not enough. The federal government would also undertake a war on poverty, extending into all those places in the nation where capitalism's promise had not reached.

"We enlist with you for the duration in the war on poverty," Reuther wired the president.[15] He eagerly embraced Johnson's initiatives, and Johnson welcomed Reuther's involvement, incorporating the UAW into the highest levels of the poverty fight. Walter served on several White House task forces empowered to draft antipoverty legislation. Johnson named Reuther's longtime assistant, Jack Conway, to direct the Community Action Program, the most innovative segment of the poverty campaign. And the federal government channeled substantial sums to the Citizens Crusade against Poverty, an advocacy program established by the UAW to supplement the federal government's initiatives.

Walter was delighted by the sudden turn in public life. "We are in the midst of a great revolutionary change of forces and people in American society," he told his advisers in 1965. "This change is of such dimensions . . . that the historians will really put [it] in the category of a major social revolution."[16] He had cause for such optimism, for never before had the UAW had such an impact on public policy. Conway tried to make the Community Action Program in the UAW's image, building local community action boards that he hoped would democratize the welfare state. Reuther himself drafted one of the most ambitious pieces of legislation of the Johnson years, the 1966 Model Cities Act, which sought to rebuild inner-city neighborhoods. Johnson even considered appointing Reuther to a cabinet post. Although none of these initiatives put into place the fundamental economic reforms that Walter had envisioned since the 1930s, he was convinced that such changes were now possible. As he worked with the Johnson administration on the poverty campaign, he pushed the president to endorse national economic planning, the public control of technological innovation, and public review of corporate pricing. When the UAW's contracts with the automakers came up for renegotiation in 1964, he insisted that the union be given a greater say over working conditions inside auto plants. The time had come, he declared, "to assert the sovereignty of the person over the machine."[17]

As quickly as it developed, however, the opening of the mid-1960s closed. White support for the civil rights movement proved to be thin; as early as 1965, more and more white Americans were insisting that African Americans were too aggressive in their demands. Many African Americans, conversely, grew frustrated at the slow pace of racial change.

Tensions mounted as conservative politicians exploited white anger and a wave of riots swept through the ghettos of the north. Johnson's escalation of the Vietnam War, meanwhile, drained federal funds from the War on Poverty and triggered inflation. Vietnam also cost Johnson the support of many liberals and radicals, who were appalled by the administration's actions in Southeast Asia. Neither the president nor the auto company executives showed any willingness to consider the union's demands to share in corporate decision making. By 1967, the hope of peaceful change had been shattered.

The nation's conflicts cut deeply through the UAW. Auto plants were beset by racial tension, made all the worse by the automakers' refusal to improve harsh working conditions. As the backlash against civil rights mounted, many white autoworkers condemned Reuther's support of the War on Poverty. Black radicals attacked Reuther as racist. The UAW leadership itself split over Vietnam. Anxious to maintain his close relationship with Johnson, Reuther supported the war. Some of his most trusted advisers opposed U.S. intervention and considered his acquiescence in LBJ's war policies to be an act of cowardice.

It was an agonizing time. Walter had invested such hope in the political opening of the mid-1960s that he did not want to admit that the moment had passed. But the searing events of 1968—the Tet offensive in Vietnam, the murders of Martin Luther King Jr. and Robert Kennedy, and the stunning success of rightwing politicians such as George Wallace—forced his hand. "American society is coming apart," he said to the union's executive board in September of that year. "I am not going to be put in a position . . . where I am charged in my own mind with having twaddled and twiddled my thumbs when the real decisions were made." Reuther thus threw himself into a frenzy of activity in a desperate effort to reestablish his union as the nation's vanguard. He came out against the Vietnam War. He renewed his commitment to the civil rights movement, backing the Poor People's Campaign, Martin Luther King's last major initiative, and pouring funds into the Memphis sanitation strike, the cause that cost King his life. He also took dramatic action to reinvigorate the labor movement. Demanding that the AFL-CIO commit to a massive organizing campaign, he withdrew the UAW from its ranks when the federation's president refused. Walter also tried to renew his own union. After his brother Roy's sudden death in 1968, he revamped the UAW's political apparatus to make it more rooted in working-class communities. And he began working on his last, great modernist dream: a state-of-the-art workers' education center, to be built in the woods of northern Michigan. These efforts consumed his last years. Indeed, they led to his death. On May 9, 1970, Walter and May took a chartered flight to the site of the UAW's education center, then under construction. The plane crashed short of the runway, instantly killing everyone aboard.

The *New York Times* in its obituary called Reuther "a crusader for a better world . . . [who] challenged not only labor but the country . . . to seek newer and broader horizons."[18] But he never realized the world he envisioned. He had dreamt that rational men and women could harness the productivity of modern America to create a more just society. And he believed that the labor movement was the force best suited to lead the transformation, to fulfill the promise of the machine age. Throughout his adult life, he struggled to make his vision a reality. When he died, it was still just a vision, a host of plans and ideas and proposals. Corporations still controlled most of the nation's economic decisions and thus shaped the lives of millions of Americans. In the three decades since Reuther's death, they have strengthened their power. In the late 1970s corporations launched a massive assault on the labor movement. Today, only 14 percent of American workers belong to unions, while the UAW has only 750,000 members, a drop of 43 percent since 1970. Businessmen now use the extraordinary productivity of the American economy not to make the world more just but to make their companies more profitable. The distribution of wealth is terribly skewed. Working people once again live in the shadow of insecurity. And the fabulous machinery of our age—from computers to the latest medical technology—still does not serve everyone. Nearly seventy years after Walter Reuther joined the UAW, the promise of modern America remains unfulfilled.

Notes

1. Kevin Boyle, "Building the Vanguard: Walter Reuther and Radical Politics in 1936," *Labor History* 30 (Summer 1989): 444.

2. Victor Reuther, *The Brothers Reuther and the Story of the UAW: A Memoir* (Boston: Houghton Mifflin, 1976), 41.

3. Kevin Boyle and Victoria Getis, *Muddy Boots and Ragged Aprons: Images of Working-Class Detroit, 1900–1930* (Detroit: Wayne State University Press, 1997), 200.

4. The phrase is Walter's, quoted in Kevin Boyle, *The UAW and the Heyday of American Liberalism, 1945–1968* (Ithaca: Cornell University Press, 1995), 20.

5. Boyle, *The UAW and the Heyday of American Liberalism,* 20–21.

6. Ibid., 22.

7. Nelson Lichtenstein, *The Most Dangerous Man in Detroit: Walter Reuther and the Fate of American Labor* (New York: Basic Books, 1995), 268.

8. Boyle, *The UAW and the Heyday of American Liberalism*, 34.

9. Ibid., 103–04.

10. Kevin Boyle, "Politics and Principle: The United Automobile Workers and Labor-Liberalism, 1948–1968" (Ph.D. diss., University of Michigan, 1990), 259.

11. Boyle, *The UAW and the Heyday of American Liberalism*, 157.

12. Boyle, "Politics and Principle," 259.

13. Boyle, *The UAW and the Heyday of American Liberalism*, 154–56.

14. Ibid., 180–81.

15. Ibid., 188.

16. Ibid., 201.

17. Lichtenstein, *The Most Dangerous Man in Detroit*, 399.

18. Damon Stetson, "Walter Reuther: Union Pioneer with Broad Influence Far Beyond the Field of Labor," *New York Times*, May 11, 1970.

Suggested Readings

Nelson Lichtenstein, *The Most Dangerous Man in Detroit: Walter Reuther and the Fate of American Labor* (New York: Basic Books, 1995), is a magisterial biography of Reuther and a masterly work of labor history. John Bernard, *Walter Reuther and the Rise of the Auto Workers* (Boston: Little, Brown and Company, 1983), and Anthony Carew, *Walter Reuther* (Manchester, Eng.: Manchester University Press, 1993), are brief but insightful biographies. Irving Howe and B. J. Widick, *The UAW and Walter Reuther* (New York: Random House, 1949), provides an intelligent contemporary evaluation of the UAW president. Victor Reuther, *The Brothers Reuther and the Story of the UAW: A Memoir* (Boston: Houghton Mifflin, 1976), and Lisa Reuther Dickmeyer, *Reuther: A Daughter Strikes* (Southfield, MI: Spelman Publishers, 1989), offer family perspectives.

There is a vast scholarly literature on the UAW. Sidney Fine, *Sit-Down: The General Motors Strike of 1936–1937* (Ann Arbor: University of Michigan Press, 1969) is the definitive account of that pivotal event. August Meier and Elliot Rudwick, *Black Detroit and the Rise of the UAW* (New York: Oxford University Press, 1979), traces racial politics and practices in the early UAW. Martin Halpern offers a critical assessment of Reuther's rise to power in *UAW Politics in the Cold War Era* (Albany: State University of New York Press, 1988). Stephen Amberg, *The Union Inspiration in American Politics: The Autoworkers and the Making of a Liberal Industrial Order* (Philadelphia: Temple University Press, 1994), is a sophisticated account of the UAW's economic programs during the Reuther years. Kevin Boyle, *The UAW and the Heyday of American Liberalism, 1945–1968* (Ithaca: Cornell University Press, 1995), details the UAW's political commitments in the same period. Nancy Gabin explores the union's gender dynamics in her important study, *Feminism in the Labor Movement: Women and the United Auto Workers, 1935–1975* (Ithaca: Cornell University Press, 1990). Steve Jefferys, *Management and Managed: Fifty Years of Crisis at Chrysler* (Cambridge, Eng.: Cambridge University Press, 1986), explores the complex relationship between the UAW leadership and union locals.

Historians have also devoted considerable attention to autoworkers' experiences on the shop floor. Nelson Lichtenstein, "Auto Worker Militancy and the Structure of Factory Life, 1937–1955," *Journal of American History* 67 (September 1980): 335–53, sets the standard for shop floor studies. Two fine collections of essays, Nelson Lichtenstein and Steven Meyers, eds., *On the Line: Essays on the History of Auto Work* (Urbana: University of Illinois Press, 1989), and Robert Asher and Ronald Edsforth, eds., *Autowork* (Albany: State University of New York Press, 1995), offer various perspectives on autoworkers' struggles. For an example of how autoworkers vied with each other, see Kevin Boyle, "The Kiss: Racial and Gender Conflict in a 1950s Automobile Factory," *Journal of American History* 84 (September 1997): 496–523.

13

In My Brother's Name
The Life and Death of Spec. 4 Bill Weber

Elizabeth Weber

Army Spec. 4 Bill Weber was killed by a Vietcong sniper on February 12, 1968, along the banks of the Diem Diem River, near the hamlet of My Lai, South Vietnam. He was the first man to die in his company, which had only recently arrived in Vietnam. One month later, on March 16, 1968, members of his company massacred every man, woman, and child in My Lai in the largest single atrocity committed by U.S. ground forces in the Vietnam War. Some of the men who participated in the rampage later claimed that revenge for Weber's death partly accounted for the killing.

Written by Weber's sister, this chapter not only chronicles the young soldier's life and death but also describes the family from which he came and the impact of his death on that family. He was a well-liked, all-American boy from Minnesota. In college, he spent so much time playing the guitar in a rock band that he flunked out and got drafted. His sister finds it bitterly ironic that after his death, the name of her guitar-picking, easygoing brother became linked with the tragedy at My Lai.

Elizabeth Weber recalls how news of her brother's death transformed every member of her family. Her parents damned Lyndon Johnson, Secretary of Defense Robert McNamara, and other national leaders. She herself went from being an honor student who attended church every Sunday to a counterculture dropout who shunned religion and stopped believing anything that politicians said. Years later, in 1996, she and her father went to Vietnam and to the spot where her brother had died. Some of their hosts were former Vietcong, one of whom may have fired the shot that killed young Weber. Surprisingly, she writes, she and her father found themselves apologizing to the Vietnamese for the war and for her brother's part in it.

Elizabeth Weber is an associate professor of English at the University of Indianapolis in Indiana. She earned an M.F.A. from the University of Montana and a Ph.D. in English literature from the State University of New York, Binghamton. She teaches creative writing and has published a book of poetry, *Small Mercies* (1984), and numerous poems and essays in literary reviews and magazines. She is currently writing a memoir of her brother.

This essay originally appeared in David L. Anderson, ed., *The Human Tradition in the Vietnam Era* (Wilmington, DE: Scholarly Resources, 2000), 83–96.

My older brother, Bill, was killed in Vietnam in February 1968, the winter of my senior year in high school. I remember the day clearly: a bone-cracking-cold Minnesota day with hardly any snow on the ground. In my bedroom over the front porch, I was studying for a calculus exam when I looked out the window to see our parish priest and a tall man in an army uniform walk up the steps to our house. Dashing for the stairs, I heard the doorbell ring. As I reached the living room, I heard my mother scream my brother's name. When she saw me, she pulled me to her and cried, "Oh, my poor baby, your brother's dead, whatever will you do?" I looked up to see the foreign exchange student staying with us standing with her back pressed to the living room wall, her eyes wide. I felt sorry for her. My father came home about then. He saw the priest and the army sergeant and said, "What's going on?" He looked as if one of the cows he worked with as a veterinarian had kicked him hard in the head. As they told him the details, he kept saying, "Huh."

My parents kept me home from school the next day. When I went back to school two days later, I took my two best friends, one by one, into the nearest girls' rest room to tell them what happened. Every time I told someone, I'd break down in tears, unable to talk. The news spread, and a few other classmates came up to me and told me they were sorry. When they did, I'd break down crying and have to run away. I took the calculus test and flunked. I had a 94 percent average until then in the class, but when midterm grades came out two weeks later, I saw the teacher had given me a C+. All my grades fell that semester. I also started to talk back to teachers, something I'd never done before. I became belligerent and developed a "fuck you" attitude. I swore at a teacher when she wouldn't let me have an extra day to study for an exam I missed because of Bill's funeral. "I guess I goddamn flunk the fucking test," I told her. Later, I felt bad and apologized to her and told her the circumstances. New to the school and out of the gossip circle, she hadn't heard about my brother's death. She still didn't cut me any slack. I forged hall passes and release-from-school passes for myself and a friend using the name of the school librarian I worked for. During study hall one day, a friend and I found a copy of a James Bond book by Ian Fleming left by someone from the period before, and we tore it up into minute pieces. When the teacher, one of our favorites, caught us with the pile of torn pages and asked why we'd done that, we told him the book was sexist and promoted violence. He shook his head and said, "I'm surprised at you. You know better. You don't tear books up for any reason." He gave us each two days of detention. I also sassed back to another favorite teacher, the man who taught German, and mispronounced all the words in a dialogue we had to memorize. "What's gotten into you?" he asked angrily. "You know better than this." I was his star student, nearly fluent in the language from the time I'd lived in Germany when I was nine and ten. I didn't know what to say to him.

The things I did may sound mild compared to what other kids did then and now. But I went to a school that had mostly University of Minnesota professors' children in it. Many students went to Ivy League colleges. The majority took school very seriously. Before my brother's death, I had been a model student, a shy recluse who never talked back to teachers, never skipped school, never turned in work late, and never flunked exams. To me, a C was a bad grade. I was captain of the soccer team and an honor roll student in the top 10 percent of my class. I obeyed all rules.

After Bill died, I just didn't care. The world I knew seemed fake, and so did the people in it. All the rules and values I'd followed until then didn't seem to matter. Those rules and values had killed my brother, who always struck me as being one of the nicest, kindest guys in the world. I looked around me, and it didn't seem that many cared about what was happening over in Vietnam because it wasn't happening to them but to others. They didn't care as long as they could go about earning their money, promoting their careers, and going to parties and football games. They did not want their lives troubled. I hated them.

I should explain that my family was against the war. My parents told me it was unjust, that the United States was imposing its will on the people of Vietnam. The war was more about money and power than the freedom of a people, they said, and the government in South Vietnam was corrupt and oppressive. From what I read about the war in magazines and newspapers, the people of Vietnam, in both the North and the South, didn't want us over there. I felt that only a few people did—those who were benefiting financially. The corrupt wanted it. I could not understand why young Americans needed to go there and die. I did not buy the domino theory. After all, weren't some countries we supported as democracies just as oppressive and corrupt? Look at the Philippines or Korea.

The staff sergeant who told us of Bill's death also talked about what was happening in the war. We were being lied to about the number of casualties, he said, and much of the news about the war was buried on the back pages of our newspapers. After that, I always looked way in the back of the paper. He also told us that we were not winning. He himself was against the war. He had been a helicopter crewman there, and finally, when he couldn't stomach any more missions, they'd given him the job of telling families their boys had died. He hated what he saw happening.

All this shattered my beliefs. Then, Martin Luther King was gunned down in April. In June, Bobby Kennedy was shot and killed. Later that summer the Democratic National Convention in Chicago brought rioting and violence. Also at that convention, I watched Hubert Humphrey, Minnesota's former senator, turn to the people behind him after he'd won the nomination and say, "Watch me wow them." He'd thought the mikes couldn't pick that up. I was disgusted.

I looked at the people with whom I had grown up, and for the first time, I saw them as shortsighted and filled with self-interest. They had killed my brother. They had sent him over to Vietnam to kill and to die. As long as it was not their sons who went and as long as their lives were not disrupted, they did not care.

I saw the leaders of this country as liars who just wanted power. They lied to the people about why we were in Vietnam, about the nature of the war over there, about who was winning, and about the number of casualties. They supported a regime that was corrupt, callous, and oppressive, and they did not care about the lives of the young men they sent to war.

I was also furious with my father and blamed him for my brother's death. Bill had been drafted into the army after flunking out of the University of Minnesota twice. For someone as smart as my brother, that must have taken some effort on his part or perhaps a sustained, concentrated lack of effort. He had gotten poor grades in high school also, mostly Cs and Ds. My brother's love in life had been music and playing the guitar. With two other guys, he first formed a folk band, then later a rock band, the Chasers, which was mildly successful locally until it dissolved when the members went off to the university in 1966.

He spent most of his high school years practicing the guitar. One of the enduring images I have of my brother is of him standing against the big picture window in our family room and playing his guitar while he looked out at the trees in the backyard. He would be totally absorbed in the music he was playing, and if I called to him then, he would not answer, or if he did, he would turn and look vacantly at me, his consciousness only coming partly back to listen. The first thing he did after he got a leave to come home right before being sent to Vietnam was to play music. I remember returning from school one afternoon in November 1967 to the sounds of the Byrds, backed by my brother's bass guitar, streaming out the front door. He had told no one he would be there, and I was the first home. I threw down my books and ran to the family room. There he stood, bass guitar in hand. "Hi, sis," he said. "So you bought the new Byrds album. Good choice."

All Bill wanted to do was play music. He spent all his time doing it, and that caused his downfall. Once during his first quarter at the University of Minnesota, I caught him playing with his band at a pep rally in our high school auditorium. He had not told us he was going to be there, and I knew he had a biology exam during that time. After the rally, I went up to him. "What are you doing?" I asked. "Didn't you have an exam at two?" He just smiled down at me and said, "Live for today, for tomorrow you die." I wanted to shake him and scream at him, "Are you nuts?" What was he doing? I was fifteen, but I knew what the consequence of flunking out of college was: Vietnam.

But back then, "Live for today, for tomorrow you die" was one of his favorite mottoes. In his last letter to me, he included a poem:

Life is like a drop of
salt water to the ocean.
From this thought arises
this question. Why waste life
on work? Why not just enjoy
what is so short.
To all who read this, search
for the answer,
I shan't.

In the same letter, he gave me this big-brotherly advice: "Always wonder, never take for granted." My brother, the philosopher. On the cover of a notebook for a college history course, he wrote, "Worry is a leak in the faucet of human potential." On a page inside, he recorded the grade for his first history theme—D+. Bill was not stupid, and he came from a home that had wall-to-wall books in the living room. When we didn't know a word or a fact, we looked it up in the dictionary or encyclopedia. Dinnertime discussions centered around politics, philosophy, or science.

My father hammered away at Bill about his grades. "Do you want to end up a ditchdigger?" he'd ask my brother, who merely stared back at him. Family opinion had it that the reason Bill did so badly in school was to get back at my father, who was a University of Minnesota professor with a Ph.D., a D.V.M., and thirteen years of college. Education was emphasized in my family. My mother had ten years of college and was only an exam away from a Ph.D. in genetics. My Grandmother Weber told us over and over that an education was the only thing no one could ever take away from you. To not do well in school was nearly a sin.

I look back on those last years of my brother's life and don't know exactly why he did poorly in school, but to say he was rebelling against my father is too simple an explanation. I know that he was embarrassed by his grades. One of his best high school friends was class valedictorian. Another graduated in the top 5 percent. One later told me that when they'd get tests back and ask Bill what he got, he would just shrug. Most of his friends said that he was not interested because he was not intellectual, but I don't agree. An intellectual even back then, I read extensively, devouring everything I could get my hands on, and from talking with my brother, reading the letters he wrote to me, and listening to the tapes he sent, I found him thoughtful and intellectual.

I also know that he could work hard. People who knew him on the few jobs he had remarked how hardworking and conscientious he was. At the Dayton's store in downtown Saint Paul where he worked in the men's department the summer before he was drafted, the manager told us that Bill had been one of his best salesclerks. In fact, I later was hired there because of his reputation. He was also a carryout boy at the local grocery store, and time and time again, I heard from women who shopped there how helpful he was. When I interviewed Bill's platoon leader and his company commander, both said that he was one of the guys they could always count on.

I watched Bill while he worked for my uncle one summer on his farm. He worked hard, getting up on time at five a.m. (unlike me), and my uncle wanted him to work for him full-time. I think Bill was a hard worker. He liked learning, reading, and thinking. But he did not like being told how to learn and what to learn and conforming to any set of rules. Also, he mostly liked playing music, pleasing people, and having people pleased with him. He worked hard at those things he liked.

My father's method of dealing with my brother's failing at school was to criticize him even more. He tried to shame him into doing well. That method worked with me because I got angry and had an "I'll show you" attitude, but it did not work with Bill. I think he began to believe he could not do well. All this may have straightened out with time, but during the late 1960s, young men did not have the luxury of gradually figuring out their lives because of the Vietnam War. So I worried about my brother and kept after him to stay in school, even if he didn't like it. But when I'd tell him that, he would just look at me as if I were clueless. Even after he flunked out and was just waiting to be drafted and I was after him to *do* something, for God's sake—go to Canada, sign up as a conscientious objector, *anything, please*—he would just stare down at me with this impervious, almost regal look. I was frantic with worry.

So when he died, I came down hard on my father. I let him know directly and regularly that I thought he had killed Bill by being too hard on him. Why hadn't he helped him more? Once when my father shouted at my younger brother, who also did not do well in school, I stood up and shouted back at my father that he had killed one of my brothers—was he now working on killing the other? Furiously, he told me to shut up or leave. I kept up my barrage at him until one day, I made him cry. I can't remember what I said to him, but he replied, "Ouch, that hurt." And I looked up to see tears in my father's eyes. I was horrified then and stopped my attacks.

As soon as I could, I left home to go to college and made sure I went to a school away from the Twin Cities, where we lived. At the time, I thought it was because I was so angry at my parents because they did nothing to help my brother. I was also angry because their way of living no longer worked for me. I wanted a different life—a life where brothers would not get sent away to wars, where wars and social injustice didn't exist. I saw everything my parents did as perpetuating those things. But now I know I also went away to be far from that house where one less person sat at the supper table and slept in a bedroom.

Unlike my brother, I did well in school and received mostly As and Bs and was on the dean's list my first two or three years of college. Majoring in biology, I thought about being pre-med, to carry on family tradition. With a love of learning and school, I was the type of student who read books for pleasure. I say this because of what subsequently happened. In college, I did not join any of the sororities because I saw them as perpetuating a system that no longer worked. How could anyone think about fraternities or sororities? They perpetuated the caste system, the materialism, the racism, the sexism, all that I felt was responsible for the way the world was. In the summer of 1968, before I went away, I addressed envelopes for Eugene McCarthy's campaign. I wrote letters to my congressmen, who, when they answered, never seemed to address the real issues but mouthed stale platitudes.

I took part in sit-ins and demonstrations. I remember two incidents most clearly. One was during a sleep-in we students held in front of the administration building in the fall of 1969 at the small college I attended. At that point, I was not what one would call a hippie, a member of the counterculture, and I remember one of the more hippie-looking students telling me to move, no one wanted me here, why didn't I go and be with my own kind? Sometimes, I found the people in the antiwar movement to be as callous as those who were prowar. In the other incident, I saw a group of students holding up placards that carried the names of those from Minnesota who had been killed in the war. On one of the signs dated 1968, I saw my brother's name. I was furious. My grief was personal and private. How dare they use his name like that? So I went over to argue with those holding the signs. Didn't they realize what they were doing? They were taking my brother and turning him into nothing but a cause, a statistic. I asked them to quit that or take his name off their sign. They tried to reason calmly with me. Didn't I want the war ended? Well, didn't I see that what they were doing was helping end the war by making people aware that actual people were dying there? I patiently explained to them how painful it was for me to see my brother's name up there. They patiently reasoned back. But our exchange ended with me screaming at them that they were as bad as the government that looked at my brother as nothing more than a tool to be used for its benefit. "Can't I have my grief? My memory of him?" I yelled in their faces. "Thank you for killing my brother twice," I raved as I snatched the sign and threw it to the ground. I walked away, aware of the murmuring at my back and the stares. I just didn't care.

During this time, I hated most people, even many of the people in the antiwar movement. Those not actively trying to stop the war I saw as murderers of my brother. And some of those in the antiwar movement I saw as sanctimonious or merely interested in the cause as a fad. Unlike most of them, I could not separate myself from the men who went to Vietnam. I did not hate the ordinary soldier who was drafted— I hated the American people; I hated those in power; I hated the generals and other commanding officers; I hated the South Vietnamese. I did not hate the Vietcong; I did not hate the North Vietnamese; and I did not hate those who went to Canada or those who didn't and fought. I did sometimes hate conscientious objectors, particularly if they took a holier-than-thou attitude. I figured they had just been graced by luck. I had utmost sympathy for the men sent to Vietnam. I saw them as my brothers.

After two years at the small private college, I transferred to the University of Minnesota. I did not like the complacent attitude most U. of M.

students had. They seemed concerned with clothes, vacations in St. Petersburg during spring break and Vail during Christmas break, their social calendars, and who was dating whom. They had queen contests in which the candidates had to be blonde, blue-eyed, and Swedish. I was none of these.

The winter of my sophomore year, a story about a massacre in the village of My Lai started to appear in newspapers. Chu Lai, Charlie Company, Americal Division, Task Force Barker, Capt. Ernest Medina, and Lt. William Calley—those names stood out. When I called my parents, they confirmed my memories: The company accused of the massacre was the one my brother had been in. Medina was the captain who had written letters to us after Bill was killed. Calley was Bill's platoon leader. In fact, Bill had been his radio operator. Some of the guys from the company had been writing to my family: Tom Turner, Ron Grzesik, Bob Lee. I remember my parents wondering how they were involved. We all read the papers anxiously to see if those names appeared.

Soon after the reports became public, some of the guys from Bill's company went to visit my parents. I was away at school. My parents asked them what had happened that day in the village. They told my parents that they didn't know. They had stayed out of it, they said, on the outskirts of the village. They knew something bad was happening and decided to stay away. We sighed with relief. If they were guilty, so was Bill, and somehow by association so were we.

I know now after all the reading I've done since the war that those soldiers were lying. My parents probably knew that at the time, and I probably intuited it, though I was only nineteen and naive. In accounts of the massacre, I find most of the names of those men solidly in the center of the events. One of them told my father that they swore for every one of them that got killed, they would kill one hundred Vietcong. One book I read reported that before they machine-gunned the villagers, some men from the company said, "And that's for Bill Weber."[1] My younger brother, who was nine at the time, told me later that one of the soldiers who visited my family looked like "someone whose vision of what the world was had been shattered, who did not recognize this world he had come back to and had found nothing yet to replace that world." He told me that the guy couldn't eat the steak my mother had served him and that even to smell it made him sick. The men and my family had gone to a hockey game at the University of Minnesota; my brother said that on the way, they had to cross a suspension bridge, and the guy smoked five cigarettes before he could cross.

Books and articles about the company and the massacre began to be published in 1970. They talked about Bill's death. I remember two accounts most vividly. The first was in an interview with Calley: "A rifle shot got my R.T.O.—my radio-telephone operator—on his radio harness, the harness shattered and it tore his kidney out. He rolled off the levee saying to me, 'I been shot.' . . . [H]e was dead a good twenty minutes before the chopper could pick him up. . . . It was horrible, but I was about to leave him floating there."[2]

Even though Calley got Bill's name wrong—he called him "Weaver"—I recognized my brother's death. In fact, many accounts got his name wrong; one called him "Ron Weber." The army had told us that Bill died instantly. The accounts I read did not seem to indicate that, and each told a different story. One described Bill as "moaning like an animal," crying, screaming, and saying, "I'm gonna die, I'm gonna die."[3] One of Bill's best friends and the medic, Doc Lee, came to aid him, but by the time the helicopter came, Bill was dead.

I wonder if most people reading such accounts think they are just like so many other stories of war and death, something read or seen in a movie. It is an impersonal death—something to cluck one's tongue about, but always something that happens to someone else. But as a twenty-year-old reading these accounts of my brother's death, I was sickened. I would slam the book shut, but every now and again, just as one picks at a scab, I would open it back up. I guess reading it and feeling the pain was one way of keeping Bill alive for me.

I also read all the accounts of the massacre I could find. I read them over and over again and tried to discover the truth about what happened. The details sickened me. I just could not imagine those guys—people who wrote to my parents, who had known Bill, and who had seemed so nice—doing such things. What had happened to them? I remembered that in his letters to us shortly before he died, Bill had mentioned that he and the others went on search-and-destroy missions. My parents were angry at that. I remember them saying, "What do you expect when you send guys out on missions like that? Particularly when it's hard to tell who's an enemy and who's a friend." They said that the generals, President Johnson, and Robert McNamara should be tried in court.

All these years later, I cannot block out the cries of those villagers. When I meet someone for the first time, I have a tendency to tell them that my brother was Lieutenant Calley's radio operator—you know, the one who was convicted of killing those villagers in My Lai. To most

Americans, My Lai is an aberration, something done by guys who went berserk and were probably a little on the edge to begin with. But for me, it is not an aberration. It is the whole war for me, and the guys who did it are my brothers. And they break my heart. I cannot separate my brother from that massacre. He has become synonymous with it. When I think of him, I think of all those people crying and screaming before they were gunned down.

In the spring of 1971, I was preparing to take an exam in organic chemistry, a course in which I had a 94 percent grade average. Instead of studying for it, I found myself drifting over to the literature section of the library and reading all the books on the shelf about Edgar Allan Poe. I passed the course with a C. The next fall, I was in an honors seminar on eighteenth-century philosophers, and when I was supposed to be studying for a midterm exam on Spinoza, Leibnitz, and Descartes, I instead stayed up all night and listened to Beethoven's Ninth and read e.e. cummings's poetry. I got the third-lowest grade in a class of sixty students. I dropped biology as a major and changed to German, a language I knew almost as well as English. After I did that, my grades improved. I went back to getting As with a few Bs thrown in here and there. German was easy. Upset that I'd changed my major, my father asked, "Why did you stop taking bread-and-butter courses?"

I began spending more time doing activities that were considered countercultural. I joined a commune, food co-ops, hardware co-ops, and a woman's health co-op. I hung out at the women's liberation office on campus. I stopped cutting my hair and let it grow long and tangled. I stopped wearing a bra, stopped shaving my legs and my underarms, and stopped wearing shoes in the summer, even in the city. I vowed not to become "part of the establishment," not to "sell out to the system," and instead I looked for alternative ways to make money. I didn't want to be part of the power structure that oppressed, robbed, and killed people. I took menial jobs. I know this upset my parents. At one point my father, on seeing the place where I lived (a condemned house off Franklin Avenue in Minneapolis), asked me how far down I thought I might go before I decided I was low enough. I just shrugged.

I went through probably about a six-month period during which I shoplifted groceries, record albums, watercolors, watercolor paper, and textbooks. I did it to get back at the capitalists who ran the country and made their money by oppressing people and who had helped kill my brother. I quit stealing for two reasons. First, the manager of the bookstore where I did a lot of my shoplifting was a very nice woman. Second,

I realized that I would never touch those who made all the money. They would simply raise the prices and pass their loss on to the people who shopped at their stores. By stealing, I hurt only the poor. So I gave it up.

I finally gave up my down-and-out counterculture life, too, and finished college. I later earned a Ph.D. in English literature and started teaching at a university. I am not one who likes to suffer much, particularly when it seems pointless, so I stopped my overt social protests. I have never regained my faith in our government, however. I still see it as basically corrupt. Also, I have never regained faith in people. Most are out to make a buck and to get as much as they can. They do not want to jeopardize their comfortable lives, and they would sacrifice their neighbors to keep living their lives as they do. I'm sorry I feel this way. I wish I didn't. I have never forgiven the people in the United States for the Vietnam War. When I walked past the Vietnam Veterans Memorial in Washington, DC, a few years ago and saw the line of people passing by and looking sad, I felt angry. What right did they have to mourn those men? What right did they have to look sad? Where were they back then? What did they do to stop the war? What did they give up to stop the killing? I found myself elbowing my way through the crowds and not caring if I hurt someone. I know it is wrong to feel this way. I know I am being unfair. But my heart hardens into a tight fist and won't let go, no matter what I say to it.

After McNamara's memoirs came out, a friend asked me what justice I thought he deserved. I decided I wanted him to feel what I felt, the pain my parents had felt. I answered that I wanted him to watch as his children were killed one by one. I know this is horrific and that such desires caused My Lai. They are evil. I have been taught that I should bless my enemies, pray for their souls. I guess I'm not there yet. I will keep trying.

I have reconciled with my father. I quit blaming him for my brother's death a long time ago. A few years ago, I wrote him a letter asking him to forgive me for ever blaming him for what happened to Bill. I have no idea why my brother seemed so bent on destruction, but he chose the way his life ended. He flunked out of school and did nothing about being drafted when he did have alternatives. He turned down officer candidate school in Germany, where, because of his fluency in German, he could have spent his time in the army, and then he put in for the most exposed position in a platoon, that of the radio operator. I told a friend right after Bill's death that I thought he had a death wish. I don't care so much anymore about reasons. I am just sad that all that potential is gone, and I'm sad that when I remember my brother, I also have to remember that miserable war.

Not long ago, my seventy-eight-year-old father, a writer friend named Bob Ross, and I traveled to Vietnam to visit the site of the My Lai massacre and to find the spot where my brother was killed. I knew my father needed to go to be at peace about Bill's death. My mother did not want us to go because she felt it uncovered things best left undisturbed. Upset at my persistence, she stopped talking to me about two months before we went and died suddenly about four weeks before our trip. Despite her angry silence, she had bought our tickets to Vietnam. I wish my mother could have made the trip. She never found peace about Bill's death. Since going, I find that I am less upset about his death. He used to come back to me in dreams. He no longer does.

My father and I met with members of the People's Committee in Quang Ngai, Duc Pho, and My Lai, all the places where Bill was during the war. One rainy day in December just before Christmas, they helped us find the place where Bill was probably killed on the Diem Diem River, near where it flows into the sea about two kilometers outside the village of My Lai. The levee where he was killed was gone, and the river had swollen far over its banks because of the never ceasing torrents of rain. The men—the same ones who, twenty-nine years earlier as Vietcong, had taken part in the battle that killed Bill—pointed to a spot about a hundred yards into the swirling river. "Over there," they said. They gestured to a far line of trees and told us that was where they were shooting from. "We knew we had killed or wounded some GI that day because we saw the helicopter land here where we stand now," they told us.

Earlier, over tea and cookies, my father and I apologized to them for my brother's part in the war. "He was a good boy. He was only doing what his country asked of him," my father said as he shook his head sadly. I told the People's Committee of My Lai that I was glad that my brother was dead because I would have hated for him to be part of that massacre. I would have hated what it would have done to his soul. Did I mean that? My friend Bob was angry at me for saying that. He told me that as he was sitting with all those former Vietcong, he had suddenly felt angry. Hadn't they killed also? What are we apologizing for? He told me my mother would be doubly angry at me now. How could I be glad my brother was dead?

These days, I keep thinking about the others in Bill's company who survived and what I have read about their lives. I also remember what my father said about Bill when he was killed: "He was probably watching the butterflies in the outfield, just as he did when he was a kid playing baseball. I'd look up and there would be old Bill daydreaming out in left field and missing all the balls hit to him."

Notes

1. Martin Gershen, *Destroy or Die: The True Story of My Lai* (New Rochelle, NY: Arlington House, 1971), 37.

2. John Sack, "The Continuing Confessions of Lieutenant Calley," *Esquire* (February 1971): 55.

3. Gershen, *Destroy or Die*, 204.

Suggested Readings

For background and analysis on the My Lai massacre, see David L. Anderson, ed., *Facing My Lai: Moving beyond the Massacre* (Lawrence: University Press of Kansas, 1998), and Michael Bilton and Kevin Sim, *Four Hours in My Lai* (New York: Viking, 1992). Moving accounts of the impact of the war on individuals are found in Myra MacPherson, *Long Time Passing: Vietnam and the Haunted Generation* (New York: Doubleday, 1984), and in the memoirs, poems, and novels of Vietnam veteran writers. For an example of the latter, see Tim O'Brien, *The Things They Carried* (Boston: Houghton Mifflin, 1990).

14

Otto Feinstein, the McCarthy Campaign in Michigan, and Campus Activism during the Cold War

Melvin Small

Like the unanticipated Tet Offensive and the killings at Kent State, another traumatic incident of the Vietnam era that deeply troubled Americans was the violence surrounding the 1968 Democratic National Convention in Chicago. In front of a worldwide television audience, the Chicago police—supported by the Illinois National Guard—followed the edict of law-and-order mayor Richard J. Daley to tolerate no disruption of the convention by protestors. Although admittedly taunted by some radicals in the crowd, the police overreacted in an orgy of beatings and mass arrests far out of proportion to the provocation. As gripping as the street scenes were, an equally fundamental drama was occurring inside the convention hall. Internal divisions within the Democratic Party paralleled the fissures in American society and revealed the inability of the political process to respond effectively to the challenge that the war presented.

Attending the Chicago convention was an alternate delegate from Michigan by the name of Otto Feinstein, who supported Sen. Eugene McCarthy as a peace candidate for the Democratic presidential nomination. Feinstein was the leader of the McCarthy Democrats, or the Concerned Democrats in Michigan, from 1966 through 1969. A refugee from Nazi Austria, he became involved in reform democratic or social democratic politics at the University of Chicago, where he founded the journal *New University Thought (NUT)*. He then taught at Wayne State University in Detroit, where he became involved in Michigan politics. In the fall of 1967, he was one of those people most influential in convincing Senator McCarthy to run for president as an antiwar candidate, and he was central to the successful insurgent effort in Democratic Party politics in Michigan. The national McCarthy campaign failed to nominate its candidate, but, as Melvin Small explains, the political changes that Feinstein and other McCarthy Democrats effected were significant. Amid the many accounts of hippies, radicals, and SDS antiwarriors,

This essay originally appeared in David L. Anderson, ed., *The Human Tradition in the Vietnam Era* (Wilmington, DE: Scholarly Resources, 2000), 175–94.

the story of adult, liberal, mostly college-related reformers such as Feinstein reveals much about reform politics within the Democratic Party.

Melvin Small is a professor of history at Wayne State University in Detroit, Michigan, and past president of the Council on Peace Research in History. His Ph.D. is from the University of Michigan. Among his many publications are *Johnson, Nixon, and the Doves* (1988), *Covering Dissent: The Media and the Anti-Vietnam War Movement* (1994), *Democracy and Diplomacy: The Impact of Domestic Politics on U.S. Foreign Relations, 1789–1994* (1996), *The Presidency of Richard Nixon* (1999), and *Anti-Warriors: The Vietnam War and the Battle for America's Hearts and Minds* (2002).

The anti-Vietnam War movement was centered on college campuses where professors and graduate students provided leadership to undergraduates who marched, rallied, leafleted, petitioned, and sometimes committed acts of civil and uncivil disobedience to demonstrate their opposition to the conflict. At no time in American history had academics figured so prominently in the creation of a political movement. They reached their peak of influence and genuine power during Sen. Eugene McCarthy's campaign for the 1968 Democratic presidential nomination.

Most of the millions who participated in the movement to end the war were liberal Democrats committed to working within the system to improve the prospects for peace and justice at home and abroad. Although the media often presented the antiwar movement as dominated by left-wing, countercultural, even anti-"Amerikan" young people, many of those who worked most effectively to end the war were middle-class adults who wore coats and ties and dresses and heels and saluted when the flag passed. They were normal people contending with critical issues that affected their personal, professional, and civic lives on individual, community, institutional, social, and cultural levels. Prof. Otto Feinstein of Wayne State University in Detroit was one of the national leaders of the McCarthy drive and executive director of the McCarthy campaign in Michigan. He was committed to working through the system, and his many earlier campus-based political activities prefigured his involvement in the attempt to nominate a Democratic presidential candidate who would end the war in Vietnam and preserve the New Deal coalition.

Feinstein was born in Vienna in 1930, the son of Abraham Feinstein and Bella Silber, both of whom came from Hasidic Jewish families. Born in the Austro-Hungarian Empire, Abraham came from Bukovina, which later became part of Romania, and Bella was from Galicia, which would become part of Poland. After serving in World War I and graduating from law school, Abraham became a successful and influential banker and commodity trader, with his business centered in Bucharest. Because of the 1929 pogroms in Romania, he moved his wife to Vienna for safety. Their first child, Otto, was born in the Austrian capital.

Otto grew up in a well-to-do household. Although his parents did not follow their families' Orthodox traditions, they were practicing Jews. At a very young age, he became aware of the anti-Semitism that he and his family confronted in a variety of ways. He also remembers well the intense political conflicts between the Left and the Right in the political cauldron that was Austria during the depression.

Four months after the 1938 Anschluss—the Nazi annexation of Austria—Abraham, a Romanian citizen, was able to obtain the aid of the Romanian consul in Vienna in escaping with his wife and two children to Zurich. He had read Adolph Hitler's *Mein Kampf* and had made careful preparations to leave any area controlled by the Nazis. Having begun public school in Vienna, Otto continued his education in 1938 and 1939 in Zurich and Lausanne. His father moved the family to London in 1939; there, after spending one day in school, Otto and his younger brother, Alfred, were evacuated to Cornwall.

Fearing a German invasion of England, Abraham arranged for his family to travel to the United States on tourist visas to see the New York World's Fair. (The U.S. immigration quota for European Jews was very small.) By the time the Feinsteins arrived in New York in May 1940, the fair and their visas had only three days until expiration. They could have been turned away at Customs, but a kind immigration official let them enter the country. Ultimately, American relatives helped the Feinsteins obtain immigrant visas.

In New York, Otto attended public schools in Jackson Heights and Manhattan before the family took up permanent residence in 1941 in Forest Hills, located in the New York City borough of Queens. By the time that he entered Forest Hills High School in 1944, he had attended nine grade schools in four countries and had been taught in three different languages. His father had established himself in the export-import business, which provided the family with a comfortable lifestyle, albeit not as comfortable as that to which it had been accustomed in Europe.

Although his father had never been involved in sectarian politics, political discussions always dominated the family mealtimes. Abraham read four newspapers daily and listened avidly to radio commentators, which was not surprising during World War II for a person concerned about the rest of his family in Europe. In the years immediately after the war, Otto traveled to the Continent with his father to search, generally in vain, for relatives who survived the Holocaust. For the rest of his life, the Holocaust would remain a central experience for him, as it did for many European—and American—Jews. His advocacy of citizen activism to promote social justice and to maintain a healthy democratic system had its roots in that experience.

At Forest Hills High School, Feinstein played on the soccer and chess teams, sang in the chorus, and excelled scholastically, although he was not Americanized enough to care about such things as the prom. He remembered that his main political ambition as a freshman was to join the U.S. Army and "get even" with the Nazis. After winning a New York State Regents scholarship in 1948, he tried to obtain admission to Columbia University but was told by a Jewish interviewer that the "quota for intelligent students had been filled." When he ran into similar indications of not-so-veiled anti-Semitism at Cornell and Syracuse, he decided (along with his brother, who had caught up with him in school) to go to the University of Chicago, which had no quota and offered an attractive general education curriculum. Under the university's Hutchins Plan, it was also possible to graduate in two years, which Otto did in 1950.

While at Chicago, Feinstein almost immediately became involved in protests against racism at the university hospital and against Illinois's anti-Communist Broyles Bill. He joined the Young Progressives of America during his first semester and soon became an officer of that wing of the Henry Wallace presidential campaign, for which he served as a poll watcher in the 1948 election. He also played on the university's soccer team, and his teammates elected him their representative to protest the Broyles Bill at a demonstration in Springfield.

Feinstein developed a lifelong interest in grassroots politics while working on local political issues in the depressed neighborhoods surrounding the university. Within the school, he became an activist in the more progressive of the two main student parties—the party involved in activities beyond the campus. Interestingly, Sander Levin, whom he would meet in Michigan Democratic Party politics twenty years later, was a leader of the more conservative student party at the University of Chicago. In 1950 the university's student council elected him to be an observer at the epochal Prague conference of the International Union of Students, an organization that could not survive the dark days of the early Cold War as an independent institution. The experience in Prague, mingling with students from both blocs, gave him firsthand exposure to the nature of the Cold War that had descended on Europe.

Throughout his years as a student, Feinstein saw a direct connection between his interest in the social sciences and political life outside the academy. He knew from the first that he would pursue a scholarly career that dealt with social issues. After graduating in 1950, he went on to the Institut des Hautes Études in Geneva, where he spent three years studying for a licentiate in international relations. At Geneva, he became active in the Swiss Federation of Students and the Swiss Union of Jewish Students and was vice president of the Association of Anti-Colonial Student Unions.

In 1953, he was drafted into the U.S. Army. During his two years at Camp Kilmer, Fort Dix, and Fort Meade, he "broadened his understanding of people from different classes and regions of the country." Using the GI Bill, he returned to the University of Chicago in 1955 to work on a Ph.D. In Geneva, he had studied traditional international relations; now, he concentrated on economic development and cultural change in the Third World. Completed under Bert Hoselitz in 1956, Otto's thesis dealt with the economic, social, and political role of foreign investment in Venezuela. As a graduate student, he also resumed his activity in campus politics, again representing his party in the student council.

Distressed with the way in which "old ideological positions developed in a different era" continued to dominate political discourse, Feinstein and a group of friends set out to publish a journal of opinion in 1959. They wanted, as they noted in their first issue, "to develop a coherent way of looking at society which can provide a rational basis for a political program for the '60s and '70s." The first issue of *New University Thought* appeared in the spring of 1960 and featured articles by Linus Pauling, David Reisman, Feinstein, and several other members of the editorial board. Published quarterly through the late 1960s, *NUT* offered nonsectarian, eclectic approaches to the problems of war and peace, race, and economic development. It boasted a "*radical* mode of analysis, radical in the original sense of going to the root."

The editors were mostly young scholars looking for ways to create a broad intellectual community in which they could use their expertise to develop new solutions to societal problems. Colleagues involved with *NUT* nationwide not only contributed to the journal but also formed study groups on their campuses to consider the issues raised in the journal.

Feinstein never forgot about the "submission of the universities and academics" to fascism in the 1930s and maintained throughout his career that the "universities had a social role critical for democratic societies." Not surprisingly, *NUT* became an essential vehicle for sharing information about the war in Vietnam and, later, about the McCarthy campaign. In its front-page article on September 16, 1960, the *Times (London) Literary Supplement* offered "an especially warm welcome" to the first volume of *NUT*, noting that Feinstein's article on Latin America deserved a "worthy place in any educated European's library."

With a press run of five thousand copies, *NUT* relied on subscriptions and a growing network of supporters in over twenty colleges, including the University of California, Berkeley, and Columbia University. The editors ran twenty thousand copies for one special 1962 issue on peace. Among the contributors to that issue were Seymour Melman, Arthur Waskow, Rep. William Fitts Ryan (D–NY), and Todd Gitlin. The journal's call for new paradigms in 1960 resembled the Students for a Democratic Society's Port Huron Statement of 1962. Both organizations were similarly dissatisfied with the contemporary political debate, but the people at *NUT* were of an older generation and were willing to work within the system, liberal warts and all.

In the fall of 1960, Feinstein took a job at Monteith College in Detroit's Wayne State University, and in December 1961, he married fellow *NUT* editor Nicolette Margaret Cecelia Carey, who was also an assistant editor of the *Bulletin of Atomic Scientists*. (Although it took Feinstein two years to make it through the University of Chicago, Carey used the Hutchins Plan to graduate in one year!) Founded in 1958, Monteith was an experimental college that employed the general studies model of the University of Chicago. In fact, several of its faculty had attended or were recruited from Chicago.

In the 1960 presidential campaign, like many of his colleagues, Feinstein did not work *for* John F. Kennedy but *against* Richard M. Nixon. In 1962, he became a Democratic Party precinct delegate and soon organized fellow delegates into the Wednesday Evening Club, a discussion-action group interested in promoting new ideas within the party. Their goal was not to take over or "subvert the party" but to invigorate its debate and move it in new and more promising directions. (Of course, party regulars did not always see things that way.) When Feinstein became vice president of the Thirteenth Congressional District Democratic Party in 1964, he established an important base from which to operate.

Open housing and the establishment of the Wayne County Community College system were among the key issues during the early 1960s in which Feinstein played a leading role. He and several colleagues also produced a local, seventeen-part public television series, *The Balance of Fear*, on the nuclear arms race, and after the Partial Test Ban Treaty was approved in 1963, other public television stations aired one of the segments in fifteen cities. The budget for the series was $180.

Feinstein was a leader of the Committee for a Sane Nuclear Policy (SANE) and a friend of its longtime director, Sanford Gottlieb, who also contributed articles to *NUT*. When Feinstein determined that the local Detroit chapter of SANE was too involved in internecine conflict with the national office, however, the tireless and always creative organizer founded Wayne SANE, which soon recruited twenty-three faculty members for its speaker's bureau. He also became one of the founders of the Center for Teaching about Peace and War (later the Center for Peace and Conflict Studies), an organization devoted not only to studying such issues in Wayne State University but also to bringing them to the community. The organization was one of the first peace and conflict centers in the United States.

In a related venture, Feinstein traveled to Columbia University to help organize the Universities Committee on the Problems of War and Peace in February 1963. In their founding document, which resembled *NUT*'s first editorial, the committee's leaders announced that they intended "to make specific use of the special talents of academic people in discovering, developing and articulating information and suggestions relating to the problems of war and peace." Feinstein was elected executive secretary of the organization, whose sponsors included Kenneth Boulding, Richard Falk, S. I. Hayakawa, Herbert Kelman, Guenter Lewy, and David Reisman. Feinstein and his wife edited the newsletter of the organization that went out to nine thousand academics on 250 campuses. The committee's membership and newsletter overlapped with those of *NUT*, but, unlike the magazine, this organization was concerned exclusively with war and peace issues.

During this period, Feinstein published a flurry of articles on disarmament and international relations in *NUT*, the *Bulletin of Atomic Scientists*, the *Saturday Review of Books*, *Current History*, and other journals, and he edited a book on development, *Two Worlds of Change* (1964). As a student of the developing world, he was well aware of the colonial war fought by the French against the Vietnamese and the American acceptance of the French burden in Vietnam in 1954. He worried as the United

States became more and more involved in Southeast Asia and doubted President Lyndon Johnson's explanation of the 1964 Gulf of Tonkin incident that led Congress to pass the Gulf of Tonkin Resolution. He was concerned about Johnson's policies in Vietnam, but he was far more worried about the prospect of Sen. Barry Goldwater's (R–AZ) election in 1964. That concern led him to organize the Republicans and Independents for Johnson in Detroit. Feinstein compared Johnson to Truman as a president with laudable domestic programs who had been led by others into dangerous Cold War policies, in part because he did not know much about international relations.

After Johnson began the sustained bombing of North Vietnam in February 1965, Feinstein and his colleagues at Wayne and throughout the *NUT* and the Universities Committee networks immediately began to hold meetings and workshops on college campuses. The bombing was the catalyst that sparked the antiwar movement in the United States and throughout the world. The Universities Committee declared March 4 a national "Vietnam Day," during which faculty, students, and community people participated in meetings and lectures on over 100 campuses, anticipating what soon came to be called "teach-ins." Feinstein and his Wayne colleagues kept in close contact and shared strategies with like-minded faculty members at the University of Michigan, some forty miles away in Ann Arbor—particularly with history professor John Weiss. It was not surprising, then, that the University of Michigan's famous teach-in of March 24–25, 1965, resembled the conference held on Wayne's campus on March 4. During that frenetic early spring, on the weekend of April 8–9, Feinstein was among the more than 100 mostly East Coast faculty members who traveled to Washington to lobby over 60 legislators on the war.

In its Summer 1965 issue, *NUT* led with an article entitled "Vietnam: The Bar Mitzvah of American Intellectuals." The journal had questioned American involvement in Vietnam as early as August 1962. Now, three years later, the editors wrote that "the most significant aspect of the recent ferment and action in academia has not been the actions themselves . . . but the potential change in what academics do and how they see their role in society." For the first time "American academics have begun to feel that they have the competence and the right to pass judgment upon our policy, to express this judgment, and to work actively in a variety of ways to make this judgment felt." They were speaking out publicly against U.S. policies in Vietnam at precisely the time in American history when "the universities and the faculty and researchers attached to them as individuals and as a class are becoming increasingly important and powerful in the functioning of our society."

The editors were pleased that "academics are beginning to learn how to use the mass media to communicate their ideas" and how to establish relationships with government officials. In the end, they predicted that academics might even form a sort of "shadow cabinet" to "evaluate present programs and propose new ones from the highest level of competence." Feinstein and his colleagues called for a careful and patient nurturing of the antiwar activities on campuses, building them into something that might lead to profound changes in the nature of the relationship of the once insular academic community to the national political culture. In the spring of 1965, that community was moving in the direction called for when *NUT* editors first presented their agenda in 1960.

In addition to bringing out the seminal *NUT* issue on the war, Feinstein helped organize antiwar meetings and petition drives. These included the "Citizens' Hearings on Vietnam" on the Wayne campus, led by two Michigan congressmen, Republican William Broomfield and Democrat Charles C. Diggs, on August 6 and 7, as well as the International Conference on Alternate Perspectives on Vietnam, held in Ann Arbor from September 14 to 18, 1965. Among those presenting papers at the Ann Arbor conference was the distinguished French scholar, Jean Lacouture.

On March 13, 1966, Feinstein, Weiss, and other antiwar Democrats established the Council for Democratic Action within Michigan. They had worked with friends in the Women's International League for Peace and Freedom (WILPF) to identify Democratic precinct delegates who desired to change administration policy at home and abroad. As its first order of business, the new council sent the Michigan Democratic State Committee its Vietnam program, which called for an end to the bombing, negotiations, and free elections open to all factions in South Vietnam. The state committee summarily rejected the proposals, but a formal process for developing opposition to the national party's policies had begun in the Detroit metropolitan area.

One outgrowth of this activity was the formation of reform caucuses in several districts, most notably the Liberal Conference in the Seventeenth Congressional District. In May 1967, Feinstein and his colleagues, now calling themselves the Conference of Concerned Democrats, announced a meeting to be held in Detroit on Wayne's campus on June 10. As many as 350 people came to hear Zoltan Ferency, the antiwar Michigan Democratic State Party chair, Detroit mayor Jerome Cavanagh, state senator Coleman Young, and Rep. John Conyers. A highlight of the meeting was a rousing speech by Wayne history professor Lynn Parsons. He urged the Concerned Democrats to elect precinct delegates, "to speak up, to work hard, to sacrifice long hours in travel and in meetings," and to work "through the political party which for most of the century has led the nation in meeting its most serious problems." The Michigan Conference of Concerned Democrats, which grew out of this gathering, served as a model used by Allard Lowenstein, Sanford Gottlieb, Bella Abzug, and others to develop a nationwide Concerned Democrats organization at a meeting in Washington later that month.

By August, the Concerned Democrats had organized units in all but two of Michigan's nineteen congressional districts. In December seven hundred Concerned Democrats attended a rally in Detroit featuring Julian Bond, John Conyers, Zoltan Ferency, and television actor Robert Vaughn, better known as "The Man from U.N.C.L.E." They responded enthusiastically to a call to action: "The time has come to proclaim the American Dream of Equality for all as the priority of our nation. For an all-out war on poverty and racism. To recognize that Vietnam has become . . . a symbol of the 'arrogance of power' and 'the major roadblock to the realization of the American Dream.' "

In office since 1963, Ferency was one of the few party chairs to oppose Johnson's reelection in 1967. His "disloyalty" came to a head at a meeting of the Michigan Democratic Central Committee in Port Huron in the early fall, when he found himself virtually the only state Democratic official unwilling to support the president's bid for a second term. Ferency decided to resign in order to help an antiwar candidate who would challenge Johnson. Drifting even further to the left after Hubert Humphrey won the Democratic nomination, Ferency founded the Human Rights Party in 1969, a third party that enjoyed very limited success in Michigan through the 1970s. Characteristically, even after disappointments in 1968 and 1969, Feinstein remained a loyal Democrat.

He and other Michigan insurgents who wanted to convince President Johnson to change his policies in Vietnam had to deal with the United Automobile Workers (UAW), the single most influential group within the state Democratic Party. The UAW was committed to many of the same progressive domestic programs as the Concerned Democrats but, nonetheless, was reluctant to criticize Johnson because it feared for the survival of those programs. Moreover, UAW president Walter

Reuther practiced a form of democratic centralism in his organization that made it difficult even for his brother, Victor, an early opponent of the war, to get his voice heard either within the executive board or among the rank and file.

By virtue of his office in the Thirteenth Congressional District, Feinstein had been appointed to the Resolutions Committee of the 1966 state convention. Although Feinstein received support from a majority of delegates in all of Michigan's counties for a resolution mildly critical of U.S. involvement in South Vietnam, Reuther, Sen. Phil Hart, Feinstein's old University of Chicago classmate Sander Levin, and other party regulars muscled through their own motion in support of the president. At one point, clever party parliamentarians prevented Feinstein from speaking even during an open debate.

Generally realistic in his approach to politics, Feinstein cannot understand to this day why the UAW would not meet his group halfway and why "they never talked to us as human beings." He was not interested in sharing power or "infiltrating" the party; he wanted only to work with all of its factions to refocus its foreign policy. The UAW was leery of groups that appeared on its left, however, and among the emerging leadership of the Concerned Democrats were a handful of former (or maybe even current) members of the Communist Party who had crossed swords with the UAW during the 1940s.

On the surface, the differences between those who supported Johnson and those who called for a change in Vietnam policy appeared slight. Both Johnson and his opponents among the Concerned Democrats called for a negotiated end to the war. The president pointed over and over to his many offers to the North Vietnamese to come to the peace table and bargain in good faith. The chief difference was that the Concerned Democrats contended that the administration had to halt the bombing before serious negotiations could begin. That was the position taken by Hanoi as well.

Feinstein never became involved directly in the organization of the major mass demonstrations that were held, generally twice a year, from 1965 through 1971. Like many others in the leadership of the antiwar movement, he wondered about the resources and energy expended on these activities. Accepting a division of labor within the movement, he spent most of his time working on campus and within the Michigan Democratic Party on electoral politics.

It was one thing to form the Concerned Democrats. It was quite another to identify a candidate willing to run against Johnson in 1968.

At some time in late 1966, Feinstein came to the conclusion that Johnson was not going to be sufficiently affected by the antiwar movement to search for a viable way to end the war. Even worse, it was clear that the Democratic Party, "the only practical vehicle for social change," was on the verge of coming apart over the war issue. From Feinstein's perspective, only New York senator Robert F. Kennedy could hold together the cumbersome New Deal coalition that stood for progressive reform in the United States. Throughout 1967, he therefore worked on both the local and the national level to try to convince Kennedy to challenge Johnson. On one occasion, prodded by David Reisman, he traveled to Boston to present his analysis of the 1968 election to John Kenneth Galbraith and other Kennedy advisers.

Even after Kennedy clearly indicated he would not throw his hat into the ring, Feinstein hoped for his candidacy because no other Democrat could keep the party together. Indeed, he was still a Kennedy man when Minnesota senator Eugene McCarthy made his important visit to Detroit on November 10, 1967, to speak at a party dinner in the Second Congressional District—and to test the political waters. James Harrison, the public relations director for Michigan's Democratic State Central Committee, had already set up the first McCarthy for President committee in the nation.

McCarthy supporters asked Feinstein, who had connections to the Sheriff's Department because of his position in Wayne County's Thirteenth District, to work with them to organize a small McCarthy-for-President rally at Detroit Metropolitan Airport. McCarthy had not yet announced his candidacy but was leaning toward running. The idea was to encourage him with an impressive show of grassroots support at the airport.

Still favoring Kennedy, Feinstein refused to get involved until he was convinced to take action by his wife, who saw McCarthy as the only viable option. Thus it was that he asked friends and colleagues to show up at the airport to greet the senator with handwritten placards calling for "Peace with McCarthy" and proclaiming "We Want Gene." This rally turned out to be one of the major early expressions of popular support for McCarthy covered by the media. Encouraged by the Michigan event and the enthusiastic response to his appearance in Berkeley, McCarthy formally announced his candidacy on November 30, 1967.

Several weeks later, Ferency asked Weiss to become chair of the Michigan McCarthy campaign and replace the Lansing-based Harrison.

Feinstein became executive director of the organization and actually ran the operation from that position. An early leader in the national McCarthy campaign, Ferency had met in October with Allard Lowenstein and Prof. Arnold Kaufman of the University of Michigan in Ann Arbor to launch the formal "Dump Johnson" movement in Michigan.

Although they established headquarters for the Michigan McCarthy campaign in a residential area of the city away from the Wayne State campus, many of those who worked at the McCarthy office were faculty, spouses, and young people connected to the university. Much of the important financial planning was handled by several faculty wives, who were of that generation of women who stayed home with the kids. The Michigan McCarthy campaign raised more money for the candidate than any other McCarthy organization in a state without a primary election. With few exceptions, the campaign workers were white and middle-class, a reflection of McCarthy's inability to connect with African Americans, a core Democratic constituency in Detroit.

Feinstein's leadership did not go unchallenged. Phil Moore, a representative from McCarthy's national headquarters, reported back from Michigan on July 1, 1968, that the candidate's people in Ann Arbor had set up their own statewide splinter group supporting the senator, and another group in the Detroit suburbs also had chosen to go it alone "because of disagreement with the leadership of Otto Feinstein." Moore also claimed that "the abrasive style of the McCarthy state-wide organization headed by Otto Feinstein . . . has alienated most of the party leadership." Unwilling to roil the waters, however, he recommended to the national headquarters that Feinstein, who would be "very good in the precinct delegate races, and with particular groups such as the Blacks," be supported as the official state McCarthy chief but that the splinter groups be permitted to do their own thing as well. Moore also recommended sending actor Paul Newman to Michigan because there were "two woman delegates who have said they will go for McCarthy if Newman calls."

A congenitally genial and gentle bear of a man, Feinstein admits that he and his people may have been "abrasive"—but only "to the national McCarthy guys," in part because they focused so narrowly on the delegate count while he and his colleagues were more interested in building a permanent progressive coalition within the Democratic Party. The McCarthy group in Michigan was involved in party politics, candidate-centered politics, and movement politics; the regular Democrats and the national McCarthy people had more narrow agendas.

NUT's January–February 1968 number was devoted to the Campus Concerned Democrats and contained a lead article by Richard Place, a friend of Feinstein's and another Wayne historian, entitled "Why McCarthy?" Place understood that many of his colleagues felt McCarthy had no chance of winning, that he was too professorial, and that he was "a one-issue candidate." Place contended, however, that whether or not McCarthy could win, "he has provided a nucleus around which those of us who despair of the entrenched leadership of both national parties can organize and show our strength as a bloc." McCarthy's candidacy was also a way to raise the question of "how to divide our resources between our world commitments as a super power and our commitment to create a viable and just society in America." Finally, although there was a chance that McCarthy might really win the nomination, Place insisted that we "can win through 'losing,' " by making "our votes, money, and actions amount to something on the national political level."

The article then listed the presidential primaries and their dates, followed by a page full of addresses and phone numbers for the national and state McCarthy headquarters. The second article, written by George W. Shepherd Jr. of the University of Delaware, dealt with the nuts and bolts of how to elect delegates to the national convention, followed by the names and addresses of Campus Concerned Democrats, which, at the time of publication, were at universities in more than thirty states. The Campus Concerned Democrats organization, of which Feinstein was executive secretary, was formed on December 3, 1967, after McCarthy had appeared at the national convention of the Concerned Democrats.

In the same *NUT* issue, Feinstein's article entitled "What You Can Do" began with his by-then common theme of how "the University reaches into all corners of our society, often having wider and deeper contacts than the political parties themselves." He described how to organize on every campus an Issues and Politics 1968 conference. At these conferences, faculty and students would present papers that would be released to the media, and thereby, it was hoped, "the political climate in the community can be affected." Feinstein was especially interested in developing speaker's bureaus on campuses that would send academics to talk to unions, social and religious groups, and parent-teacher associations about the war and domestic politics. Considering the growing number of "Concerned" faculty members, he hoped to create two thousand such groups. Although he fell well short of his goal, faculty and graduate students on many campuses did appear before community groups and—just as important—in print and on electronic media to try to win the battle for the hearts and minds of Americans. John Weiss, for one, remembers making presentations in Michigan communities and elsewhere every other week for one year.

The special issue of *NUT* concluded with a useful article by Sanford Gottlieb of SANE explaining community organizing, followed by a long list of materials available to McCarthy campaigners. Considering that McCarthy declared for the presidency less than a month before and that his supporters built the organization from scratch, the level of activity and wide range of resources made available in *NUT* was impressive and a tribute to the mostly academic activists behind it. Although readers with experience in politics did not need the simple instructions on how to operate within the party system to effect change, many of those in the McCarthy campaign were inhabitants of "ivory towers" who knew little if anything about grassroots politics. It was also important to spell out in detail a common strategy for the campaign. Involved in such activities since high school, Feinstein understood those subjects quite well.

The Michigan McCarthy organization helped raise money to send nine thousand young people, including high school students, to primaries in New Hampshire, Wisconsin, and Indiana. Feinstein recruited Peace Corps veterans who had the maturity necessary to lead their younger comrades and who were experienced at operating in "foreign" environments. Ferency himself went with McCarthy to New Hampshire to show the poet-politician how to campaign at plant gates. According to Ferency, the candidate was "not really in tune with politics." In fact, he had not considered making a run for the presidency—only a symbolic protest against the war—until he did well in New Hampshire and "got the fever."

After McCarthy almost won in New Hampshire, Robert Kennedy declared his candidacy on March 16, 1968, four days after the primary. Some in the McCarthy camp immediately joined Kennedy, but Feinstein and Ferency felt a certain loyalty to the Minnesota senator and his many young supporters who resented Kennedy's late and seemingly opportunistic candidacy. Thus, Feinstein decided to stick with McCarthy even though Kennedy was more likely to defeat Johnson and unite the party. Making the difficult decision to stay with their candidate suggested a strain of quixotic idealism—or perhaps morality—among the McCarthy people that is rare in the political game. But their dual strategy of keeping both men in the race to gain enough votes to deny Humphrey the nomination on the first ballot at the national convention in Chicago and then convincing McCarthy to release his delegates to Kennedy on the second ballot might not have been so quixotic after all. Despite the hard feelings that existed between the McCarthy and Kennedy groups in Michigan, leaders of the McCarthy camp were able to present unity slates of delegates from district conventions, who were elected to the August 30–31 state convention.

For these leaders the main and insurmountable problem in Michigan was that those who would elect the delegates to the national convention had been chosen in 1966. Consequently, the May 1968 precinct elections and the county, district, and state conventions, in which the newly elected McCarthy delegates would compete, could only have an indirect impact on who would represent Michigan in Chicago. If the McCarthy people made significant gains throughout the state, Feinstein reasoned, the party regulars could not, in all conscience (or political wisdom) ignore them—that is, if they had a conscience. Certainly, they had to be impressed by such events as the Tiger Stadium rally at which at least twenty-five thousand people turned out to hear McCarthy on July 27, 1968, the largest political rally in the state that year. Prominent Ford family member William Clay Ford, who owned the Detroit Lions, helped pay for the event, and Detroit mayor Jerome Cavanagh, an anti-war Democrat, provided buses.

The McCarthy and Kennedy people were able to pass resolutions favorable to their cause in many district conventions. Typical was the Seventeenth Congressional District of Johnson loyalist Rep. Martha Griffiths, where one of the leaders of the Liberal Conference Caucus, William Broadhead, went on to become a long-term member of Congress from the district. Twenty percent of the winners in the 1966 district elections were favorable to the McCarthy-Kennedy cause. In the 1968 elections, that number rose to between 45 and 51 percent. Thus, the Concerned Democrats had achieved one of their main goals and were on the verge of having enough influence in the party to affect its domestic and international policies.

Feinstein helped organize a petition drive that attracted more than 100,000 registered voters. The petition asked the state Democratic Party to acknowledge the influence of the McCarthy forces and award their leaders an appropriate share of the 24 at-large seats in the Michigan delegation. That delegation had 94 votes, or 100 delegates, at the national convention, of which 76 had already been elected at district meetings in May.

New party chair Sander Levin told Feinstein to negotiate with Sam Fishman, the powerful head of the UAW's Community Action Program (CAP), about obtaining a "fair portion" of the at-large delegates. An old-line anti-Stalinist who Feinstein claims was "still fighting the battle of the Barcelona Post Office," Fishman rejected Otto's plea for recognition for his group, even after Feinstein promised that the ten thousand paid-up members of the McCarthy for President organization would join the Democratic Party. (At the time, the entire paid-up membership of the state party was only two thousand.) Feinstein, however, would not promise to support Humphrey on the second ballot as a price for those seats. Ultimately, the state party grudgingly agreed to give the McCarthy forces two at-large seats. From Feinstein's perspective, the decision by the UAW and the state politicos to refuse to treat his people with generosity helped to weaken the Michigan Democratic Party and later paved the way for the Republicans to make statewide gains.

Feinstein attended the Chicago convention as an alternate delegate from his district. He did not expect McCarthy to win the nomination but thought that he and his colleagues might be able to move Humphrey and the rest of the party closer to their positions on the war and civil rights. Mayor Richard J. Daley's cordoned-off convention center reminded him of a concentration camp, but he felt even more ostracized by the convention organizers who marginalized the members of his delegation, even to the point of housing them in a motel far from the main action. Feinstein returned to Detroit one day before the convention ended to try to keep a lid on the protests that were simmering among his supporters over the police riot in Chicago. He addressed rallies and meetings, explaining that it was still necessary to support the party, considering the alternative. He felt that he helped to "avoid a major confrontation and contained the anger." Other parties, especially those in New York and California, suffered far more fragmentation and internal warfare than the one in Michigan.

The McCarthy-Kennedy forces controlled almost a majority of the votes of delegates to the state convention in August, two weeks after the national convention—demonstrating just how far they had come in Michigan in 1968. Many who attended wore black armbands in mourning for Chicago. The state convention dropped unit rule, censured Mayor Daley and the Chicago police, and adopted the minority plank on Vietnam that the national convention had rejected. In a close vote, 1,100 to 1,000, the state convention also defeated a resolution that would have condemned the Democratic National Committee's handling of the national convention and vowed never to hold another convention in Chicago as long as Daley remained mayor.

Although the McCarthy forces were not welcomed as a group in the state Humphrey campaign, many members worked individually for the candidate. McCarthy himself was extremely slow to endorse Humphrey. Feinstein met with him and William Clay Ford when the senator was in Detroit for the 1968 World Series in early October. He was disappointed to hear McCarthy explain that he was withholding his support from Humphrey as a way to compel him to move toward his own position on the war. Ultimately, McCarthy endorsed Humphrey at the eleventh hour, when it did the Democratic standard-bearer little good. Humphrey carried Michigan nonetheless, in part because the unions convinced hundreds of thousands of their members to switch their allegiance from third-party candidate George Wallace.

After the election, many insurgents dropped out of Democratic Party work. Some were disappointed and disillusioned by what they had witnessed during the year. Campus-based activists returned to their research and teaching, concerned once again about tenure and promotion. As party pros had predicted, they were one-issue activists who, after failing to stop the war, no longer were interested in the tedious and unglamorous work of local politics. Feinstein, by contrast, was in the struggle for the long haul and did not lose faith, even after the election of Richard Nixon. In fact, supported by new activists he had helped to bring into his party, he ran for state Democratic Party chair in 1969. He was a reluctant candidate, but the Concerned Democrats could not find anyone else who was willing to enter the race.

According to his campaign literature, Feinstein was the "only candidate who has worked intensively with the new forces that have come into the Party . . . the young people, the professionals and intellectuals, the urban and rural poor, the various minority and ethnic groups. We need these people in the Party—if it is to win"; he was described as "uniquely qualified to provide the kind of leadership that can unite the disparate forces in the Party." Otto came in second on the first ballot at the January 1969 state convention with 21 percent of the vote, and an ally who finished fourth took another 10 percent. It was not a bad showing for an amateur politician—an academic with a slight foreign accent (both New York and European) who was confronting the savvy party regulars dominated by labor. Further, Feinstein won two of the nineteen congressional districts (his own Thirteenth and the Liberal Conference-dominated Seventeenth) and received 29 percent of the votes in the

Detroit metropolitan area. The main problem, as he pointed out in his own February 4, 1969, postmortem, was that "we have been particularly weak in the more outlying counties." An attempt by sectarian forces to reconfigure the Michigan Concerned Democrats and to impose a far more bureaucratic structure on the organization caused Feinstein to resign from his position as executive secretary in March. Paradoxically, some of those who led the attempt to restructure the organization were the same people—formerly old leftists—who had once caused party power brokers such as Sam Fishman to see red.

Like so many other academics involved in leadership roles during those heady days, Feinstein never again participated so directly in party politics, although he remained a precinct delegate and did heavy campaigning in 1972 and 1976. It had been a remarkable moment in history when college professors and sometimes even graduate students negotiated almost as equals with senators, mayors, and party chieftains over issues that dramatically affected American politics. Although he would not again enjoy such a position, he continued his lifelong effort to develop mechanisms and institutions that would involve the academy with social problems. In 1971, he was the prime mover behind the creation of the Southeast Michigan Ethnic Heritage Studies Center, which was devoted to ethnic conflict resolution. In 1973, he became director of Wayne's innovative University Studies and Weekend College Program, which, in eighteen months, enrolled thirty-six hundred adult students. Among other activities, the new college produced one thousand broadcast programs for its telecourses, making it the second largest telecourse producer in the world. Feinstein's To Educate the People Consortium, which grew out of the program modeled on England's Open University, adapted the Wayne model to thirty-five other universities and ultimately, with support from the United Nations Educational, Scientific, and Cultural Organization (UNESCO), branched out into the European Community.

Feinstein also organized the City-University Consortium in Detroit, which sponsored joint city-university projects, often involving students, on key urban issues. Finally, in his own department, he developed the Civic Literacy and Urban Society module for the basic introductory political science course, which, among other things, offered students the opportunity to participate in voter registration projects in Detroit.

From those early days at the University of Chicago in the late 1940s to the present, Otto Feinstein has never relinquished his dream of creating a university community closely tied to the outside world, a community in which scholars would offer their special talents and expertise in practical ways to improve the chances for peace and justice at home and abroad. The failure of the McCarthy campaign was only one transitory, if bitter and enervating, setback for Feinstein in an admirable career of creating valuable programs and institutions that affected the quality of life for tens of thousands of students and faculty and the millions of citizens of the national and international communities with whom they interacted.

Author's Note

Unless otherwise noted, all Otto Feinstein quotes are the product of a series of interviews I conducted with him over several months during the fall of 1997. Quoted material from Democratic Party documents and broadsides comes from Feinstein's personal archive as well as the personal archive compiled by Pat Thornton for the Liberal Conference, which is in my possession. Zoltan Ferency's observations about Eugene McCarthy are quoted from Zoltan Ferency Oral History, July 15, 1988, p. 40, Walter P. Reuther Library of Labor and Urban Affairs, Wayne State University, Detroit, Michigan.

Suggested Readings

For the McCarthy campaign, see George Rising, *Clean for Gene: Eugene McCarthy's 1968 Presidential Campaign* (Westport, CT: Praeger, 1997); Eugene J. McCarthy, *The Year of the People* (Garden City, NY: Doubleday, 1969); Jeremy Larner, *Nobody Knows: Reflections on the McCarthy Campaign of 1968* (New York: Macmillan, 1969); and Ben Stavis, *We Were the Campaign: From New Hampshire to Chicago for McCarthy* (Boston: Beacon Press, 1969). For discussion of media images of the antiwar movement, see Melvin Small, *Covering Dissent: The Media and the Anti-Vietnam War Movement* (New Brunswick, NJ: Rutgers University Press, 1994).

15

César Chávez
The Serpent and the Dove

Frank Bardacke

Until the general upheaval of the 1960s, California farmworkers, hampered by their geographical, racial, and political isolation, had been unable to build a lasting union, although not for lack of trying. Native Californians, European American outcasts, and Chinese, Japanese, East Indian, Filipino, and Mexican immigrants, each in turn, fought their bosses in periodic strikes and rebellions. California agribusinessmen, however, captains of the most industrialized agricultural enterprise in human history, were able to defeat (or wait out) these battles and did what they could to keep California's rural working class separated from their potential allies in America's cities.

By the midtwentieth century, the political friends of U.S. agribusiness had legally codified the second-class status of agricultural workers. Farmworkers were excluded from the National Labor Relations Act and were not entitled to the fruits of the working-class victories of the 1930s: social security, unemployment insurance, workers' compensation, a minimum wage, and prohibitions against child labor. Moreover, starting in World War II and for the next twenty-four years, a major portion of the agricultural labor on the largest farms in California (and Texas) was done by braceros, contracted workers from Mexico, whose ability to organize was highly restricted by their legal status.

César Chávez, born on a homestead farm in Arizona and thrust into the California migrant stream in the 1930s, did more than any other single person to end the crippling isolation of U.S. farmworkers. Along with Gilbert Padilla, Dolores Huerta, and Helen Chávez, he founded what was to become the United Farm Workers (UFW) in 1962. Under his guidance the UFW quickly took advantage of the strike wave that followed the end of the Bracero Program in 1965 and pushed itself into the center of contemporary American politics. Combining militant farmworker strikes with extensive consumer boycotts, Chávez built a wide coalition of forces that helped California farmworkers win significant gains in their wages and working conditions. Despite serious setbacks in the fields in the mid-1980s, his UFW established itself as the most powerful farmworker union in U.S. history.

This essay originally appeared in Clark Davis and David Igler, eds., *The Human Tradition in California* (Wilmington, DE: Scholarly Resources, 2002), 209–24.

Frank Bardacke, a California public school teacher, argues that Chávez was not only largely responsible for the UFW victories, but he was also implicated in its later defeats. Historically, Bardacke contends, Chávez will be noted more for his role in the birth of the Chicano movement than for his success as a farmworker leader.

The politics are transparent; the historical significance is opaque. The law that made March 31, the birthday of Mexican American labor leader César Chávez, a mandated holiday for state employees and an optional "day of service" for California public school students included no benefits for California farmworkers. No political mystery here: at the end of the twentieth century, Sacramento politicians found a way to please Latino voters while not taking any money out of the pockets of agribusiness. But what is the historical meaning of this conveniently structured holiday? At the very least, it suggests an irony: César triumphed in California while farmworkers continued to lose.

Nor does this contrast between the honoring of César Chávez and the dishonoring of farmworkers stand alone. The same legislators and governor who created César Chávez Day rejected a bill that would have held California growers jointly responsible for their labor contractors' labor code violations. They thereby continued the legal fiction that growers do not employ the farmworkers who make them rich. And here the irony deepens: labor contractors replaced Chávez's defeated United Farm Workers (UFW) in the early 1980s, and were the major instrument through which growers attacked farmworker wages and working conditions. That attack was not entirely successful. Workmen's compensation, unemployment insurance, and a favorable farm labor law—all won during the height of the UFW's power in the late 1960s and 1970s—remain intact. But the grower offensive was powerful enough. By the time of César's death in 1993, farmworker wages had fallen at least 25 percent from their highs in the 1970s, and conditions in the fields were nearly as bad as when César first entered farmworker politics in 1962.[1]

So the question remains, how are we to understand the contradictory juxtaposition of César's symbolic victory and the farmworkers' material defeat? My answer depends on a distinction between César's unofficial position as "first president of the Chicano Nation" and his official position as president of the United Farm Workers. Once those two roles are considered separately, some of the César Chávez Day irony disappears. Chávez can be celebrated, without reservation, as a Mexican American leader, an inspiration to the short-lived Chicano Nation, and an example of the possibilities of Latino political power. But the celebratory mood ends when we turn to César's record as a union leader. His relationship to the farmworker movement is so fraught with contradiction and difficulty, so filled with betrayal and tragedy, that a proper historical account evokes emotions that dwarf these common ironies.

César as First President of the Chicano Nation

In the summer of 1966, after scores of striking farmworkers and hundreds, even thousands, of supporters walked the length of California's San Joaquin Valley, a triumphant Luis Váldez, cofounder of Teatro Campesino, predicted the future, using the past tense: "Under the name of *huelga* [labor activism], we had created a Mexican American *patria* [nation], and César Chávez was our first *presidente*." Both tenses proved true. César Chávez became a combination hero and godfather to what came to be called the Chicano Nation. But the past tense was equally accurate: Chávez's position as Mexican American president was rooted in his farmworker union leadership, which first gained national attention with this dramatic pilgrimage through the San Joaquin Valley.

The Mexican American college students who created the Chicano Nation in the late 1960s and early 1970s needed the farmworker movement as much as (and probably more than) that movement needed them. Consider Jorge García, a Fresno State College senior in 1966, one of only sixty-five Spanish-surnamed students in that school of 14,000. His parents were farmworkers in Dinuba. He had spent a good part of his own youth in the fields. Getting to college had required hard work. In order to do well in school, he had focused so intently on his English (with the help and support of his parents but the disapproval of his grandparents) that he began to lose his Spanish. After high school he went to a seminary in Fresno, then to a community college, and finally to Fresno State. Once there, he could say good-bye to the fields. He was on his way to becoming a teacher, a successful Mexican American, when the pilgrimage came through town. "I went to the rally and it changed my life," García recalled. "It was like looking in the mirror and seeing the rest of myself, the part that I had left behind in my struggle to get out of the fields. I thought college was a ticket to paradise. I realized then that I couldn't be in paradise unless I could be there as a whole person. And that meant helping farmworkers."[2]

Jorge García and thousands of Mexican American students like him from rural and urban communities entered politics as supporters of César Chávez and the UFW. They set up student organizations whose first order of business was to help the farmworkers whom they had either literally or figuratively left behind. They visited Delano, the union's birthplace, bringing money, clothes, and food; they picketed grocery stores that handled "scab" grapes; they demanded that their schools begin to teach farmworker history. To create a new identity, they needed to reconstruct their connection to their real or imagined past. Through acts of solidarity with struggling farmworkers, they could reject the professional world they were about to enter and declare themselves part of the working-class *raza* (race) they were about to leave. They proudly took as their new name a derisory word that had meant a low-caste Mexican north of the border. They were no longer aspiring Mexican Americans; they were now Chicanos.

Never abandoning farmworker solidarity, the members of the new Chicano movement sought to make a place for themselves and their own history in their colleges and universities. They fought for Chicano studies or, together with others, for Third World studies. They pressured campus administrators to admit more persons of color and provide them financial support. They tried to build ties to various barrio groups and organizations so they could use their education to serve their old communities. Many opposed the Vietnam War, and through the antiwar movement came to identify with the national and international left. They fought in defense of undocumented workers and called for open borders. And some rejected the American two-party electoral system and made various attempts to set up independent political parties.

César Chávez remained a hero to these students, but he was not one of them. He was older, born twenty miles north of Yuma, Arizona, in 1927, a child of the depression and a veteran of World War II, the two great events that shaped the previous Mexican American generation. Moreover, he had sharp differences with many of the political positions of the new Chicano generation he had inspired. He was not a Chicano nationalist; he was dubious about the celebration of Aztlán, opposed open borders, and did not like all the *raza* talk. The mature César did not need militant nationalism. He was not anxious about his own identity; he could appreciate other cultures and ways of life. But some of his rejection of Chicano nationalism was politically convenient, even necessary. In the late 1960s, amid the fledgling Chicano movement, César was building a diverse coalition of grape boycotters, of which Chicano students were but one part. Chávez could not afford to be a separatist if he wanted to hold together a coalition that included unions, churches, and antipesticide consumers.

César was especially critical of any attempt at independent political action, and risked isolating himself from his most fervent Chicano support by openly opposing the La Raza Unida Party. Again, the requirements of the boycott coalition were primary. The Democratic Party, chief losers if La Raza Unida were to be successful, actively supported the boycott. But César's defense of the Democrats went far beyond this particular tit for tat. He worked in tandem with the Democratic Party throughout his entire political career. His first political act, in 1952, was registering Mexican Americans to vote in San Jose, a campaign that was clearly in the interest of Democrats and could not have been successful without Democratic Party assistance. Throughout the 1950s, César—along with Fred Ross, Gilbert Padilla, and Dolores Huerta—built the Community Service Organization into the country's most powerful Mexican American group by registering 300,000 new and mostly Democratic voters, mobilizing them to go to the polls, and then pressuring politicians to respond to their agenda. In 1958, César was such an important player in California Democratic Party politics that he could get Governor Pat Brown on the phone. In the mid-1960s he extended his influence to the Kennedy wing of the National Democratic Party; and his long-term cooperation with Pat Brown's son Jerry contributed to the UFW's greatest political triumph, the 1976 California Farm Labor Law. This commitment to Democratic Party politics even survived César's death, as the UFW's greatest political asset today is its ability to register and mobilize Latino voters and to win concessions from Democratic Party politicians. Even César Chávez Day is, to a certain extent, one of those concessions.

But if César Chávez opposed the Chicano movement's separatist impulse, withdrew himself from many of their struggles, and opposed their most important political initiatives, how did he simultaneously remain their hero? To a certain extent, Jorge García's experience has already answered that question: the farmworker movement was a precondition for the new Chicano identity and the politics that followed. Throughout the 1960s and 1970s, Chávez and the UFW continued to inspire even those activist Chicanos with whom he seriously differed.[3] But César's seminal role in the Chicano movement does not completely explain his remarkable staying power. After all, César remained a hero even after the Chicano movement stalled and disintegrated in the mid-1970s, after the Democrats lost the California governorship and Chávez lost much of his political access in the early 1980s, and after the UFW was defeated in the fields in the mid-1980s. What sustained his reputation despite this string of political defeats?

The answer is that César Chávez was not and is not a hero just to Mexican Americans and other Latinos. During the mid- and late 1960s he became an exemplary hope of American liberals. At the time of the 1966 farmworker pilgrimage, the liberal/radical cooperation of the early civil rights movement was over, and white liberals could find no home in the new movement for Black Power. They were horrified by the northern ghetto riots. Moreover, liberal president Lyndon Johnson, soon after defeating conservative Barry Goldwater, escalated the war in Vietnam—and initially, most liberals stuck by his side. There was war at home and war abroad. Many people who had been so hopeful at the beginning of the 1960s now watched the twin terrors of the nightly news: black rioters burning American cities, white radicals burning American flags.

Enter César Chávez and the grape boycott. César provided a constructive, nonviolent political alternative to those horrified by the rioters and radicals. "Boycott, Baby, Boycott," UFW picketers chanted to make sure everyone got the point. The simple, peaceful act of not eating grapes would help grateful farmworkers win a union contract. The simplicity and hopefulness of the appeal attracted millions. In the midst of the campaign, in the cataclysmic year of 1968, César fasted. He did so, he said, to remind his own followers to be nonviolent. He appeared on the cover of *Time*. Many other major magazines and newspapers wrote feature stories about him, warning that if his movement did not prevail, a more violent alternative would take its place. The press championed César as the new Chicano leader, and attacked or ignored the two possible alternatives—Corky Gonzalez and Reis Tijerina—who were almost as important to the early Chicano movement as César but could not receive an official seal of approval because they denounced the two-party political system and advocated self-defense. With this wide support, the grape boycott became the most successful consumer boycott in American history. Thousands worked in the boycott campaign, and polls reported that one-third of all adult Americans had committed themselves to not eating grapes. The contract was won, and although the victory did not belong to liberals alone, it was one of their few achievements of the late 1960s and early 1970s. Is it any wonder that César won a permanent place in liberal hearts? Or that thirty years later, after the larger hopes of the Chicano left had come to grief, his triumphant grape boycott would still be remembered and honored?

But César cannot be dismissed as the Latino most favored by white liberals. Yes, he became a liberal hero, but he was also the leader of the farmworker movement and a chief inspiration to the new Chicano youth before most liberals ever heard about him. The liberal media did not make him; he was picked up by them. He is often called the Mexican American Martin Luther King, and he deserves the title, although King was more troublesome to larger numbers of people in his time and widely celebrated only after he was assassinated. (César was celebrated during his lifetime and was bothersome to a narrower, albeit powerful, sector: California agribusiness.) And César was Martin Luther King and Jackie Robinson, too: he was the first Mexican American to play in the political big leagues and, just like Robinson, he refused to alter his style once he got there. César was not a nationalist and certainly not a separatist, but he was not an accommodating assimilationist either. He did not win power by ingratiating himself to liberal, white America. He did not remake himself in order to be accepted. He was proud of his Mexican heritage, his farmworker roots, and his bilingual intelligence. And he was proud of the collective struggle that had propelled him into prominence. When we honor him, we can honor all of that. There need be no irony.

César as Defeated Farmworker Leader

The rise and fall of the Chicano movement, unmistakable in its broad sweep, cannot be precisely located in time. It began in the mid- to late 1960s and ended about a decade later. The trajectory of the UFW, however, is much easier to chart chronologically, its fortunes bouncing between dramatic highs and lows. Starting with nothing in 1962, the union won a few labor contracts in the mid-1960s, and then, after the successful boycott in 1970, had almost the entire California table grape industry under contract, covering tens of thousands of workers. In 1973, however, the growers refused to re-sign with the UFW, and since then the union has never been able to reestablish itself in the table grape industry. But the union bounced back in 1975 when Governor Jerry Brown and the California legislature passed the Agricultural Labor Relations Act, which provided for state-supervised elections in the fields. The UFW won a majority of those elections, and contracts covering half of the vegetable industry. Then, in 1979, the union won a major vegetable strike—pushing wages up significantly—and some sectors of agribusiness publicly declared that they now accepted the union's continued presence in the fields. But within the next few years, the union lost almost all of its vegetable contracts, was reduced to a couple of thousand workers under contract, and retreated from active organizing in the fields. That retreat lasted nearly a decade, as it was not until after César's death in 1993 that the union tried to reenter the fields, with mixed results.

What happened? To a certain extent, the union was simply overwhelmed by the power of agribusiness, its friends in high places (especially Republican George Deukmejian, who became governor in 1982), and a conservative, antiunion ethic that swept the country in the mid-1980s. But that is not even half of the story. Quite unexpectedly, after the 1979 strike victory, the UFW tore itself apart. Many of its top organizers left or were forced out, and a virulent internal faction fight ripped the union asunder, leaving it incapable of countering the 1980s grower offensive. No full answer to the question of how the growers defeated the union can ignore the prior question of how and why the union wrecked itself. And here we reach a sad, even tragic, conclusion. César Chávez, so responsible for the union's victories, was also deeply implicated in its demise—not just he personally, of course, but the strategic policies, leadership style, and religious commitment that he impressed upon the union.

This story begins with the contradictions inherent in the boycott victory. The triumphant table grape boycott transformed the UFW into a peculiar twin-souled institution: a cross between a culturally diverse farmworker advocacy group, highly skilled at boycott activities, and a mostly Mexican and Mexican American, Catholic farmworker union. Under the skillful guidance of Chávez, these two souls reinforced each other, especially in the early years when boycotts and threats of boycotts so directly and obviously led to fundamental improvements in farmworkers' lives. But even at the beginning, the two souls occasionally lived in contradiction. Sending farmworkers to work in the boycott offices of U.S. cities, for example, was a major factor in making the boycott so successful, as the workers themselves became the best advocates for the boycott and the UFW. But placing workers in boycott cities also meant that the most dedicated and articulate strikers did their political organizing work among boycotters, not among farmworkers. This tactic was part of a strategy that reduced the importance of farmworker organizing and focused on supporters instead. As such, it was neither wrong (the UFW needed outside support to win) nor impossible to reverse, but it turned out to be the first intimation of a coming disaster.

Similarly, and even more perniciously, in the later stages of the boycott—when all hope of winning the grape contracts in the fields had been abandoned—the UFW often mobilized farmworkers into staged events whose purpose was neither to educate the workers nor to directly improve their lives, but rather to mobilize the support of distant boycotters. What UFW strategists called "legitimacy strikes," sometimes involving hundreds of workers, were not meant to win, but rather to legitimize later boycotts.[4] Such strikes may have helped the boycotts, but they often embittered the farmworker participants against the UFW. Later, this technique degenerated into "publicity strikes," whose sole purpose was to produce anti-grower and anti-Teamster publicity but whose defeats only added to the list of farmworkers suspicious of the UFW.[5]

What began as an intimation, a small contradiction within a successful strategy, ended in a major internal conflict. In 1979, in the midst of the most successful strike in UFW history, in a period when boycotts had become less effective and farmworkers—their dues and their strikes—had become a larger part of the UFW's power, a debilitating internal struggle broke out over the relationship between the two souls of the union. This was an open struggle, with most of the union staff on one side and the rank-and-file leaders of the Mexican farmworker membership on the other. It broke into public view at the 1979 Salinas UFW convention, when farmworkers on the floor of the convention began chanting, "*Huelga, huelga, huelga,*" while members of the executive board and other officials sitting on the stage answered with a competing chant of "Boycott, boycott, boycott."[6] In this internal struggle, César Chávez led those who upheld the boycott as the essence of the UFW, and then subsequently (in 1981) purged from the union the leading farmworkers (and the few union staffers) who had opposed him.[7]

César's role was no great surprise. By the time this internal UFW debate burst into full bloom, César had grown much more comfortable at organizing boycotters than at organizing farmworkers, and had already told many admiring newsmen and biographers that the boycott, which he described as "the most nearly perfect instrument of nonviolent change," was his greatest contribution to the farmworker movement.[8] He had no patience with those—in his own union!—who questioned its effectiveness. Furthermore, by the time these questions were raised, César had become accustomed to forcing out those on the union staff who he suspected might oppose him. On this question the opponents were right out in the open. The earlier staff purges had harmed the UFW, but not mortally. This time, however, César fired the leaders of the farmworker movement, demoralizing them and their followers and alienating them from the union. The successful grower offensive soon followed.[9]

The issue of religion in the UFW repeats and reinforces this dynamic in a minor key. Once again, that which propelled the UFW to victory eventually contributed to its defeat, and César was right in the middle of both the rise and the fall. César was a serious Catholic whose religious beliefs were rooted in the folk piety of his mother and the religious instruction of his convent-trained grandmother. As a child he had taken to that training so well that a Yuma priest waived the requirement that he submit to further Church-directed religious instruction before receiving his first Holy Communion. Later he became an altar boy, an adult who regularly attended Mass, and a committed *cursillista*—a member of a Church-directed movement for lay Catholic renewal. He was first recruited to politics by a Catholic priest who introduced him to Catholic Social Action, and he self-consciously constructed the early UFW on the principles of Catholic worker associations spelled out in 1891 by Pope Leo XIII in *Rerum Novarum*. Periodically, when the UFW found itself in a particularly difficult political predicament, Chávez responded with a dramatic act of personal penitence, fully within the traditions of the Catholic Church and Mexican folk piety.

Although his religion was not essentially a political device, César's faith turned out to be extremely useful. The UFW used religious symbols to help organize the overwhelmingly Catholic farmworkers and elicit sympathy from supporters. César's piety—especially his dramatic 1968 fast—helped pull the union together and situated the boycott as the exemplary nonviolent alternative to those turbulent times. But César's religious intentions also contributed to the UFW's fall, as the internal life of the organization came to resemble a religious order rather than a labor union. One of the people who lived in the union headquarters at La Paz—an isolated, former tuberculosis sanitorium in the Tehachapi Mountains—and who witnessed firsthand César's attempt to mesh trade unionism and religious commitment, put it this way: "César never wanted to be just a trade union leader, he wanted to be Mother Teresa."[10]

La Paz was not only supposed to be the union's chief administrative and political headquarters; César also tried to make it into a kind of ashram, an intentional beloved community. But a beloved community has a unity of belief and purpose, a suspicion of difference and dissent that is inimical to a trade union representing tens of thousands of workers. It was at La Paz, in César's efforts to build a religious community around him, that the first large purges began. And while the union's center at La Paz was going through the travails of forced unanimity, the life of the union staff, working in field offices throughout California, began to mimic the internal culture of the Catholic Church. In the union, as in the Church, those who disagreed with official policies kept their differences to themselves, and if they stepped out of line, they were disciplined through transfer or excommunication. And when people left the union they left quietly, unwilling to share their criticisms with people outside the faith.

The UFW, however, needed a democratic ethic—not a hierarchical, Catholic one—in order to thrive. UFW members were a diverse group; they worked at different jobs, under different contracts, in widely scattered areas. They did not share the common commitment that is assumed in a religious community. They had different interests that required open political discourse to resolve. They also had differences over what they wanted from their union and what they thought the best union strategy might be. But there was little space in the UFW for the expression of such differences. People were expected to follow César's directions, which came to be beyond question. When a group of ordinary farmworkers wanted to see him about a grievance that they could not resolve locally, they did not make an appointment, a *cita*. They had to get an *audiencia*, an audience, as if they were going to see the pope.

The union's hierarchical Catholic ethos was reinforced by a thoroughly antidemocratic structure. Until 1980 no farmworker could be elected to a full-time UFW staff position. People were appointed to the staff and owed their positions to those who appointed them, rather than to the rank and file from which they came. Nor were there any locals in the union—it has remained one body since its inception. Also, until 1980, the only structural loci of democratic control in the union were the local ranch committees and the biannual national convention. But ranch committee members continued to work in the fields and were not on the staff. Usually they ended up with much less power than the local "field office," where people appointed by La Paz worked as full-time union officers. Eventually, most ranch committees became nothing but transmission belts for union policy, and only occasionally sounding boards for disagreement from the ranks. Similarly, the national conventions were primarily staged affairs, marked by near unanimity, as the assembled delegates endorsed the proposals of the unopposed executive board candidates.

This kind of rigid, antidemocratic structure could not survive serious internal disputes, and the union fragmented in the wake of the 1979 strike. It was during that 9-month strike—one of the most powerful strikes in California agricultural history—that the dispute between boycotters and strikers first surfaced. César ordered the strike called off and replaced by a boycott. But the strike leadership, elected by their fellow strikers and supported by a few staff members, refused to obey the order. After this defiance the strike won an amazing victory, which included as a new provision in the contracts the election by the rank and file of full-time representatives ("paid reps") who would become part of the union staff and would be paid as if they continued to work in the fields. This meant that for the first time people came onto the staff who owed their positions not to other staffers (and ultimately to César) but rather to the rank and file that had elected them. And those elected were largely the victorious strike's leaders, the very people who had defied César's wishes and then won their own victory.

The final calamity unfolded quickly. The new staffers fought for their own power inside the union; César interpreted their fight as an attempt to take the union away from him and blocked their every initiative. The newly elected leaders then sought to run their own partial slate of candidates for the executive board against César's handpicked candidates. César controlled the convention and through a series of maneuvers denied the opposition the right even to vote for their own candidates. The opposition walked out of the convention and took their complaints to the press. César responded by firing them from their jobs as paid reps. Workers in the fields, the ones who had elected the representatives to begin with and whose issues the paid reps were championing when they initially locked horns with César, were mostly confused by the fight between their immediate leadership and their, by then, famous president. Those who were not demoralized divided into two opposing factions. Feuding workers sat in different sections of the buses that took them to the fields, refusing to talk to one another. The growers, emboldened by the division, moved against the union. The workers could not get themselves together to respond and César, defeated, stopped organizing in the fields and withdrew to his beloved community.

Over the next ten years, César presided as the UFW became less a union and more a cross between a farmworker advocacy group and a small family business. During another long fast in 1988, Chávez successfully focused public attention on pesticides in the fields and unsuccessfully tried to renew a table grape boycott. In 1993, César Chávez died in his sleep, not far from the Arizona homestead where he had been born. His good friend and colleague, Leroy Chatfield, who had seen him shortly before, said that although César was only sixty-six, he seemed more like 122, as he had compressed so much living into one overloaded lifetime.

An Interethnic Complication and a Conclusion

My easy distinction between César, the Latino icon, and César, the farmworker leader, is useful for this essay, but it obscures several complications. I will mention just one. César Chávez was thoroughly Mexican American. His paternal grandfather voted in Texas elections and homesteaded a 100-acre Arizona farm a few years before Arizona even became a state. César grew up on that farm, in what he remembered as an idyllic childhood filled with games and chores. In the late 1930s, César's father lost both the homestead and his own adjacent farm to falling agricultural prices, a flash flood that destroyed a homemade irrigation system, and a scheming Anglo lawyer. At the age of eleven, César was thrust with his family into the migrant stream, where the youngster's life became a calamity. A short-handled hoe replaced his childhood toys; cheating contractors humiliated his proud father, a master horseman; the family's 1930 Studebaker became their home. Like so many other Mexican American farmworkers who returned from World War II, César did not go back to the hated fields. He was working in a San Jose lumberyard when Father Donald McDonnell started him on his organizing career by introducing him to the ideas of Catholic Social Action.

When César first started organizing farmworkers in 1962, he began in an area and a crop where many Mexican American families lived and worked. Their life stories were somewhat different from his—they did not typically come from failed homesteads elsewhere in the United States—but they shared his Mexican American roots, and many of their parents or grandparents had come to the United States in the 1920s. These folks, these grape workers, were César's first constituency. But after the end of the Bracero Program in 1965 (when as a matter of semi-official policy the Mexican border was thrown open to illegal immigration), the character of California farmworkers changed. Mexican immigrants became the overwhelming majority of farmworkers by the mid-1970s, replacing Mexican Americans, Filipinos, Anglos, and others who had dominated the labor force since the 1920s.

Mexican Americans who continued to work in the fields often viewed the new immigrants with suspicion, believing them to be a threat to their jobs and union. César Chávez shared and encouraged this view. Angered by the use of undocumented workers against UFW strikes, he campaigned vigorously against illegal aliens. He not only blamed them for lost strikes but had some of them removed from union jobs. In 1974 he initiated a national campaign against "illegals," testified in Congress for increased activity by the Immigration Service, and ordered UFW staffers to finger illegals to the Border Patrol.[11] Ultimately, this policy rebounded sharply against the UFW in the fields, where the growing majority of workers had friends and relatives who were undocumented. The union's reputation of being against illegals hurt it immensely and was partly responsible for its many defeats in table grape elections after the passage of the Agricultural Labor Relations Act.

The final internal battle that so debilitated the union shared this same interethnic dimension. In the fight between the old union staff, led by César, and the rank-and-file union leadership, the union staff were primarily Mexican Americans—or, as they still called themselves at the time, Chicanos—while the rank-and-file leadership and membership were overwhelmingly Mexican immigrants. The dispute was not only about boycotts versus strikes and staff power versus rank-and-file power; it was also a struggle between Chicanos and Mexicans. That battle covered a world of differences: language, relationship to Mexico, and, most important, the place of agricultural work in peoples' lives. For many Mexican immigrants the California fields are not a disaster, as they had been for César. Rather, they are a step up in the world. Wages in the United States are, and have been over time, about ten times higher than wages in Mexico, and a job in the California fields can mean either the well-being of a family back home in Mexico or the possibility of successful family emigration to the United States. Certainly, the work is hard and people do not want their U.S.-born children to do it, but many immigrant farmworkers are quite successful on their own terms.

This was especially true for the paid reps who battled César Chávez for some power within the UFW. They were all Mexicans as opposed to Chicanos. Many were well-paid skilled farmworkers for whom the fields had been a success story. They were confident in their own abilities and had just led a great strike victory. They were not deeply religious people; many of them came from the anticlerical tradition inside the Mexican left. They were not comfortable with the UFW's pious style. They did not want to wear old work clothes when they went to news conferences—as was standard UFW practice—nor appeal for support on the basis of their downtrodden condition. They sought solidarity, not charity. The cultural difference between their worldview and the dominant worldview within the union staff was enormous. In some sense, César was right. Such people could not be granted significant power within the union without changing the whole nature of the enterprise.

So we come upon a final irony. César, the Latino icon, was partly undone by contradictions within the Latino community. But history is filled with ironies, as action is always rife with unintended consequences. In the case of César Chávez, Latino politicians and liberal admirers have been so anxious to establish him as a hero that they have bowdlerized the ironies from his story. They need not. Irony does not automatically degenerate into cynicism. It does not drive out hope—it leavens it. When César Chávez's tale is reduced to hagiography, it loses most of its historical and political value. And those who can celebrate César's life and triumphs only by exorcising that which is uncomfortable, or by blurring the contradictions and betrayals, mask the tragedy of his political trajectory, make him banal, and rob his story of its anguish and its grandeur.

Notes

1. *San Jose Mercury News*, December 23, 1990; *Sacramento Bee*, December 8–11, 1991; John C. Hammerback, *The Rhetorical Career of César Chávez* (College Station, TX, 1998).

2. Jorge García, interview by author, December 11, 2000.

3. Carlos Muñoz Jr., *Youth, Identity, Power: The Chicano Movement* (New York, 1989), 7.

4. Larry Itliong, interview by Jacques Levy, in possession of author, April 4, 1969.

5. Robert García, interview by author, October 20, 1994.

6. Hermilio Mojica, interview by author, October 3, 1994; Jerry Cohen, interview by author, June 25, 2001.

7. *Los Angeles Times*, September 6, October 25, 1981; *New York Times*, December 6, 1981; *Village Voice*, August 14, 1984.

8. Dick Meister and Anne Loftis, *A Long Time Coming: The Struggle to Unionize America's Farm Workers* (New York, 1977), 144.

9. The list of staff purged or forced out is long. Among the most prominent were executive board members Philip Vera Cruz, Gilbert Padilla, Jessica Govea, Marshall Ganz, and Eliseo Medina, along with top aides Jerry Cohen and Nick Jones. The best-

known rank-and-file leaders fired by Chávez were Mario Bustamonte, Hermilio Mojica, Aristeo Zambrano, Rigoberto Pérez, Sabino López, and Berta Batres.

10. Gretchen Lamb, interview by author, March 12, 1995.

11. Agenda, Monthly Newsletter of the National Council of La Raza, November 1974; *Riverside Daily Enterprise*, July 11, 1973; "Illegals Project 1974," Folder 4, Box 7, United Farm Workers Archives, Wayne State University Library, Detroit, Michigan; Gilbert Padilla, interview by author, December 20, 1997.

Suggested Readings

Coplon, Jeff. "César Chávez's Fall from Grace." *Village Voice*, August 14 and 21, 1984.

Daniel, Cletus E. "César Chávez and the Unionization of California Farm Workers." In Melvyn Dubofsky and Warren Van Tine, eds., *Labor Leaders in America*. Urbana and Chicago: University of Illinois Press, 1987.

Dunne, John Gregory. *Delano*. New York: Farrar, Straus, and Giroux, 1967.

Jenkins, Craig J. *The Politics of Insurgency: The Farm Worker Movement in the 1960s*. New York: Columbia University Press, 1985.

Levy, Jacques E. *César Chávez*. New York: W. W. Norton and Co., 1975.

London, Joan, and Henry Anderson. *So Shall Ye Reap*. New York: Thomas Crowell Co., 1970.

Majka, Linda C., and Theo J. Majka. *Farm Workers, Agribusiness, and the State*. Philadelphia: Temple University Press, 1982.

Matthiessen, Peter. *Sal Si Puedes: César Chávez and the New American Revolution*. New York: Dell Publishing Co., 1969.

Muñoz, Carlos, Jr. *Youth, Identity, Power: The Chicano Movement*. New York: Verso Books, 1989.

Taylor, Ronald B. *Chávez and the Farm Workers*. Boston: Beacon Press, 1975.

16

Alix Kates Shulman
Novelist, Feminist, Twentieth-Century Woman

Charlotte Templin

A best-seller, *The Memoirs of an Ex-Prom Queen* was celebrated in its day and was reissued in a twenty-fifth anniversary edition. Its author, Alix Kates Shulman, not only wrote about the women's liberation movement but also participated as a pioneering activist. She was a member of the early feminist organizations founded in New York City in the late 1960s, and with these groups she took part in actions such as the protest at the Miss America Pageant in 1968. Shulman exemplifies the revolutionary changes in women's lives and expectations that came about as a result of the women's movement. She experienced the conflicts and tensions that were inevitable while leading several lives—mother, wife, writer, activist—but she could not go back to the values of her mother's generation. At age fifty she began to spend her summers alone on a Maine island, and her experiences there resulted in the memoir, *Drinking the Rain*. Most recently she wrote a book about her parents' final illnesses and deaths and her role in their last years. She truly demonstrates the dramatic changes in women's lives in the twentieth century.

Charlotte Templin is professor of English at the University of Indianapolis in Indiana. She received a Ph.D. from Indiana University and is the author of *Feminism and the Politics of Literary Reputation: The Example of Erica Jong* (1995) and the editor of *Conversations with Erica Jong* (2003).

Alix Kates Shulman's *Memoirs of an Ex-Prom Queen* (1972) has been recognized as the first important novel to emerge from the women's liberation movement. Shulman was inspired to write it, as she was inspired to become a writer and a novelist, because of her personal involvement in the movement from its origins in the 1960s, when it began in small neighborhood groups engaging in discussions, "speak-outs," and demonstrations, through its evolution into a powerful national movement. Her steadfast commitment to women's equality and freedom, her political activism (for civil rights and against the Vietnam

This essay also appears in David L. Anderson, ed., *The Human Tradition in America since 1945* (Wilmington, DE: Scholarly Resources, 2003), 189–204.

War as well as in the women's movement), and her contributions to literature as a feminist novelist and memoirist earn her a place in twentieth-century history.

The body of Alix Kates Shulman's work charts the changing position of women in American society. She explores the new feminist consciousness in *Memoirs of an Ex-Prom Queen* and *Burning Questions* and the challenges of motherhood in *In Every Woman's Life . . .* and other novels. In the memoir, *Drinking the Rain*, she describes the experience of starting life over at fifty and discusses ecological concerns; and in *A Good Enough Daughter*, she writes about reconnecting with her family and seeing her parents through their final years. Shulman is the author of twelve books: four novels, two memoirs, three children's books, a biography of Emma Goldman, and two edited collections of essays by Emma Goldman.

Young men and women born in recent decades find it hard to imagine society as it existed before the changes brought about by the women's liberation movement. Advertisements for job openings were segregated according to sex, and women were paid nearly 40 percent less than men for the same work. Banks denied women credit for mortgages or loans. No women were anchors on television or radio news broadcasts since it was thought that their voices were too strident. There were virtually no women CEOs or firefighters or police officers. The number of women professors, doctors, and lawyers was miniscule, and female college students were funneled into certain "feminine" occupations: teaching elementary school, nursing, and secretarial work. There was no awareness of sexual harassment and date rape (and no language to describe them). Moreover, there was a belief among the general public (and the police) that women who were raped had "asked for it." Abortion was illegal but performed illegally at great risk to the woman. Shulman and other feminist activists transformed society and were themselves transformed in the process.

Alix Kates was born in Cleveland, Ohio, in 1932 to Samuel Kates, an attorney and labor arbitrator, and Dorothy Davis Kates, a community volunteer and activist and also an art collector. Both were Polish Russian Jews and first-generation Americans. Dorothy Kates, who had been a teacher until she married, also worked for the New Deal's Works Progress Administration (WPA) until the end of World War II as a designer of history projects. After the war, like other women of her generation, she accepted the postwar redefinition of their role that generally excluded married women from paid employment. Samuel and Dorothy's second child, Alix, was named for Alexander B. Cook, Samuel Kates's mentor at law. She had one older brother, Bob, her cousin by birth, who was adopted by her parents after his mother died in childbirth.

Alix graduated from Cleveland Heights High School and lived at home while attending Western Reserve University, where she majored in philosophy. In *A Good Enough Daughter*, she recounts her life as a teenager, punctuated by episodes of rebellion: an instance of shoplifting, a bearded boyfriend with an antiestablishment attitude. She speculates that her adolescent strivings were fueled by her sense that she, not her adopted brother, bore the birthright or father's blessing: "Had our parents never had another child, Bob would have kept the birthright. But as the one true Kates, I got it. Here was something new, a girl, a secondborn, with a boy's name and the birthright. Fertile soil in which to grow a feminist."[1]

After her college graduation, Alix moved to New York City to enter graduate school in philosophy at Columbia University. Her departure for New York represented a deliberate break with her family and her midwestern past. Her flight did not bespeak any lack of love or of appreciation for her parents but rather a deep need to be herself. Shulman likens her departure to the American immigrant experience or the attraction to the frontier—the imperative need to seek out the unexplored.

At Columbia she completed the coursework for a doctorate. She discovered, however, that in the early 1950s, it was all but impossible for a woman to be a philosopher, and it became clear that there would be no job in her chosen field. She married a graduate student in the English Department and dropped out of school to support him: "It was just a given that between the two of us, as between two of practically any academic couple in those days, the one whose career mattered was the man, and the one whose job it was to support the career was the woman. It wasn't my husband's evil. It was the way things were."[2] To keep the couple solvent, she took jobs as a receptionist, bookkeeping machine operator, librarian, researcher for the city's Board of Higher Education, and encyclopedia editor.

In 1956, Alix accompanied her husband to Europe when he was awarded a Fulbright scholarship. Soon after they returned to New York, they divorced, and she married again, to Martin Shulman, in 1959. They had a son and a daughter: Theodore, in 1961, and Polly, in 1963. This marriage, which, according to Shulman, "had initially been very romantic," began to disintegrate after the children were born: "He started wandering as soon as I was the wife home with the baby."[3] Although

Shulman had willingly embarked on a traditional marriage, she endured many frustrations. Deeply committed to her children, she nonetheless felt trapped in a domestic role and resented her husband's expectations that she take complete responsibility for the children and the housework while he pursued his career and his own interests, including extramarital affairs.

In the late 1960s, Shulman heard an announcement over the radio about a women's liberation meeting, and she attended with a friend. She immediately recognized that feminism could "give an explanation of my misery that could enable me to change it." She felt the exhilaration of being part of "an emotional transformation, an explosion, a feeling all over the country that things must be different and ideas about how they should be."[4] Shulman joined several feminist groups: New York Radical Women, Redstockings, WITCH (Women's International Terrorist Conspiracy from Hell), and New York Radical Feminists. These groups met to discuss and oppose male supremacy. Shulman recalls that she "understood for the first time that things did not have to be the way they were, that they could be changed. A lot of us felt that way, and that's how the movement started. It was a thrilling thing to be alive and to be there at that moment. It changed my life."[5] Redstockings focused on theoretical critique while the focus of WITCH was action. Shulman estimates that when she first became involved in 1967, there were perhaps one hundred women active in radical groups. There were thousands by the 1970s. In these groups, there was a conscious attempt to overcome class divisions. As a Redstockings statement proclaimed, "We define the best interests of women as the best interests of the poorest, most insulted, most despised, most abused woman on earth."[6]

The discussions held at women's liberation meetings evolved into what became known as consciousness-raising. In these groups, women explored their common gender experiences. The slogan "The Personal Is Political" meant that the oppression women felt in their personal lives was more than an individual private matter, but rather arose from society's treatment of women as a class. Shulman explains that until she encountered feminism, she believed that she had to accept her lot as inevitable: "Until then, I only felt the anguish of it, and felt that it was demeaning to complain. This was my fate: I was a woman, I was a mother, and to complain about it would be beneath me. So I couldn't complain about it. But I had my secret thoughts."[7] Consciousness-raising was not therapy but rather modeled on the Chinese practice called "Speaking Bitterness." Women tried to get at the truth of how they felt and what they experienced in society with the aim of figuring out how to change their situation. There was an emotional outpouring on the subject of sex, as they expressed their outrage about being used sexually. Women came to see that all aspects of their lives were connected. They could start anywhere in their analysis—jobs, sex, housework—and find interconnections relating to the fact that their entire lives were permeated by sexism.

Influenced by the media hype about the sexual revolution, Shulman was amazed to hear from women who came of age in the 1960s that sexual liberation, far from bringing them freedom, was really another form of victimization. Women in the New Left complained that not only were they expected to do the drudgery of the movement, but they were also expected to be sexually available: "These women saw an intimate connection between the way men treated them in their organizations and the way they treated them sexually; they were two sides of a single demeaning attitude toward women—one that would not take them seriously."[8]

Shulman belonged to the radical wing of the movement, which asserted that women's subordination in the larger social realm was connected to their subordinate role in the family. Radical feminists critiqued the family, marriage, romantic love, heterosexuality, and rape. They insisted on legal and safe contraception, legal abortion, and accessible child care. They attacked the media's objectification of women.

Feminism taught Shulman useful skills as well as enabling her to follow her own inner promptings. One memorable moment was the time she made her first public speech: "My knees shook. It was so difficult. It was for a Redstockings event, and we had agreed that everyone should do everything so that we would develop skills. So I gulped and volunteered. But I was terrified. Terrified. And then afterward, I was strong. I was never afraid to speak again. It was such a liberating and rewarding experience. And I had it over and over again. I wasn't afraid of what would happen to me; I was just afraid of stepping across that line."[9]

In September 1968, Shulman took part in the first national women's liberation demonstration at the Miss America Pageant in Atlantic City. This demonstration, which focused on women's exploitation as sex objects, drew the attention of the nation to the new movement. While some feminists went inside the convention hall and unfurled a banner that read "Women's Liberation," Shulman and others demonstrated outside, crowning a live sheep Miss America and throwing the accouterments of female oppression—high-heeled shoes, girdles, hair curlers, brooms, *Playboy* magazines—into a "freedom" trash can. One of the most striking posters was "a replica of a display ad for a popular steakhouse depicting a woman's naked body charted with the names of beef cuts."[10] Women's liberationists would speak only to female reporters (of whom there were very few). Since the movement was little known or understood at the time, the demonstrators were ridiculed: "Many onlookers and reporters were incensed; it was at that demonstration that feminists became known as 'crazy bra burners,' though no bra was burned. So acceptable was the practice of valuing women for their sexual attractiveness that many people genuinely believed that the demonstrators must be ugly women, motivated by simple jealousy of the contestants, proclaiming a politics of sour grapes."[11] It was on the Atlantic City boardwalk that Shulman got the idea for her first novel, *Memoirs of an Ex-Prom Queen*: "I suddenly could see my life in terms of this junior high and high school beauty focus. I was never a prom queen myself, but I knew that milieu very well."[12]

The next year, against her husband's wishes, she attended the Redstockings speak-out on abortion, where she revealed her own abortions motivated by diaphragm failure. Women explained the anguish and trauma they had to endure to get abortions. The country was stunned because, Shulman believed, the prohibition against abortion was tied to the "deeply held feeling that sex outside of marriage must be punished."[13] The speak-out was founded on the feminists' belief that there can be no equality between men and women without abortion rights. Like others in the movement, Shulman had an FBI file. The FBI was infiltrating the women's movement all along, and feminists got hold of a large file through the Freedom of Information Act. Of hers, Shulman says that "it consisted mostly of reviews of my books. I mean, they hadn't a clue."[14]

Beginning in the late 1960s, Shulman wrote articles on topics related to women's liberation. A 1970 article for the feminist journal *Up from Under* on equitable marriage attracted considerable attention and was harshly criticized. Early in 1969 she had drawn up what she called "A Marriage Agreement." Her marriage with the father of her two children was seriously strained, and the couple talked about divorce. They explored the possibilities for joint custody but found that such an arrangement was not possible at the time. (Changes came later with New York's 1975 divorce law reform.) Eventually, they decided to stay together for the sake of Theodore and Polly, and Shulman drafted an agreement that would introduce equality into their relationship. She first wrote down every household task, no matter how small. Then, applying the analytical and critical skills learned in her training in philosophy, she produced a work with the astonishing premise that the paid work of the husband was a privilege and did not excuse him from sharing the common tasks of domestic life.

The agreement went on to assert that each partner had a right to spend free time as he or she wished and to insist on complete sharing of child care. The agreement was reprinted in many popular magazines and in textbooks, including a casebook on contract law produced at Harvard. In *A Good Enough Daughter*, Shulman marvels that "a simple proposal to divide the tasks of childcare and housework equally between husband and wife" was at the time "so controversial as to merit a six-page spread in *Life*, more than two thousand letters from *Redbook* readers, and attacks by Norman Mailer and the *New York Times*."[15] The novelist Mailer quoted from the agreement in his notorious attack on feminism, *The Prisoner of Sex*. Shulman took the attack as a compliment. Feminists had succeeded in cracking wide open the assumption that women should be tied to the home while men were freed for careers, hobbies, and male pleasures by women's domestic services.

Shulman was interested in the idea of sharing household tasks and child care not only as a matter of simple justice but also because she thought it would transform child rearing. Redstockings subjected the institution of marriage to intense scrutiny, but the group did not put itself in opposition to marriage, as some radical feminists did. Its aim was instead to transform marriage to make men more responsible. Shulman was gratified that after she and her husband had put into effect the agreement, one of her children said, "You know, I used to love Mommy more, but now I love you both the same."[16]

Female sexuality was another important topic for feminists and for Shulman. Historically, the patriarchy restrained women's sexual experience in order to control them. Shulman and other feminists believed that women should have complete freedom to seek sexual pleasure. One of her earliest articles was written at the request of her women's group and directly addresses the subject. At the beginning of the essay, "Organs and Orgasms," her focus is not love-making but rather the myths about female anatomy that have hindered female pleasure. One of the things that attracted Shulman to the work of Emma Goldman was Goldman's impassioned defense of free love. Shulman demanded sexual freedom for herself, although she had entered into a monogamous relationship when she married the man who became the father of her children. (Later, after he had affairs, she also took lovers.) Her passionate affair with her undergraduate philosophy professor is fictionalized in

Memoirs of an Ex-Prom Queen as both a sexual and an intellectual awakening.

Shulman states unequivocally that the women's liberation movement made her a writer. She first intended to be a lawyer like her father, then fell in love with philosophy in her undergraduate years. As a young mother, it occurred to her that she could write and still take care of her children at home. She thought that she could write better children's books than those she was reading to Theodore and Polly, and she published three children's books in the early 1970s. Along with other women, she founded Feminists for Children's Media to analyze sexism in children's literature, and they presented their research to an astonished American Library Association meeting. At this time, Shulman also wrote several stories for adults. She had been writing for about a year when she attended her first women's liberation meeting. Her writing, like her life, was transformed by the encounter.

When given an opportunity to write a biography of a forgotten woman for an American biography series for young adults, Shulman chose to write about Emma Goldman, an anarchist, feminist, and, as noted, proponent of free love. At that time, writers were often criticized in the movement as "elitist" opportunists who might benefit by describing the movement. As a children's author, Shulman had been largely safe from criticism. She welcomed the chance to pen the biography of Goldman because she could bring her identities of feminist and writer together and make her work "serve, not subvert, feminism."[17]

When an opportunity arose to write a novel, Shulman was ready. She encountered a man in publishing whom she had known earlier. He had read one of her stories in a feminist journal and told her to contact him if she ever wrote a novel. She went home and immediately started *Memoirs of an Ex-Prom Queen*, based on her own experiences of growing up in Cleveland and her early years in New York. "I knew that there was another view of women's experience that hadn't been expressed in fiction, or hardly ever, a view that was just starting to take hold in the country, a new interpretation of experience. I wanted to dramatize that interpretation," she explained. "And I knew there was an audience who needed to hear it. I wasn't sure if I could reach them, or whether I could do it well. But I knew we had to come together, somehow. That was why I became a writer."[18]

The novel's protagonist is Sasha Davis, who is deeply influenced by society's prescriptions for women. The dominant goal in her life is her quest for beauty or, in other words, for male recognition. Sasha believes that "there was only one thing worth bothering about: becoming beautiful."[19] Being pretty, however, does not bring her much joy: "Could it be that the prettier I grew, the worse I would be treated? Much likelier, I thought, I wasn't really pretty."[20] In spite of the fact that she considers males largely a nuisance and a threat, she will do anything for their approval. She drops out of college and marries, terrified at the thought of life without a man. She sacrifices her ambitions for her men again and again, not gaining a sense of herself until her beauty fades.

In this novel as in her later work, Shulman focuses on the structural relations between the individual and society. Although the novel can also be read as a psychological study, for Shulman it is an exploration of social forces. She published the novel under the name Alix Kates Shulman, adding Kates to the name she had previously used as an author. Later, she said that she regretted that she had not dropped Shulman altogether. (In her private life, she now goes by Alix Kates.) The novel sold over one million copies and was adopted by the Literary Guild. Although it had many readers and many admirers, not everyone understood the tone of wry humor that characterized it. While some reviewers were positive, others did not grasp the point of view of women's liberationists and failed to see the novel as satire.[21]

That *Memoirs of an Ex-Prom Queen* spoke to women was clear even before its publication, when the novel was handed around by secretaries employed in the publishing firm. Noting this reaction to the novel, the men in charge realized that they had a publishing phenomenon on their hands. As a result, when *Memoirs* was auctioned for reprinting in paperback, it sold for the highest amount that any first novel had brought up to that time.

In her next novel, *Burning Questions* (1977), Shulman set out to write a historical novel of the rise of the women's movement. Shulman had read Emma Goldman's revolutionary autobiography and became interested in the genre, seeking out other examples. The change in consciousness caused by feminism is the subject of the novel. Zane IndiAnna, the protagonist, first flirts with rebellion by joining the Beatniks, a bohemian movement in the 1950s. But it becomes clear that bohemia offers no more for women than does mainstream society. Zane's discovery of the women's movement in early adulthood, as a wife and mother, ends her quest for self-fulfillment and puts her in solidarity with other women. The novel includes a dramatic account of the march down Fifth Avenue to commemorate the fiftieth anniversary of the vote for women.

In *On the Stroll* (1981), Shulman takes on the subject of runaway girls and homeless women in the menacing environment of the city. Robin, an abused teenager, runs away to New York from home in rural Maine and falls into the clutches of Prince, a pimp. As Robin struggles to disentangle herself from Prince, she becomes connected to Owl, a homeless woman. Shulman had planned from the beginning to have Robin and Owl move toward each other: "I knew the ending was going to be that. This bonding among women is the solution. That's my feminist outlook."[22] The novel earned an Outstanding Book citation from the *New York Times* in 1981.

In addition to consulting published sources about her subject, Shulman and a friend ran a coffee hour for bag ladies in the basement of a seedy Times Square hotel as part of an outreach program sponsored by Franciscan nuns. Shulman spent hours in the shelter talking to homeless women. At the time, unlike homeless men, these women had drawn little attention. As the traditional support system for women began to fall apart, some feminists had fears about an impoverished old age. Shulman wanted to find out the truth about the lives of homeless women and demythologize the subject. She also talked to runaway teenage girls who were interviewed by the police in the Port Authority Bus Terminal. At the time she was aware of scandals connected with runaway girls —one involved luring young blondes from Minnesota to New York City.

In her days as a feminist activist, Shulman had participated in a conference on prostitution. She was bothered by members of the audience heckling the prostitutes who had been invited to be on the program: "I decided someday I was going to write about prostitution—from the inside, or as far inside as I could get."[23] She was also inspired by Emma Goldman, who had written about prostitutes and viewed them as victims, not victimizers.

Motherhood figures as an important theme in many of Shulman's works. The challenges and frustrations of being a mother in the male-dominated society of her day provided much food for thought. In the early days of the feminist movement, the question of whether women should marry and have children in the misogynist climate of the time was discussed. Already a mother, Shulman considered it her duty to explain and defend motherhood. She herself found no contradiction between being a mother and a feminist. Indeed, feminism showed her that she could be a mother and also be active in the outside world.

In Every Woman's Life . . . (1987) poses the question, "To marry or not to marry?" Ultimately, the novel views marriage as an institution of the family. Shulman comments, "Otherwise, why marry? Even if the feeling dies in marriage, if you have children, you have certain responsibilities. I wasn't divorced until after my children graduated college, which is not an uncommon story. I think people take the responsibility of parenting quite seriously, and even if they no longer have the relationship they had when they first got together, they stay together for the children. I'm not sure that's a bad thing."[24]

Rosemary, the protagonist of *In Every Woman's Life . . .* , and her husband maintain their marriage largely so they can join together in the task of parenting. Everyone in the family is involved in a secret affair, but everyone opts for marriage, including the daughter, even though marriage is not highly regarded by the young. The institution may be problematic, but it refuses to die, even though much of the time it seems at odds with sexual pleasure. Eroticism and a woman's right to sexual pleasure are at the center of the novel, and, as usual, Shulman relates events with a wry sense of humor. In spite of the difficulties with marriage, Shulman is careful not to make her male characters the villains. Her aim is to show the structural relations that cause women's sufferings: "If I made one man a villain, the rest would be off the hook. I'm interested in the system of oppression."[25]

In the early 1980s, in middle age, Shulman reevaluated her life and decided to begin anew rather than slowly fade away. Her children were grown, and her marriage had all but disintegrated; she divorced in 1985. A new generation treading on her heels seemed to take for granted the improvements in women's lot and to be uninterested in furthering the cause. One could say that she felt the weight of the years, but that was not all. To someone who had spent a lifetime pondering culture's definitions, the contempt of the culture for aging women was another burden. She was busy with friends, political projects, and her writing, but being busy did not satisfy her. She wanted to start life over like Mother Jones, who found her career as a union organizer at fifty. In 1982, at the age of fifty, Shulman spent the summer on an island off the coast of Maine, where the family had a vacation cottage without electricity, plumbing, or a phone. She continued to summer on the island in subsequent years, living there from May to October. Her experiences formed the basis for the memoir *Drinking the Rain* (1996), published fourteen years after her first summer alone. In the book she wanted to show that a simple life is possible and rewarding: "People can live as I did without falling apart. I thought it was important for people to understand that we don't need everything that our culture tells us we have to have to be satisfied."[26]

She had rarely spent more than a few days alone, and on the island she learned to adapt to natural rhythms, to slow down, and to be receptive. One day she undertook the chore of pushing a cart to the island's sole grocery store only to find that the usual limp vegetables had already sold out. On the way home she noticed the native edible plants (lamb's-quarter, sorrel) she had formerly used only as a garnish and stopped to pick enough for an entire salad. It was the beginning of a diet harvested from the land and the sea. She found that mussels and other sea creatures could provide all the protein she needed. *Drinking the Rain* has an ecological theme: nature is bountiful. Moreover, the sociopolitical state of the nation can be read in the food supply: "Our society has very much limited our choices, even unto the food we think acceptable. A lot of those 'weeds' that I gathered on the island used to be common foods, but when the corporations took over our food supply—when farming became a corporate venture, and the distribution of food became corporate—the variety of foods that were considered good diminished greatly."[27] Furthermore, unbothered by the contempt of the culture for domestic work that makes many women resent cooking, Shulman had always viewed cooking as creative and rewarding. If cooking is devalued female drudgery, enjoying it was a way to defy the culture's misogyny. In New York she had cooked for family and friends. On the island she cooked elaborate meals for herself, experimenting with the wild produce she harvested every day.

In all her writing from *Memoirs* onward, Shulman had addressed society's propensity to shape women for its uses and then to despise them for being different (the "female taint," she calls it in *Drinking the Rain*). She found it satisfying to be alone on the island, where in solitude there was neither male nor female: "What a relief to have that weight of womanhood rise like a gull and fly away. To be where nothing I did had a scripted meaning. Where keeping house and cooking were not female chores but simple tasks of pleasure and survival."[28] On the island, Shulman embraced solitude, and her life became a spiritual experience. In subsequent years, while she continued to spend almost every summer on the island, she learned that she could carry her new understanding away from the island too.

Having devoted most of her life to political activism, Shulman could hardly fail to be struck by the contradiction between the life of political engagement—the effort to change the world—and the life of enjoyment and contemplation that she led on the island. To deal with the contradiction, she turned to the words of James Baldwin, who enunciated the paradox that one can hold in one's mind two contradictory ideas: the idea of acceptance of life without bitterness, and the idea that one must never accept injustice but continue to struggle against it. Shulman's time on the island enabled her to live that paradox.

Her life in the mid-1980s is recounted in *Drinking the Rain*. With her marriage at an end and divorce in the offing, she accepted an appointment as Visiting Writer-in-Residence at the University of Colorado at Boulder. (Not her first stint at teaching—she has taught writing workshops at New York University and the universities of Southern Maine, Arizona, and Hawaii.) With a female anthropologist friend, she hiked through the Colorado mountains. She visited Hare Krishna groups and joined a demonstration against CIA recruiters on campus. She was courted long distance by a former high-school sweetheart, and the two met and resumed a romantic relationship from thirty years earlier. When her lover visited her in Santa Fe, where she spent the summer, they took part in a Los Alamos protest against the atomic bomb on the fortieth anniversary of Hiroshima. (Shulman married Scott York in 1989.) In the last part of *Drinking the Rain*, Shulman's ecological theme deepens. Amid rumors that the mussels are not safe to eat and with a red tide of pollution heading for the island and the appearance of an itchy rash, Shulman's awareness that everything is connected for good or ill deepened. *Drinking the Rain* won the Body Mind Spirit Award of Excellence and was a *Los Angeles Times* Book Prize finalist.

In the 1990s, as her parents' health declined, Shulman had an opportunity to reconnect with them. In her parents' last years, she made many visits to Cleveland to help them sell their house and move to a retirement home. She saw them through their final years until the death of Dorothy at eighty-nine and Samuel, some months later, at ninety-five. Coming back into their lives gave her the chance to explore the influences of family, which she had pushed to one side in her earlier work in favor of exploring the forces in the larger society.

During these years, she set out to know her mother and father as people, not just as a daughter knows her parents. After leaving home at age twenty to take charge of her own life, Shulman almost never looked back. When her parents settled in the retirement home and she returned to their empty house, she lamented: "I open the door on the sudden smell of [my mother's] perfume and the breath-stopping knowledge, like a blow to the solar plexus, of what I've thrown away in the name of freedom and can never regain."[29] She was fortunate, however, to find that she could regain some of what she had lost.

Trying to make up for past neglect, she insisted that her father's papers recording his arbitration decisions be preserved, and she found a home for them in the Ohio Historical Society. She made sure that her mother's art collection (including works by de Kooning, Motherwell, and Frankenthaler) was properly disposed of. Although she had not come home when her mother was diagnosed with cancer, her elderly parents insisted that she never let them down. Caring for them in their old age was deeply satisfying for her. It also left her with the realization that old age is the last stage in a journey, a ripening rather than a decline. In a recent interview, she reflected: "When you witness the end of a life up close day by day, you begin to understand time and mortality in profound ways. You see time's relativity and death's necessity."[30]

Alix Kates Shulman is an ordinary woman—student, librarian, receptionist, encyclopedia editor, wife, mother—but she became extraordinary as a result of being reborn as a feminist in the 1960s.

Notes

1. Alix Kates Shulman, *A Good Enough Daughter* (New York: Schocken, 1999), 32.

2. Leora Tanenbaum, "The Liberation of an Ex-Prom Queen," *Ms.* (November/December 1997): 82.

3. Ibid.

4. Alix Kates Shulman, interview with author, March 22, 2000.

5. Ibid.

6. Quoted in Lisa Maria Hogeland, *Feminism and Its Fictions: The Consciousness-Raising Novel and the Women's Liberation Movement* (Philadelphia: University of Pennsylvania Press, 1998), 10.

7. Tannenbaum, "Liberation," 84.

8. Alix Kates Shulman, "Sex and Power: Sexual Bases of Radical Feminism," *Signs* 5 (Summer 1980): 592.

9. Tannenbaum, "Liberation," 84.

10. Shulman, "Sex and Power," 595.

11. Ibid.

12. Shulman interview.

13. Shulman, "Sex and Power," 595.

14. Shulman interview.

15. Shulman, *A Good Enough Daughter*, 114.

16. Alix Kates Shulman, "A Marriage Disagreement, or Marriage by Other Means," in *The Feminist Memoir Project: Voices from Women's Liberation*, ed. Rachael Blau DuPlessis and Ann Snitow (New York: Three Rivers Press, 1998), 219.

17. Alix Kates Shulman, "Living Our Life," in *Between Women: Biographers, Novelists, Critics, Teachers, and Artists Write about Their Work on Women*, ed. Carol Ascher, Louise DeSalve, and Sara Ruddick (Boston: Beacon Press, 1984), 4.

18. Shulman interview.

19. Alix Kates Shulman, *Memoirs of an Ex-Prom Queen* (New York: Penguin Books, 1997), 22.

20. Ibid., 49.

21. For more discussion of the reception of feminist novels, see Charlotte Templin, *Feminism and the Politics of Literary Reputation: The Example of Erica Jong* (Lawrence: University Press of Kansas, 1995).

22. Shulman interview.

23. Ibid.

24. Ibid.

25. Ibid.

26. Ibid.

27. Ibid.

28. Alix Kates Shulman, *Drinking the Rain* (New York: Penguin Books, 1996), 90.

29. Shulman, *A Good Enough Daughter*, 10.

30. Shulman interview.

Suggested Readings

Echols, Alice. *Daring to Be Bad: Radical Feminism in America, 1967–1975*. Minneapolis: University of Minnesota Press, 1989.

Rosen, Ruth. *The World Split Open: How the Modern Women's Movement Changed America*. New York: Viking Press, 2000.

Ryan, Barbara. *Feminism and the Women's Movement*. New York: Routledge, 1992.

Shulman, Alix Kates. *Burning Questions*. New York: New Space Press, 1977.

_____. *In Every Woman's Life . . . .* New York: Knopf, 1987.

_____. *On the Stroll*. New York: Knopf, 1981.

_____. "Organs and Orgasms." In *Woman in Sexist Society: Studies in Power and Powerlessness*, ed. Vivian Gornick and Barbara K. Moran. New York: Basic Books, 1971.

_____. *To the Barricades: The Anarchist Life of Emma Goldman*. New York: Crowell, 1971.

_____, ed. *Red Emma Speaks: Selected Writings and Speeches by Emma Goldman*. New York: Schocken, 1983.

Templin, Charlotte. "An Interview with Alix Kates Shulman." *Missouri Review* 24 (Spring 2001).

17

Mary Crow Dog
A Story of the American Indian Movement and the United States

Michelle Mannering

Lakota people believe that actions unfold through seven generations. Mary Crow Dog's life story chronicles the often-bitter consequences of American policies designed over centuries to solve "the Indian problem." In the 1970s many of those policies sparked one of the most explosive confrontations between American Indians and the U.S. government in recent memory, and Mary was there. She was born in 1953 into the Lakota people, on the Pine Ridge reservation in South Dakota. She grew up in government housing without telephones, electricity, or running water. In the 1950s federal policy relocated thousands of Indians to cities, where the American Indian Movement (AIM) began. Although still living on the reservation, Mary joined AIM as a teenager. Under provisions of the Indian Reorganization Act of 1934, Richard Wilson served as tribal chairman at Pine Ridge. There, in 1973, a few hundred AIM members and supporters, Mary among them, reclaimed sacred ground at Wounded Knee, the site of the 1890 massacre of the Ghost Dancers—over 300 Lakota men, women, and children. Heavily armed FBI agents, federal marshals, and government troops joined Wilson's private force, which styled itself Guardians of the Oglala Nation, to besiege Wounded Knee for seventy-one days. In the middle of the fighting, Mary Crow Dog gave birth to her first child. The ghosts of Crazy Horse, the Ghost Dancers, and even General George Armstrong Custer walked through the events of Mary Crow Dog's life. The story of this Lakota woman makes clear a fundamental condition of human existence: each person's life resounds with the repercussions of the past.

Michelle Mannering is associate professor of history at Butler University, Indianapolis. She received a Ph.D. from Indiana University, Bloomington, and is associate editor of *Always a People: Oral Histories of Contemporary Woodland Indians* (1997).

Mary Crow Dog was born Mary Brave Bird in 1953 on the Pine Ridge reservation in South Dakota and joined the American

This essay also appears in David L. Anderson, ed., *The Human Tradition in America since 1945* (Wilmington, DE: Scholarly Resources, 2003), 171–88.

Indian Movement (AIM) as a teenager in 1971. Two years later, in the small town of Wounded Knee on the Pine Ridge reservation, she gave birth to her first child in the middle of a firefight with U.S. marshals, FBI agents, and specially trained police armed with .50-caliber machine guns and M-16 rifles. The 200 American Indian men, women, and children inside the town had fewer than three dozen guns, some so old that ammunition for them was hard to find. Mary Crow Dog's tales of AIM, of what happened at Wounded Knee and why, and of how she came to be there belong with the stories of those turbulent years now often called, simply, the Sixties. Many histories of that period, however, leave out AIM and Wounded Knee altogether. The story of Mary Crow Dog explains why American Indians share a history with the United States unlike that of any other people in the country. The uniqueness of the Indian relationship with the rest of U.S. society shaped every aspect of the Indian rights movement and of the life of Mary Crow Dog.

The little settlement of Wounded Knee on the Pine Ridge reservation became AIM's last battleground in a decade-long uprising of Indians against the U.S. government. For seventy-one days in 1973, AIM members inside the town withstood continuous fire from federal forces and from Indian mercenaries hired by the chairman of the Lakota tribe at Pine Ridge, Richard Wilson. Wilson's assault on AIM at Wounded Knee, funded by the United States and reinforced by federal troops, epitomized the reasons for AIM's existence and the purpose of the Indian rights movement. From the perspective of AIM members, Wilson had sold his identity, his heritage, and his history for money, power, and approval. Official recognition by Washington of Wilson's regime at Pine Ridge assured a continuous flow of federal dollars to Wilson and his tribal government.

Wilson supported, and AIM members opposed, a policy for Indians called "assimilation," which had been the basis of U.S. Indian policy for almost one hundred years. Through assimilation, the federal government intended to transform Indians into typical Americans indistinguishable from any other citizens of the United States. Successful implementation of assimilation meant that Indians would be absorbed into the larger society and would disappear as a distinct ethnic culture.

At Wounded Knee, Mary Crow Dog and AIM fought for the right to be recognized as different from other American citizens. They fought for the right not to disappear into the larger society. Mary Crow Dog declared, "I do not consider myself a radical or revolutionary."[1] The federal government labeled her that way, however, because she was a member of AIM and because AIM challenged its authority. Specifically, AIM challenged the right of federal officials to carry out policies that the government believed best served American society but that AIM believed meant the destruction of Indian peoples.

In 1990, Mary Crow Dog described this destruction in an autobiographical account of her life in the Indian rights movement. She titled it *Lakota Woman*, and it won an American Book Award in 1991. With both the book and its title she challenged her readers to recognize not only her identity but also the history of the Indian nation to which she belongs. She did not use the word "Sioux" in the title, the name that most Americans know for the Lakotas, and thereby highlighted her nation's own name for its people. Beginning with its title, Mary Crow Dog's book attempts to narrow the gulf of misconceptions that divides other Americans from American Indians. In *Lakota Woman*, she describes who the Lakotas have been in the country's history, the degradation that U.S. Indian policies brought to them, and the almost unimaginable conditions on the reservations that drove Mary Crow Dog and other Lakotas to join AIM.

For Mary Crow Dog and AIM's other Lakota members, Wounded Knee was not only a battle for the right to remain Indian but also a continuation of the struggle to remain Lakota—a struggle that their grandparents and great-grandparents had lost nearly a century before. By 1890, the Lakotas had been stripped of their land and were sequestered on reservations. They had been denied the life that their ancestors had led for centuries and were forced by the United States to accept that in the future they would have to live like white men and women. Desperate to survive as a people, the Lakotas of the late nineteenth century embraced a new ceremony, the Ghost Dance, given to a Paiute medicine man, Wovoka, in a vision. Wovoka promised that if the people kept dancing in this new way, their dead would return, the buffalo would come back, and the whites would vanish in a cataclysm of destruction. The dancing caused panic among white settlers and federal agents, and in 1890 a detachment of the U.S. Army's 7th Cavalry was dispatched to the Lakota reservations. On December 29 the cavalry massacred a small band of Ghost Dancers—300 Lakota men, women, and children— caught at Wounded Knee. When AIM members arrived at the town in 1973, "we all felt the presence," Mary Crow Dog wrote, "of the spirits of those lying close by."[2]

Only twenty-two years before the 1890 massacre at Wounded Knee, the U.S. government had negotiated a peace treaty with the Lakotas and other Plains peoples, the Treaty of Fort Laramie of 1868. The treaty established a reservation—lands reserved for the Lakotas—in what is now the state of South Dakota west of the Missouri River. By the treaty's provisions, no white settlers were permitted on Lakota lands without Lakota consent. The fate of the Lakota nation after the 1868 Treaty of Fort Laramie was evidence, according to AIM, that the United States had practiced deceit and had attempted the destruction of Indian peoples.

Within a decade of signing the Fort Laramie treaty, the United States had broken the agreement, waged war on the Lakota people, and reduced them to the status of impoverished subjects dependent on the federal government. The lands that the Lakotas had retained by the 1868 treaty were rich in mineral resources and ripe for both exploitation and settlement. The discovery of gold in the Black Hills, granted to the Lakotas by the 1868 treaty as part of their lands, prompted the war. The Black Hills are sacred to the Lakotas, and they refused to cede them to the United States. Three armies, under Generals George Crook, George Armstrong Custer, and Alfred H. Terry, were sent to drive out the Lakotas. In 1876 the great Lakota chiefs and their allies won their famous victory at the Little Big Horn River and annihilated Custer and the 7th Cavalry, but that victory was fleeting. Within two years most of the Lakotas had surrendered.

Because the government's war against the Plains peoples had abrogated the 1868 treaty, AIM added another charge of criminality to its case against the United States. Nations usually sign treaties with equals, with sovereign powers like themselves, and breaking a signed treaty can be tantamount to breaking international law. By signing treaties with the Lakotas and with other Indian nations—the United States signed over three hundred of them—the federal government seemingly recognized that American Indians were members of sovereign nations and separate from, although within, U.S. boundaries. A case could be made that the Indians had rights unique to them, derived from the sovereign status of their nations and different from the rights of other citizens. Thus, because the United States had signed the 1868 treaty, Lakotas in 1968 could claim that it had recognized the Lakota nation as a sovereign state with the right to use or dispose of its lands as the Lakota peoples saw fit.

After the defeat of the Plains peoples, the United States instituted the policy of assimilation, which was, to AIM, merely a new method, short of war, by which the federal government destroyed Indian cultures, obliterated Indian identities, and robbed Indians of the lands they had left. The basis of AIM's case against assimilation was the General Allotment Act, more commonly known as the Dawes Act, passed by Congress in 1887 and the bedrock of the federal government's assimilation policy.

The Dawes Act broke up reservations across the United States, stripped more land from them, and, according to AIM, began the systematic impoverishment of Indian peoples. The Dawes Act decreed that each head of household would receive an allotment of 160 acres, although the size of some allotments was modified by later amendments. Allotments were held in trust for a period of years by the United States, under the provisions of the Dawes and later acts, until the Indians who held them were deemed capable of managing their own affairs. The rest of the acreage on the reservations was designated surplus land, bought for pennies per acre by the federal government, and sold to white settlers.

As part of the assimilation program instituted by the Dawes Act, the United States agreed to provide schools and teachers so that Indians could be taught good citizenship, learn the ways to prosper in white society, and, from the government's point of view, overcome the limitations of their Indian cultures. A number of Americans believed that assimilation provided Indians with their best chance for survival in a white world. The schools were supervised by the Bureau of Indian Affairs (BIA), created in 1834 as the Indian Bureau in the War Department and transferred to the Department of the Interior in 1849.

Federal officials charged with implementation of assimilation decided that a strict military regimen was needed to teach nomadic Indians the discipline required to become productive Americans, and the federal laws and programs, many still in place when Mary Crow Dog and other activists grew up, instilled in many AIM members a bitter resentment of federal policy. Children were taken from their families and sent to boarding schools where they faced severe punishment for speaking their own language. The supporters of assimilation believed that children could more easily and more speedily be indoctrinated into white society if removed from their Indian families and cultures. Indian religious practices, traditional ceremonies, and dress were outlawed. The male children who endured boarding school learned vocational skills; the female children learned domestic housekeeping. The schools turned out thousands of illiterate carpenters, shoemakers, and maids for whom few jobs existed on the reservations.

The continued acquisition by white owners of Indian lands provided more evidence for AIM that the federal government instituted with the Dawes Act the systematic impoverishment of the Indian peoples. In 1887, Indians still retained 138 million acres of land. After allotment, periodic removal of trust restrictions for some Indians often led to fraud, which stripped more acres from Indian holdings. Other lands were sold or leased under the supervision of the BIA. Governmental studies of Indian poverty during the Great Depression acknowledged that many of the individual allotments were either too small or too infertile to sustain a single family. By the start of World War II, roughly fifty million acres were left, and 25 percent of what remained was leased to whites for their use.

The poverty under which Mary Crow Dog grew up testifies to the dismal failure of assimilation programs. Her family had a one-room cabin without heat, running water, or electricity. "With a blizzard going," Mary Crow Dog reported in *Lakota Woman*, "a trip to the privy at night is high adventure."[3] Some families added on to their dwellings by attaching the broken-down bodies of old automobiles. Others made do in the tar-paper shacks that dotted the reservation. "The little settlements we lived in," she wrote, "were places without hope where bodies and souls were . . . destroyed bit by bit."[4]

Mary Crow Dog's experience in boarding school adds further testimony to the misery that resulted from U.S. assimilation policy. Her family sent her to a Catholic mission school in St. Francis, South Dakota, even though three generations of Brave Bird women—her sister Barbara, her mother, and her grandmother—had run away. Mary ran away from the school, too, and, like all of the women in her family, was beaten for disobedience. "It is almost impossible," she wrote, "to explain to a sympathetic white person what a typical old Indian boarding school was like."[5]

According to the reminiscences of other AIM members and Indian activists, the BIA schools taught hatred. "We underwent what seemed to be a constant challenge to our will to live," said Robert Burnette, a former tribal chairman of the Rosebud reservation in South Dakota who entered the Rosebud boarding school at age five.[6] "They did their best," remarked George Mitchell, one of AIM's founders, "to beat the Indian out of us. Actually, I think they beat the Indian *into* us."[7]

The disintegration of identities and cultures had accelerated after passage of the Indian Reorganization Act (IRA) of 1934. John Collier, the commissioner of Indian affairs under Franklin Roosevelt, was sympathetic and meant the IRA to be a reform of assimilation policy that returned some power to the Indian nations. But Collier drew his model for tribal governance from white corporate structures, and the IRA ended up undermining the traditional ways in which Indians had governed themselves. The IRA eventually brought power to tribal chairmen such as Richard Wilson at Pine Ridge and helped create AIM's confrontation with Wilson and the U.S. Army at Wounded Knee. Under the IRA, tribal members, by majority vote, elected tribal chairmen and tribal councils that implemented policy according to tribal constitutions written under the supervision of the Department of the Interior and the BIA. All of these measures reflected an American, but not an American Indian, style of governance.

After passage of the IRA, many tribal chairmen were, like Wilson, corrupted by the money and support that came from Washington when the BIA approved of the way in which they ran a reservation. Wilson and other tribal chairmen funneled federal dollars meant for educational and economic assistance programs to relatives and friends—those who could get them reelected—rather than to the neediest populations on their reservations. Under a regime such as Wilson's at Pine Ridge, tribal councils ended up doing the bidding of the tribal chairman rather than attending to the needs of the peoples they were supposed to serve. By the 1960s and 1970s, Burnette testified, tribal councils, established under the IRA of 1934, had "degenerated to the point where the young and the old on reservations . . . [could] no longer use the normal channels to communicate with the men that supposedly represent[ed] them."[8]

After World War II, the United States created a new federal policy called "termination," designed to bring about the complete assimilation of Indians into American society, or, as the Indians saw it, their complete obliteration from the American landscape. On August 1, 1953, Congress passed House Concurrent Resolution 108, which recommended termination of the trust relationship between the Indian nations and the federal government. The resolution expressed the will of Congress, "as rapidly as possible, to make the Indians . . . subject to the same laws and entitled to the same privileges and responsibilities as are applicable to other citizens of the United States."[9] Termination, a name derived from a shorthand reference to the congressional resolution, remained federal policy for two decades. Under termination, tribal lands could be broken up and proceeds distributed among individual tribal members; tribal funds would be disposed of in the same way; and tribal peoples would also be broken up and become individual citizens, no longer members of Indian nations.

By 1953, a strong pan-Indian movement dedicated to advocacy of Indian rights had developed in the United States, and the arguments put forth by its leaders against assimilation, now to be finished under termination, shaped the political agenda of AIM and other Indian activist groups. The National Congress of American Indians (NCAI), organized in 1944 and still an advocate on behalf of Indians today, led the development of pan-Indianism. The NCAI built a successful, grass-roots, pan-Indian organization by emphasizing the value of all American Indian cultures and the common history that Indians shared with the United States, namely, the making of treaties. Thus, the NCAI worked into the national consciousness the ideas that Indians had rights different from other Americans and were, in fact, sovereign peoples. The NCAI also raised issues of land fraud and treaty violations and their formative effect on Indian poverty. The organization united Indians behind causes common to all: tribal sovereignty, treaty violations, reclamation of lands unjustly taken, and compensation for land cessions for which they had been denied adequate payment.

The NCAI's linkage of sovereignty, treaty violations, land fraud, and poverty drew the attention of young Indians, many of them destitute and confronted with termination, which threatened to take away almost all they had left: their identities as American Indians and their cultures. On the reservations, the poverty of the peoples worsened through the 1950s and 1960s. As Indian nations were terminated by congressional act—termination bills were introduced in Congress for six nations in 1953—some Indians quickly dissipated their assets, for a variety of reasons. Others were forced to sell their holdings. They charged that food rations were cut for those who opposed termination. "We had to sell our land to live," lamented a Blackfoot woman.[10]

The addition of the BIA's Urban Relocation Program to Congress's policy of termination produced young, urban Indians whose hostility to federal policy reflected the fears of their peers on the reservations. The Urban Relocation Program removed the peoples from their reservations, ostensibly provided them with vocational education, and relocated them in cities where they were to seek jobs and eventually blend into the larger society. In 1956, 5,000 workers—more than 12,000 Indians when their families were included—were relocated to cities, but the average rate of unemployment for Indians remained at 40 percent through the 1960s. The House Subcommittee on Indian Affairs reported a failure rate of 30 percent under the BIA's relocation program, that is, 30 percent of those relocated had to return to their reservations. Non-federal agencies reported a failure rate of 60 percent.

AIM's founders and many of its members came from the Indian ghettos in American cities that sprang up from the BIA's Urban Relocation Program. Clyde Bellecourt and Eddie Banai, both Ojibwa and two of AIM's founders, met in a Minnesota prison. Dennis Banks, who became one of AIM's leading spokesmen, spent fourteen years in BIA boarding schools, did a stint in the Air Force, and returned to Minneapolis and St. Paul where, he said, "there were no jobs, no nothing."[11]

In 1964, Bellecourt created a group in Minneapolis patterned after the local community organizations that were so effective in the civil rights movement. He attempted to organize the Indians in Minneapolis's ghettos to seek recognition of their rights. He also sought educational and economic opportunities for Minneapolis's urban Indians. "I tried to work within the System for four years, demanding a fair share of it for my people," said Bellecourt, "but all the money was controlled by the churches and bureaucracies, and they weren't interested in any programs that might have led toward real economic independence for the Indians."[12]

Bellecourt recreated his organization in 1968; he modeled the group on the Black Panthers and called it AIM. In Oakland, the Black Panthers, armed with shotguns, trailed police charged with brutality against the African American community. In Minneapolis and St. Paul, AIM members armed with cameras followed police charged with brutality against American Indians. Arrests among the Indian community decreased, and AIM spread chapter by chapter to other cities. AIM members built community centers for urban Indians in the BIA's relocation cities. In addition, AIM sought economic and educational opportunities for Indians, and its members led protests against racial discrimination, poor housing, and illegal arrests.

Veterans of other Indian activist groups joined AIM demonstrations in between their own protests. Among the most notable of these organizations was the National Indian Youth Council (NIYC). Organized in 1961, the NIYC led a series of "fish-ins" in Washington State that spread to other Indian peoples. NIYC members used civil disobedience, a classic tactic of the civil rights movement, to protest restrictions imposed by state laws on fishing rights guaranteed to the Indian peoples by treaties signed with the United States.

Veterans of Alcatraz, a shorthand term for the occupation by Indians in 1969 of the abandoned federal prison on Alcatraz Island in San Francisco Bay, also came to AIM activities. The occupiers of Alcatraz named their organization Indians of All Nations and claimed the prison property on behalf of Indians. The protestors stayed on the island for nineteen months without heat, running water, or electricity until U.S. marshals removed them on June 11, 1971. After Alcatraz, land reclamation protests sprang up across the United States.

In the summer of 1971, AIM members, NIYC members, and Veterans of Alcatraz gathered on the Rosebud reservation in South Dakota, where Mary Crow Dog met them for the first time. Indians came to Rosebud because Leonard Crow Dog, the man whom Mary Brave Bird later married after the Wounded Knee siege, held a Sun Dance, a ceremony sacred to the Lakotas, at Crow Dog's Paradise, the name that the family had given to its original allotment. The Crow Dog family is famous among the Lakotas. "Every Crow Dog," Mary wrote, "seems to be a legend in himself."[13] Leonard Crow Dog was the first medicine man to join AIM. His great-grandfather, his grandfather, and his father were all medicine men. The Crow Dogs had preserved the Sun Dance in secret at Crow Dog's Paradise during the years when the ceremony was outlawed by the United States as barbaric, because the Sun Dance requires a tearing of the flesh, a ritualized suffering for the sake of a loved one or for the sake of one's people.

The members of AIM made an immediate impression on Mary Crow Dog. They "hit our reservation like a tornado," she explained. AIM members wore Indian dress, and some of the men wore braids. These were unusual sights on the reservations in the 1970s after almost a century of assimilation. AIM members also moved with confidence—"swaggering," as Mary Crow Dog remembered—among the peoples gathered at Crow Dog's Paradise. "They had a new look about them," she recalled, "not that hangdog reservation look I was used to." That year she traveled with AIM members who were demonstrating across the country at courthouses where Indians were on trial, at anthropology digs to protest the removal and display of the bones of the dead, and at any place, she said, that sported a sign reading "No Indians Allowed."[14]

Mary Crow Dog, fellow AIM members, and other activists gathered at Crow Dog's Paradise for the Sun Dance in 1972. They planned a national demonstration on behalf of Indian rights for that fall in Washington, DC. The murders of two Indians—Richard Oakes in California and Raymond Yellow Thunder in Nebraska—had prompted the activists gathered at Rosebud to go to Washington. Oakes, a leader of the Alcatraz occupation, was unarmed when he was shot and killed by a white man in Santa Rosa, California. In Gordon, Nebraska, two white men stripped Yellow Thunder, a fifty-one-year-old Lakota from Pine Ridge, from the waist down and, at gunpoint, made him dance for a crowd of white men and women at a local bar. He was found beaten and dead in the trunk of a car. At an informal gathering after the Sun Dance, Robert Burnette called for at least two hundred Indians to descend on BIA headquarters in Washington in order to bring Indian grievances before the government.

Burnette, AIM, and other activists organized the demonstration, which became known as the Trail of Broken Treaties. It was scheduled for November 1972, just before the presidential election. The BIA offered to assist the organizers and to facilitate consultations with government officials. Several churches and community centers volunteered housing and food. AIM members prepared a twenty-point position paper for discussion with government leaders; among the points were settlement of treaty grievances, economic development on reservations, an end to termination, and a congressional inquiry into the workings of the BIA.

When the several hundred Indians who joined the Trail of Broken Treaties arrived in Washington on November 1 and 2, they discovered that the BIA intended to renege on its offers of assistance. An assistant secretary in the Department of the Interior, Harrison Loesch, had ordered the BIA to provide no assistance whatsoever to the protestors, and apparently he telephoned the local churches and community centers to stop them from aiding the demonstration. An abandoned church turned out to be the only lodging available. Mary Crow Dog had just gotten into her sleeping bag, she recounted in *Lakota Woman*, when she spied "the biggest and ugliest" rat she had ever seen walk across her bedroll.[15] Pandemonium erupted inside the church when more rats appeared, and those Indians inside poured out of the church and headed for the BIA.

Rage led to the takeover of the BIA building by Indians on November 2. Through part of that day, protestors negotiated with BIA and Department of the Interior officials over housing. By afternoon, government officials had agreed to allow the demonstrators to stay inside the BIA until suitable accommodations could be found. Police showed up at 4 P.M. and tried to evict the demonstrators, however. The protestors fought back, and a riot broke out. The police withdrew after receiving orders from the White House to leave. The presidential election was only a week away, and scenes of Indians being removed from the BIA was not, President Richard Nixon's advisers reasoned, in the best interests of his reelection campaign. But the order came too late. The Indians at the BIA had barricaded themselves inside.

The takeover of the BIA building lasted a week and earned AIM its reputation for radical militancy, even though many of the participants in the Trail of Broken Treaties were not AIM members. AIM attracted media attention, and its members often spoke, in fiery language, before national television cameras on behalf of all of the demonstrators. After days of negotiation, federal officials promised to appoint an interagency task force to respond to the twenty-point position paper that the demonstrators had brought to Washington, and on November 8 the participants in the Trail of Broken Treaties left the BIA building. Two months later the task force rejected all of their proposals, and BIA officials, with support from some tribal chairmen, denounced the occupiers as militant renegades who had no concern for Indians.

When Mary Crow Dog and other AIM members left Washington, they departed, in the judgment of many federal officials, as radicals dangerous to the stability of the U.S. government and American society. The FBI joined forces with the BIA in a combined effort to put a stop to AIM. Federal officials expected AIM members to head for the Pine Ridge reservation, where tribal chairman Richard Wilson and the residents of Pine Ridge opposed to Wilson were on the brink of civil war. The federal government sent U.S. marshals, FBI agents, and specially trained BIA police to Wilson's tribal headquarters.

The federal government had a useful ally in Wilson. He had faced several charges of fraud for diverting tribal funds to friends and supporters but had never been convicted. Thus, the BIA viewed its support of Wilson as the defense, from dangerous renegades, of a tribal chairman duly elected under the rules of the IRA set down in 1934 and still in effect in the early 1970s. The BIA ignored complaints from Pine Ridge residents that Wilson had established a "reign of terror," the phrase most often used to describe his regime. The BIA supported Wilson because he opposed AIM.

As opposition to Wilson from Pine Ridge residents grew, he hired his own mercenaries, the Guardians of the Oglala Nation (GOONS), and was more than willing to deploy them against AIM. Most residents at Pine Ridge were members of the Oglala band of the Lakota nation, and they were the first to call Wilson's mercenaries "goons," a name that his forces decided to adapt for themselves. Beatings by the GOONS silenced some of Wilson's critics; GOONS burned down the houses of other Wilson opponents.

Many of Pine Ridge's residents supported AIM. The organization was popular on the reservation for a variety of reasons. Residents shared AIM's anger at the death of Raymond Yellow Thunder, who had been well liked and well respected. In addition, one of AIM's most prominent leaders, Russell Means, was an Oglala and a member of the Oglala Sioux Landowners Association at Pine Ridge. Some of Means's family lived in the town of Porcupine on the Pine Ridge reservation, some ten miles from Wounded Knee, and Means knew firsthand the terror Wilson employed against the Oglala at Pine Ridge. When Means attended a meeting of the landowners' association after his return from Washington, he was beaten by Wilson's GOONS and hospitalized.

In February 1973 residents on the Pine Ridge reservation appealed to Means and to AIM for help in removing Wilson from office, and that appeal resulted in the siege of Wounded Knee. By February, Leonard Crow Dog recalled, "the goons were running wild. Things had gotten to where the people just could not endure it any longer. . . . The goon squad beat up people every day."[16] On the night of February 27, fifty or so cars filled with AIM members and supporters drove around the heavily guarded bunker that had become Wilson's office and rolled on into Wounded Knee.

AIM intended to occupy the town and force negotiations with the BIA until Wilson was removed, but the siege of Wounded Knee immediately became a showdown between AIM and the U.S. government. By the afternoon of February 28, more U.S. marshals, FBI agents, BIA police, and some of Wilson's GOONS had blockaded Wounded Knee, which consisted of the houses belonging to the town's few residents, a church, a museum, and a trading post, the latter owned by a white family long hated on the reservation for garish advertisements inviting tourists to visit the mass grave of the Lakotas killed in 1890 at Wounded Knee.

U.S. authorities assembled a heavily armed force of 300 men on the Pine Ridge reservation that reflected the ferocity with which federal officials regarded AIM. More than 100,000 rounds of ammunition arrived for the M-16s carried by the combined federal forces. Sharpshooters equipped with night-vision scopes on their rifles joined the forces at Wounded Knee. Helicopters and spotter planes were also brought in for the siege, and guard dogs patrolled the perimeter.

To many Indians, Wounded Knee symbolized the climax of an uprising against the federal government. Although the occupiers inside the town never numbered more than about 200, as many as 2,000 Indians and non-Indians participated in the siege, slipping in and out of the town by walking back trails at night to bring food, medicines, supplies, and occasionally guns and ammunition to the besieged. Indians across the country also held demonstrations in support of those at Wounded Knee.

About midway through the siege, on April 11, the birth of Mary Crow Dog's first child was a day of rejoicing for the Indians inside the town. "I really thought then," she recalled, "that I had accomplished something for my people." On the morning of her son's birth, a firefight erupted between federal troops and the occupiers, and several women who were attending Mary Crow Dog as midwives moved her to a trailer home out of the worst of the barrage. All of the occupiers, except for those returning fire from bunkers inside the town, gathered around the trailer. When one of the midwives held the new baby up to a window, "a great cheer went up. They were beating the big drum and singing the AIM song." "My heart," Mary remembered, "beat with the drum." At that moment, six armored personnel carriers roared up to the perimeter of the town and opened fire. When the federal forces heard the drum, Mary Crow Dog believed, they thought the occupiers were preparing a suicide charge, certainly not celebrating the birth of a baby.[17]

Mary left Wounded Knee with her son one week before the siege ended. Her uncle, Buddy Lamont, was killed in a firefight, one of two Indians who died of gunshot wounds inside the town. Mary Crow Dog left when her relatives asked her to help with his funeral. She negotiated a deal with federal officials. She was allowed to leave and was free to go to her relatives, but she also submitted to arrest and spent a day and a night in jail.

After seventy-one days, the siege ended with no resolution to any of the issues that had brought AIM to Wounded Knee. Its members had demanded a federal investigation of Wilson's conduct on the Pine Ridge reservation; a congressional investigation of the Department of the Interior, the BIA, and the implementation of their policies on the reservations; and a federal commission to review violations to the 1868 Treaty of Fort Laramie. Eventually the government agreed to a review of the 1868 treaty and to consultations between its officials and Indians about federal policies. Government officials also agreed that if those occupiers with federal charges pending against them would agree to arrest, then federal prosecutors would not seek to set bail or try to restrict terms of release. On May 8 the occupiers of Wounded Knee surrendered the town to federal authorities.

Federal officials immediately broke the agreement that they had negotiated to end the occupation. When those arrested at Wounded Knee appeared for arraignment, federal prosecutors asked for and got bail set at $150,000 for a number of the defendants. On May 30, several hundred Lakotas gathered at the home of Frank Fools Crow, the most respected medicine man in the Lakota nation, to begin consultations with government officials as scheduled. No federal representatives showed up; a U.S. marshal delivered a letter from Leonard Garment, one of President Nixon's domestic policy advisers, reaffirming the administration's commitment to the 1871 congressional act that had abolished treaty making with Indian nations.

Richard Wilson continued his reign of terror on the Pine Ridge reservation until he was defeated for reelection in 1976. Between 1973 and 1976 the murder rate at Pine Ridge was ten times the rate in Detroit, then considered the murder capital of the United States. Among the hundreds of Lakotas killed during those years were a niece, a nephew, and a sister of Leonard Crow Dog.

After Wounded Knee, the U.S. government followed a simple strategy to put an end to AIM: AIM leaders spent the next five to seven years either in jail or on trial for a succession of offenses. By the end of the decade, Means had been indicted five times in federal courts and seven times in state courts on thirty-seven felony counts and three misdemeanors. All but one of the charges were dismissed. Leonard Crow Dog served eighteen months in maximum security prisons, often in solitary confinement, on charges of interference with federal postal inspectors and armed robbery. During the siege at Wounded Knee, Leonard Crow Dog and other AIM members had intercepted four men carrying concealed weapons who said they were postal inspectors. Leonard Crow Dog took away their guns—hence, the conviction on armed robbery—before he let them go.

The policy of termination was formally rescinded under the Nixon administration. In 1975, Congress created the American Indian Policy Review Commission to investigate federal practices. In 1977 the commission recommended an end to the BIA and establishment of an independent federal body with more power returned to the Indian nations. The final report of the commission recognized the validity of Indian claims of sovereignty and the validity of claims against the United States for violations of the treaties. Most of its recommendations were not enacted. Lawsuits brought by Indians, however, continue over land reclamation, just compensation for lands taken, treaty violations, and Indian rights.

Mary Crow Dog followed her husband from prison to prison in the early years of their married life. They had three children together before separating. Mary Crow Dog remarried in 1991 and, as Mary Brave Bird, published in 1993 a second autobiographical work, *Ohitika Woman*. Poverty on the reservations had become much worse than when AIM was active. "AIM is not what it used to be," she admitted; "many of its leaders are dead, or burned out, or too old to fight."[18] But tribal governments now carry on programs established by AIM chapters to save Indian languages, revive tribal cultures, and revise and evaluate school textbooks so that more accurate accounts of American Indians and their history are included.

Although many former members have said that AIM is dead, Mary Brave Bird denies it. At the Sun Dance in 1991 at Crow Dog's Paradise, participants asked the veterans of Wounded Knee—Mary Brave Bird and Clyde Bellecourt among them—to rise and sing an honor song for them. "We're still working for the people," Mary Brave Bird reflected after the tribute. "We are still here."[19]

Few Americans today wish Indian cultures to vanish into a homogeneous white society as federal officials planned. In the 1960s and 1970s, AIM and other organizations brought the Indian fight for survival to the public's attention, and many Americans since then have come to value Indian cultures. Perhaps, most of all, AIM, alongside the NCAI, NIYC, and individual Indian activists, made it possible for thousands of young Indians in the 1960s and 1970s to refuse assimilation, to insist on retaining their identity, and to survive into another century.

Notes

1. Mary Crow Dog and Richard Erdoes, *Lakota Woman* (New York: HarperPerennial, 1991), 111.

2. Ibid., 126.

3. Ibid., 43.

4. Ibid., 15.

5. Ibid., 28.

6. Robert Burnette and John Koster, *The Road to Wounded Knee* (New York: Bantam Books, 1974), 46.

7. Ibid., 48.

8. Ibid., 192.

9. Francis Paul Prucha, ed., *Documents of United States Indian Policy*, 2d ed. rev. and exp. (Lincoln: University of Nebraska Press, 1991), 233.

10. Quoted in Angie Debo, *A History of the Indians of the United States*, Civilization of the American Indian, no. 106 (Norman: University of Oklahoma Press, 1970), 376.

11. Quoted in Peter Matthiessen, *In the Spirit of Crazy Horse* (New York: Penguin Books, 1992), 35.

12. Quoted in ibid., 34.

13. Mary Crow Dog and Erdoes, *Lakota Woman*, 9.

14. Ibid., 73, 75, 79.

15. Ibid., 85.

16. Leonard Crow Dog and Richard Erdoes, *Crow Dog: Four Generations of Sioux Medicine Men* (New York: HarperCollins, 1995), 187.

17. Mary Crow Dog and Erdoes, *Lakota Woman*, 163–64.

18. Mary Brave Bird and Richard Erdoes, *Ohitika Woman* (New York: Grove Press, 1993), 226.

19. Ibid., 118.

Suggested Readings

Brave Bird, Mary, and Richard Erdoes. *Ohitika Woman.* New York: Grove Press, 1993.

Burnette, Robert, and John Koster. *The Road to Wounded Knee.* New York: Bantam Books, 1974.

Churchill, Ward. *Agents of Repression: The FBI's Secret Wars against the Black Panther Party and the American Indian Movement.* Boston: South End Press, 1990.

Crow Dog, Leonard, and Richard Erdoes. *Crow Dog: Four Generations of Sioux Medicine Men.* New York: HarperCollins, 1995.

Crow Dog, Mary, and Richard Erdoes. *Lakota Woman.* New York: HarperPerennial, 1991.

Debo, Angie. *A History of the Indians of the United States.* Civilization of the American Indian, no. 106. Norman: University of Oklahoma Press, 1970.

Deloria, Vine, Jr. *Behind the Trail of Broken Treaties: An Indian Declaration of Independence.* 2d ed. Austin: University of Texas Press, 1985.

Fixico, Donald L. *Termination and Relocation: Federal Indian Policy, 1945–1960.* Albuquerque: University of New Mexico Press, 1986.

Matthiessen, Peter. *In the Spirit of Crazy Horse.* New York: Penguin Books, 1992.

Means, Russell, and Marvin J. Wolf. *Where White Men Fear to Tread: The Autobiography of Russell Means.* New York: St. Martin's Press, 1995.

Steiner, Stan. *The New Indians.* New York: Harper and Row, 1968.

Takaki, Ronald. *A Different Mirror: A History of Multicultural America.* New York: Little, Brown, 1993.

18

Harvey Milk
San Francisco and the Gay Migration

Laura A. Belmonte

Harvey Milk (1930–1978) was born on Long Island, New York, during the Great Depression. After an average childhood, he graduated from New York State College for Teachers and served in the U.S. Navy. Then came the social revolution of the 1960s. By 1970, Milk was a budding social activist and producer for such Broadway hits as *Hair* and *Jesus Christ Superstar*. He was also gay, and in 1972 he headed to San Francisco to settle permanently. For the next five years, Milk worked tirelessly as both a gay and community activist, demonstrating an adroit skill at forging political alliances in this cosmopolitan city. In 1977 his efforts were rewarded with his election as a city supervisor, making Milk the nation's first openly gay elected municipal official. One year later, however, he was assassinated in his own office. His death, along with the rise of the New Right movement of the late 1970s, reenergized the gay liberation movement, which itself would be sustained by the challenge of meeting the AIDS epidemic.

Milk's journey from the eastern seaboard to the Pacific Coast was a search for self-definition, one shared by many Americans of the politicized 1960s and the "me decade" of the 1970s. His story reinforces the argument that many parts of the West have always been places of diversity and cultural intersection, which sometimes leads to cooperation and innovation but at other times ends in violence.

Laura A. Belmonte is associate professor of history at Oklahoma State University. In the fall of 2003, she will publish *Speaking of America: Readings in U.S. History*. Her *Selling America: Propaganda, National Identity, and the Cold War* is forthcoming.

O n the morning of November 27, 1978, former San Francisco supervisor and ex-policeman Dan White loaded his .38-caliber pistol and filled his pockets with hollow-point ammunition. After getting

This essay originally appeared in Benson Tong and Regan A. Lutz, eds., *The Human Tradition in the American West* (Wilmington, DE: Scholarly Resources, 2002), 209–25.

a ride to City Hall, he crawled in through a basement window and made his way to the office of Mayor George Moscone. When Moscone refused to reappoint him to his former post, White shot the mayor twice. He then walked over to the wounded man and pumped two dumdum bullets into his head. As he reloaded his gun, White walked to the offices of the supervisors. He asked Harvey Milk, his former colleague, to join him across the hall. After the two men entered the room, White closed the door. Seconds later, Milk shouted, "Oh, no!" White shot Milk three times and then fired two dumdum bullets into Milk's head. He then ran from the building and went to a diner to call his wife. A devout Catholic, he asked her to meet him at Saint Mary's Cathedral. Shortly thereafter, he turned himself in to the police and confessed to the murders.[1]

The killings gained worldwide attention. That evening some 40,000 San Franciscans gathered for a candlelight march in honor of the fallen men. Both Moscone and Milk were hailed as committed politicians with promising futures. To gay and lesbian people everywhere, Milk represented unprecedented visibility and influence, but his fate also reminded them of the conflicts such power could engender.[2] Harvey Milk's life remains an example of progressive politics in America and of the continuing role of westward expansion in pursuit of individual happiness, community, and freedom.

Since World War II the Castro district of San Francisco has become a symbol of liberation for the gay community. Inspired by the New Left and the counterculture of the 1960s, gays and lesbians claimed an entire neighborhood as their own and forged a powerful cultural and economic force. They continued a long history of Americans who moved to the West in pursuit of individual fulfillment, but their motives obviously differed from those of the Mormons, the gold miners, or other pioneers. For the first time, emigrants moved westward seeking sexual freedom and identity—a lure that proved as powerful as religious freedom, potential wealth, or landownership.

Long before the gay migration of the 1970s, gay life in San Francisco was already a visible reality. During the height of the gold rush of the 1850s, the population of San Francisco was approximately 90 percent male, and it remained disproportionately male for decades. This environment proved conducive to homosexual activity—especially when one considers that the majority of these men were under forty years of age and isolated from women. There are legendary stories about all-male square dances in which the man dancing the "woman's" part was identified with a red bandanna on his arm. Extensive evidence about homosexual subcultures among other predominantly male groups—including sailors, pirates, and cowboys—can be extrapolated to San Francisco.[3]

Nonetheless, public discussion of same-sex activities in San Francisco did not begin until the 1890s. Police arrested male prostitutes catering to military troops stationed at the Presidio. Stories of "passing women" who masqueraded as men in order to gain better jobs, political rights, or marry women appeared in local papers. In 1908 city officials closed down The Dash, San Francisco's earliest known gay bar. In 1933 the repeal of Prohibition sparked the emergence of new gay establishments, especially in North Beach, the predominantly Italian neighborhood that soon became a mecca for artists, bohemians, and writers.[4]

No event transformed the lives of gays and lesbians more than World War II. Drawn together by military service or wartime employment, thousands of these individuals found each other in the sex-segregated environments created by the war. Because San Francisco served as one of the major dispatch points for troops heading to the Pacific theater, discharged soldiers often remained in the city rather than return to their hometowns with a "blue discharge."[5] By V-J Day, San Francisco's gay community burgeoned to unprecedented levels. The next decade, however, proved more challenging. Against the backdrop of Cold War rhetoric, the homophobia and anticommunism in the broader society created stereotypes of gays as predatory, contagious, and weak-willed. San Francisco authorities continued to raid gay clubs, theaters, and "cruising" spots. Despite the hostile climate, moderate homophile groups, including the male-dominated Mattachine Society (established in 1950) and the lesbian-controlled Daughters of Bilitis (founded in 1955), began challenging legal oppression. Meanwhile, gays and lesbians kept packing gay bars, and private house parties flourished. Long before Harvey Milk arrived, *Life* magazine christened San Francisco the nation's "gay capital" in 1964.[6]

Little in Harvey Milk's early life portended his future role as a gay rights activist. Born in Woodmere, New York, on May 22, 1930, he was known for his quick wit and amiability, and he was a popular high school athlete. No one suspected that he led a secret gay life, but at seventeen he was arrested for being shirtless in a police raid of a "cruising" section of Central Park. Milk never told his family, but he always remembered the indignity of the incident. After graduating from college and serving in the navy, he settled into a comfortable job at an insurance company and a seven-year relationship with a young drifter named Joe Campbell. Milk paid little attention to McCarthyism's impact on gays or police harassment at gay establishments. He remained closeted to his family and coworkers. His politics were staunchly conservative.[7]

In the mid-1960s, however, Milk began to change. Bored with insurance, he became a researcher for a Wall Street investment firm. His math skills, memory, and charm enabled him to rise quickly through the ranks. After his relationship with Campbell ended, he began a romance with Jack McKinley, another younger man. When McKinley became stage manager for avant-garde theater director Tom O'Horgan, Milk began socializing with artists whose lives were the antithesis of his own. Intrigued, he quit his job, grew his hair long, and became a producer for O'Horgan's hit shows *Hair* and *Jesus Christ Superstar*. He began adopting more liberal political views and abandoning the trappings of his buttoned-down life. When the *Hair* tour took McKinley to San Francisco, Milk followed. Although he got a job as a financial analyst there, he criticized the wealthy elite who controlled San Francisco politics and excluded gays, minorities, and the poor. In April 1970, following the U.S. invasion of Cambodia, Milk burned his BankAmericard in an antiwar rally at the Pacific Stock Exchange. Displeased by Milk's blooming radicalism, his employers fired him. He spent the next two years traveling with various O'Horgan productions.[8]

While Milk was changing, so were gay politics. In late June 1969 the Stonewall riots in New York raged for three days, sparking the gay liberation movement. By 1973 almost 800 gay and lesbian organizations had been formed all over the United States. More gay bars opened, but so did gay churches and synagogues, health clinics, community centers, and hosts of businesses and nonprofit services. Gay political clubs and newspapers proliferated. Urging their cohorts to "come out" and challenge antigay stereotypes and laws, gay liberation groups claimed that homosexuals were an oppressed minority. Gays and lesbians began openly celebrating their sexuality and rejecting self-loathing and hiding in favor of pride and visibility.[9]

In the wake of Stonewall some San Francisco gay activists adopted more confrontational tactics. They questioned the homophiles' reliance on liberal politicians and working "within the system." They adopted the strategies of the Marxist, women's liberation, and radical political groups pervading the Bay Area. New gay militant groups formed.[10] In the early 1970s both militant and moderate gay activists scored victories in San Francisco. In 1969, California state assemblyman Willie

Brown introduced legislation decriminalizing all sexual acts between consenting adults. Gay political groups provided crucial support in the elections of City Supervisor Dianne Feinstein and Sheriff Richard Hongisto. In 1972 the San Francisco Board of Supervisors passed an ordinance prohibiting antigay discrimination by city contractors.[11]

These gains were countered by the deep divisions within the city's estimated population of 80,000 gays in 1971. Moderate activists criticized radical attempts to include gays in a larger progressive coalition of minorities, the poor, and the elderly. Gay people of color accused white activists of racism. Lesbians, especially separatists, accused gay men of sexism. Poorer queers denounced elitism among wealthy gays. Drag, transgender, sadomasochistic, and leather groups felt marginalized. It would take a remarkable leader to unify such a diverse lot.[12]

No one would have guessed that Harvey Milk would become that leader. In 1972, Milk and his new lover, Scott Smith, returned to San Francisco. They moved to Castro Street in the heart of the Eureka Valley district, a deteriorating Irish neighborhood, and opened Castro Camera, living above the sprawling storefront. They joined an influx of gay men transforming the local demographics.[13]

To Milk, moving to Eureka Valley meant a chance to take part in city politics. Infuriated by the Watergate hearings, sales taxes, and underfunded schools, he decided to enter the 1973 election for the San Francisco Board of Supervisors.[14] Milk's answers to a questionnaire given to all candidates are quite revealing. He had no experience in local politics or community projects. He listed his net worth as "$2,000 in debt." He had no endorsements. He expected to "pass the hat for dollars and coins" in order to finance his campaign.

If Milk's resources were limited, his political vision definitely was not. He said he was running for the board to stop the waste of taxpayers' money and end prosecution for "victimless crimes," including prostitution, consensual sex, and marijuana use. When asked to specify the voters to whom he was appealing, Milk crossed out all of the subcategories and wrote, "I campaign for all." If elected, he intended to expand health care for the elderly and to create better job opportunities for minorities and the young. He denounced the city's increasing reliance on tourism and real estate development that displaced poor and minority San Franciscans. He advocated free public transportation and stricter environmental laws. Milk also outlined an ambitious civil rights agenda, supporting the aims of "all—especially gay, black, Mexican, Oriental." "For a city made of minorities," he added, "there is no excuse."[15]

The sweeping agenda of the audacious newcomer stunned local liberal politicians. Some thought that the ponytailed, mustached Milk was a crazy hippie. Even if they liked his personality and ideas, gay moderates worried that his unpredictable nature could harm the gay political movement. Having spent years building the local movement, they viewed Milk as an arrogant opportunist. They remained wedded to the idea that gays should rely on straight liberals to implement gradual civil rights reforms.

Milk emphatically rejected this logic. Believing that gays should run for office themselves rather than rely on anyone else, he launched impolitic attacks on moderate gay activists. Needless to say such tactics did not win him the endorsement of the Alice B. Toklas Memorial Democratic Club, the biggest gay political group in the city. But radicals loved him. Drag queens, bar owners tired of police raids, and marijuana users supported him in droves.

Milk combined his fiscal conservatism with fiery progressive oratory. He became skilled at the art of getting press coverage. Despite his hippie image and failure to secure gay political endorsements, he received 17,000 votes, finishing tenth out of thirty-two candidates. Even with a meager $4,500 campaign budget, Milk managed to win substantial support in heavily gay neighborhoods and counterculture enclaves. Convinced that gays would support one of their own, he decided to run again. Making two concessions to political reality, he cut his hair and vowed never to smoke pot or go to a gay bathhouse again. A populist was born.[16]

While Milk prepared for his political future, San Francisco's booming service economy drew gays from around the country. Beginning in 1973 the gay invasion of Eureka Valley skyrocketed. Drawn by inexpensive Victorian homes, gays began renovating scores of houses and opening new businesses. The neighborhood changed dramatically. The maternity shop became All-American Boy, a men's clothing store catering to gay styles. The historic Castro Theater reopened and showed the Hollywood classics beloved by many gays. The family florist evolved into a leather shop.[17]

Castro Camera served as the center of the changing community. Milk became known for his relentless efforts in advocating for the neighborhood at City Hall. Old ladies facing eviction, troubled teens, and gay activists gathered in his storeroom. Local Teamsters leaders noticed Milk's growing influence and asked for his help in their boycott of six antiunion beer distributors. Milk agreed to help in exchange for a promise that the union would admit gay employees, and he quickly convinced gay bars to join the boycott. Five distributors agreed to settle. Thrilled at Milk's organizational skills and the success of their boycott, the Teamsters began hiring gay and lesbian drivers.[18]

Inspired by his success, Milk escalated his political activities. Insisting that gays had no right to complain about politics unless they participated, he registered 2,350 new voters. He tried to organize the neighborhood's gay and straight merchants. When the Eureka Valley Merchants Association refused to admit gay businesspeople, Milk organized the gay merchants into the Castro Valley Association (CVA). The subtle name change gained enormous significance as gay residents began referring to the neighborhood as the Castro instead of Eureka Valley. Throughout 1974, Milk promoted CVA and extolled the tremendous potential of gay economic power. To prove his point, he organized the Castro Street Fair in August. Over 5,000 people attended. Thrilled at the business created by the fair, some straight merchants joined CVA.

A number of older residents were appalled by the growing power of the Castro gays. Often, tensions erupted into violence. Gay bashings were frequent. Arsonists targeted gay establishments. Policemen shouted antigay epithets and harassed gays with unwarranted disorderly conduct tickets. Usually covering their badge numbers first, a few cops even beat gays. After a series of particularly brutal attacks over Labor Day weekend in 1974, gay attorney Rick Stokes filed a $1.375 million lawsuit against the San Francisco Police Department. Although the affair prompted a decline in police harassment, Milk used the melee to emphasize the need for gays to enter the San Francisco political establishment.[19]

He planned to lead the way himself. In March 1975, Milk announced his candidacy for a second run for the Board of Supervisors. He stressed his opposition to prosecution for victimless crimes and support for fairer taxation and improved schools. Although his work on the beer boycott had earned him scores of labor endorsements, gay moderates continued to shun him. Undeterred, Milk ran his campaign amid the chaos of Castro Camera. He relied on volunteers and often catapulted virtual strangers to positions of authority. Unable to afford expensive advertisements, he rose at 5:30 A.M. in order to shake hands with commuters. He spent his days campaigning in parks, churches, bars, and cafés. He was not always greeted warmly. Some people refused to take his leaflets, and in Golden Gate Park someone shouted, "What are you running for, dairy queen?" Milk took such hostility in stride. "If I turned around every time somebody called me faggot," he explained to a local reporter,

"I'd be walking backwards and I don't want to walk backwards."[20] Finishing just one spot short of the top six vote-getters elected to the board, he narrowly lost the election.

Nonetheless, Milk saw the election of 1975 as a victory. He established himself as a power broker for his neighborhood. Scores of gay-friendly and liberal candidates won office. District Attorney Joseph Frietas pledged to stop prosecution for victimless crimes. Promising to challenge the city's powerful real estate interests, George Moscone was elected mayor by a powerful coalition of the city's minorities, poor, elderly, and gays. Moscone recognized the importance of San Francisco's growing gay population. Accordingly, he rewarded Milk with an appointment to the city's Board of Permit Appeals.[21]

Milk, however, had bigger plans. Just five weeks after being sworn in, he announced his intention to run for the Democratic nomination for the Sixteenth Assembly District seat representing east San Francisco in the state legislature. Moscone was furious. The mayor and most of the city's other Democratic leaders had already endorsed another candidate, Art Agnos. Milk was undeterred. After Moscone fired him, he launched a populist crusade against the wealthy and political elites. Agnos, he claimed, was the tool of a "machine" dominating city politics. The "Milk versus the Machine" campaign concluded with Milk losing to Agnos by 3,600 votes. He was, however, gaining substantial support, and he carried the Castro decisively.[22]

The Castro was undoubtedly becoming a force with which to be reckoned. By 1977, 20,000 gay men had moved to the neighborhood, and thousands more visited each weekend to experience the sexual energy pulsating through the district's bars. "The Castro was like Mardi Gras every weekend," one gay couple remembers. Gay softball leagues, a gay chorus, a tap-dancing troupe, and other gay clubs provided a host of community activities. The Castro Street Fair, Halloween, and Gay Freedom Day Parade drew massive crowds.[23]

Gays were also making striking gains nationwide. By 1977 almost forty cities had adopted ordinances outlawing antigay discrimination in housing, employment, and public accommodations. Eleven states were considering adopting statewide gay rights bills. And sodomy statutes were being repealed across the country.[24]

The gay community's growing power prompted a nationwide backlash as well. In January 1977, when Dade County, Florida, adopted a gay rights law, former Miss America runner-up and Florida Citrus Commission spokesperson Anita Bryant launched a campaign to rescind the law. On June 7, Dade County voters repealed the gay rights law by an overwhelming margin. A little-known California state senator, John Briggs (R-Fullerton), was inspired by Bryant's success. Hoping to advance his gubernatorial aspirations, he introduced legislation banning gays and lesbians from working in public schools.[25]

Throughout Bryant's crusade in Florida, reports of antigay violence in San Francisco soared. The attacks also took rhetorical forms. In August, Board of Supervisors candidate Dan White released an ominous brochure proclaiming that he was "not going to be forced out of San Francisco by splinter groups of radicals, social deviates, and incorrigibles." White called for "frustrated, angry people" to "unleash a fury that can and will eradicate the malignancies which blight our beautiful city."[26]

The antigay backlash only increased Milk's determination to win election to the Board of Supervisors. In 1976, San Franciscans had voted to replace citywide elections with district elections. Neighborhoods—including the Castro—could now elect their own representatives. In November 1977, after his third campaign for election to the Board of Supervisors, Milk defeated sixteen other candidates and won the District 5 seat. At a joyous victory party, he told his gay supporters: "This is not my victory, it's yours, and yours, and yours. If a gay can win, it means that there is hope that the system can work for all minorities if we fight." But Milk also recognized that his victory may have endangered his life. A week later, he taped a political will to be read in case he was assassinated. "If a bullet should enter my brain," he declared with chilling foresight, "let that bullet destroy every closet door."[27]

Whatever his personal safety concerns, Milk was determined to represent the Castro well. In January 1978 he was sworn in as the city's first gay supervisor, joining the first Chinese, the first unwed mother, and the first African American on the most diverse Board of Supervisors in San Francisco history. Dan White, a former policeman and fireman, was also inaugurated that day.

Milk quickly proved himself a hardworking legislator. At times he was abrasive and crude, but even his opponents admired his humor, eloquence, and dedication. He challenged corporate interests and defended minorities and the poor. Appalled by spiraling real estate prices, he pushed for a strict antispeculation tax. After his hilarious demonstrations of the city's "dog poop" problem gained wide media attention, Milk lobbied for legislation requiring pet owners to clean up after their pets. Although his colleagues defeated many of his proposals, he protected his constituents—gay and straight. He successfully fought for road improvements, street cleaning, and traffic signs in his district. He prevented closure of the community's elementary school and public library. In March, Milk won passage of the long-awaited city gay rights law by a ten-to-one vote. Outlawing antigay discrimination in employment, housing, and public accommodations, the ordinance culminated decades of Bay Area gay activism.[28]

Milk thrived on the board, but Dan White found his own experience frustrating. Moody and inflexible, he was ill suited to the vicissitudes of politics. His biggest disappointment came when his colleagues voted six to five to construct a psychiatric facility in his district despite his vociferous opposition. At first, Milk had sided with White, but he changed his vote after learning more about the project. Enraged, White refused to speak to him for months and retaliated by attacking Milk's gay rights bill, casting the lone dissenting vote. In the months that followed, White opposed every gay-related issue put before the board. He also allied himself with the wealthy real estate developers whom Milk so disdained.[29]

Facing a continued antigay backlash, Milk paid little attention to White's ranting. Throughout early 1978, an organization called California Defend Our Children quietly gathered the 500,000 signatures needed for a statewide vote on the Briggs initiative, officially named Proposition 6. Gay activists were stunned at the breadth of the proposal. The bill not only barred anyone who engaged in "public homosexual conduct" from working in the public school system but also employed a sweeping definition of the word "public." Under Proposition 6, anyone "advocating, soliciting, imposing, encouraging or promoting private or public homosexual activity" in an educational setting could be dismissed. Attorneys warned that the Briggs bill posed a threat to the freedom of speech of all school employees regardless of sexual orientation. The news that voters in St. Paul, Minnesota, Wichita, Kansas, and Eugene, Oregon, had repealed gay rights ordinances did little to cheer San Franciscan gays.[30]

Milk refused to be cowed. As his popularity increased, so did the number of death threats he received. Despite a morass of personal and financial problems, he continued to devote himself to his job. He also knew that gays could not ignore their increasingly powerful opponents. He emerged as the leader of several groups fighting the Briggs initiative. Putting aside their differences, gays and straights worked together to raise funds, canvass voters, and lobby politicians.[31]

Throughout the fall, Milk campaigned tirelessly against Proposition 6. He and Briggs made dozens of public appearances debating the proposal and the issue of homosexuality. The contests featured exchanges of various statistics and interpretations of the Bible. "This is not a civil rights question. This is not a human rights question. It is simply a question of morality," Briggs insisted. Milk shot back, "If Senator Briggs thinks he's better than Christ, that he can decide what's moral, then maybe we should have elected him Pope."[32]

Milk often used humor to deflect Briggs's outrageous charges. When Briggs argued that a quarter of gay men had over 500 sexual partners, Milk retorted, "I wish." Briggs repeatedly asserted that children needed good role models and should be protected from homosexuals who wished to "recruit them." "Children do need protection," Milk responded, "protection from the incest and child beatings pandemic in the heterosexual family." As for role models, he reminded his audiences that if children emulated their instructors, there would be "a helluva lot more nuns running around."[33]

Milk was not alone in opposing the Briggs initiative. When September 1978 polls showed that over 60 percent of California voters supported Proposition 6, many people realized Briggs could not be ignored and began publicly attacking his proposal. Gays realized that even in laid-back California, they could not take their civil rights for granted. In the weeks prior to the election, statewide polls showed Californians evenly split over Proposition 6. Briggs had proven himself an inept spokesman. Unable to persuade politicians to join him, he surrounded himself with fundamentalist preachers. Only three state groups—the Ku Klux Klan, the Nazi Party, and the Los Angeles County Deputy Sheriffs' Association—endorsed Proposition 6.

On election day, California voters defeated the Briggs initiative by a significant margin. Seattle voters rejected an attempt to repeal that city's gay rights law. The antigay tide had turned. Milk was the nation's most prominent gay activist. Supported by a progressive coalition of gays, minorities, and the poor, he expected easy reelection. Life was good for Supervisor Milk.[34]

Dan White was not so lucky. Unable to work as a fireman while serving on the board, he struggled to support his wife and newborn son on his $9,600 supervisor's salary. After he closely aligned himself with local real estate interests, a developer helped him attain a potato stand at Pier 39, the city's newest tourist attraction. White and his wife, Mary

Ann, worked long hours to make ends meet. White grew depressed and distant. He stopped shaving and stayed in bed for days. Citing his financial problems, he resigned from the board on November 10, 1978. Six days later, he changed his mind. He explained that his sixteen brothers and sisters had offered financial assistance and that his supporters had urged him not to quit. Returning White's letter of resignation, Moscone proclaimed, "As far as I'm concerned, Dan White is the supervisor from District 8. . . . A man has the right to change his mind."[35]

But then Moscone exercised the same prerogative. He announced that the city's attorneys had advised him that White could not rescind his resignation. Although he could legally reappoint White, the mayor hesitated. Citing several complaints about the former policeman, Moscone stated that he would not reappoint White unless he provided evidence of substantial support in District 8. At the same time, an "unnamed supervisor" told reporters that White was "a nice guy" but a poor supervisor who opposed gays and minorities in order to curry the favor of the wealthy.

It did not take a genius to figure out that White's critic was Harvey Milk. Behind the scenes, Milk reminded Moscone that White had been the swing vote on many six-to-five defeats. Milk also let the mayor know that San Francisco's gays would not look favorably on the reappointment of the homophobic White. With gays now composing a quarter of the city's electorate, Moscone knew he could not afford to alienate the city's 100,000 gays and lesbians or his liberal constituents. Distracted by the news that 900 members of the San Francisco–based People's Temple had committed suicide in the jungles of Guyana, few citizens paid much attention to Moscone's dilemma. They were about to receive another shock.[36]

On November 27, Dan White murdered Moscone and Milk. For the next week the stunned city mourned its fallen leaders. Flags were lowered to half-staff. Businesses closed. President Jimmy Carter expressed "a sense of outrage and sadness at the senseless killings." Thousands attended memorial services for Moscone and Milk. While the city grieved, police booked White on two counts of first-degree murder. His confession left no doubt who had committed the crimes. His colleagues and neighbors portrayed him as an intensely moral and competitive man who had snapped under the pressure of financial problems. Yet his jailers noted White's eerily calm demeanor.[37]

Although several details about the murders emerged in the next few months, nothing prepared San Franciscans for White's dramatic trial.

He pleaded not guilty and faced a possible death sentence. Jury selection began in April 1979. Douglas Schmidt, White's attorney, questioned potential jurors about the death penalty, gay organizations, psychiatry, and Moscone and Milk. After only three days of selection, Schmidt and Assistant District Attorney Thomas F. Norman accepted an all-white, all-straight jury.[38]

In his opening argument on May 1, Schmidt presented White as "a good man" who "cracked" after a long struggle with depression. White was, he said, an "honest and fair" public servant who "tried very hard to be tolerant of different lifestyles." "Good people—fine people with fine backgrounds," Schmidt concluded, "simply don't kill people in cold blood."[39] Norman's bland recounting of the murders proved no match for Schmidt's sympathetic portrait of White.[40]

Norman was no more adept at challenging Schmidt's psychiatric experts. Three of the four defense experts claimed that White lacked the mental capacity to commit premeditated murder. He was, they said, a conflicted man who lacked friends and confidants. Furthermore, White's frequent episodes of deep depression were exacerbated by a diet made up exclusively of junk food.[41]

The so-called Twinkie defense made legal history, and Norman's prosecution was lackluster and ineffective. After Schmidt made an eloquent closing argument imploring the jury to spare White's life, Norman embarked on a four-and-a-half hour summation that put jurors, bailiffs, and even District Attorney Joseph Frietas to sleep.[42] On May 21, after thirty-six hours of deliberation, the jury convicted White of two counts of voluntary manslaughter. He would serve a maximum sentence of seven years and eight months.

The lenient verdict generated an enormous uproar. An incredulous Mayor Dianne Feinstein declared, "As far as I'm concerned, these were two murders." Many San Franciscans agreed. The evening after the verdict was announced, 5,000 predominantly gay demonstrators marched from the Castro to City Hall. Invoking Milk's fervent belief in nonviolence, several speakers attempted to calm the crowd, but their pleas fell on deaf ears. A riot erupted. Flinging a lighted match into a police car, one demonstrator told a reporter, "Make sure to put in the paper that I ate too many Twinkies." By the time the White Night Riot ended, demonstrators destroyed $1 million of city property. Dozens of gays and cops were injured. Over fifty people were arrested.[43]

Fears that Milk's death would stymie the gay community's growing political power proved groundless. On May 22, 1979, the night after the White Night Riot, a peaceful crowd of 4,000 gathered in the Castro to commemorate Milk's forty-ninth birthday. The event became an annual celebration of the activist's life. In the 1980s, when AIDS began to decimate San Francisco's gay male population, the city became a worldwide model for its educational and medical response to the epidemic. The crisis prompted unprecedented cooperation between gay men and lesbians. By the 1990s gay people held prominent positions throughout San Francisco government, politics, and business. Confronting increasingly hostile national opposition, the city's queer community worked to overcome its racial, ethnic, economic, and sexual divisions. Although Milk would have disdained the Castro's evolution into a pricey gay tourist trap, he would have been thrilled that the neighborhood embodies the visibility and power he wanted for gays everywhere.[44]

Harvey Milk's life and death continue to inspire human rights advocates throughout the world. His colorful lifestyle and courageous message have been depicted in books, an Oscar-winning documentary, plays, a television show, a musical, and an opera. His progressive vision and concern for justice stir all people who hope for a world in which diversity and dignity triumph over discord and derision.

Notes

1. The definitive account of Harvey Milk's life and assassination is Randy Shilts, *The Mayor of Castro Street: The Life and Times of Harvey Milk* (New York: St. Martin's Press, 1982). See also Mike Weiss, *Double Play: The San Francisco City Hall Killings* (New York: Addison-Wesley, 1984).

2. See Shilts, *Mayor of Castro Street.*

3. Susan Stryker and Jim Van Buskirk, *Gay by the Bay: A History of Queer Culture in the San Francisco Bay Area* (San Francisco: Chronicle Books, 1996), 13–19.

4. The San Francisco Lesbian and Gay History Project, " 'She Even Chewed Tobacco': A Pictorial Narrative of Passing Women in America," in *Hidden from History: Reclaiming the Gay and Lesbian Past*, ed. Martin Duberman, Martha Vicinus, and George Chauncey Jr. (New York: Meridian Books, 1989), 183–94; Stryker and Van Buskirk, *Gay by the Bay*, 18–19.

5. "Blue discharge" refers to the paper on which dishonorable discharges for homosexuality were printed. Such discharges often prevented gays from attaining private employment. See Allan Bérubé, *Coming Out under Fire: The History of Gay Men and Women in World War Two* (New York: Free Press, 1990).

6. On the impact of McCarthyism on gays, see John D'Emilio, "The Homosexual Menace: The Politics of Sexuality in Cold War America," in *Passion and Power: Sexuality in History*, ed. Kathy Peiss and Christina Simmons (Philadelphia: Temple University Press, 1989), 226–40; Geoffrey Smith, "National Security and Personal Isolation:

Sex, Gender, and Disease in the Cold-War United States," *International History Review* 14 (May 1992): 307–35; and Bérubé, *Coming Out under Fire*, 255–79. On the homophile movement, see John D'Emilio, *Sexual Politics, Sexual Communities: The Making of a Homosexual Minority in the United States, 1940–1970* (Chicago: University of Chicago Press, 1983), 121–22, 177–95; Stryker and Van Buskirk, *Gay by the Bay*, 43–47.

7. Shilts, *Mayor of Castro Street*, 3–22. On Milk's interest in the arts and his life with Joe Campbell, see Harvey Milk–Susan Davis Alch correspondence, San Francisco History Collection, San Francisco Public Library (hereafter cited as SFHC, SFPL).

8. Shilts, *Mayor of Castro Street*, 24–46.

9. Martin Duberman, *Stonewall* (New York: Plume, 1994).

10. On these protests, see *San Francisco Chronicle*, July 2, 1969, November 1, 1969, November 4, 1969, and November 19, 1969.

11. Ibid., October 18, 1971; Shilts, *Mayor of Castro Street*, 60–65.

12. On these divisions, see Stryker and Van Buskirk, *Gay by the Bay*, 54–62. The term "queer" is not used pejoratively; rather, it is used to reflect the wide diversity of the gay community, encompassing gay, lesbian, bisexual, and transgendered people.

13. Shilts, *Mayor of Castro Street*, 43–46, 65.

14. For Milk's motivations in running for office, see Shilts, *Mayor of Castro Street*, 69–72.

15. San Francisco Board of Supervisors Study, August 7, 1973, Vertical File on Harvey Milk, SFHC, SFPL.

16. Shilts, *Mayor of Castro Street*, 69–80. See also 1973 Campaign Brochure, Vertical File on Harvey Milk, SFHC, SFPL.

17. On the development of the Castro and reaction of residents, see Peter L. Stein, *The Castro in the series Neighborhoods: The Hidden Cities of San Francisco*, produced by Peter L. Stein (San Francisco: KQED Books and Tapes, 1997), videocassette; Shilts, *Mayor of Castro Street*, 112.

18. Shilts, *Mayor of Castro Street*, 81–84.

19. Ibid., 87–93; Stein, *Castro*.

20. *San Francisco Chronicle*, March 17, 1975, and October 23, 1975. See also 1975 Campaign Brochure, Vertical File on Harvey Milk, SFHC, SFPL.

21. Shilts, *Mayor of Castro Street*, 95–110; *San Francisco Chronicle*, January 30, 1976.

22. Shilts, *Mayor of Castro Street*, 127–152; *San Francisco Chronicle*, March 10, 1976, June 9–10, 1976; 1976 Campaign Brochure, Vertical File on Harvey Milk, SFHC, SFPL.

23. Stein, *Castro*; Frances Fitzgerald, "The Castro—I," *The New Yorker* (July 7, 1986): 34–54.

24. For a chronology of these developments, see Mark Thompson, ed., *Long Road to Freedom: The Advocate History of the Gay and Lesbian Movement* (New York: St. Martin's Press, 1994).

25. Stein, *Castro*; Shilts, *Mayor of Castro Street*, 155–58; *San Francisco Chronicle*, April 21, 1977, and June 8–10, 1977.

26. *San Francisco Chronicle*, June 23, 1977, and July 1, 1977; Shilts, *Mayor of Castro Street*, 161–63.

27. Shilts, *Mayor of Castro Street*, 169–85.

28. Ibid., 189–97, 203; *San Francisco Chronicle*, March 21, 1978.

29. On White's temperament, see Shilts, *Mayor of Castro Street*, 198–200.

30. *San Francisco Chronicle*, January 12, 1978, and April 27, 1978; Thompson, *Long Road to Freedom*, 163.

31. Shilts, *Mayor of Castro Street*, 204–6, 214–18, 221–26.

32. Ibid., 229–30.

33. Ibid., 230–31.

34. Ibid., 242–51.

35. *San Francisco Chronicle*, November 11 and 18, 1978, and, on White's behavior prior to his resignation, May 2, 1979.

36. Ibid., November 21–22, 1978; Shilts, *Mayor of Castro Street*, 254–55.

37. *San Francisco Chronicle*, November 28 and December 2, 1978.

38. Ibid., February 10, 1979, April 20, 1979, April 22, 1979, and April 28, 1979.

39. Ibid., May 2, 1979.

40. Ibid., May 4, 1979.

41. Ibid., May 8–10, 1979.

42. Ibid., May 12, 1979, and May 15–16, 1979.

43. Ibid., May 22–23, 1979.

44. Ibid., May 23, 1979; Stryker and Van Buskirk, *Gay by the Bay*, 85–142; Stein, *Castro.*

Suggested Readings

Bérubé, Allan. *Coming Out under Fire: The History of Gay Men and Women in World War Two.* New York: Free Press, 1990.

D'Emilio, John. *Sexual Politics, Sexual Communities: The Making of a Homosexual Minority in the United States, 1940–1970.* Chicago: University of Chicago Press, 1983.

Shilts, Randy. *The Mayor of Castro Street: The Life and Times of Harvey Milk.* New York: St. Martin's Press, 1982.

Stryker, Susan, and Jim Van Buskirk. *Gay by the Bay: A History of Queer Culture in the San Francisco Bay Area.* San Francisco: Chronicle Books, 1996.

19

William O. Douglas
The Environmental Justice

Adam M. Sowards

William O. Douglas (1898–1980) is best known for his tenure as a justice of the U.S. Supreme Court. Named by President Franklin Delano Roosevelt in 1939, the forty-year-old Douglas became the Court's second-youngest appointee ever. Less well known, however, are Douglas's contributions to the environment. Though born outside the West, he grew up near the Cascade Mountains, and personal tribulations shaped his lifelong ties to the physical landscape. His career later took him to the East, but outdoor leisure activities repeatedly pulled him back to the Pacific Northwest. Like the preservationist John Muir, Douglas was reverent toward nature, and like the conservationist thinker Aldo Leopold, he embraced an ethical response to the land. His understanding that the wilderness frontier made men and women strong and Americans great—which reminds us of the ideas of Frederick Jackson Turner and Theodore Roosevelt—also shaped his commitment to the environment.

This love of wilderness was articulated in several decisions the Court handed down during his tenure as well as in his books on nature. Douglas's public life reflected the emergence of an early environmentalism in the West, one that stressed the health of ecosystems and the biological well-being of the planet. Certain changes after World War II gave this movement its momentum. The prosperity experienced in U.S. cities in the postwar years made Americans less concerned with scarcity and more concerned with the quality of life. Yet that same prosperity also fueled more investments, which engendered continual opposition from wilderness preservation advocates.

Adam M. Sowards earned his doctorate at Arizona State University in Tempe and is an assistant professor of history at the University of Idaho. Currently, he is completing an environmental biography of William O. Douglas. He has published essays and articles on John Muir and the American Southwest as well as other works on Douglas.

I n early 1939, U.S. Supreme Court Associate Justice Louis Brandeis announced his plans to retire. President Franklin D. Roosevelt made

This essay originally appeared in Benson Tong and Regan A. Lutz, eds., *The Human Tradition in the American West* (Wilmington, DE: Scholarly Resources, 2002), 155–70.

no secret that he wished to appoint a westerner to the nation's highest tribunal to balance regional representation on the Court. A front-runner for the position seemed to be a senator from Washington State named Lewis Schwellenbach, a loyal New Dealer who even faithfully supported Roosevelt's ill-advised Court-packing plan.[1] William O. Douglas, chair of the Securities and Exchange Commission (SEC), was also a possibility, but Roosevelt initially dismissed him as an easterner. To borrow Schwellenbach's characterization, Douglas, though he had grown up in Washington State, "was anything but a 'technical' Westerner." In fact, he had been a member of the eastern intelligentsia since the 1920s—as a Wall Street attorney, a law professor at Columbia and Yale University Law Schools, and a commissioner and eventually the chair of the SEC. An individual who had spent his entire professional life on the East Coast clearly would not fit Roosevelt's bill.[2]

Despite those nonwestern qualifications, Douglas and his allies maneuvered to emphasize his western experience and sensibilities, as well as demonstrate regional support. The pro-Douglas campaign worked, especially after the well-known William Borah, a Republican senator from Idaho, announced that Douglas would make a fine representative of the West on the Court. In March, Roosevelt sent his name to the Senate for confirmation, and in short order, William O. Douglas became a U.S. Supreme Court justice.[3]

That Roosevelt could have considered Douglas too "eastern" in 1939 comes as a surprise today, for no member of the Court or perhaps all of Washington, DC, during his tenure could match his image as a westerner—rugged individualist, expert outdoorsman, famous for his marked informality. He cultivated this image deliberately and linked it inextricably to the West's reputation of individualism and its celebrated landscapes. Douglas may have spent his professional life largely in Washington, DC, but his heart remained in his native Pacific Northwest. His favorite cause, conservation, confirmed that western identity, for environmental debates and activism were always a central feature of western politics and culture. As the Supreme Court's environmental justice, he drew deeply from his western roots and experiences.

In the foreword to his 1950 autobiography, *Of Men and Mountains*, Douglas remarked, "The boy makes a deep imprint on the man." That truism seems especially apt in the case of William O. Douglas. Orville, as he was known as a child and youth, was born in Maine, Minnesota, in 1898 to Julia Fisk Bickford Douglas and William Douglas, a Presbyterian minister. Later in life, he recalled little about Minnesota, since soon after his birth his father transferred to a new pastorate in Estrella, California, and soon thereafter the family made another move to Cleveland, Washington. From Cleveland, Douglas first glimpsed the two principal natural features of the Pacific Northwest that would ultimately prove so important in his upbringing and later career—the Cascade Mountains forty miles to the west and the Columbia River thirty miles to the south. For Douglas the river and the range formed an emotional, almost spiritual, bond to this land.[4]

Now settled in the Northwest, which he would call home in one way or another for the rest of his life, Douglas developed an intense attachment to the dry, sagebrush-covered hills of central Washington. That affection only deepened during the funeral for his father, who had died in August 1904 of complications following surgery for stomach ulcers. Now fatherless and understandably scared, the five-year-old boy wanted to escape the church service, but at the cemetery he "became afraid—afraid of being left alone, afraid because the grave held my defender and protector." As young Orville started to cry the minister told him, "You must be a man, sonny." Douglas's gaze gradually lifted to Mount Adams in the distance: "As I looked, I stopped sobbing. My eyes dried. Adams stood cool and calm, unperturbed by the event that had stirred us so deeply that Mother was crushed for years. Adams suddenly seemed to be a friend. Adams subtly became a force for me to tie to, a symbol of stability and strength." As Douglas remembered the episode, no doubt embellishing it over the years, the Cascades became an anchor for him and remained so from that day forward.[5]

If being fatherless at age five was not difficult enough, Douglas contended with extreme poverty and his own severe illness. Julia Douglas moved her family—three children under the age of seven—to Yakima, Washington. There she built a house at 111 North Fifth Avenue with part of the life insurance money her husband left behind, and she invested the remainder in a highly speculative irrigation project that soon failed. Housed but penniless, the Douglas family struggled financially. Orville washed store windows, swept out businesses, picked fruit in the productive Yakima Valley, and worked at other odd jobs. The money that he, his older sister, Martha, and his younger brother, Arthur, earned "often meant the difference between dinner and no dinner." At Christmas time the Douglases received a box from the Presbyterian Home Mission. This and other charity made Christmas a "grubby occasion" for Douglas, who felt such welfare mostly assuaged the psyche of the rich who donated the cast-off clothing, with only slight benefit to the poor recipients. These childhood holiday episodes helped form his substantial distrust toward what he routinely referred to throughout his career as "the Establishment" and created an indelible class consciousness. Even in Yakima, a small but growing center for agricultural production, the Establishment affected Douglas, as it contrasted sharply with his family's poverty. "Because of our poverty," he wrote in *Go East, Young Man* (1974), the first volume of his autobiography, "we did occasionally feel that we were born 'on the wrong side of the railroad tracks.' " That feeling of being outcast and the resentment it engendered remained strong within Douglas and later permeated his jurisprudence and extrajudicial writings, speeches, and other activities.[6]

Although poverty made a deep impact on Douglas's worldview, another factor more profoundly shaped the course of his life. While still in Minnesota, he contracted a minor case of polio. Despite his mother's near-constant attention, including massaging Douglas's limbs every two hours and praying continually for weeks, the young boy's legs remained weak. However, contrary to doctors' prognoses and in contrast to the experiences of many other polio victims, Douglas eventually regained the use of his legs, though his mother still made excuses for his understandable weakness. "He's not as strong as other boys," he remembered her telling others; "he has to be careful what he does—you know, his legs were almost paralyzed." Predictably, he was afraid of "being publicly recognized as a puny person—a weakling." On the way to school, classmates teased, "Look at that kid's skinny legs. . . . Did you ever see anything as funny?" At a loss, Douglas cried, confirming, at least in his own mind, his weakling status.

He resolved to rise above his peers in academics, which he did. Yet a boy's world, especially in the American West just past the turn of the century, required strength. Men were expected to exemplify the strenuous life that Theodore Roosevelt celebrated in his early-twentieth-century salute to the masculine accomplishments of the American westering spirit. Drawing a parallel with the natural world and heavily incorporating Darwinian language, Douglas later explained his fears: "The physical world loomed large in my mind. I read what happened to cripples in the wilds. They were the weak strain that nature did not protect. They were cast aside, discarded for hardier types. . . . Man was the same, I thought. Only men can do the work of the world—operating trains, felling trees, digging ditches, managing farms. Only robust men can be heroes of a war." The western world in which he wished to live and which was enshrined in popular culture had no room for a "cripple" or a weakling.[7]

So, in a fashion to be repeated time and again, Douglas set out to meet a challenge and conquer his fear, for he knew that "man is not ready for adventure unless he is rid of fear." He longed for adventure, and the foothills north of Yakima provided an ideal testing ground. After meeting a Sunday school classmate who had been climbing those hills under a doctor's orders, Douglas knew instinctively that he would strengthen his legs similarly. "First I tried to go up the hills without stopping," the justice explained. "When I conquered that, I tried to go up without change of pace. When that was achieved, I practiced going up not only without a change of pace but whistling as I went." After several seasons of regular hiking, Douglas's legs grew strong. He defeated his weakness, learned to appreciate nature in the mountains, and developed a passion for hiking in magnificent western landscapes. In the process, his childhood disease, the method he used to overcome it, and the place of his recovery made lasting imprints on a young man destined for a life that led him away from his beloved hills near the Cascade Mountains.[8]

Douglas's uncommon determination and his imposing intellect led to his graduating as valedictorian of his high-school class and earning a scholarship to Whitman College in Walla Walla, Washington. He worked his way through college at a Norwegian immigrant's jewelry store, as a janitor, and as an agricultural worker in summertime, where he worked and conversed with Wobblies—members of the radical Industrial Workers of the World union. At Whitman, Douglas met influential science and literature professors, rebelled against religious dogma, and nursed his suspicion of the Establishment. His successful college career led first to a stint teaching high school back in Yakima and then on to Columbia Law School in 1922, after shepherding a flock of sheep on the railroad from eastern Washington to Chicago to pay for his transportation. The departure from his beloved West was not without misgivings: "All the roots I had in life were in the Yakima Valley." Whenever he thought of the Cascades while in the urban corridors of New England, New York, and Washington, DC, Douglas "felt an almost irresistible urge to go West. It was the call of the Cascade Mountains." For him, then, the West was home in spirit, if not always in fact.[9]

As Douglas made his meteoric rise from professor of law to SEC commissioner to SEC chair to Supreme Court justice in just a few years, he garnered national press attention as a leading New Deal liberal. Notably this attention fixed partly on his previous western life. Richard L. Neuberger, Oregon journalist and eventual U.S. senator, wrote a feature entitled "Mr. Justice Douglas" in the August 1942 edition of *Harper's*. The complimentary article depicted the young justice dressed in "the five-gallon Western hat he invariably wears." Neuberger maintained that everyone called Douglas "Bill," emphasizing an informality cultivated from his western background. Finally, the journalist explained Douglas's political appeal, drawn unmistakably from his humble Yakima beginnings: "He has a grassroots personality, a homespun Lincolnesque appearance, and the nearest thing to a log-cabin background there is in American politics today." Neuberger's portrait was an accurate homage from a friend. He made clear to readers of *Harper's* that William O. Douglas personified the West. As was revealed in a 1946 letter to the editor of *American Mercury*, the public accepted such an image and early on identified the justice with the outdoors: "Douglas suggests the strength and ruggedness of the giant oaks of his own Wallowa Mountains of Oregon." Surely this characterization would have pleased Douglas, even if his botanical knowledge and outdoor experience told him oaks were relatively rare in the pine-dominated Wallowas. Throughout American political history a western identity held appeal, conveying as it did the image of a rugged individual from the frontier past.[10]

At the time Neuberger's article appeared in *Harper's*, rumors that President Roosevelt might reshuffle his cabinet for the wartime emergency led to conjectures that Douglas might receive a cabinet appointment. Neuberger speculated and actively promoted Douglas for such positions as director of the War Production Board or secretary of war. Douglas's leading qualifications were, first, his proven administrative acumen and, second, his ability to represent the needs and desires of the Far West. For their part, western liberals and progressives readily praised his qualities and urged his reassignment. "The west has an especial regard for Justice Douglas," stated an editorial in southern Oregon's *Coos Bay Times*. The editorialist went on to claim that the "west" knew Douglas from his time as a student, lawyer, and perennial visitor. "The northwest has found Justice Douglas, as has the east, a man of intellectual vigor, of impeccable honesty, with a *restless physical verve* so necessary for high offices in conduct of war. Douglas gets things done. . . . This area knows he would make a valuable addition to any reconstituted cabinet the president may select." In a similar endorsement the *Oregon Labor Press* offered even higher praise. After complaining that there were "too few Westerners" in the war program, an editorialist announced "the common people of the country—and especially the common people of the West—know that Mr. Douglas understands their problems." These northwestern newspapers sanctioned Douglas's westernness and accepted him as an able regional representative. If these editorials at all reflected their readers' opinions, western communities, especially the liberal constituencies, happily claimed him as one of their own.[11]

The national and regional press clearly offered praise and prominence for this symbol of American liberalism. Although Douglas would always wear with pride the liberal badge he earned in the 1930s and 1940s, he increasingly donned other political apparel. Beginning in 1949 he became a world traveler extraordinaire, visiting Asia, the Middle East, and the Soviet Union and writing books filled with observations and policy recommendations not always popular with conservative politicians during the Cold War. With his considerable stature as a public figure and his self-conscious image as an outdoorsman, Douglas brought to conservation a ready influence. By the mid-1950s he regularly took a visible public role in conservation matters. A hiker and fisherman nearly all his life, he found it necessary to lead environmental causes into the public fray. In that role, he may have achieved his greatest lasting significance.

Occasionally, Douglas wrote letters in the 1940s to friends and acquaintances about fishing resources or trail conditions in the Pacific Northwest. Not until the 1950s, however, did he bring his penchant for outdoor activities and his weighty influence to bear on conservation causes. His first publicized fight involved the Chesapeake & Ohio Canal near Washington, DC, adjacent to which some hoped to build a scenic highway. Douglas frequently hiked along the historic canal and enjoyed the birds and other wildlife and especially the solitude. In 1954, long before most Americans were aware of or interested in environmental matters, he challenged the editors of the *Washington Post*, who had publicly approved the idea of a parkway, to a hike along the 189-mile canal from Cumberland, Maryland, to Washington, DC. Soon the Wilderness Society, private citizens, and government officials clamored for a voice and a place among the hikers. For a week the hike held the national news media's attention. The *Washington Post* editors changed their minds, and in 1961, after a long battle and annual reunion hikes to maintain the issue's prominence in the public's eye, President Dwight D. Eisenhower declared the canal a national monument. In 1971 it was designated a national historic park, and by 1977 it was dedicated to Douglas. Assuredly, the controversy surrounding the Chesapeake & Ohio

Canal was an eastern environmental battle, and that was fitting for a justice who lived three out of four seasons in the Beltway. Nevertheless, Douglas's early foray into public conservation activism served as a significant precedent and established patterns for his later environmental contests in the West.[12]

Not long after beginning his activism on behalf of the canal, Douglas took up a cause closer to his favored home in the Pacific Northwest. On Washington's Olympic Peninsula, where he owned a summer cabin, local business interests wanted to build a new road that would wind along an ocean beach contained within the Olympic National Park. Although such a roadway would make automobile travel for commercial and tourist purposes easier within the relatively remote peninsula, Douglas wrote Conrad L. Wirth, director of the National Park Service, in 1957 to express his concern. "I have hiked this primitive beach," he explained, "[and] as a result of that hike I fell in love with that primitive beach and its great charm and beauty, and its abundant wildlife." He continued, citing his worry that if the road were allowed close to the beach, the traffic would "drive out the game and we'd end up with just another *ordinary* beach." The justice wanted anything but an *ordinary* beach. Taking a page from his C & O Canal book, he led a three-day, twenty-two-mile hike to protest the road, with sponsorship and organization provided by the Wilderness Society and the Federation of Western Outdoor Clubs. Despite evidence to the contrary, he maintained that the group was "not fighting a road." Clearly, of course, they were fighting a road, but Douglas meant more was at stake than merely this strip of macadam.[13]

In his first book of nature writing, *My Wilderness: The Pacific West*, published in 1960, Douglas devoted a chapter to this Pacific beach and explained the deeper issues involved in the 1958 fight. He described the flora and fauna of the region and wove human and natural history together by commenting on the native history of the coast and even describing how the ocean connected, rather than divided, North American and Asian populations. Besides offering these portraits, Douglas embedded his prose with ecological lessons. He carefully explained how downed timber littered the forest floor, making traveling with a horse quite treacherous; however, he noted that the timber was "being reclaimed and turned to humus," returning basic nutrients to the soil. He extended his ecological discussion to the marine life as well, offering a series of miniature biology lessons for readers who were likely ignorant on the subjects he addressed.[14]

Moreover, the beach proved inspiring at a spiritual level. Like many before him, Douglas felt an almost obligatory humility before the force of the oceans: "I realize how small and minute man is in the cosmic scheme." Furthermore, he coupled that humility with fear of humans' growing technological prowess and ability to despoil natural areas. Humans had become "bold and aggressive and dangerous," Douglas warned, adding that "now [humanity] has unlocked the secrets and can destroy and sterilize for eons the good earth from which we all came." He emphasized how threatened the beach had become in the technological world of post–World War II America.[15]

With his reasons for protecting the Pacific beach outlined, Douglas's protest hike in the late 1950s seemed justified. By the time the hike began, the group had grown to seventy individuals—"safari proportions," according to a Seattle newspaper. Among the safari members were the central leaders in American conservation circles, including Harvey Broome, president and cofounder of the Wilderness Society; Olaus J. Murie, famed wildlife biologist and director of the Wilderness Society; Howard Zahniser, secretary of the Wilderness Society; and Conrad Wirth, director of the National Park Service. The group represented some of the most important founders of the postwar environmental movement, suggesting the significance of the event and the esteem in which the participants held Justice Douglas. Such a notable roster inevitably led to media exposure.[16]

The ocean strip of the Olympic National Park should be off-limits to road building, the protest group maintained, primarily because it was wilderness protected in a national park. Through Douglas, their spokesperson, group members suggested alternatives to a road in the park. "We can have both the road and a stretch of wilderness sea shore," Douglas explained. "Let's not put roads everywhere. Let's leave some of the state, some of the country, free from roads and from the effects of civilization that roads always bring." Confronting a protester who met the hiking group at the trail's end, he elaborated, "We'll settle for a road east of Lake Ozette. We'll give you 99 per cent of the U.S. but save us the other 1 per cent, please." Proponents of the highway hailed those very "effects of civilization"—tourist dollars for fuel, food, and lodging—that Douglas and the others hoped to avoid.[17]

It is important to note that, given the weak economy of the region based on forest exploitation, the peninsula economy needed to turn to tourism. The conflict involved a cast of characters that presaged countless environmental battles in the American West. Areas with economies that were dependent on natural resources increasingly looked to tourist development to cure their economic ills and frequently encountered opposition from environmentalists. Moreover, opponents of preservation often equated wilderness protection with locking up resources and the eventual and certain onset of poverty. This episode on the Pacific beach portended the western environmental future. In this instance, Douglas and the road's opponents emerged triumphant. No road has yet been built.[18]

This Olympic Peninsula protest was not the only instance when Douglas faced environmental issues before most others recognized them, and *My Wilderness: The Pacific West* was not the only forum he used to popularize his ideas. A companion volume—*My Wilderness: East to Katahdin*—was published the following year, in 1961. Both books consisted of chapters devoted to different places and landscapes, such as the Brooks Range in Alaska, the Middle Fork of Idaho's Salmon River, Baboquivari in southern Arizona, and the Florida Everglades. Douglas described the natural features of each place and typically educated the reader on a specific issue of ecology or conservation politics. Thus, readers were treated to portraits of some of America's fabulous landscapes while simultaneously being imbued with an environmentalist ethic. Perceiving an especially dire environmental situation in Texas, Douglas devoted an entire book to the state, titled *Farewell to Texas: A Vanishing Wilderness* (1967). Although he employed many of the same rhetorical devices as in his earlier works, his stance was decidedly more strident and his message more pessimistic because he grew increasingly exasperated that progress in raising environmental consciousness proved so slow. In each of these books of nature writing, Douglas allowed the western landscape to fill the pages, as he hoped readers would share his profound awe of the places and his fervent hope to prevent industrial and agricultural economies from wreaking ecological havoc. His books seldom addressed the people who made their livelihood from working the land, thus revealing a weakness shared by many others in the wilderness movement—the inability to reconcile the conflicting needs of humans and nature.[19]

In addition to leading protest hikes and writing books, Justice Douglas used his position on the Supreme Court to argue on nature's behalf. After people began farming and ranching more extensively and intensively in the arid American West in the nineteenth century, obtaining sufficient water became a ubiquitous concern. In the twentieth century new and expanding western manufacturing and population centers also needed cheap power. For both reasons, dams blocked portions of all the major western rivers, generating hydroelectricity and storing water for irrigation and against drought. By the middle of the twentieth century dam proponents became a favored target of environmentalists. Douglas, an avid fisherman and frequent rafter, joined the antidam sentiment.

Delivering the opinion of the Court in *Udall v. Federal Power Commission* (1967), Douglas questioned the wisdom of building another dam on the Columbia-Snake river system, this time at High Mountain Sheep on the Snake River. Douglas quickly turned to "the question whether any dam should be constructed." He looked to three existing laws to argue against the Federal Power Commission (FPC) granting a private power company a permit to build the proposed dam. Using a phrase in the 1920 Federal Power Act that named "recreational purposes" as a public use in river development, the justice claimed the dam would likely destroy or significantly diminish the salmon population and thus ruin recreational possibilities. In addition, the Fish and Wildlife Coordination Act of 1958 forced agencies to address wildlife conservation in water development projects with "equal consideration" given to other development factors. Finally, the recently passed Anadromous Fish Act (1965) discouraged river development that would harm salmon runs. Douglas had all the law he needed to determine that no dam should be built. According to western legal expert Charles F. Wilkinson, his opinion in the case was "trailblazing." The justice located relatively minor parts of relevant statutes and forced the FPC to reexamine the potential dam site further before issuing a permit, effectively quashing the power project by emphasizing recreational and conservation values for free-flowing rivers. Wilkinson claimed that the opinion "has stood as a bright model of vigilant judicial review in complex natural resources litigation." It would be difficult to find a better Supreme Court case that encompassed so many aspects of western history.[20]

For most of Douglas's tenure, though, comparatively few cases with environmental components came to the tribunal. When they did, Douglas as often as not dissented from the majority opinion. Thus, he made little actual impact on existing law, which is how constitutional scholars tend to evaluate a justice's importance. In Douglas's estimation, however, a dissent was "an appeal to the brooding spirit of the law, *to the intelligence of a future day*, when a later decision may possibly correct the error into which the dissenting judge believes the court to have been betrayed." So it was from his position as a dissenting justice that Douglas most commonly expressed his environmentalist values. Although his arguments rarely won over legal scholars or his brethren on the Court, hopeful environmentalists await "the intelligence of a future day."[21]

His most important dissent came in the early 1970s when he argued his most radical philosophy in *Sierra Club v. Morton* (1972). In the 1960s, Walt Disney Enterprises, the company that portrayed the West in the idealized Frontierland and unrealistic depictions of wildlife, wanted to transform the Sierra Nevadas' Mineral King Valley into a ski resort, carving it out of a portion of the Sequoia National Forest. In protest the Sierra Club touched off a long legal debate focusing on the issue of legal standing. Traditionally, litigants must prove they suffered some injury themselves to be able to sue. The Sierra Club hoped to establish a new precedent by arguing that Mineral King Valley itself had legal standing to sue. Such a ruling would have expanded greatly the notion of natural rights. The majority of the Court held that the Sierra Club had suffered insufficient harm and thus lacked standing. The Court would not grant inanimate natural objects rights.[22]

In his dissent, Douglas embraced an expansive reading of the law on legal standing and pushed back the envelope of environmental ethics, law, and philosophy, reaching the zenith of his environmental thinking. He began simply arguing that a federal rule was needed to allow "environmental issues to be litigated before federal agencies or federal courts in the name of the inanimate object about to be despoiled, defaced, or invaded by roads and bulldozers and where injury is the subject of public outrage." The case, he explained, would then properly be named *Mineral King v. Morton*, reflecting the valley's legal interest that superseded any human representation. Giving inanimate objects rights was surely not revolutionary: as Douglas pointed out, ships had legal personalities, and corporations acted as "people" in the law. These legal fictions were unproblematic, "so it should be as respects valleys, alpine meadows, rivers, lakes, estuaries, beaches, ridges, groves of trees, swampland, or even air that feels the destructive pressures of modern technology and modern life," he maintained. To solve the logistical question, he suggested that people who know and have "a meaningful relation" to the inanimate natural system are "its legitimate spokesmen." With such advocates, "the voice of the inanimate object . . . should not be stilled." Douglas's reasoning failed to move a majority of his colleagues, although two other justices dissented from the Court's ruling.[23]

Judging Douglas as an environmental advocate on the bench becomes a complicated task. Compared to the opportunities presented to the Supreme Court after his retirement in 1975, few cases of lasting environmental significance were presented in his record thirty-six-year career. In those that did, Douglas could be counted on to vote for what he believed was nature's best interest. In the two examples offered here, one can see how he at times worked within the law, finding obscure passages to support his viewpoint, as in *Udall v. FPC*. At other times, he pioneered new legal terrain—something critics fault him for doing—as he did in *Sierra Club v. Morton*. Environmental law specialist Christopher D. Stone argued that with his dissent in *Sierra Club v. Morton*, Douglas "instated himself as the leading judicial champion of the environment." Wilkinson concurred, explaining that the opinion was "daring" but adding that, nonetheless, "its influence is intangible and lies in the scholarship and the public mind rather than in the Supreme Court's opinions." Such ambiguity establishes the complexity of evaluating Douglas's role as a justice.[24]

Judged by any standard, Douglas's life story is remarkable. Whether he could have lived in the same way had he been born and raised in the East is unlikely. The ready access to public lands in which to hike and explore, so common in the West, influenced him to take an interest in conservation. It is telling that the entirety of his first *My Wilderness* book and nearly half of the second concerned western places. In addition, he devoted an entire book to Pacific Northwest mountains and another to Texas. Douglas traveled widely through America and the world, and the places he came to know, love, and revere were, by and large, located within the American West. Consequently, many of the causes he hiked for, wrote about, or passed judgment on involved western landscapes and ways in which to prevent them from what he perceived as further despoliation or exploitation.

In a memorial written the year after his death in 1980, Cathy H. Douglas, the justice's widow, reflected on how he led his life. She acknowledged that Douglas drew from his own life experience: "He may . . . be best remembered for the way in which he incorporated the experiences of his own life into the fabric of the law and his work on the Court." Of the many experiences that shaped his life, Cathy wrote at length about his time in Goose Prairie, Washington, his summer retreat in the Cascade Mountains. On one occasion there, Douglas led a hesitant deer to safety, away from a pack of wild dogs. That rescue, Cathy was certain, played in his mind during the following term, when the justice wrote his dissent in *Sierra Club v. Morton*. In her memorial, Cathy only discussed two cases with any depth, and the inclusion of the Mineral King case resonates with the argument that Douglas was, at heart, a western environmentalist. He built that identity self-consciously and deliberately but also from lived experience. It is a legacy for which he shall always be remembered.[25]

Notes

1. During the New Deal, the Supreme Court declared several of Roosevelt's reforms unconstitutional. To counter the seeming obstinacy of the Court, the president proposed granting his office the power to add federal judges once sitting judges turned seventy. The proposition was a thinly veiled power play designed to force conservative judges off the bench. It was Roosevelt's most serious political blunder of his presidency.

2. "Douglas, Jurist: Appointment to Supreme Court Puts Hard Hitter on the Bench," *Newsweek* (March 27, 1939): 13.

3. James F. Simon, *Independent Journey: The Life of William O. Douglas* (New York: Harper and Row, 1980), 191–94; William O. Douglas, *Go East, Young Man: The Early Years—The Autobiography of William O. Douglas* (New York: Random House, 1974), 456–63.

4. William O. Douglas, *Of Men and Mountains* (1950; reprint, San Francisco: Chronicle Books, 1990), xi.

5. Douglas, *Go East, Young Man*, 11, 12; idem, *Men and Mountains*, 29.

6. Douglas, *Go East, Young Man*, 15, 19.

7. Douglas, *Men and Mountains*, 32, 33–34; for Roosevelt and the "strenuous life," see Roderick Nash, *Wilderness and the American Mind*, 3d ed. (New Haven: Yale University Press, 1982), 149–50.

8. Douglas, *Men and Mountains*, x, 35.

9. Douglas, *Go East, Young Man*, 94–113; quotes in Douglas, *Men and Mountains*, 15, 5.

10. Richard Neuberger, *They Never Go Back to Pocatello: The Selected Essays of Richard Neuberger*, ed. Steve Neal (Portland: Oregon Historical Society Press, 1988), 108–25, quotes on 112, 116, 125; Hugh Russell Fraser, letter to "The Open Forum," *American Mercury* 62 (February 1946): 251; Michael P. Malone and F. Ross Peterson, "Politics and Protests," in *The Oxford History of the American West*, ed. Clyde A. Milner II, Carol A. O'Connor, and Martha A. Sandweiss (New York: Oxford University Press, 1994), 501–33.

11. Neuberger, *They Never Go Back*, 109; "Douglas for the Cabinet," *Coos Bay (Oregon) Times*, May 9, 1942, 2 (emphasis added); "When Will Douglas Enter War Effort," *(Portland) Oregon Labor Press*, n.d., 2.

12. See letters concerning the C & O Canal in William O. Douglas, *The Douglas Letters: Selections from the Private Papers of Justice William O. Douglas*, ed. Melvin I. Urofsky and Philip E. Urofsky (Bethesda, MD: Adler and Adler, 1987), 236–41; "The C and O Walkathon," *American Forests* 60 (May 1954): 18–19, 54; William O. Douglas, *My Wilderness: East to Katahdin* (Garden City, NY: Doubleday, 1961), 181–211;

and Stephen Fox, *The American Conservation Movement: John Muir and His Legacy* (Madison: University of Wisconsin Press, 1981), 241–43.

13. Douglas, *Douglas Letters*, 241–42 (emphasis added); "Justice Douglas, 70 Hikers to Begin Wilderness Trip," *Seattle Times*, August 18, 1958, 10.

14. William O. Douglas, *My Wilderness: The Pacific West* (Garden City, NY: Doubleday, 1960), 32–49 passim, quote on 34.

15. Ibid., 40.

16. Byron Fish, "Olympic Wilderness Hikers Hope to Chill Coast-Road Plan," *Seattle Times*, August 19, 1958, 30; "Highway Boosters, Primitive Lovers Will Take Hike along Coastline," *Seattle Times*, August 10, 1958, 22; "Justice Douglas and Hiking Party Complete Trip," *Seattle Times*, August 21, 1958.

"68 Footsore Hikers Wind Up Beach Trek near LaPush," 1958.

see Hal K. Rothman, *Devil's Bargain:* (Lawrence: University Press of Kan- *Landscapes and Failed Economies: The* land Press, 1996).

; idem, *My Wilderness: East to Katahdin*; ss (New York: McGraw-Hill, 1967). ttle, Brown, 1965) and *The Three Hun-* er (New York: Random House, 1972) n more political and philosophical per- American West. Richard White most ble problem of humans and nature in a or Do You Work for a Living?': Work *Reinventing Nature*, ed. William Cronon

57); Charles F. Wilkinson, "Justice Dou- *Pass This Way Again": The Legacy of Justice* ttsburgh: University of Pittsburgh Press, 239.

21. Quoted in James C. Duram, *Justice William O. Douglas* (Boston: Twayne Publishers, 1981), 102–3 (emphasis added).

22. *Sierra Club v. Morton*, 405 U.S. 727 (1972); Wilkinson, "Douglas and Public Lands," 242–44; Roderick Frazier Nash, *The Rights of Nature: A History of Environmental Ethics* (Madison: University of Wisconsin Press, 1989), 130–31; John Warfield Simpson, *Visions of Paradise: Glimpses of Our Landscape's Legacy* (Berkeley: University of California Press, 1999), 220–35 passim.

23. *Sierra Club v. Morton*, 741, 743, 745, 749; Wilkinson, "Douglas and Public Lands," 242–44; Nash, *Rights of Nature*, 130–31; Simpson, *Visions of Paradise*, 220–35.

24. Christopher D. Stone, "Commentary: William O. Douglas and the Environment," in *"He Shall Not Pass This Way Again": The Legacy of Justice William O. Douglas*, ed. Stephen L. Wasby (Pittsburgh: University of Pittsburgh Press, for the William O. Douglas Institute, 1990), 231; Wilkinson, "Douglas and Public Lands," 244.

25. Cathleen H. Stone, "William O. Douglas: The Man," in *Supreme Court Historical Society, Yearbook* (1981): 6–9.

Suggested Readings

Nash, Roderick. *Wilderness and the American Mind.* 3d ed. New Haven: Yale University Press, 1982.

Rothman, Hal K. *The Greening of a Nation? Environmentalism in the United States since 1945.* Fort Worth, TX: Harcourt Brace, 1998.

Simon, James F. *Independent Journey: The Life of William O. Douglas.* New York: Harper and Row, 1980.

Wasby, Stephen L., ed. *"He Shall Not Pass This Way Again": The Legacy of Justice William O. Douglas.* Pittsburgh: University of Pittsburgh Press, for the William O. Douglas Institute, 1990.

Index

Volumes in the Human Tradition in America series:

David L. Anderson, ed., *The Human Tradition in America since 1945* (2003). Cloth ISBN 0-8420-2942-7   Paper ISBN 0-8420-2943-5

Eric Arnesen, ed., *The Human Tradition in American Labor History* (2004). Cloth ISBN 0-8420-2986-9   Paper ISBN 0-8420-2987-7